EARLY CHILDHOOD EDUCATION TODAY

EARLY CHILDHOOD EDUCATION TODAY

Fourth Edition

George S. Morrison

Florida International University

Merrill Publishing Company
A Bell & Howell Information Company
Columbus   Toronto   London   Melbourne

Cover Photo: © Photo Edit, Myrleen Ferguson

Published by Merrill Publishing Company
A Bell & Howell Information Company
Columbus, Ohio 43216

This book was set in Leawood.

Administrative Editor: David Faherty
Production Editor: Molly Kyle
Art Coordinator: Pete Robison
Cover Designer: Cathy Watterson
Text Designer: Cynthia Brunk

Photo credits: American Montessori Society, p. 78; Art Resource, Inc., p. 23; Ben Asen/
Envision, p. 362; Jeff Bates, p. 403; Joan Bergstrom/Merrill, p. 41; Bettman Archive, p. 11;
Constance Brown/Merrill, p. 352; Rich Bucurel/Merrill, p. 450; Tim Cairns/Merrill, p. 412;
CDMRC, p. 114; Ben Chandler/Merrill, pp. 10, 17, 31, 39, 46, 49, 59, 69, 70, 82, 84, 87, 91,
93, 94, 111, 117, 135, 140, 144, 160, 224, 226, 228, 235, 261, 263, 316, 456; Children's
Hospital, Columbus, Ohio, p. 461; Paul Conklin, pp. 28, 288, 416; Celia Drake/Merrill,
pp. 114, 226; Kevin Fitzsimons/Merrill, pp. 295, 386; Joan I. Glazer, pp. 1, 226; Tom
Hutchinson/Merrill, p. 336; Bruce Johnson/Merrill, pp. 50, 248, 253, 300, 340, 466; Joanne
Kash, p. 379; Korver/Thorpe Ltd., p. 51; Lloyd Lemmerman/Merrill, pp. 149, 156, 162,
187, 193, 202, 312, 365, 390, 395, 396, 408; Med.-Tech./Merrill, p. 460; George Morrison,
pp. 3, 5, 15, 55, 133, 184, 282; NEA/Joe DiDio, p. 356; Phillips Photo Illustrators, p. 106;
Michael Siluk, pp. 25, 56, 114, 190, 195, 221, 230, 452; David S. Strickler/Strix Pix, pp. 339,
444; Larisa Wilson, p. 328; Gale Zucker, pp. 239, 376.

Library of Congress Catalog Card Number: 87-61794
International Standard Book Number: 0-675-20799-1
Printed in the United States of America
1 2 3 4 5 6 7 8 9—92 91 90 89 88

This book is affectionately dedicated to B. J., a very able helpmate

Preface

The world of early childhood education is constantly changing. The decade of the '90s promises to be an exciting and challenging time for children, parents, and teachers. Just as we professionals make important transitions in our lives, so, too, we must be willing and prepared to help young children make transitions in their lives.

The fourth edition of *Early Childhood Education Today* provides information and practices related to early childhood issues, the history of the profession, infant and toddler development and education, preschool and kindergarten programs, child care, children's special needs and behavior guidance, parent involvement, and becoming a professional. The content is applicable to infant and toddler programs, nursery schools, child care, kindergartens, preschools, programs of curriculum and instruction, child development, Head Start, and early special education programs.

Changes in the field of early childhood education make the fourth edition of *Early Childhood Education Today* different from the third edition in several ways. A new chapter on infants and toddlers has been added, and the contents of two chapters have been incorporated into other chapters. Chapters on preschool and kindergarten education and child care have been greatly expanded by the inclusion of child development information and additional material related to teaching and child care practices. Throughout this fourth edition, vignettes of programs conducted by practicing professionals illustrate the real-life applications of current educational theory and help the reader with the difficult but exciting task of translating theory into practice. In this sense, the textual material shows a continuity of education from birth to age eight and builds bridges between theory and practice.

The fourth edition of *Early Childhood Education Today* has several purposes: first, to help early childhood educators understand theory so they can implement exemplary practices in their own programs; second, to help early childhood educators understand what is developmentally and educationally appropriate for young children; and third, to promote the competence and effectiveness of early childhood professionals.

As with the earlier editions, I have written this fourth edition with a deep sense of pride for all who teach, care for, and parent young children. I agree with Froebel, Montessori, and Dewey that teaching is a redemptive calling and that early childhood educators should strive to achieve their best to help children and their families. This view of teaching is echoed in the vignettes of the Teachers of the Year in Chapter 15.

During the revision process, I met and talked with many people who are deeply involved with and committed to educating young children. I am always impressed and touched by the openness, honesty, and unselfish sharing of ideas that characterize these professional colleagues. Those who shared of themselves and their ideas are Virginia Boone, Beverly McGhee, Silvia La Villa, Pat Doyle, Maxine G. Roberts, Constance Kamii, Miriam Mades, Jamie Southworth, Joyce McCalla, Sally de Vicentis, Charlotte Kadison, Christine Taylor, Gail Harris, Kathryn Semple, Bernice Hardeman, Eugene Ramp, Marsha Poster, Natalie Kaplan, Odalys Figueroa, Donna McClelland, Patricia Boyles, Mary Wilson, Brenda McDaniel, Alicia Castro, Jane DeWeerd, E. Dollie Wolverton, Gina Barclay-McLaughlin, Ann Dehan, Harriet Midget, Charles Sherwood, Sally Schur, John Staley, Russ Lofthouse, Janice Fitzsimmons, Nanci Maes, Donna Viveiros, Laurie Jones, and Glenna Markey.

I also appreciate the helpful comments of these reviewers: Dr. Robert R. McClune of Edinboro University; Dr. Judith Reitsch of Eastern Washington University; Dr. Mary Link of Miami University; Dr. Ethel Minzey of Illinois State University; Dr. Leslie Morrow of Rutgers University; and Dr. Joseph Lawton of the University of Wisconsin.

Contents

6 **Infants and Toddlers:
Rediscovering the Early Years**   **185**

7 **The Preschool Years:
Readiness for Learning**   **217**

8 **Kindergarten Education:
More Than ABC's**   **249**

9 The Primary Years: The Process of Schooling 289

10 The Federal Government and Early Childhood Education: Helping Children Win 313

11 Teaching Children with Special Needs: Developing Awareness 353

12 Guiding Behavior at Home and School: Helping Children Become Responsible

387

13 Parent Involvement: Key to Successful Programs

413

14 Contemporary Concerns: Educating Children in a Changing Society

433

15 Responsible Caregiving and Teaching: Becoming a Professional

457

EARLY CHILDHOOD
EDUCATION TODAY

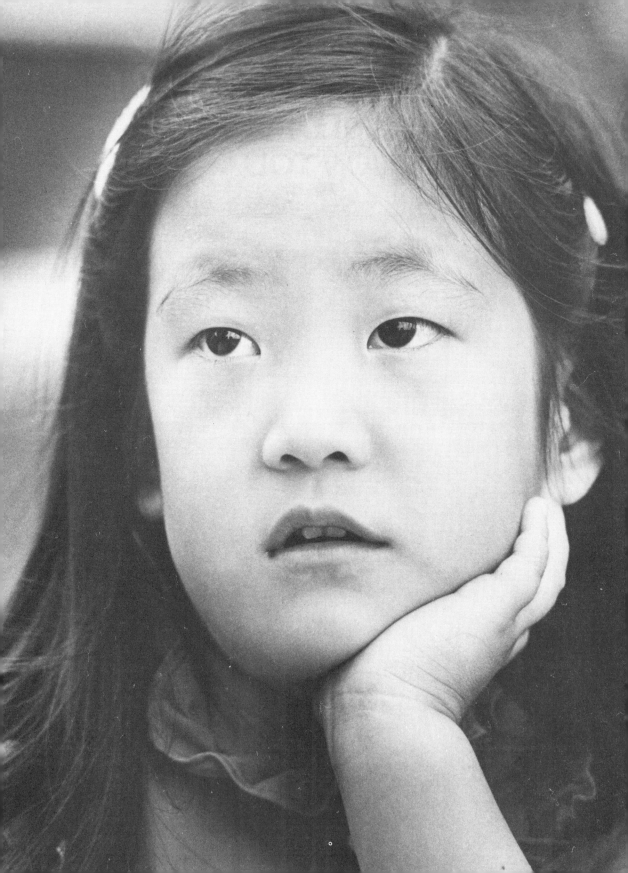

1

Interest and Issues: What's All the Fuss About?

As you read and study:

Identify reasons for the great interest in early childhood education.

Identify contemporary influences that create interest in early childhood education.

Understand and use the terminology of early childhood education.

Identify and describe types of early childhood education programs.

Recognize the importance of the ecology of early childhood education.

Analyze the influence of the concept of "the competent child" on child rearing and education.

Consider influences that hurry, pressure, and encourage children to grow up too soon, too fast.

Examine adults' views of children and explain the implications of these views for rearing and educating children.

Examine social, political, economic, and educational issues that influence child rearing, teaching, and policy development.

Understand how the public's desire for basic education influences early childhood education programs.

POPULARITY OF EARLY CHILDHOOD EDUCATION

For early childhood education, the 1990s will resemble the '60s, '70s, and '80s. While all areas of early childhood education have captured the public's attention, the fastest growing and most popular is the education and care of the very young, from birth to age three. More parents—and the public at large—recognize the importance of the early years to learning and later development. Many upwardly mobile parents believe they have only a few years to set the course of their children's development and futures. They are extremely goal-directed about their careers and their children. Given this attitude, it is likely that the popularity of early childhood education and interest in the early years will continue unabated.

Problems such as child abuse and the numbers of children who live in poverty are perennial sources of controversy and concern, to which early childhood professionals continue to seek new solutions. Topics such as infant stimulation and infant child care have caught early educators' attention. The continual emergence of new ideas and issues relating to the education and care of young children and the quest to provide educationally and developmentally appropriate programs keeps the field in a state of disequilibrium by constantly challenging early childhood professionals to determine what is best for young children and their families.

Continued Interest in the Early Years

Evidence of the public's interest in early childhood is all around us. Popular magazines, many of them targeted to meet the insatiable needs of parents for child rearing information, stress the importance of the early years for learning. They advise parents how to rear "smart" children who wil be capable of taking their places in the corporate world. Newspaper advertisements proclaim the advantages of preschools that emphasize academic excellence. Toy manufacturers market systematic approaches to learning through toy-of-the-month plans. Parents enroll themselves and their infants and toddlers in self-improvement programs promoted as physically and cognitively stimulating. Courses designed for expectant parents, new parents, and harried parents are now a standard part of the curriculum of many community colleges and schools. During one semester at a local community college, parents could select from these courses: Parent/Infant Enrichment, Play Activities with the Preschool Child, Discipline Strategies That Work, Movement and Play Activities, Creative Learning-Storytelling/Drama, Toilet Learning, Choosing a Preschool for Your Child, Building Your Child's Self-esteem, and Developmental Screening for Infants. Many of the courses required registration of both parents and their young children! Citizens' groups focus their advocacy efforts on issues such as eliminating violence from children's television programs, convincing manufacturers to reduce the amount of sugar, salt, and other additives in children's food products, and preventing more children and their families from sinking into poverty.

Parent groups discuss prevention of child abuse; how to reduce stress in children's lives; the demise of childhood; how to nurture in the nuclear age; ways to develop curricula for peace; how to extend more rights to children; and how to parent in these increasingly stressful and permissive times.

Economic issues fuel the controversy and conversation surrounding the future of the nation's young. The federal government's budget cuts, undertaken in efforts to decentralize the federal role in education, continue to strain the ability of programs to provide for the needs of disadvantaged children. As federal monies become increasingly scarce, early childhood educators and parents seek ways to garner private support to keep programs open and operating. Private agencies are asked to subsidize many programs previously supported by the federal government.

Stimulation/enrichment programs help popularize the importance of the very early years. Infant-parent stimulation programs catch the fancy and serve the needs of young parents, especially upwardly mobile parents. They want "the best" for their children and are willing to spend time, effort, and money to see that they get the best. This, in turn, makes it possible for early childhood educators to address the importance of the early years. It also creates a climate of acceptance for very early education and an arena in which early childhood educators are heard. Infant stimulation programs stimulate more than infants.

More and more parents seek out-of-home care and education for their children, at younger ages, in a wide variety of settings.

Males, once rarely seen in early childhood programs, are now accepted and expected to participate in classrooms, nurseries, delivery rooms, and child care centers. Increasing numbers of fathers-to-be attend prepared-childbirth seminars and actively seek advice and counseling about child rearing. Men are now recognized as competent, skillful caregivers.

In short, young children have captured the attention of the nation. They compete with budget deficits, nuclear arms treaties, and summit meetings for media attention. Young children are prime-time subjects. Consequently, early childhood educators must learn more about how to care for, educate, and rear children so they can advise parents, legislators, and those who formulate public policy when they look to them for guidance in determining what is best for the nation's children.

TERMINOLOGY OF EARLY CHILDHOOD EDUCATION

Terminology is frequently a problem when discussing early childhood education. Early childhood educators are not always clear with terms they use in their work, so it is important to have some knowledge of common definitions, and a command of the terminology used by the National Association for the Education of Young Children (NAEYC) and most early childhood professionals.

Throughout this text, *early childhood* refers to the child from birth to age eight. This is a standard and accepted definition used by the NAEYC.[1] The term frequently refers to children who have not yet reached school age, and the public often uses it to refer to children in any type of preschool.

Early childhood settings provide "services for children from birth through age eight in part-day and full-day group programs in centers, homes, and institutions; kindergartens and primary schools, and recreational programs."[2]

Early childhood education consists of the services provided in early childhood settings. It is common for educators of young children to use the terms *early childhood* and *early childhood education* synonymously.

Other terms frequently used when discussing the education of young children are nursery school and preschool. *Nursery school* is a program for the education of two-, three-, and four-year-old children. Many nursery schools are half-day programs, usually designed for children of mothers who do not work outside the home, although many children who have two working parents do attend. The purpose of the nursery school is to provide for active learning in a play setting. In some instances the kindergarten curriculum has been pushed down into the nursery school. As a result, a child-centered program in an informal play setting that characterizes a good nursery school has been replaced by a formal teacher-centered setting. *Preschool* generally means any educational program for children prior to their entrance into kindergarten.

When a public school or other agency operates one program for five-year-olds and another for four-year-olds, the term *kindergarten* is applied to the former and *nursery school* or *preschool* to the latter. Some school districts refer to their kindergarten as a preschool; others consider it part of their regular educational program.

Children should be the focal point of any discussion of education. Our primary concern should be: What is best for children?

The term *prekindergarten* is growing in usage to refer to a program for four-year-olds attending a program prior to kindergarten. Another term, *transitional kindergarten*, designates a program for children who are not ready for kindergarten and who can benefit from another year of the program. The term *transitional* also refers to grade-school programs that provide additional opportunities for children to master skills associated with a particular grade. Transitional programs do not usually appear beyond the second and third grades.

Junior first grade or *pre-first grade* are transitional programs between kindergarten and first grade developed to help five-year-olds get ready to enter first grade. Not all children are equally "ready" to enter first grade because of the wide range of mental ages and experiential backgrounds, and children frequently benefit from such special programs designed to meet their needs.

Preprimary refers to programs for children prior to their entering first grade; *primary* means grades first, second, and third. With increasing frequency, primary children are being taught in classes that include two grade levels. In these *split* or *nongraded, classes*, first and second graders and second and third graders are taught in a single class. Split classes are seldom composed of upper-elementary children. Reasons for split classes are decreasing school enrollments, influences of open education practices, and teacher contracts that limit class size.

A *parent cooperative preschool* is a school formed and controlled by parents for their children. Programs of this type are generally operated democratically with the parents hiring the staff. Often, some of the parents are hired to direct or staff the program. Being part of a cooperative means parents have some responsibility for assisting in the program.

The term *child care* encompasses many programs and services for preschool children. The more common term is *day care*, but most people engaged in the care of young children recognize this as outmoded. *Child care* is more accurate because it focuses on the children themselves. The primary purpose of child care programs is to care for young children who are not in school and for school-age children of working parents before and after school hours. Child care programs may have an educational orientation, or may offer primarily babysitting or custodial care. Many programs have a sliding fee schedule based on parents' ability to pay. Quality child care programs are increasingly characterized by their comprehensive or full-range services that address children's total needs—physical, social, emotional, creative and intellectual.

A large number of *family day care* programs provide child care services in the homes of the caregivers. This alternative to center-based programs usually accommodates a maximum of four or five children in a *family day care home*. Home care programs were formerly custodial in nature, but there is a growing trend for caregivers to provide a full range of services in their homes.

Church related or *church-sponsored* preschool and elementary programs are quite common, and are becoming more popular. These programs usually have a cognitive, basic skills emphasis within a context of religious doctrine and discipline. The reason for the popularity of these church-sponsored programs, which often charge tuition, is their emphasis on the basic skills and no-nonsense approach to learning and teaching.

Head Start is a federally sponsored program for children from low-income families. Established by the Economic Opportunity Act in 1965, the program is intended to overcome the effects of poverty. *Follow Through* extends Head Start programs to children in grades 1 through 3, and works with school personnel rather than apart from the schools.

There are not as many federal programs providing services to children, parents, and families as there were in the 1970s, but these programs have had a tremendous influence on early childhood education. For example, *Home Start* was a demonstration program within Head Start designed to deliver a comprehensive program of services to children and parents in the home. Today, many Head Start programs provide children and families a *Home Base* option for delivery of services. Table 1–1 delineates the purposes of the various types of early childhood programs.

The *Child and Family Resource Program* was a Head Start demonstration program. Services included education, parent involvement, and health and social ser-

TABLE 1–1 Types of Early Childhood Programs

Program	Purpose	Age
Early childhood	Multipurpose	Birth to third grade
Child care	Play/socialization; babysitting; physical care; provide parents opportunities to work; cognitive development	Birth to 6 years
Employer child care	Different settings for meeting child care needs of working parents	Variable; usually as early as 6 weeks to the beginning of school
Corporate child care	Same as employer child care	Same as employer child care
Industrial child care	Same as employer child care	Same as employer child care
Proprietary care	Provide care and/or education to children; designed to make a profit	6 weeks to entrance into first grade
Nursery (public or private)	Play/socialization; cognitive development	2–4 years
Preschool (public or private)	Play/socialization; cognitive development	2½–5 years
Parent cooperative preschool	Play/socialization; preparation for kindergarten and first grade; babysitting; cognitive development	2–5 years
Babysitting cooperatives (Co-op)	Provide parents with reliable babysitting; parents sit for others' children in return for reciprocal services	All ages
Prekindergarten	Play/socialization; cognitive development; preparation for kindergarten	3½–5 years
Junior kindergarten	A prekindergarten program	Primarily 4-year-olds
Senior kindergarten	Basically the same as regular kindergarten	Same as kindergarten
Kindergarten	Preparation for first grade; developmentally appropriate activities for 4½-to 6-year-olds	4–6 years
Developmental kindergarten	Same as regular kindergarten. Often enrolls children who have completed one or more years in an early childhood special education program	5–6 years

TABLE 1-1 continued

Program	Purpose	Age
Transitional kindergarten	Extended learning of kindergarten; preparation for first grade	Variable
Preprimary	Preparation for first grade	5–6 years
Primary	Teach skills associated with grades 1, 2, and 3	6–8 years
Toy lending libraries	Provide parents and children with games, toys, and other materials that can be used for learning purposes; housed in libraries, vans, or early childhood centers	Birth through primary years
Lekotek	Resource centers for families who have children with special needs; sometimes referred to as a *toy* or *play library* (*Lekotek* is a Scandinavian word that means *play library*)	Birth through primary years
High school child care programs	Provide child care for children of high school students, especially unwed parents; serve as an incentive for student/parents to finish high school and as a training program in child care and parenting skills	Six weeks–5 years
Drop-off child care centers	Provide care for short periods of time while parents shop, exercise, or have appointments	Infancy through the primary grades
Infant stimulation programs (also called parent/infant stimulation programs)	Programs for enhancing sensory and cognitive development of infants and young toddlers through exercise and play; activities include general sensory stimulation for children and educational information and advice for parents	3 months–2 years
Pre-first grade	Preparation for first grade; often for students who "failed" or did not do well in kindergarten	5–6 years

TABLE 1–1 continued

Program	Purpose	Age
Junior first grade	Preparation for first grade	5–6 years
Split class	Teach basic academic and social skills of grades involved	Variable, but usually primary
After school care	To provide child care for children after school hours	Children of school age; generally K–6
Family day care	Provide care for a group of children in a home setting: generally custodial in nature	
Head Start	Play/socialization; academic learning; comprehensive social and health services; prepare children for first grade	2–6 years
Private schools	Provide care and/or education	Usually preschool through high school
Health and Human Services	Same as Dept. of Children, Youth, and Families	All
Health and Social Services	Same as Dept. of Children, Youth, and Families	All
Follow Through	Extend Head Start services to grades 1, 2, and 3	6–8 years
Home Start	Provide Head Start service in the home setting	Birth–6 or 7 years
Laboratory school	Provide demonstration programs for preservice teachers; conduct research	Variable; from birth through senior high
Child and Family Resource Program	Deliver Head Start services to families	Birth–8 years
Montessori School (preschool and grade school)	Provide programs that use the philosophy, procedures, and materials developed by Maria Montessori (see Chapter 3)	1–8 years
Open education	Child-centered learning in an environment characterized by freedom and learning through activities based on children's interests	2–8 years
British primary school	Implement the practices and procedures of open education	2–8 years

Good early childhood programs provide stimulating and enriching activities that are developmentally appropriate.

vices, with the family as the central focus in providing services to children. The Child and Family Resource Program enrolled families with children from birth to age eight. This program, more than any other, was responsible for focusing the attention of early childhood educators on the importance of families in the lives of children. It also broadened the vision of early childhood professionals and made them realize that helping families solve their problems, frequently with the intervention of social service agencies, can be just as important as working directly with children.

Demonstration programs of many kinds are operated by public and private agencies including colleges and universities, hospitals, and industries. Many colleges and universities with schools of education have a *laboratory school* used primarily for research in teaching methods, demonstration of exemplary programs and activities, and for training teachers. Many of these schools also develop materials and programs for children with handicaps and learning disabilities.

As the name implies, a *toy library* makes toys and other learning materials available to children, parents, child care providers, and teachers. Toy libraries are housed in many different settings, such as libraries, shopping malls, churches, preschools, and vans. Many toy libraries are supported by user fees and parent and community volunteers.

Early Childhood Labels

Professionals in early childhood education use certain labels to refer to children of different ages, as outlined in Table 1-2. Just as professionals use certain terms to refer to children, so too, there are also labels for the various adults who work with young children, as shown in Table 1-3.

THE ECOLOGY OF EARLY CHILDHOOD

Ecology is the study of how people interact with their environments and the results and consequences (good and bad) of these interactions. There is growing interest in how children interact with their environments—home, child care center, and school—and the effect of these interactions on children. Early childhood educators realize they must pay greater attention to children's environments.

Early childhood ecological considerations apply at three levels. The first level is an examination of the environments and how they are structured and arranged to promote children's maximum growth. For example, early childhood educators are more aware than ever of the role the child care environment has in influencing health, safety, and physical and intellectual development. Sensitive professionals seek ways to structure environments so they are less stressful, more healthful, less dangerous, and more accommodating to children's developmental needs.

TABLE 1-2 Labels for Children

Label	Description	Age
Baby	Generic term referring to a child from birth through the first two years of life	Birth to two years
Neonate	Child during the first month of life; from Latin term *neo* (new) *natus* (born). Usually used by nurses, pediatric specialists, and people working in the area of child development	Birth to one month
Infants	Children from birth to the beginning of independent walking (about 12 months of age)	Birth to one year
Toddlers	Children from the beginning of independent walking to about age four; the term *toddler* is derived from the lunging, tottering, precarious balanced movement of children as they learn to walk	Thirteen months to three years
Preschoolers	Children between toddler age and age of entrance into kindergarten or first grade; because kindergarten is becoming more widespread, it is customary to refer to four-year-olds as preschoolers	Three to five years
Child/Children	Generic term for individuals from birth through the elementary grades	Birth to eight years
The very young	Used to identify and specify children from birth through preschool	Birth to five years

At a second level, early childhood educators focus on how environments interact with each other. For example, early childhood educators are part of children's environments, and how they interact with parents, who are also part of children's environments, affects children. Urie Bronfenbrenner, a leading proponent of the importance of ecological studies in education, says, "A child's ability to learn to read in

TABLE 1–3 Adults Who Work with Young Children

Label	Description
Early childhood educator	Works with young children and has committed oneself to self-development by participating in specialized training and programs to extend professional knowledge and competence
Early childhood teacher	Responsible for planning and conducting a developmentally and educationally appropriate program for a group or classroom of children; supervises an assistant teacher or aide; usually has a bachelor's degree in early childhood, elementary education, or child development
Early childhood assistant teacher	Assists the teacher in conducting a developmentally and educationally appropriate program for a group or classroom; frequently acts as a co-teacher, but may lack education or training to be classified as teacher (many people who have teacher qualifications serve as an assistant teacher because they enjoy the program or because the position of teacher is not available); usually has a high school diploma or associate degree and is involved in professional development
Early childhood associate teacher	Plans and implements activities with children; has an associate degree and/or the CDA credential; may also be responsible for care and education of a group of children
Aide	Assists the teacher and teacher assistant when requested; usually considered an entry-level position
Director	Develops and implements a center or school program; supervises all staff; may teach a group of children
Home visitor	Conducts a home-based child development/education program; works with children, families, and staff members of the program
Child Development Associate	Has completed a CDA assessment and been awarded the CDA credential*
Caregiver	Provides care, education, and protection for the very young in or outside the home†; includes parents, child care workers, and early childhood teachers
Parent	Provides the child with basic care, direction, support, protection, and guidance††

*CDA National Credentialing Program, *Child Development Associate Assessment System and Competency Standards* (Washington, D.C.: CDA National Credentialing Program, 1985), p. 551.

†George S. Morrison, *The Education and Development of Infants, Toddlers, and Preschoolers* (Boston: Little, Brown, 1988).

††George S. Morrison, *Parent Involvement in the Home, School and Community* (Columbus, Ohio: Merrill Publishing Company, 1978), p. 28.

the primary grades may depend no less on how he is taught than on the existence and nature of ties between the school and home."[3] Early childhood educators demonstrate they are attuned to the importance of the interactions of educational settings and homes when they initiate programs of parent involvement and family support.

Political and social environments represent a third, more abstract, level of interaction. For example, the Florida legislature recently mandated compulsory kindergarten for all children five years of age as of September first. What effects does such political policy have on young children? Some people worry that children who are five by September first are "too old" when they enter kindergarten. Others are concerned about the cost and trauma parents undergo to find quality child care because their children were born a month or a day too late. Others see an advantage to the September first age limit in that children are older when they come to school, and therefore will be "ready" to learn. The point is that members of the early childhood profession, parents, social workers, legislators, and others are beginning to care about such ecological relationships, which will undoubtedly play an even more important role in early childhood as the years go by. Increasing numbers of early childhood educators are writing position statements about the effects of social and public policy on children. Child advocacy agencies are drafting public policies on topics ranging from developmentally appropriate curricula for young children to the pros and cons of developing public school programs for four-year-olds.

At no time in American history has there been so much interest and involvement on the part of educators in the development of public policy. This political reality is beneficial to all—children, parents, families, and early childhood professionals—for it helps to assure that children's best interests will be considered when decisions are made that affect them.

THE COMPETENT CHILD

The decade of the 1960s ushered in a renewal of interest in very young children and how they learn. Many research studies (see chapter 2) focused on the importance of the early years and challenged educators and parents to reconsider the role early learning plays in life-long learning. A result of this renewed interest in the early years was that parents placed great *intellectual* importance on early learning. This change in parental attitudes toward early learning resulted in what David Elkind calls the "concept of the competent infant." Elkind believes the image of the competent infant is promoted and reinforced by such social conditions as divorce, increasing numbers of single parents, and two-career families. According to Elkind, "The concept of the competent infant is clearly more in keeping with these contemporary family styles." Contemporary social forces and lifestyles create a need to view children as competent. As Elkind explains,

> A competent infant can cope with the separation from parents at an early age. He or she is able to adjust with minimal difficulty to babysitters, day care centers, full day nursery schools and so on. If some parents feel residual pangs of guilt about leaving their young offspring in out-of-home care, they can place their youngster in a high-pressure academic program. If the child were not in such a program, the parents tell themselves, he or she would fall behind peers and would not

be able to compete academically when it is time to enter kindergarten. From this perspective, high pressure academic programs are for the young child's "own good."[4]

Many parents embrace the concept of the competent infant as compatible with what they want to achieve in their own lives. An upwardly mobile career parent wants a child who can achieve at an early age. Parents want to begin early to assure success and advancement for their competent children. Susan Littwin sums up the new attitude toward child rearing:

> What the child care experts did do, at least indirectly, was create the idea of the professional parent. With all the advice available on television talk shows and in magazines and paperback books, raising children could no longer be something that you did by tradition or whim or common sense. There was a right way and a wrong way to put a child to bed, to leave him with a baby-sitter, to get him started at school, to have a friend over. Being a parent was a career; the harder you worked the more you gained.[5]

CHILDHOOD STRESS

The scene of children being left at a child care center or preschool for the first time is familiar to anyone who has worked with young children. Some children quickly become happily involved with new friends in a new setting; some are tense. They cling fearfully to their parents, and cries of despair pierce the air. For many children, separation from the ones they are attached to is a stressful experience that causes them and others a great deal of trauma. Crying, fear, and tension are the *stress responses*, the symptoms or outward manifestations of children's stress.

Young children are subjected to an increasing number of situations and events that cause them stress. Some of these *stressors* include their parents' divorce, being left at home alone before and after school, parents who constantly argue, the death of a parent or friend, being hospitalized, living in a dangerous neighborhood, and fears of nuclear war, poverty, riots, and child abuse. Children are also subjected to stress by parents who hurry them to grow up, to act like adults, to get into school, and to succeed. Other causes of stress are the rush to early schooling, the emphasis on competency testing, and basic skills learning.

Parents and early childhood professionals are becoming aware of the effects stress can have on children. These can include sickness, withdrawal, shyness, loss of appetite, poor sleep patterns, urinary and bowel disorders, and general behavioral and discipline problems. Some early childhood educators believe that one way to alleviate stress is through play. They feel children should be encouraged to play as a therapeutic antidote to the effects of stress. Others think the best way to relieve stress in children is to stop hurrying and pressuring them. They think children should be free from parental and societal demands so they can enjoy their childhood. Unfortunately, society is as it is; we cannot and should not want to return to the "old days." The tempo of twentieth-century America is hectic, and demands for individual achievement are increasing. Despite our wishes, the pace of life is not going to slow down.

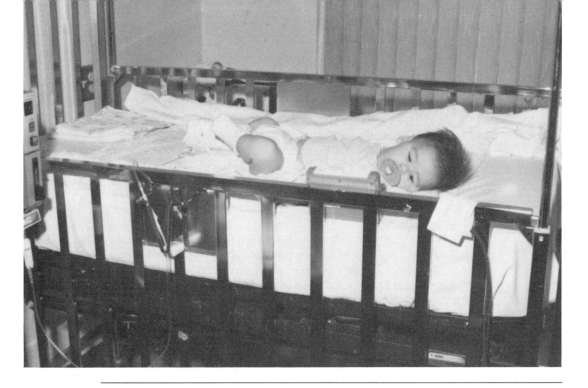

Young children experience greater stress than ever before. Some of this stress results from the benefits of new advances in health care; other stress results from the pressures of living in a fast-paced society.

Another solution is to teach children how to alleviate the effects of stress. From preschool on, children should be taught stress reduction techniques, including relaxation and breathing exercises, yoga, physical exercises, meditation, and regular physical activity. Since we cannot slow the pace of society, we need to teach children coping skills. The amount and kinds of stress on children and its effect is causing more early childhood educators and caregivers to become involved in programs and agencies that work for solutions to societal issues and forces that cause children stress. Reducing stress is one of the premier issues in early childhood education. Events and actions that cause stress in children, and educators' searches for ways to reduce or eliminate stress, help keep young children and early childhood education in the forefront of the educational scene.

THE DISAPPEARANCE OF CHILDHOOD

There is growing concern that childhood as we knew it or remember it is disappearing. Children are often viewed as pseudoadults; they even dress like adults, in designer jeans, tops, and running shoes. Some believe that childhood is not only endangered, but already gone. Neil Postman deals with the demise of childhood in his book, *The Disappearance of Childhood*. Postman says that before the Renaissance, there was no such period as childhood. The invention of the printing press and books brought childhood into being, because children now had to earn their right to adulthood by learning to read, so as to gain access to adult information and knowledge.

With the advent of books came schools, where children were taught to read and prepared to become literate adults. Postman says the hundred-year period from 1850 to 1950 represents the highwater mark of childhood, and was also the period during which the stereotype of the "modern" family developed. The introduction of television assured the end of childhood, because television presents information that is available to all in an undifferentiated form. The whole family—infants, toddlers, teenagers, and parents—watch the same programs together:

> We may conclude, then, that television erodes the dividing line between childhood and adulthood in three ways, all having to do with its undifferentiated accessibility: first, because it requires no instruction to grasp its form; second, because it does not make complex demands on either mind or behavior; and third, because it does not segregate its audience.... Given the conditions I have described, electric media find it impossible to withhold any secrets. Without secrets, of course, there can be no such thing as childhood.[6]

Vance Packard expresses concern and alarm over "a deep malaise" that has come swiftly over child rearing in America. Packard believes that changes in the family have contributed to an overall deterioration in the quality of parenting. He finds these societal forces responsible:

1. An antichild culture that confronts children with a cool, hard world outside their homes
2. The surge of married women—including millions of mothers—into jobs outside the home
3. An increase in the splitting up of parents and the reverberating impact on the millions of children involved[7]

Perhaps even more disturbing, Packard detects a growing sentiment against children. He believes that many people are consciously deciding not to have children, and a childless lifestyle is viewed by some as the "ultimate liberation." Children are no longer considered emotionally necessary to the fulfillment of an individual lifestyle or married life. On the contrary, children are perceived as obstacles to fulfillment, obstacles to a career, an economic burden, and impediments to marital happiness. People who consider children unnecessary to their own fulfillment and as obstacles and economic burdens are less likely to be concerned about the welfare of children in general. They will be less inclined to consider programs for children a top national priority.

VIEWS OF CHILDREN

Views of children determine how people teach and rear them. As you read about the different views of children, try to clarify and change what you believe. Also identify social, environmental, and political factors that tend to support each particular view. Sometimes, of course, views overlap, so it is possible to synthesize ideas from several views into a particular personal view.

Children's views of themselves result partly from how society and adults view them.

Miniature Adults

What early childhood educators and parents identify as childhood has not always been considered a distinct period of life. During medieval times, the notion of childhood did not exist; little distinction was made between children and adults. The concept of children as miniature adults was logical for the time and conditions of medieval Europe. Economic conditions did not allow for a long childhood dependency. The only characteristics that separated children from adults were size and age. Children were expected to act as adults in every way, and they did so.

In many respects the twentieth century is no different, because children are still viewed and treated as adults. In many third world countries of Latin America, Africa, and Asia, children are, of necessity, expected to be economically productive. They are members of the adult world of work at the ages of four, five, or six.

In the United States, where child labor laws protect children from the world of adult work and exploitation, there are those who advocate allowing children to enter the workplace at earlier ages and for lower wages. In some rural settings, the young child still has economic value. Approximately one million migrant children pick crops and help their parents earn a livelihood (see Chapter 10). At the other end of the spectrum, child actors and models engage in highly profitable and what some call glamorous careers. National publicity about child abuse and drug usage dramatizes the extent to which young children are involved in prostitution and drugs.

Encouraging children to act like adults and hurrying them toward adulthood causes conflicts between capabilities and expectations, particularly when early childhood educators demand adultlike behavior from children and set unrealistic expectations.

The Child as Sinful

Based primarily on the religious belief in original sin, the view of the child as sinful was widely accepted in the fourteenth through eighteenth centuries, particularly in Colonial North America during the Puritan era of the sixteenth and seventeenth centuries. Misbehavior was a sign of this inherent sin. Making children behave and using corporal punishment whenever necessary was emphasized. Misbehavior was taken as proof of the devil's influence, and beating the devil out of the child was an acceptable solution.

This view of inherent sinfulness persists, and is manifested in the belief that children need to be controlled through rigid supervision and insistence on unquestioning obedience to and respect for adults. Educational institutions are perceived as places where children can be taught "right" behavior. The number of private and parochial or religious schools that emphasize respect, obedience, and correct behavior is growing because of parents' hopes of rearing children who are less susceptible to the temptations of crime and drugs.

Blank Tablets

The English philosopher John Locke (1632–1704) believed that children were born into the world as *tabula rasa*, or *blank tablets*. After extensive observations, Locke concluded: "there is not the least appearance of any settled ideas at all in them; especially of ideas answering the terms which make up those universal propositions that are esteemed innate principles."[8] Locke believed that children's experiences, through sensory impressions, determined what they learned and, consequently, what they became. The blank tablet view presupposes no innate genetic code or inborn traits; that is, children are born with no predisposition toward any behavior except what is characteristic of human beings. The sum of what a child becomes depends upon the nature and quality of experience; in other words, the primary determinant of what a person becomes is environment.

The blank tablet view has several implications for teaching and child rearing. If children are seen as empty vessels to be filled, the teacher's job is to fill them—to present knowledge without regard to their needs, interests, or readiness for learning. What is important is that children learn what is being taught. Children become what adults make of them.

This view of children deemphasizes individual differences, and assumes that as children are exposed to the same environmental influences, they will tend to behave and even think the same. This concept is the basis for many educational beliefs and practices in socialist countries. Children begin schooling early, often at six weeks of age, and are taught a standard curriculum that promotes a common political consciousness. They are expected to behave in ways that are consistent with and appropriate to how a citizen of the state should behave.

Growing Plants

Another viewpoint is that of children as growing plants. The role of the educator or parent is similar to that of a gardener, and classrooms and homes are greenhouses where children grow and mature in harmony with their natural growth patterns. A natural consequence of growth and maturing is that children *unfold*, much as the bloom of a flower unfolds under the proper conditions. In other words, what children are to become results from natural growth and a nurturing environment. Two key ingredients of this natural growth and unfolding are *play* and *readiness*. The content and process of learning are included in play, and materials and activities are designed to promote play.

Children become ready for learning through motivation and play. This concept prompts teaching subjects or skills when children reach the point where they can benefit from appropriate instruction. Lack of readiness to learn indicates that the child has not sufficiently matured; the natural process of unfolding has not occurred.

Belief in the concept of unfolding is evident in certain social and educational policies, such as proposals to increase the age requirements for entry into kindergartens and first grade so that children have more time to mature and get ready for school. Many people also believe each child's maturation occurs in accordance with an innate timetable; that there is a "best time" for learning specific tasts. They believe it is important to allow time for children's inner tendencies to develop, and that teachers and parents should not "force" learning. This maturation process is as important, if not more so, than children's experiences. Many contemporary programs operate on the unfolding concept, whether or not it is explicitly stated.

Property

The view has persisted throughout history that children are the property of their parents or of institutions, justified in part by the idea that, as creators of children, parents have a right to them and their labors. Children are, in a real sense, the property of their parents. Parents have broad authority and jurisdiction over a child. Few laws interfere with the right of parents to control their child's life.

Laws (although difficult to enforce) protect children from physical and emotional abuse. Parents must send their children to school where there are compulsory attendance laws. Generally, however, parents have a free hand in dealing with their children. Legislatures and courts are reluctant to interfere in what is considered a sacrosanct relationship. Parents are generally free to exercise full authority over their children. Within certain broad limits, most parents feel their children are theirs to do with and for as they please. Parents who embrace this view see themselves as decision makers for their children and may place their own best interests above those of their children.

Investments in the Future

Closely associated with the notion of children as property is the view that children represent future wealth or potential for parents and a nation. Since medieval times, people have viewed child rearing as an investment in the future. Many parents assume (not always consciously) that, when they are no longer able to work or must retire, their children will provide for them. Consequently, having children becomes a means to an end. Seeing that children are clothed and fed assures their future economic contribution to their parents.

Over the last several decades, many social policies in the U.S. have been based partly on the view that children are future investments. Many federal programs were built on the underlying assumption that preventing problems in childhood leads to more productive adulthood. An extension of this attitude is that prevention is less expensive than curing a problem. Many local educational programs emphasize identifying the problems of children and their families early, so as to take preventive rather than remedial action. The rationale is that it is less costly in the long run to prevent in the preschool and primary years than it is to remediate in the high school or later years. As educators, we also know that besides being more expensive, remediation is not as effective as prevention.

Particularly during the 1960s, many federal programs were based on the idea of conserving one of the country's greatest resources—its children. Head Start, Follow Through, and child welfare programs are products of this view, which has resulted in a "human capital" or "investment" rationale for child care and other services. As expressed by the Research and Policy Committee of the Committee for Economic Development,

> The most important investment this nation can make is in its children. Although many institutions influence our children's education and development—the family, the community, the church, the media—the focus of this policy statement is on the institution in which the public plays a direct and dominate role: America's public schools.
>
> . . .
>
> We are convinced that the earliest stages of educational development are where we will receive the best return on our investment in education. This means a stronger focus on the elementary schools and on well-designed preschool programs for children from disadvantaged backgrounds.[9]

The public believes a primary goal of education is to develop children who will be productive and will help protect the nation against "foreign" competition. Therefore, the early education of young children in "good" programs is seen as one way to strengthen the U.S. economically. Thus, the country's best defense against outside forces is a well-educated, economically productive population. From this perspective, then, investing in children is seen as an investment in the United States. One problem with this view is that it fails to consider children's intrinsic human worth. Trying to make a nation stronger through its children tends to emphasize national priorities over individuals.

CHILDREN'S RIGHTS

A contemporary legal and humanistic view recognizes children as individuals with rights of their own. While children are often still treated as economic commodities and individuals who need protection, their rights are beginning to be defined. Since children are not organized into political groups, others must act as their advocates. Courts and social service agencies are becoming particular champions and defenders.

The International Year of the Child, sponsored by the United Nations in 1979, helped focus attention on the UN's view of the basic rights of children as adopted by the General Assembly. The UN Declaration of the rights of the child included these points:

- ☐ The right to affection, love, and understanding.
- ☐ The right to adequate nutrition and medical care.
- ☐ The right to full opportunity for play and recreation.
- ☐ The right to a name and nationality.
- ☐ The right to special care if handicapped.
- ☐ The right to be among the first to receive relief in times of disaster.
- ☐ The right to learn to be a useful member of society and to develop individual abilities.
- ☐ The right to be brought up in a spirit of peace and brotherhood.
- ☐ The right to enjoy these rights, regardless of race, color, sex, religion, national or social origin.
- ☐ All children, without any exception whatsoever, shall be entitled to these rights, without distinction or discrimination.

Many professions and child advocacy groups also have goals and statements that advocate extension of certain basic rights to children. The National Child Health Goals of the American Academy of Pediatrics are an example:

- ☐ All children should be wanted and born to healthy mothers.
- ☐ All children should be born well.
- ☐ All children should be immunized against the preventable infectious diseases for which there are recommended immunization procedures.

- ☐ All children should have good nutrition.
- ☐ All children should be educated about health and health care systems.
- ☐ All children should live in a safe environment.
- ☐ All children with chronic handicaps should be able to function at their optimal level.
- ☐ All children should live in a family setting with an adequate income to provide basic needs to insure physical, mental and intellectual health.
- ☐ All children should live in an environment that is as free as possible from contaminants.
- ☐ All adolescents and young people should live in a societal setting that recognizes their special health, personal and social needs.[10]

Societal attitudes toward children's rights are often ambivalent. Child abuse laws tend to protect children from physical and emotional abuse; on the other hand, the courts do not consider corporal punishment of school-age children cruel and inhumane treatment. Contemporary advocates of children's rights, such as Richard Farson, feel that society does not recognize the right of children to full humanity:

> Our world is not a good place for children. Every institution in our society discriminates against them. We all come to feel that it is either natural or necessary to cooperate in that discrimination. Unconsciously we carry out the will of a society which holds a limited and demeaned view of children and which refuses to recognize their right to full humanity.[11]

Some children's rights supporters believe children need advocates to act on their behalf because they are politically disenfranchised, economically disadvantaged, have passive legal status, are the personal property of their parents, and because their lack of experience makes them vulnerable to abuse and exploitation. On the other hand, many people, including parents, feel they should be allowed to raise their children as they think best, free of interference.

Rights are being extended to children in ways that would not have been thought possible ten years ago. Particularly in the area of fetal rights, parents are encountering conflicts between their rights and the lives of their unborn children. Many localities require places that sell liquor to post a sign that says: "Warning: Drinking alchoholic beverages during pregnancy can cause birth defects." Major controversies are arising between the rights of the unborn and the rights of pregnant women. Questions such as "What rights of the pregnant woman supersede those of her unborn child?" and "Does the government or other agency have the right to intervene in a woman's life on behalf of her unborn child?" are not easy to answer.

Generally speaking, people who teach and care for young children are more accepting of laws that extend children's rights. In a survey of early childhood educators, Kerckhoff and McPhee found that 78 percent favored laws giving children more protection, 67 percent favored giving children more rights, 72 percent favored providing an advocate for children, and 51 percent favored making it illegal to sell war toys for children. Further, 41 percent of those surveyed favored providing children with attorneys when their parents are divorcing, and 42 percent favored making it illegal for parents to ridicule their children.[12]

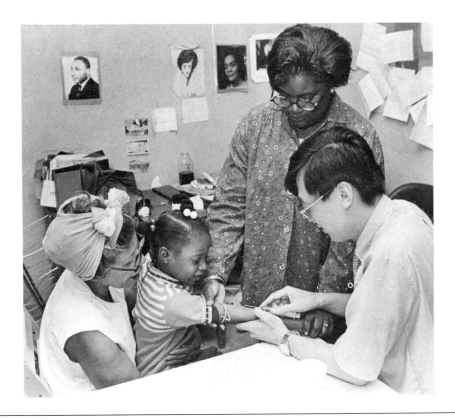

Among children's basic rights, one is freedom from preventable diseases.

The debate will undoubtedly continue throughout the next decade, and the rights of children will be further defined and clarified through the judicial system. The rights of all children will be examined, and more special interest groups will join the trend to gain even more rights for children.

A review of the ways we see children leads to some intriguing questions. In this generation, are parents and teachers as child-centered as they should be? Are early childhood educators interested in helping children receive the best so they can realize their best? What we know we should do and what we do are often two different things. Public and social policies often supersede our interest in children. Wars, national defense, and economics sometimes take precedence over questions of what is best for our nation's (and other nation's) children.

CONTEMPORARY INFLUENCES ON EARLY CHILDHOOD EDUCATION

The field of early childhood education is constantly changing as a result of social, political, and economic conditions. These areas influence not only how children are taught, but where and by whom. Economic influences often determine whether we can afford to teach and provide basic care for children. A number of forces and topics influence the nature of early childhood. Some have exerted influence for many years; others are only now emerging, and the exact nature of their influence is yet to be determined.

Women's Movement

The women's movement has had a tremendous and long-lasting influence on young children and early childhood education. A major reason for the interest in infants and infant care is that women want quality out-of-home care for their infants. The National Organization of Women (NOW) is working for a federally funded, 24-hour child care program. True equality for women depends partly on relieving them of the constant care of children. The women's movement liberates women and gives them opportunities to make choices about how to best conduct their lives and the lives of their children. These choices have resulted in more women entering the work force, more divorces, single parenting, and demand for more and better comprehensive child care. The women's movement has helped enlighten parents regarding their rights as parents, including helping them learn how to advocate on behalf of themselves and their children for better health services, child care, and programs for earlier education. Previously, the public supposed that because parents conceived children, they knew how to provide experiences that would promote intellectual, social, and emotional growth. Today, more people seek help to become effective parents because of the programs and efforts of the women's movement.

Working Parents

More and more families find that both parents need employment to make ends meet. Over 50 percent of mothers with children under six are currently employed or are actively seeking employment, creating a greater need for early childhood programs (see Figure 1–1, p. 26). This need has brought a beneficial recognition to early childhood programs and prompted early childhood educators to try to meet parents' needs. Unfortunately, the urgent need for child care has encouraged people who are ill-prepared and who do not necessarily have children's or their parents' best interests in mind to establish programs. Demand is high enough that good programs have not had a chance to drive inferior programs from the child care marketplace.

For their part, some parents are not able or willing to evaluate programs and select the best ones for their children, which also encourages poor quality programs to stay in operation.

Rising Incomes

Ironically, while the need for two incomes generates interest in early childhood, rising incomes are also a factor. Many parents with college degrees and middle-level incomes are willing to invest money in early education for their children. They look for nursery schools and preschool programs they feel will give their children a good start

The growing demand for child care services creates interest in early childhood programs and helps raise public expectations about the nature and quality of the programs.

in life, and many Montessori schools and franchised operations have benefited in the process. In the last several years, the Montessori system has experienced a tremendous boom, both in the number of individuals seeking Montessori teacher training and in preschool enrollments. Many parents of three- and four-year-olds spend almost as much in tuition to send their children to good preschools as parents of eighteen-year-olds spend to send their children to state-supported universities.

Single Parents

The number of one-parent families is increasing, as shown in Figure 1–2 (p. 27). In 1986, more than 25 percent of American families with children were headed by a single parent. People are single parents for a number of reasons. It is estimated that half of all marriages end in divorce. Some people choose single parenthood; others, such as teenagers, become parents by default. Liberalized adoption procedures, artificial insemination, surrogate childbearing, and general public support for single parents make this lifestyle an increasingly attractive option for some people.

No matter how people become single parents, the reality and extent of single parenthood has tremendous implications for early childhood educators. Early child-

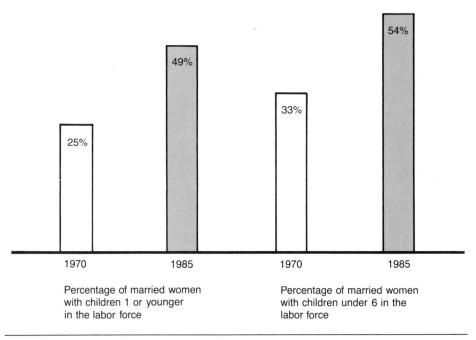

FIGURE 1–1 Increase in the Percentage of Mothers in the Labor Force (Source: Brad Edmondson, "The Education of Children," *American Demographics* 8 [1986]: 28)

hood programs are having to develop curricula to help children and their parents deal with the stress of family breakups, and teachers are called upon to help children adjust to the guilt they often feel and to their altered family pattern. In addition to child care, single parents frequently seek help in child rearing, especially in regard to discipline. Early childhood educators are often asked to conduct seminars to help parents gain these skills.

A decade ago, early educators were not as concerned about how to help and support single parents and children from single-parent families, but today they recognize that single parents want and need their help. How well early educators adjust to accommodate the needs of single parents may well make the difference in how successful many single parents are in their new roles.

Fathers

One of the biggest changes in early childhood today is that fathers have rediscovered the joys of parenting and working with young children. Many men are playing an active role in providing basic care, love, and nurturance to their children. The definition of father is changing; a father is no longer stereotypically unemotional, detached from everyday responsibilities of child care, authoritarian, and a disciplinarian. Fathers no longer isolate themselves from child rearing only because they are

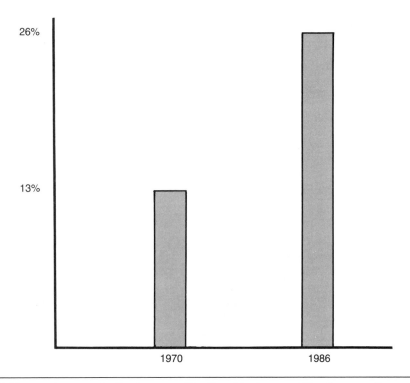

FIGURE 1-2 Increase in Single-parent Families: Single-parent Families as a Percentage of all Families, 1970–1986 (Source: Bureau of the Census)

male. Men are more concerned about the role of fatherhood and their participation in family events before, during, and after the birth of their children. Fathers want to be involved in the whole process of child rearing. Because so many men feel unprepared for fatherhood, agencies such as hospitals and community colleges are providing courses and seminars to introduce fathers to the joys, rewards, and responsibilities of fathering.

Fathers no longer quietly acquiesce to giving up custody of their children in a divorce. Men are becoming single parents through adoption and surrogate childbearing. Fathers' rights groups have tremendous implications for the family court system and traditional interpretations of family law.

Fathers are also receiving some of the employment benefits that have traditionally gone only to women. Paternity leaves, flexible work schedules, and sick leave for family illness are just a few examples of how fathering has come to the workplace.

Early childhood educators are having to readjust their thinking. They are learning how to work with and involve both parents and single fathers. In particular, they are learning how to help fathers overcome cultural stereotypes and prejudices. While one dad who provides family child care or one househusband doesn't create the attention it might have several years ago, taken collectively, males are a strong influence and a definite sign of a growing trend toward equality in parenting roles.

Fathers have rediscovered the joys of parenting and working with young children and are being encouraged and supported in their new roles of shared parenting.

Teenage Parents: Children Having Children

Teenage pregnancies are on the rise. Each year one out of ten teenagers—1.1 million—become pregnant. These facts about teenage pregnancy dramatically demonstrate its extent and effects:

☐ One out of ten girls between the ages of 15 and 19 becomes pregnant each year

☐ Fifteen percent of all pregnant teenagers will become pregnant again within a year

☐ Many teenagers are emotionally and physically unprepared for parenthood

☐ Becoming a teenage parent often means a sudden drastic change in lifestyle

☐ Complications during pregnancy are more likely among teenage girls because their bodies may not yet be physically mature

☐ Children born to mothers under 18 face greater hazards than those born to older mothers

☐ Many teen parents are forced to reconsider career and educational plans in trying to fulfill the role of parents[13]

Concerned legislators, public policy developers, and national leaders view teenage pregnancy as further evidence of the breakup of the family. They worry about the demand for public health and welfare services; envision a drain on the taxpayer's dollars; and decry the loss of future potential because of school dropouts. From an early childhood point of view, teenage pregnancies create greater demand for infant and toddler child care and the need to develop programs to help teenagers learn how to parent. The staff of an early childhood program must often provide nurturance for both child and parent, because the parent herself may not be emotionally mature. Emotional maturity is necessary for a parent to engage in a giving relationship with children. When teenage parents lack parenting characteristics of any kind, early childhood educators must help them develop them.

Federal Cuts in Social Service and Education Programs

Beginning about 1980, the federal government began cutting many program budgets, and private agencies and state governments have had to take over support of some programs. Other programs have had to close, so that some families and children must cope with reduced services or no services at all. Federal monies had a stimulating effect on early childhood programs in the 1960s and 1970s, but the current cuts are having a dampening effect. Federal budget cuts that affect early childhood and related programs are likely to continue, and federal officials suggest that support from private agencies, contributions, and volunteerism constitute legitimate alternatives to federal funds.

Critics of the declining federal presence in early childhood programs maintain that the results are harmful to women, children and families. They cite increases in the number of women and children living in poverty and a higher infant mortality rate to support their argument. Reduced funding for early childhood programs requires early childhood educators to be strong advocates on behalf of children and their families. Early educators should be in the vanguard of efforts to influence public policy and develop public awareness about providing for children in the early years.

Programs that commit to and depend on federal monies must recognize their vulnerability to shifts in political attitudes and swings, both up and down, in federal support. Agencies that provide money can also take away money. Part of the solution to this dilemma is strong advocacy for and development of programs based on multiple funding sources rather than a single source.

The Basic Education Movement

The basic education movement in early childhood advocates early teaching of the basics—reading, writing, arithmetic, and the skills and concepts associated with learning them. While writing might not actually be taught to preschoolers, skills such as holding a pencil, making straight and curved lines, letter identification, and eye-hand coordination activities would be included in the curriculum. The same would be true for reading and mathematics.

The basic education movement has tended to create a sense of urgency in parents, and an accompanying tendency to start schooling at an earlier age, which some people cite as evidence of hurrying, pressuring, and making children grow up too fast.

The issue of what to teach often polarizes between advocates of basic education on the one hand and of progressive education on the other. The basic education viewpoint is the belief that certain basics should receive priority in teaching–reading, writing, arithmetic, and cultural heritage. Those who support this point of view generally advocate a no-nonsense approach to education that includes, among other elements, homework, tests, memorization, and strict discipline. The school is a place where hard work and obedience to teacher authority are expected, and the functions of the school are to impart factual knowledge, preserve the cultural heritage, promote basic values such as hard work, and guard the status quo.

Those who believe the school should be child-centered advocate a curriculum based on the "whole child" and developed out of his interests and abilities. John Dewey is credited with fathering the progressive education movement. The progessive curriculum currently finds expression in the open education method.

It is possible to teach just about anything (content) with just about any methodology (process). For example, it is possible to teach basic skills (content) in an open education setting (process) and in a traditionalist or back-to-basics classroom (process). Some parents and educators feel that a particular process precludes teaching a particular content, but this is not so.

THE PUBLIC SCHOOLS AND EARLY EDUCATION

Traditionally, the majority of preschool programs were operated by private agencies or by agencies supported wholly or in part by federal funds to help the poor, unemployed, working parents, and disadvantaged children, but times have changed. Now working and single parents exert great pressure on public school officials and state legislatures to sponsor and fund additional preschool and early childhood programs. The public schools of 14 states provide some degree of funding for programs for four-year-olds. Consequently, public school programs for four-year-olds are a growing reality.

Parents lobby for public support of early childhood education for a number of reasons. First, because working parents cannot find quality child care for their children, they believe the public schools hold the solution to child care needs. Second, the persistent belief that children are a nation's greatest wealth makes it seem sensible to provide services to young children to avoid future school and learning problems. Third, many people believe that early public schooling, especially for children from low-income families, is necessary if the U.S. is to promote equal opportunity for all. They argue that low-income children begin school already far behind their more fortunate middle-class counterparts, and the best way to keep them from falling hopelessly behind is for them to begin school earlier. Fourth, many parents cannot afford the cost of quality child care. They believe preschools, furnished at the public's expense, are a reasonable and cost-efficient way to meet child care needs.

A fifth reason for the demand for public school involvement relates to the "competent child." Parents want academic programs for their children at an earlier age, and look, naturally, to the public schools to provide programs that will help their children succeed in life. Sixth, baby-boom parents are the best educated in American history. One in four men and one in five women have college degrees.[14] These well-educated parents are causing a boom in preschool programs that emphasize earlier and more comprehensive education for young children.

There have been discussions at the federal level about how to link programs such as Head Start more closely to the public schools. With continuing cuts in educational programs, there may be greater effort to effect such linkages, and many public schools have already moved into the area of child care. There are several arguments in favor of such a realignment. First, some educators don't think it makes sense to train nonteachers for preschool work when trained teachers are available. Second, some educators think it is reasonable to put the responsibility for educating and caring for the nation's children under the sponsorship of one agency—the public schools. For their part, public school teachers and the unions that represent them are anxious to bring early childhood programs within the structure of the public school system.

Television has given today's children a door to the world of adulthood. Television offers entertainment and educational benefits, but also exposes children to violence and a degree of sophistication that earlier generations did not have to deal with.

There is by no means consensus that there should be universal public schooling or even anything approaching it. Critics of the effort to place preschool programs in the public schools cite three reasons against such a policy. First, they cite the failure of public education to do a good job of teaching young children. They ask how public schools can handle an expanded role if they have not done a good job with what they are already supposed to do. Second, some critics say that public school teachers are not trained in the specific skills needed in Head Start, child care, and other preschool programs. A third, more convincing argument relates to money: the cost of having the public schools assume the responsibility of preschool programs would probably cost over several billion dollars, which taxpayers are unlikely to be willing to pay.

These are some of the influences on and interests in early childhood education during the last decade of the twentieth century that should challenge early childhood educators to seek the best ways to educate children in turbulent and exciting times. More is demanded of parents and teachers than ever before, and teaching and parenting thus require more and different skills. But it is the issues, concerns, and emerging influences that make early childhood such an exciting profession. If everything were stable, if all the questions were answered, if all the issues were settled, there would be no problems to deal with! Early childhood education is a vibrant profession composed of dedicated individuals willing to address issues and problems creatively and sensitively. As John Naisbitt says, "What a fantastic time to be alive!"[15] And perhaps even more importantly, what a fantastic time to be an early childhood educator!

FURTHER READING

Cleverley, Joan, and D. C. Phillips. *Visions of Childhood: Influential Models from Locke to Spock*, Revised Edition (New York: Teachers College Press, 1986) Updated focus on major ideas and theories of child rearing and educational practices. Examines major contributions of Freud, Piaget, Dewey, and many others; provides solid foundation of philosophy and fundamentals of early childhood education.

Elkind, David. *The Hurried Child: Growing Up Too Fast, Too Soon* (Reading, Mass.: Addison-Wesley, 1981) Examines today's concern about pressure on children of all ages and addresses their fears of failure.

Greenberg, Martin. *The Birth of a Father* (New York: Continuum, 1985) The author states, "The event of fatherhood is a momentous occurrence in the life cycle of man. It inevitably triggers . . . emotions that are multifaceted and often tumultuous." Prospective parents need to read Greenberg's book.

Kagan, Jerome. *The Nature of the Child* (New York: Harper and Row, 1984) Describes the author's personal vision of child development, combining science and philosophy as they interrelate in human nature.

Littwin, Susan. *The Postponed Generation: Why America's Grown-up Kids Are Growing Up Later* (New York: William Morrow, 1986) Explores the "startling trend" of a generation of young people who are postponing the responsibilities and autonomy of adulthood and the social, economic, and emotional factors that have caused this turnabout in traditional expectations.

Miller, Mary Susan. *Childstress! Understanding and Answering Stress Signals of Infants, Children, and Teenagers* (Garden City, N.Y.: Doubleday, 1982) Helps adults pick up stress signals from children at an early stage, and provides guidelines for coping with stress.

Postman, Neil. *The Disappearance of Childhood* (New York: Delacorte Press, 1982) Postman argues convincingly that childhood is disappearing at "dazzling speed." He credits the Renaissance with creating childhood as a social structure and psychological condition, and blames electronic media for the disappearance of childhood.

FURTHER STUDY

1. Observe a young child whose parents you know, and decide how the child's mannerisms (speech and ways of doing things) are similar to those of the parents. Which mannerisms do you expect will remain with the child through life?

2. Give general definitions of the terms *heredity* and *environment.* Which of the two seems to pose the more immediate problem in educating children? Give reasons for your choice. Do you think heredity and environment play an equal role in growth and development? Why or why not?

3. Interview people in education and other professions. How do they view the relationship between heredity and environment? In what ways do you agree or disagree?

4. Would you consider sending your own child to a nursery school (or any other type of care setting) at age four? Why or why not?

5. Interview parents who are actively involved in children's programs and others who are not. Are there noticeable differences in their children or in the parents?

6. Visit and observe at least three different types of child care programs, then list the "stressors" you feel are present for young children in each of these different centers. Compare your lists.

7. Visit a church-related program or church-sponsored preschool program. How are they different from other programs you have visited? How is their structure different? Their curriculum? Their routines? How are they similar?

8. Compare the program philosophy of a Head Start program to that of a private, for-profit child care program. How are they similar? Different?

9. List your opinions of corporate child care, then visit a program. Now go back and review your pre-visit ideas to compare your opinions after your visit. List the pros and cons of corporate child care, and explain how your opinions changed.

10. Interview the director of a corporate child care program, and ask about the program's philosophy, primary goals, concerns, and ideas.

11. Research the theories of children as "growing plants" and as "property." How have these theories influenced today's views of children?

12. Contact different governmental agencies to gather information about single parenting, teenage parenting, legal separation rights, and custody of young children. How are these social forces affecting early childhood education programs in your state and local community?

13. Find out about your state and local government assistance programs for child care programs. Are cuts anticipated that will threaten this type of governmental assistance? What does the future hold for children in this area?

14. Identify and define terms that summarize how young children are viewed in today's society.

15. Observe parent-child relationships in public settings such as supermarkets, laundries, and restaurants. What do these relationships tell you about parent-child interactions and how parents rear their children? What implications do these relationships have for how the child is taught in school?

16. Critique the issues presented in this chapter. What issues are most significant? What other issues do you feel should be included? Defend your selections.

17. Given a limited amount of community resources to spend on education for young children, how would you spend it? Establish priorities for services.

18. Find out if your state legislature or local school district has identified certain *basic skills* the schools will teach. Do you agree with these identified basic skills? Why or why not?

19. Find out what problems teachers in your schools face as a result of divorce, abuse, and other types of stress in children's lives.

20. Find out what types of nursery school programs are available in your community. Who may attend them? How are they financed? What percentage of the children who attend have mothers who work outside the home?

21. Observe a kindergarten or nursery school with a cognitive emphasis and one with a socialization emphasis. Compare the two programs. How are they similar? How are they different? Which would you prefer to teach in? Why?

22. Make a telephone survey of tuition costs of early childhood programs in your area. Do you think tuitions are generally reasonable? Why or why not?

23. Find advertisements for child care in the classified ads of newspapers and the yellow pages of the telephone directory. Call or visit one of these programs. Tell why you would or would not send your child to the program.

24. Visit attorneys, legal aid societies, juvenile courts, and other agencies. List the legal rights children already have. Do you think children have some rights they should not have? Which ones? Why?

25. List certain rights that children do not have that you think should be extended to them. Justify your response.

26. List factors that support the argument that childhood is disappearing or has disappeared, then make a list to support the opposite viewpoint, that childhood is not disappearing.

27. What actions do you think government, schools, and other agencies could take to curtail the disappearance of childhood?

28. What useful purposes does childhood serve?

29. Interview teachers, early childhood professors, and child care workers for their opinions about public school programs for four-year-olds. Summarize their opinions.

2

Historical Influences:
Who Are These People?

As you read and study:

Identify reasons it is important to know about the ideas and theories of early educators.

Analyze and develop a basic understanding of the beliefs of Luther, Comenius, Locke, Rousseau, Pestalozzi, Froebel, Montessori, Dewey, and Piaget.

Describe the contributions of great educators to modern educational thought and practice.

Identify basic concepts that are essential to good early childhood education.

Identify and develop an appreciation for events, professional accomplishments, and contributions in the field of early childhood education.

Understand how people, agencies, and legislation influence early childhood education.

There are at least five good reasons to know about the ideas and theories of early educators. First, by reading of the hopes and ideas of people your profession has judged famous, you will realize that today's ideas are not necessarily new. Old ideas and theories have a way of being reborn. Topics such as individualizing instruction, compensatory education, open education, behavior modification, and basic education have been discussed since the 1400s. Maria Montesorri, for example, was a proponent of today's open education. We can more fully appreciate the premises of open education by having at least a rudimentary understanding of Montessori and some of the thinkers who influenced her, such as Pestalozzi and Froebel. The influence of Montessori, in turn, can be found in modern materials and activities.

Second, many of the earlier educators' ideas are still dreams, despite the advances we think modern education has made. In this regard, we are the inheritors of a long line of thinkers going back to Socrates and Plato. We should acknowledge this inheritance and use it as a base to build meaningful teaching careers.

Third, the ideas expressed by the early educators help us better understand how to implement current teaching strategies. For instance, Rousseau, Froebel, and Montessori all believed children should be taught with dignity and respect. This attitude toward children is essential to an understanding of good educational practice and often makes the difference between good and bad teaching.

Fourth, theories about young children decisively shape educational and child rearing practices. Many parents and teachers may not realize, however, what assumptions form the foundations of their daily practices. Studying and examining beliefs of the great educators helps parents and educators clarify what they do and gain insight into their actions. In this sense, knowing about theories liberates the uninformed from ignorance and empowers professionals and parents. As a consequence, they are able to implement practices with confidence.

Fifth, exploring, analyzing, and discovering the roots of early childhood education helps *inspire* professionals. Recurring rediscovery forces people to examine current practices against what others have advocated. Examining sources of beliefs helps clarify modern practice, and reading and studying others' ideas makes us rethink our own beliefs and positions. In this regard, the history of the great educators and their beliefs can keep us current. When we pause long enough to listen to what they have to say, we frequently find a new insight or idea that motivates us to continue our quest to be the best we can be.

MARTIN LUTHER

While the primary impact of the Protestant Reformation was religious, other far-reaching effects were secular. Two of these were universal education and literacy.

In Europe, the sixteenth century was a time of great social, religious, and economic upheaval, due partly to the Renaissance and partly to the Reformation. Great emphasis was placed on formal schooling to teach children how to read, the impetus

The great educators have always stressed that parents and teachers should help children develop the social and cognitive skills they need for success in life. Reading to children provides a warm emotional context in which to learn one of life's most basic skills.

for which is generally attributed to the father of the Reformation, Martin Luther (1483–1546).

The question of what to teach is an issue in any educational endeavor. Does society create schools and then decide what to teach, or do the needs of society determine what schools it will establish to meet desired goals? In the case of European education, the necessity of establishing schools to teach children to read was an issue raised by Martin Luther. Simply stated, Luther replaced the authority of the hierarchy of the Catholic Church with the authority of the Bible. Believing that each person was free to work out his own salvation through the Scriptures meant that people had to learn to read the Bible in their native tongue.

This marked the real beginning of teaching and learning in the people's native language, the *vernacular,* as opposed to Latin, the official language of the Catholic Church. Before the Reformation, only the wealthy or those preparing for a religious vocation learned to read or write Latin. One of the early tasks undertaken by Luther was the translation of the Bible into German; the Bible thus became available to the people in their own language, and the Protestant Reformation, under the impetus of Luther, encouraged and supported popular universal education.

Luther believed the family was the most important institution in the education of children. To this end, he encouraged parents to provide religious instruction and vocational education in the home. Luther also believed a strong state-supported system of education was necessary to counter the control the Catholic Church exercised over education. He believed a reformed church also needed a reformed educational system.

Throughout his life Luther remained a champion of education. He wrote letters and treatises and preached sermons on the subject. His best known letter on education is the *Letter to the Mayors and Aldermen of All the Cities of Germany in Behalf of Christian Schools,* written in 1524. In this letter, Luther argues for public support of education.

> Therefore it will be the duty of the mayors and council to exercise the greatest care over the young. For since the happiness, honor, and life of the city are committed to their hands, they would be held recreant before God and the world, if they did not, day and night, with all their power, seek its welfare and improvement. Now the welfare of a city does not consist alone in great treasures, firm walls, beautiful houses, and munitions of war; indeed, where all these are found, and reckless fools come into power, the city sustains the greatest injury. But the highest welfare, safety, and power of a city consists in able, learned, wise, upright, cultivated citizens, who can secure, preserve, and utilize every treasure and advantage.[1]

Out of the Reformation came other religious denominations, all interested in preserving the faith and keeping their followers within the fold of their church. Most of the major denominations such as Calvinism and Lutheranism established their own schools to provide knowledge about the faith. Education and schooling were considered not only socializing forces, but also means of religious and moral instruction. Many religious groups have always had rather extensive school programs, for this is one way to help assure that children born into the faith will continue in the faith. Religious schools are a means of defending and perpetuating the faith as well as a place where converts can learn about and become strong in the faith.

JOHN AMOS COMENIUS

Comenius (1592–1670) was born in Moravia, a former province of Czechoslovakia, and became a minister of the Moravian faith. Comenius spent his life serving as a bishop, teaching school, and writing textbooks. Of his many writings, those that have received the most attention are *The Great Didactic* and the *Orbis Pictus* (*The World in Pictures*), considered the first picture book for children.

Just as Luther's religious beliefs formed the basis for his educational ideas, so too with John Comenius. In fact, throughout this discussion of the influence of great men and women on educational thought and practice, you will see a parallel interest in religion and education. It has always been obvious to religious followers that what they believe gives shape, form, and substance to what they will teach, and to a large

Play allows opportunities for sensory experiences and for learning cognitive skills and concepts.

degree, what is taught determines the extent to which the religious beliefs are maintained and extended.

Comenius believed that humans are born in the image of God, and that it was therefore an obligation and duty to be educated to the fullest extent of one's abilities to fulfill this Godlike image. If so much depends on education, then, as far as Comenius was concerned, it should begin in the early years.

> It is the nature of everything that comes into being, that while tender it is easily bent and formed, but that, when it has grown hard, it is not easy to alter. Wax, when soft, can be easily fashioned and shaped; when hard it cracks readily. A young plant can be planted, transplanted, pruned, and bent this way or that. When it has become a tree these processes are impossible.[2]

Comenius became an advocate of universal education that began at an early age and continued through adulthood. He also believed in the essential goodness of man, in direct opposition to the belief that man's natural depravity predisposed behavior contrary to accepted religious practice. His religious beliefs help explain Comenius's interest in early education and lifelong learning.

Since one of Comenius's fundamental beliefs was that people are essentially good, he believed that education should be a positive learning experience that includes freedom, joy, and pleasure. This contrasts sharply to the concept of education as discipline, consisting partly of a rigid, authoritarian atmosphere designed to control children's natural inclination to do bad things. In modern terms, the argument is whether children learn better in an authoritarian setting characterized by traditional classrooms, or in a child-centered setting that encourages autonomy and self-regulation.

Another basic belief of Comenius was that education should follow the order of nature. Natural order implies a timetable for growth and learning, and one must observe this pattern to avoid forcing learning before the child is capable, or before the necessary steps to that learning have been taught. This belief is reflected in Montessori's concept of sensitive periods, Piaget's stages of development, and the perennial issue of readiness for school and learning.

> It is now quite clear that that order, which is the dominating principle in the art of teaching all things to all men, should be, and can be, borrowed from no other source but the operations of nature. As soon as this principle is thoroughly secured, the processes of art will proceed as easily and as spontaneously as those of nature. Very aptly does Cicero say: "If we take nature as our guide, she will never lead us astray," and also: "Under the guidance of nature it is impossible to go astray." This is our belief, and our advice is to watch the operations of nature carefully and to imitate them.[3]

Comenius also thought that learning is best achieved when the senses are involved, and that sensory education formed the basis for all learning.

> Those things, therefore, that are placed before the intelligence of the young, must be real things and not the shadows of things. I repeat, they must be *things;* and by the term I mean determinate, real, and useful things that can make an impression on the senses and on the imagination. But they can only make this impression when brought sufficiently near.
>
> From this a golden rule for teachers may be derived. Everything should, as far as is possible, be placed before the senses. Everything visible should be brought before the organs of sight, everything audible before that of hearing. Odours should be placed before the sense of smell, and things that are tastable and tangible before the sense of taste and of touch respectively. If an object can make an impression on several senses at once, it should be brought into contact with several.[4]

We see an extension and refinement of this principle in the works of Montessori and Piaget and in contemporary programs that stress manipulation of concrete objects.

Comenius gave some good advice when he said that the golden rule of teaching should be to place everything before the senses. Because of his belief in sensory education, Comenius thought children should not be taught the names of objects apart from the objects themselves or pictures of the objects. His *Orbis Pictus* helped children learn the names of things and concepts through pictures and words. As the name implies, *Orbis Pictus* pictured the world as it was during Comenius's time.

Comenius's emphasis on the concrete and sensory is a pedagogical principle early childhood educators are still trying to fully grasp and implement. Many modern-day programs, such as those derived from Montessori's ideas, stress sensory learning. Many early childhood materials promote learning through activities that use the senses. The concept of learning through the senses and by doing is not new. So much of early education tends to be conducted in the abstract, by talking to and telling about an object in the absence of concrete examples. Teaching then becomes one-dimensional via the telling and listening (oral and aural) mode rather than multidimensional and multisensory as it should be.

A broad view of Comenius's total concept of education can be gained by an examination of some of his principles of teaching:

> Following in the footsteps of nature we find that the process of education will be easy
> (i)   If it begins early, before the mind is corrupted.
> (ii)   If the mind be duly prepared to receive it.
> (iii) If it proceed from the general to the particular.
> (iv)   And from what is easy to what is more difficult.
> (v)   If the pupil be not overburdened by too many subjects.
> (vi)   And if progress be slow in every case.
> (vii) If the intellect be forced to nothing to which its natural bent does not incline it, in accordance with its age and with the right method.
> (viii) If everything be taught through the medium of the senses.
> (ix)   And if the use of everything taught be continually kept in view.
> (x)   If everything be taught according to one and the same method.
> These, I say, are the principles to be adopted if education is to be easy and pleasant.[5]

There is a noticeable trend in education today to make learning, as Comenius suggested, easier and more pleasant.

Probably the two most significant contributions of Comenius to today's education are textbooks with illustrations and the emphasis in most early childhood programs on training the senses. We take the former for granted, and naturally assume that the latter is necessary as a basis for learning.

The writings of Comenius echo many of Luther's ideas and in a sense anticipate and provide a basis for the ideologies of Pestalozzi and other educators. Comenius's emphasis on sensory perception found expression in Pestalozzi's ideas about the concrete and direct sensory experience in learning. The current emphasis on the family and its importance in educating children is evidence of society's unwillingness or inability to put into practice many of the ideas that it has known for centuries were worthy. It seems as though we are constantly reinventing the wheel, rather than learning from and building on the good ideas developed by educators such as Comenius.

JOHN LOCKE

As mentioned in chapter 1, John Locke (1632–1704) popularized the *blank tablet* view of children. This and other of his views influence modern early childhood education and practice. Indeed, the extent of Locke's influence is probably unappreciated by many who daily implement practices based on his theories. More precisely, Locke developed the theory of and laid the foundation for *environmentalism*—the belief that it is the environment, not innate characteristics, that determine what a person will become.

Locke, born in Somerset, England, was a medical doctor, philosopher, and social scientist. His ideas about education were first applied when his cousin and her husband asked him for child rearing advice. His letters to them were published in 1693 as *Some Thoughts Concerning Education.* Many of his philosophical ideas that directly relate to education are also found in *An Essay Concerning Human Understanding.* Locke's assumption of human learning and nature was that there are no innate ideas, which gave rise to his theory of the mind as a blank tablet or "white paper":

> Let us suppose the mind to be, as we say, white paper void of all characters, without ideas. How comes it to be furnished? Whence comes it by that vast store which the busy and boundless fancy of man has painted on it with an almost endless variety? Whence has it all the materials of reason and knowledge? To this I answer, in one word, from *experience;* in that all our knowledge is founded, and from that it ultimately derives itself.[6]

For Locke, then, the environment forms the mind. The implications of this idea are clearly reflected in modern educational practice. The notion of the primacy of environmental influences is particularly evident in programs that encourage and promote early education as a means of overcoming or compensating for a poor or disadvantaged environment. Based partly on the assumption that all children are born with the same general capacity for mental development and learning, these programs also assume that differences in learning and achievement are attributable to environmental factors such as home background, early education, and experiences. Programs of early schooling, especially the current move for public schooling for four-year-olds, work on the premise that children's differences arise because disadvantaged children fail to have the experiences of their more advantaged counterparts that are necessary for school success. In fact, it is not uncommon, as evidenced by Head Start and programs in Texas and Florida, to limit early schooling to those who are considered disadvantaged and to design it especially for them. Because Locke believed that experiences determine the nature of the individual, sensory training became a prominent feature of the application of his theory to education. He and others who followed him believed that the best way to make children receptive to experiences was to train their senses. In this regard, Locke exerted considerable influence on others, particularly Maria Montessori, who developed her system of early education based on sensory training.

JEAN JACQUES ROUSSEAU

Jean Jacques Rousseau (1712–1778) was born in Geneva, Switzerland, but spent most of his life in France. He is best remembered by educators for his book *Émile,* in which he raises a hypothetical child from birth to adolescence. Rousseau's theories were radical for his time. The opening lines of *Émile* not only set the tone for Rousseau's educational views, but for many of his political ideas as well. "God makes all things good; man meddles with them and they become evil."[7]

Rousseau advocated a return to nature and a natural approach to educating children, called *naturalism.* To Rousseau, naturalism meant abandoning society's artificiality and pretentiousness. A naturalistic education would permit growth without undue interference or restrictions. Rousseau would probably argue against such modern practices as dress codes, compulsory attendance, minimum basic skills, frequent and standardized testing, and ability grouping, because they are "unnatural." There is some tendency in American education to emphasize naturalism by replacing practices such as regimentation, compulsory assignments, and school-imposed regulations with less structured processes.

According to Rousseau, natural education promotes and encourages qualities such as happiness, spontaneity, and the inquisitiveness associated with childhood. In his method, parents and teachers allow children to develop according to their natural abilities and do not interfere with development by forcing education upon them or by protecting them from the corrupting influences of society. Rousseau felt that Emile's education occurred through three sources: nature, people, and things.

> All that we lack at birth and need when grown up is given us by education. This education comes to us from nature, from men, or from things. The internal development of our faculties and organs is the education of nature. . . . It is not enough merely to keep children alive. They should learn to bear the blows of fortune; to meet either wealth or poverty, to live if need be in the frosts of Iceland or on the sweltering rock of Malta.[8]

Rousseau believed, however, that although we have control over the education that comes from social and sensory experiences, we have no control over natural growth. In essence, this is the idea of *unfolding,* in which the nature of children—what they are to be—unfolds as a result of maturation according to their innate timetables. We should observe the child's growth and provide experiences at appropriate times. Some educators have interpreted this notion as a *laissez-faire* approach.

Educational historians point to Rousseau as dividing the historical and modern periods of education. Rousseau established a way of thinking about the young child that is reflected in innovators of educational practice such as Pestalozzi and Froebel. His concept of natural unfolding echoes Comenius and appears in current programs that stress readiness as a factor of learning. The developmental stages of Jean Piaget reinforce Rousseau's thinking about the importance of natural development. Educational practices that provide an environment in which children can become autonomous and self-regulating have a basis in his philosophy. The common element in all the approaches that advocate educating in a free and natural environment is the view of children as essentially good and capable of great achievement. It is the responsibility of teachers and parents to apply the right educational strategy at the right period of readiness for this potential to be fulfilled.

Perhaps the most famous contemporary example of the laissez-faire approach to child rearing and education is A. S. Neill's *Summerhill* (also the name of his famous school), which presents a strong case for freedom and self-regulation. Neill and his wife wanted "to make the school fit the child—instead of making the child fit the school."

> We set out to make a school in which we should allow children freedom to be themselves. In order to do this, we had to renounce all discipline, all direction, all suggestion, all moral training, all religious instruction. We have been called brave, but it did not require courage. All it required was what we had—a complete belief in the child as good, not an evil, being. For almost forty years, this belief in the goodness of the child has never wavered; it rather has become a final faith.[9]

JOHANN HEINRICK PESTALOZZI

Pestalozzi (1746–1827) was born in Zurich, Switzerland. He was greatly influenced by Rousseau and his *Émile*. Originally, Pestalozzi was so impressed by Rousseau's back-to-nature concepts that he purchased a farm that he hoped would become a center for new and experimental methods in agriculture. While engaged in farming, Pestalozzi became more and more interested in education and, in 1774, started a

Activities of daily living offer young children opportunities to learn responsibilities and to develop skills associated with formal learning.

school called Neuhof at his farm. At Neuhof, Pestalozzi developed his ideas of the integration of home life, vocational education, and education for reading and writing. Because the cost of trying his ideas was much greater than the tuition he was able to collect, this educational enterprise went bankrupt.

Pestalozzi spent the next twenty years writing about his educational ideas and practices. From such writings as *Leonard and Gertrude,* which was read as a romantic novel rather than for its educational ideas, Pestalozzi became well known as a writer and educator. He spent his later years developing and perfecting his ideas at various schools throughout Europe.

The influence of Rousseau is most apparent in Pestalozzi's belief that education should follow the child's nature. His dedication to this concept is demonstrated by his rearing his only son, Jean Jacques, using *Émile* as a guide. His methods were based upon harmonizing nature and educational practices.

> And what is this method? It is a method which simply follows the path of Nature, or, in other words, which leads the child slowly, and by his own efforts, from sense-impressions to abstract ideas. Another advantage of this method is that it does not unduly exalt the master, inasmuch as he never appears as a superior being, but, like kindly Nature, lives and works with the children, his equals, seeming rather to learn with them than to teach them with authority.[10]

Unfortunately, Pestalozzi did not have much success rearing his son according to Rousseau's tenets, as evidenced by Jean Jacques's inability to read and write by the age of twelve. This may be due either to his physical condition (he was thought to be epileptic), or to Pestalozzi's inability to translate Rousseau's abstract ideas into practice. Pestalozzi was able, however, to develop his own pedagogical ideas as a result of the process.

Probably the most important lesson from Pestalozzi's experience is that educators cannot rely solely on a child's initiative for learning to occur. While some children are able to teach themselves to read, someone created the climate and conditions for that beginning reading process. To expect that children will be or can be responsible for learning basic skills by themselves is asking too much.

Pestalozzi believed all education is based on sensory impressions, and that through the proper sensory experiences, the child's natural potential could be developed. This belief led to "object lessons." As the name implies, Pestalozzi thought the best way to learn many concepts was through manipulative experiences, such as counting, measuring, feeling, and touching. Pestalozzi believed the best teachers were those who taught children, not subjects. He also believed in multiage grouping. Pestalozzi anticipated by about 150 years the many parent programs that teach parents to work with young children in the home. He believed mothers could best teach their children and wrote two books, *How Gertrude Teaches Her Children* and *Book for Mothers,* detailing procedures for doing this. He felt that "the time is drawing near when methods of teaching will be so simplified that each mother will be able not only to teach her children without help, but continue her own education at the same time."[11]

FRIEDRICH WILHELM FROEBEL

Born in Germany, Froebel (1782–1852) devoted his life to developing a system for the education of young children. While his contemporary, Pestalozzi, with whom he studied and worked, advocated a system for teaching, Froebel actually developed a curriculum and methodology. In the process, Froebel earned himself the distinction of "father of the kindergarten." As a result of his close relationship with Pestalozzi and of reading the works of Rousseau, Froebel decided to open a school and put his ideas into practice. Like many other great people, Froebel was not eminently successful in either his personal or professional life. Some of the reasons for the lack of recognition during his lifetime were his inability to find educators who were interested in his ideas and accompanying personal problems. In his early years, Froebel was supported both financially and emotionally by his brother's widow, who as a result of this support had expectations of marriage. When this union did not materialize, Froebel's relatives mounted an attack on him and his ideas. This animosity lasted throughout his life and prevented, in several instances, the adoption of his ideas by others. It was only at the end of his life that he and his methods received the recognition they so richly deserved.

Froebel's primary contributions to educational thought and practice are in the areas of learning, curriculum and methodology, and teacher training. His concept of children and how they learn was based, in part, on the idea of unfolding, held by Comenius and Pestalozzi before him. The educator's role, whether parent or teacher, was to observe this natural unfolding and provide activities that would enable children to learn what they are ready to learn. The teacher's role, in essence, was to help children develop their inherent qualities for learning. In this sense, the teacher was a designer of experiences and activities. This notion of teacher as facilitator would be reinforced later by both Montessori and Piaget, both undoubtedly influenced by Froebel, who believed that:

> Therefore, education in instruction and training, originally and in its first principles, should necessarily be *passive, following* (only guarding and protecting), *not prescriptive, categorical, interfering.*
>
> Indeed, in its very essence, education should have these characteristics; for the undisturbed operation of the Divine Unity is necessarily good—cannot be otherwise than good. This necessity implies that the young human being—as it were, still in process of creation—would seek, although still unconsciously, as a product of nature, yet decidedly and surely, that which is in itself best; and, moreover, in a form wholly adapted to his condition, as well as to his disposition, his powers, and means.[12]

Consistent with his idea of unfolding, comparable to the process of a flower blooming from a bud, Froebel compared the child to a seed that is planted, germinates, brings forth a new shoot, and grows from a young, tender plant to a mature fruit-producing one. He likened the role of the educator to that of a gardener. In his kindergarten, or "garden of children," he envisioned children being educated in close harmony with their own nature and the nature of the universe. Children unfold their uniqueness in play, and it is in the area of play that Froebel makes one of his greatest contributions to the curriculum of the preschool.

Froebel compared the child to a seed, and likened caregivers to gardeners.

Play is the purest, most spiritual activity of man at this stage, and, at the same time, typical of human life as a whole—of the inner hidden natural life in man and all things. It gives, therefore, joy, freedom, contentment, inner and outer rest, peace with the world. It holds the sources of all that is good. A child that plays thoroughly, with self-active determination, perseveringly until physical fatigue forbids, will surely be a thorough, determined man, capable of self-sacrifice for the promotion of the welfare of himself and others. Is not the most beautiful expression of child-life at this time a playing child?—a child wholly absorbed in his play?—a child that has fallen asleep while so absorbed?

As already indicated, play at this time is not trivial, it is highly serious and of deep significance. Cultivate and foster it, O mother; protect and guard it, O father! To the calm, keen vision of one who truly knows human nature, the spontaneous play of the child discloses the future inner life of the man.

The plays of childhood are the germinal leaves of all later life; for the whole man is developed and shown in these, in his tenderest dispositions, in his innermost tendencies.[13]

Froebel knew from experience, however, that unstructured play represented a potential danger and that it was quite likely, as Pestalozzi learned with his son Jean

Learning and socializing should be joyful experiences.

Jacques, that a child left to his own devices does not learn much. Without guidance and direction, and a planned environment in which to learn, there was a real possibility that no learning or the wrong kind of learning might occur. Unfortunately, not all teachers have learned this lesson. Some believe that meaningful learning can occur in a context of free play in which the child is allowed to do anything he wants to do.

According to Froebel, the teacher is responsible for guidance and direction so children can become creative, contributing members of society. To achieve this end, Froebel developed a systematic, planned curriculum for education of the young child. The basis for his curriculum were "gifts," "occupations," songs he composed, and educational games. Gifts were objects for children to handle and use in accordance with the teacher's instructions so they could learn shape, size, color, and concepts involved in counting, measuring, contrasting, and comparison. The first gift was a set of six balls of yarn, each a different color, with six lengths of yarn the same colors as the balls. Part of the purpose of this gift was to teach color recognition.

Froebel felt that the ball (meaning a round, spherical object) played an important role in education; consequently, he placed a great deal of emphasis on its use. He also believed the ball was a perfect symbol for man's unity with the divine, a concept he felt was important but is difficult for us to understand. Froebel said of the ball:

> Even the word *ball*, in our significant language, is full of expression and meaning, pointing out that the ball is, as it were, an image of the all; but the ball itself has such an extraordinary charm, such a constant attraction for early childhood, as well as for later youth, that it is beyond comparison the first as well as the most important plaything of childhood especially.[14]

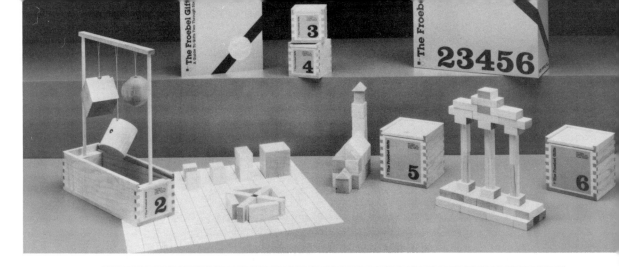

These modern reproductions of some of Froebel's "gifts" attest to the renewed interest in Froebelian ideas and materials.

The second gift was a cube, a cylinder, and a sphere. The directions for the use of the second gift give an insight into Froebel's educational methods and philosophy.

> The importance of the consideration of the presence and absence of an object and its utilization for play, and in playing with the child, has been already noticed (with the ball, see first gift). With this we will now add a continuation to the play; for repeating the same experience in different ways with the same object serves to develop as well as to strengthen the child. Hence the mother hides the cube in her hand while she sings to her child:
>
> > I see now the hand alone.
> > Where, oh, where can cube be gone?
>
> The mother thus leads the gaze and attention of the child to her hand, which he will therefore watch intently; the gaze, and even the little hand of the child, will make an effort to find the cube. As if yielding to this effort, the concealing hand opens, and the mother says or sings to the child:
>
> > Aha! aha!
> > My hand has hid the cube with care,
> > While you looked for it everywhere.
> > See, it is here!
> > Look at it, dear.
>
> By this play the child is not only again made to notice that the cube fills space, but his attention is also called to the precise form of the cube; and he will look at it sharply, unconsciously comparing it with the hand, to which his eyes were first attracted. But the form of the cube appears to him, up to this point, as too large a whole, and composed of too many kinds of parts; the child's view of it must therefore be clarified by single perceptions.
>
> Therefore the mother or nurse clasps the cube again in her hand, but so that one surface is still perceptible, singing to the child:
>
> > Only one side here you see
> > Where can now the others be?[15]

"Occupations" were materials designed for developing various skills, primarily psychomotor, through activities such as sewing with a sewing board, drawing pictures by following the dots, modeling with clay, cutting, bead stringing, weaving, drawing, pasting, and paper folding. Many of the games or plays Froebel developed were based on his gifts.

The following "Taste Song" from Froebel's *Mother's Songs, Games, and Stories* is typical of how he felt mothers could talk to, play with, and provide their children with sensory impressors. Froebel wanted mother and child to actively engage in the process of learning.

Through the Senses, Nature plainly speaks to Baby here:
Mother, see that he finds Nature through their accents clear.
Through the Senses, there's a pathway to the inmost door;
But the mind must light this pathway, light on darkness pour.
In the Senses, Baby's soul lies open, fair and pure;
Train the Senses truly, Mother, with a hope that's sure.
You may hope that little Baby will avoid much pain,
And for clearness, joy and gladness may prepare the reign.
  For in Nature's every word
  God's own Father-voice is heard.
  A Child's sense we must early rouse to trace
  The inner meaning in the outward face.
  Once let a Baby this connection seize,
  He'll find his own way to his goal with ease.
  He to whom Nature Law and God reveals,
  Finds that about him God's own peace he feels.

I
Open your mouth, my little Pet!
Something very nice you'll get.
Bite this soft, ripe, purple plum;
Use your tongue in tasting some.
What's the taste? Dza, dza! it's nice!
Sweet things will the tongue entice.

II
Bite this rosy apple here!
It is also eaten, Dear.
Oh! your mouth is drawn like paper,
When it's burnt in fire or taper.
"Sour!" you say. " 'Tis sour, I find.
Give me sweet things, Mother kind!"

III
Bitter almond kernel try;
You will like it by-and-by.
Bitter things do good, I think,
Though your mouth will rather shrink.
Bitter things you'll often meet,
But Life soon will make them sweet.

IV

If you eat harsh, unripe things,
Pleasure after-evil brings.
Unripe things you must not touch, Dear;
They will hurt you very much, Dear.
Nothing, Dear, is good for you,
That is not quite ripe all through.[16]

These are some of Froebel's explanations and comments about the "Taste Song":

What is more important, Mother, for your child than the improvement of the senses, and especially the improvement of the sense of Taste, in its transferred moral meaning as well? Who likes to be accused of having "common and low Taste," and who is not glad when it can be said of him: "He has fine, elevated, good Taste?"

Now, why is it that people praise the improvement of a man's Taste? Because it is Taste that proclaims and reveals the inner part, the essence, the soul, the mind of the thing, its principle of life or death.

If even at this early age, it is important to improve the senses, whether of Sight, or more especially of Smell and Taste, in order to avoid much that is harmful and unwholesome, this improvement is above all important for the development and ennobling of the disposition and mind, and for the awakening of the will for activity.

For since it is in the senses that the soul, the very spirit's own activity, lies open, even in a child, so it is the senses which are, in their turn, like leaders to our knowledge of what is most intellectual—above all, the sense of taste, physical as well as intellectual taste.[17]

Froebel is not called the "father of the kindergarten" simply because he coined the name, but because he devoted his life to developing both a program for the young child and a system of training for kindergarten teachers. Many of the concepts and activities of the "gifts" and "occupations" are similar to activities that many kindergarten programs provide.

Froebel's recognition of the importance of learning through play is reinforced by modern teachers who intuitively structure their programs around play activities. Other features of Froebel's kindergarten that remain are the play circle, where children arrange themselves in a circle for learning, and singing songs to reinforce concepts taught with "gifts" and "occupations." Froebel was the first educator to develop a planned, systematic program for educating young children and the first to encourage young, unmarried women to become teachers. This break with tradition caused Froebel no small amount of criticism and was one reason his methods encountered opposition.

All the educators discussed so far have had certain basic premises in common. First, they believed strongly in the important role of the family in educating the child and providing the background for all future learning. Second, they felt it was important to begin educating the child early in life. Consequently, they advocated schooling either in the home or in a school setting. Third, they felt that parents needed training and help to be good teachers for their children. They recognized that for education to begin early in life, it was imperative that parents have materials and training to do a good job. (As we will discuss in Chapter 13, there is renewed interest in procedures for involving parents in children's learning experiences.)

Educators and politicians are rediscovering how important parents are in the educational process. Parent involvement is being encouraged in public schools and other agencies, and we are learning what great educators knew—that parents are their children's first, and perhaps best, teachers.

MARIA MONTESSORI

Maria Montessori (1870–1952) was born in Italy, and devoted her life to developing a system for educating young children. Her system has influenced virtually all subsequent early childhood programs. A precocious young woman who thought of undertaking either mathematics or engineering as a career, she instead chose medicine. Despite the obstacles to entering a field traditionally closed to women, she became the first woman in Italy to earn a medical degree. Following this achievement, she was appointed assistant instructor in the psychiatric clinic of the University of Rome. Since it was customary not to distinguish between the mentally retarded and the insane, her work brought her into contact with the mentally retarded children who had been committed to insane asylums. Although Montessori's first intention was to study children's diseases, she soon became interested in educational solutions for problems such as deafness, paralysis, and idiocy.

At that time she said, "I differed from my colleagues in that I instinctively felt that mental deficiency was more of an educational than medical problem."[18] Montessori became interested in the work of Edward Seguin, a pioneer in the development of an educational system for mentally defective children, and of Jean Itard, who developed an educational system for deaf mutes. Montessori read the works of both Itard and Seguin and credits them with inspiring her to continue her studies with mentally retarded children. Of her initial efforts at educating children, she says:

> I succeeded in teaching a number of the idiots from the asylums both to read and to write so well that I was able to present them at a public school for an examination together with normal children. And they passed the examination successfully.[19]

This was a remarkable achievement, which aroused interest in both Montessori and in her methods. Montessori, however, was already considering something else:

> While everyone else was admiring the progress made by my defective charges, I was trying to discover the reasons which could have reduced the healthy, happy pupils of the ordinary schools to such a low state that in the intelligence test they were on a level with my own unfortunate pupils.[20]

While continuing to study and prepare herself for the task of educating children, the opportunity to perfect her methods and implement them with normal school-age children occurred quite by chance. In 1906 she was invited by the Director General of the Roman Association for Good Building to organize schools for young children of families who occupied the tenement houses the association had constructed. In the first school, named the *Casa dei Bambini,* or Children's House, she had the opportunity to test her ideas and gain insights into children and teaching that led to the perfection of her system.

Montessori was profoundly religious, and a religious undertone is reflected throughout her work. She often quoted from the Bible to support her points. At the dedication ceremonies of the first Children's House, she read from Isaiah 60:1–5, and ended by saying, "Perhaps, this Children's House can become a new Jerusalem, which, if it is spread out among the abandoned people of the world, can bring a new light to education."[21] Her religious dedication to the fundamental sacredness and uniqueness of every child and subsequent grounding of educational processes in a religious conviction undoubtedly account for some of her remarkable achievements as a person and as an educator. Thus, her system functions well for those who are willing to dedicate themselves to teaching as if it were a religious vocation.

JOHN DEWEY

John Dewey (1859–1952) represents a truly American influence on American education. Through his positions as professor of philosophy at the University of Chicago and Columbia University, his extensive writing, and the educational practices of his

Optimum cognitive development occurs in environments that are rich in opportunities for children to interact with people and things. Siblings offer that interaction.

many followers, Dewey did more to alter and redirect the course of American education than any other person.

Dewey's theory of schooling, usually called *progressivism,* emphasizes the child and his interests rather than subject matter; from this emphasis come the terms *child-centered curriculum* and *child-centered schools.* The progressive movement also maintains that schools should be concerned with preparing the child for the realities of today rather than for some vague future time. As expressed by Dewey in *My Pedagogical Creed,* "education, therefore, is a process of living and not a preparation for future living."[22]

What is included in Dewey's concept of children's interests? "Not some one thing," he explained, "it is a name for the fact that a course of action, an occupation, or pursuit absorbs the powers of an individual in a thorough-going way."[23] In a classroom based upon Dewey's ideas, children are involved with physical activities, utilization of things, intellectual pursuits, and social interaction. Physical activities are expressed through running, jumping, and other autonomous activities. In this phase the child begins the process of education and develops other interest areas. The growing child learns to use tools and objects. Dewey felt that an ideal expression for this interest was daily living activities or occupations such as cooking and carpentry.

John Dewey believed that teachers can use young children's interests and activities as a context for teaching concepts and skills.

To promote an interest in the intellectual—solving problems, discovering new things, and figuring out how things work—the child is given opportunities for inquiry and discovery. *Social interest* refers to interactions with persons; Dewey believed this interest was encouraged in a democratically-run classroom.

While Dewey believed the curriculum should be built on the interests of children, he also felt it was the teacher's responsibility to plan for and capitalize on opportunities to weave traditional subject matter through and around the fabric of these interests. Dewey describes a school based on his ideas:

> All of the schools ... as compared with traditional schools ... [exhibit] a common emphasis upon respect for individuality and for increased freedom; a common disposition to build upon the nature and experience of the boys and girls that come to them, instead of imposing from without external subject-matter standards. They all display a certain atmosphere of informality, because experience has proved that formalization is hostile to genuine mental activity and to sincere emotional expression and growth. Emphasis upon activity as distinct from passivity is one of the common factors.[24]

Teachers who correlate subjects, utilize the unit approach, and encourage problem-solving activities are philosophically indebted to Dewey.

There has been a great deal of misinterpretation and criticism of the progressive movement and of Dewey's ideas, especially by those who favor a traditional approach that emphasizes the basic subjects and skills. Actually, Dewey was not opposed to teaching basic skills or subject matter. He did believe, however, that traditional educational strategies *imposed* knowledge on children, whereas their interests should be a springboard for involvement with skills and subject matter.

> The accumulation and acquisition of information for purposes of reproduction in recitation and examination is made too much of. "Knowledge," in the sense of information, means the working capital, the indispensable resources of further inquiry; of finding out, or learning, more things. Frequently it is treated as an end itself, and then the goal becomes to heap it up and display it when called for. This static, cold-storage ideal of knowledge is inimical to educative development. It not only lets occasions for thinking go unused, but it swamps thinking. No one could construct a house on ground cluttered with miscellaneous junk. Pupils who have stored their "minds" with all kinds of material which they have never put to intellectual uses are sure to be hampered when they try to think. They have no practice in selecting what is appropriate, and no criterion to go by; everything is on the same dead static level.[25]

JEAN PIAGET

Jean Piaget (1896–1980) was born in Switzerland. He was a precocious child who published his first article at the age of ten. He received his baccalaureate degree from college at eighteen and earned his doctorate three years later. His training in biology was influential in the development of his ideas about knowledge, and the primary basis for his theory of intellectual growth is biological.

Piaget studied in Paris, where he worked with Theodore Simon at the Alfred Binet laboratory, standardizing tests of reasoning for use with children. (Binet and Simon developed a scale for measuring intelligence.) This experience provided the

FROM LUTHER TO PIAGET: BASIC CONCEPTS ESSENTIAL TO GOOD EDUCATIONAL PRACTICES

As They Relate to Children

Everyone needs to learn how to read and write.

Children learn best through using all their senses.

All children are capable of being educated.

All children should be educated to the fullest extent of their abilities.

Education should begin early in life.

Children should not be forced to learn, but should be taught what they are ready to learn and should be prepared for the next stage of learning.

Learning activities should be meaningful to children.

Children learn through guided and directed play.

Children can learn through activities based on their interests.

As They Relate to Teachers

One must show love and respect for all children.

Teachers should be dedicated to the profession.

Good teaching is based on a theory, a philosophy, and goals and objectives.

Children's learning is enhanced through the use of concrete materials.

Teaching should move from the concrete to the abstract.

Observation is a key to determining children's needs.

Teaching should be a planned, systematic process.

Teaching should be child-centered rather than adult-centered.

Teaching should be based on children's interests.

As They Relate to Parents

The family is an important institution in education.

Parents are their children's primary educators.

Parents must provide guidance and direct young children's learning.

Parents should be involved in any educational program designed for their children.

Everyone should have some training for child rearing.

foundation for Piaget's clinical method of interviewing, used in studying children's intellectual development. As Piaget recalls, "Thus I engaged my subjects in conversations patterned after psychiatric questioning, with the aim of discovering something about the reasoning process underlying their right, but especially their wrong, answers."[26] The emphasis on this method helps explain why some developers of a Piaget-based early childhood curriculum emphasize the teacher's use of questioning procedures to promote thinking.

Following his work with children in Paris, which established the direction of his lifework, Piaget became associated with the Institute J. J. Rousseau in Geneva and began studying intellectual development. Piaget's own three children played a major role in his studies, since many of his consequent insights about how children develop intellectually are based on his observations and work with them. Using his own children in his studies has caused some to criticize his findings. His theory, however, is based not only on this research, but also on literally hundreds of studies involving thousands of children.

Although Piaget's work has been known in Europe since the early 1930s, it was not until the 1960s that it began to receive attention in the United States, so the study of Piaget's theory and its application to education is a relatively new phenomenon. Based on his research, Piaget came to these conclusions about early childhood education.

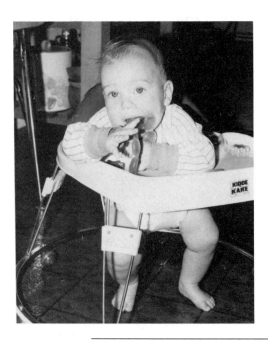 

One of a child's earliest adaptive behaviors is the sucking mechanism, which begins at birth.

☐ Children play an active role in their own cognitive development
☐ Mental and physical activity are important for children's cognitive development
☐ Experiences constitute the raw materials children use to develop mental structures
☐ Children develop cognitively through interaction with and adaptation to the environment
☐ Development is a continuous process
☐ Development results from maturation and the *transactions* or interactions between children and the physical and social environments

Piaget also popularized the age/stage approach to cognitive development and influenced others to apply this age/stage theory to other processes such as moral, language, and social development. He encouraged and inspired many psychologists and educators to develop educational curricula and programs utilizing his ideas and promoted interest in the study of young children's cognitive development that has in turn contributed to the interest in infant development and education.

THE RECENT PAST

The most rapid growth of interest in early childhood education has occurred since about 1965. The beginning of the current interest dates back to the 1950s, to three events that have had a far-reaching and long-lasting impact on all education. The first event was the general acceptance of claims that the public schools were not successfully teaching reading and related skills. The second event was the boycott of city buses by blacks in Montgomery, Alabama, on December 1, 1955. The third event was the launching of Sputnik by the Soviet Union on October 4, 1957.

The public schools have frequently been under attack for their inability to teach basic skills. A host of articles and books detailing why children couldn't read followed publication of Rudolf Flesch's book *Why Johnny Can't Read* in 1955. Flesch criticized the schools for the way reading was taught. Critics and parents began to question the methodology and results of the teaching of reading and other basic skills. Parents demanded schools and programs that would teach these skills. Many parents felt that traditional play-oriented preschools and public school programs that emphasized socialization were not preparing their children for college or for earning a living. Preschools that stressed cognitive learning became popular with parents who wanted to give their children both an early start and a good foundation in learning.

A critical re-examination of the schools—their purposes, products, and teaching methods—occurs about every twenty years. In the early 1980s, the public schools were again in the throes of another back-to-basics movement.

The Montgomery bus boycott set in motion a series of court cases and demonstrations for civil rights and human dignity. The fight for civil liberties spread quickly to the school arena. As a result, the rights of children and parents to public education were and are being clarified and extended. Many of the new federal and state regulations and laws that deal with handicapped, disadvantaged, and abused children are essentially civil rights legislation rather than purely educational legislation. As such, while they have tremendous educational implications, they also broaden and extend civil rights. Consequently, children have been granted rights to a free, appropriate, individualized education, as well as to humane treatment.

Spurred by the Soviet Union's early lead in space exploration, the U.S. government passed the National Defense Education Act in 1958 to meet national needs particularly in the sciences. As a result of the renewed interest in our education system, Americans became more interested in other educational systems, including that of the Soviet Union. What made it possible for the Soviets to launch Sputnik? Examination of the Soviet educational system led to the conclusion that it provided educational opportunities at an earlier age than did the U.S. public schools. Some educators began to wonder if we could have more intelligent adults by teaching children at a younger age. This idea sparked a controversy about early education that continues to the present.

Indeed, with the current interest in day care and the possibility that more and more children will need day care services, there is increased interest in Russian day care programs and that country's long experience in child care.

Research

At the time the Soviet achievement brought a reappraisal of our system of education, research studies were also influencing our ideas. These studies led to a major shift in basic educational premises concerning what children should be able to achieve. This shift can be attributed in part to works by B. S. Bloom and J. McV. Hunt. One of Bloom's conclusions was that:

> When a number of longitudinal studies are compared with each other and allowances are made for the reliability of the instruments and the variability of the samples, a single pattern clearly emerges. . . . Both the correlational data and the absolute scale of intelligence development make it clear that intelligence is a developing function and that the stability of measured intelligence increases with age. Both types of data suggest that in terms of intelligence measured at age 17, about 50% of the development takes place between conception and age 4, about 30% between ages 4 and 8, and about 20% between ages 8 and 17.[27]

In *Intelligence and Experience,* Hunt draws these conclusions:

> In view of the conceptual developments and the evidence coming from animals learning to learn, from neuropsychology, from the programming of electronic computers to solve problems, and from the development of intelligence in children, it would appear that intelligence should be conceived as intellectual capacities based on central processes hierarchically arranged within the intrinsic portions of the cerebrum. These central processes are approximately analogous to the strategies for information processing and action with which electronic computers are programmed. With such a conception of intelligence, the assumptions that intelligence is fixed and that its development is predetermined by the genes are no longer tenable.

In the light of these considerations, it appears that the counsel from experts on child-rearing during the third and much of the fourth decades of the twentieth century to let children be while they grow and to avoid excessive stimulation was highly unfortunate....

Further in the light of these theoretical considerations and the evidence concerning the effects of early experience on adult problem-solving in animals, it is no longer unreasonable to consider that it might be feasible to discover ways to govern the encounters that children have with their environments, especially during the early years of their development, to achieve a substantially faster rate of intellectual development and a substantially higher adult level of intellectual capacity.[28]

We can draw four inferences from this research. First, the period of most rapid intellectual growth occurs before age eight. The extent to which children will become intelligent, based on those things by which we measure intelligence and school achievement, is determined long before many children see the inside of a classroom. This process of shaping intelligence implies that children benefit from home environments that are conducive to learning and early schoollike experiences. Some educators believe both conditions should occur simultaneously, but there is no general agreement in this regard.

Second, it has become increasingly evident that a child is not born with a fixed intelligence. This outdated concept fails to do justice to people's tremendous capacity for learning and change. In addition, evidence supports developmental intelligence. The extent to which individual intelligence develops depends upon many variables, such as experiences, child rearing practices, economic factors, nutrition, and the quality of the prenatal and postnatal environments. Inherited genetic characteristics set a broad framework within which intelligence will develop. Heredity sets the limits, while environment determines the extent to which the limits will be achieved. For example, the child's genetic makeup carries the capacity for language development, but a child who is reared in an environment devoid of opportunities for conversation with adults will not become as linguistically competent as the child who has such opportunities.

Third, children who are reared in homes that are not intellectually stimulating may also lag intellectually behind their counterparts reared in a more advantaged environment. Hunt's implications concerning the home environment are obvious. While questions have been raised about how well school achievement indicates real life achievement and success, experience shows that children who lack an environment that promotes learning opportunities will be handicapped throughout life. On the other hand, homes that offer intellectual stimulation tend to produce students who do well in school.

A fourth conclusion implied by the studies is this: If 80 percent of childrens' intellectual development occurs by the time they are eight, then the environment will have its greatest impact during the first eight years. If intelligence does develop at the rates and in the proportions Bloom states, then the concepts, attitudes, and ways of looking at the world that children learn early in life will essentially remain with them for life. The things children learn early in life, especially from their parents, are hard to change later. A child reared in an environment of noncommunication may well experience difficulty in communicating. Enrichment of the child's life, therefore, should be undertaken earlier than the age of six, the traditional age for admittance to school.

More contemporary studies of the influence of the family background on children tend to support the earlier research of Hunt and Bloom. Christopher Jencks and his colleagues analyzed the effects of inequality of opportunity and concluded:

> We found that family background had much more influence than IQ genotype on an individual's educational attainment. The family's influence depended partly on its socioeconomic status and partly on cultural and psychological characteristics that were independent of socioeconomic level. The effect of cognitive skill on educational attainment proved difficult to estimate, but it was clearly significant. We found no evidence that the role of family background was declining or that the role of cognitive skill was increasing. Qualitative differences between schools played a very minor role in determining how much schooling people eventually got.[29]

Another study that supports the role and influence of the family in the educative process was conducted by Mayeske and his associates; they concluded:

> This study has demonstrated that family background plays a profound role in the development of achievement, not only through the social and economic well-being of the family but through the values its members hold with regard to education, and the activities that parents and parental surrogates engage in with their children to make these values operational.[30]

After examining the influences of people and the environment on young children, Burton White drew this conclusion:

> In our studies we were not only impressed by what some children could achieve during the first years, but also by the fact that the child's own family seemed so obviously central to the outcome. Indeed, we came to believe that the informal education that families provide for their children *makes more of an impact on a child's total educational development than the formal educational system.* If a family does its job well, the professional can then provide effective training. If not, there may be little the professional can do to save the child from mediocrity. This grim assessment is a direct conclusion from the findings of thousands of programs in remedial education, such as Head Start and Follow Through projects.[31]

There are dangers in assuming that preschool experiences totally determine a child's achievement. It becomes too easy to adopt a fatalistic and uncaring attitude toward the child. Such an attitude usually results in blaming the home for the child's lack of achievement, and can also lead to a deterministic point of view that not much will help the child; the damage has already been done. My response to this attitude has always been that if the teachers of the world are not optimistic about and hopeful for children, then who will be?

Schools are a basic social service. The manner and extent to which this service is provided makes a difference in how well and how much children achieve. The quality of education depends on the interest of professional educators in providing it to all children who come to school: the handicapped, the gifted, the poor, the slow learner, the quick learner, and all those children we label "average."

How should we respond to the research that seems to indicate the family has an extremely powerful influence on the child's achievement? As with so many controversies, the middle ground is often the best position. We cannot ignore or minimize the influence of the family on the child. Schools and society should do everything possible to involve parents in schooling and help do the best job of nurturing, rearing, and educating. On the other hand, schools and teachers must be willing to respond creatively and with a broad range of services to all children without blaming anyone or any institution for a poor job. The responses of the school to family conditions and their effects on the child is critical in determining how well schools fulfill the functions of education and socialization.

Poverty

During the 1960s, the United States rediscovered the poor and recognized that not everyone enjoyed affluence. In 1964, Congress enacted the Economic Opportunity Act. The EOA was designed to wage a war on poverty on several fronts. Head Start, one of the provisions of the EOA, attempted to break generational cycles of poverty by providing education and social opportunities for the preschool children of poor families (see chapter 10).

Head Start has probably done more than any other single force to interest the nation in the business of educating the young child. Although programs for children had been sponsored by the federal government during the Great Depression and World War II, these were primarily designed to free mothers for jobs in defense plants. Head Start marked the first time that children were the intended beneficiaries of the services.

MODERN IMPLICATIONS

To what extent are we influenced by the great educational thinkers of the past? While it is difficult to ascertain exactly in what areas and to what degree, it is obvious that we can find evidence of their thinking in current educational practices. Although much of today's jargon would be alien to Froebel, many of the strategies would not. Terms such as *open education* and *individualized prescribed instruction* are merely new names for old methods.

Open Education

Open education is an attempt to restructure preschool and primary classrooms into settings that support individuality, promote independence, encourage freedom, and demonstrate respect for children. In this context, open education is a logical extension of many of the ideas of Montessori, Dewey, and Piaget. Open education is an attitude that encourages children to become involved in their own learning. Teachers allow children to make choices about how and what they learn. Teachers can conduct an open program regardless of the physical, social, or financial setting of the school or community.

Open education is an environment in which children are free from *authoritarian* adults and *arbitrary* rules. Contrary to popular misconception, children are not free to do everything they choose. Within broad guidelines, however (ideally established by teachers, students, and administrators), children are free to move about the room, carry on conversations, and engage in learning activities based on their interests.

Open education is child-centered learning. Adults do not do all the talking, decision making, organizing, and planning when it is children who need to develop these skills. Open education seeks to return the emphasis to the child, where it rightfully belongs.

Historical Influences

We can trace the foundations of open education to Pestalozzi, Froebel, Montessori, and Dewey, although they did not use the same terminology. Montessori might be called the first modern open educator, because she allowed children to enjoy freedom within a prepared environment. She also encouraged individualized instruction, and most important, insisted on respect for children.

Interest in open education in the U.S. began in the 1960s when many educators and critics called attention to the ways schools were stifling student initiative, freedom, and self-direction. Schools were characterized as similar to prisons. Critics described students sitting apathetically in straight rows, passively listening to robotlike teachers, with little or no real learning taking place. In short, classrooms and learning were assumed to be devoid of enthusiasm, joy, and self-direction. Educators and schools were challenged to involve students in learning and abolish policies and procedures that were detrimental to students' physical and mental health. In essence, schools were challenged to become happy places of learning.

Concurrently, school reformers in the U.S. discovered the British Primary School, a comprehensive education program characterized by respect for children, responsiveness to children's needs, and learning through interests. The terms *open education, open classroom, British Primary School,* and *British Infant School* are often used interchangeably.

THE TEACHER'S ROLE

Just as Montessori conceptualized a new role for the teacher, so does open education encourage redefinition of the role. The teacher who believes that open education is possible has surmounted the first obstacle; many teachers are afraid to try it. An open education teacher respects children and believes they are capable of assuming responsibility for their own learning. The teacher considers herself primarily a teacher of children, not of subject matter, and feels confident with all students in all subject areas. Like the Montessori directress, she is a keen observer of children, for many of the decisions regarding instruction and activities depend on thorough knowledge of what the children have accomplished. Adjectives that describe the teacher's role include *learner, guide, facilitator, catalyst,* and *director.*

A CHILD'S DAY IN AN INFORMAL CLASSROOM[32]

An open or informal classroom is organized in many different ways. Many activities and processes must have taken place before a good program can be implemented. In this case, Keith's teacher, Ms. Walsh, has done several important things during the first three weeks of school. She has:

1. Observed her children to determine their levels of maturity, levels of learning, and how they interact with each other and the learning environment.
2. Assessed academic strengths and weaknesses through informal and formal testing, observation of work skills, and verbal interaction.
3. Identified, assessed, and recorded children's interests.
4. Begun informal grouping of children based on all data collected. Grouping is homogeneous and flexible, and used primarily for reading.
5. Designed and established learning centers and areas based on the interests of children, skills that need to be learned, and limitations of the learning environment.

Since Keith lives fairly close to his neighborhood school, he walks, and arrives at about 8:45 A.M. He is one of thirty children in a second/third grade split classroom taught by Ms. Walsh and a full-time aide.

Upon arriving, Keith records his own attendance by flipping his name tag on an attendance board, and proceeds to a learning center of his choice. Today he chooses the "Word Hunt" Center. This center is based on the children's interests and designed to build on and extend vocabulary words already learned.

At 9:00, Keith begins work in an integrated language arts program block. The first part of the block consists of a formal reading lesson during which Ms. Walsh informally assesses Keith's vocabulary and word attack skills while he takes part in reading a story on how to make chocolate chip cookies. When the formal reading lesson is finished, Keith and about eight of his classmates go to the cooking area, and under the guidance of the teacher aide, begin to make plans for making the cookies they read about. Their planning includes a discussion of what utensils and ingredients will be needed, health considerations, such as washing, and how long their activity will take. Working as a group and from a simple recipe, the children make and bake their cookies. The teacher aide serves a facilitating function, and assesses how children handle such tasks as measuring and whether they understand what is being done. This assessment and verification is accomplished in part through skillful questioning. Through such a process, plans will be made for reteaching, reinforcing, and extending concepts and skills.

During the morning "break," Keith and his group serve the cookies to their classmates which gives the group an opportunity to share the cookies and tell how they made them and what they would do differently the next time. After the sharing experience, Keith writes the recipe to take home to his parents. In addition, he and two of his friends write the recipe for inclusion in the class recipe book.

Keith's next activity is in the art area, where he makes an illustration of the steps involved in baking the cookies. This illustration will be placed in one of the display areas, and may be used as one of the illustrations in the class cookbook.

During the cooking activity, the teacher aide observed that Keith was not measuring ingredients as easily as he should be able to. This observation prompts both Ms. Walsh and the teacher aide to note that they will involve Keith in activities for improving his measuring skills.

At 11:30, Keith goes to lunch in the cafeteria. While Ms. Walsh is not required or expected to eat with the children, she chooses to do so. She feels this gives her an opportunity to learn even more about her students. After lunch, Keith and his classmates go outside, where they are supervised by Ms. Walsh.

The afternoon begins with a short rest period, during which Keith reads a book to the rest of the class while they relax on the carpeted floor. Keith then decides to work in the science area on a science project, because of his interest in science. He could have chosen to go to the social science area first instead of later. Keith is very much involved in leaf collecting. He works on a project of collecting, labeling, and classifying the leaves, using the abundant reference materials available.

Part of the curriculum of Keith's school involves a program of creative movement. At 1:30, it is his class's turn to meet with the movement therapist. Today he participates in an activity designed to help in learning to follow directions as well as general motor coordination.

About 2:00, Keith begins a social studies activity that involves writing a script for a "news broadcast." This activity is done in cooperation with a group of his friends, and serves as a culminating activity or recap for the day's activities. The script includes highlights of the day's activities such as the baking, the movement class, what they liked best, etc. Once the script is finished, it is taped with a tape recorder and played for the rest of the class during the planning period that ends the day. Also during this time, assignments are given for the next day and assignments completed during the day are reviewed.

Several important concepts about the informal classroom as it is implemented in Keith's school and I.U. #19 apply to the majority of open/informal educational programs.

Keith's program is implemented in a self-contained classroom, which reinforces the idea that open education is an attitude and that large open spaces are not necessary for open education concepts to be effectively implemented. There can be freedom within the space of a classroom.

Ms. Walsh has a prescribed curriculum she must follow. This prescribed curriculum is a function of both the state and the local school district. Sometimes teachers feel that a specified curriculum precludes the implementation of open education. However, Ms. Walsh uses requirements as a core around which she plans her program.

Ms. Walsh has developed an integrated program focusing on communication and the prescribed curriculum. This integration provides for reading, writing, speaking, and listening skills throughout the entire curriculum. Basic skills are taught all day, not just at one specified time period.

Parent involvement is an important program component. Ms. Walsh and the other faculty and administrators want and encourage parent involvement. As parents participate in the program, they come to understand and support it. Also, as parent involvement increases, they become advocates for more and better change.

Informal education can and does work with a wide range of children. The programs of I.U. #19 are evidence of this fact.

This look at an open classroom is only representative of what can occur. The ways the day can be organized depend upon the interests of the children and teachers, the creative energies they bring to the classroom, the kinds of schools in which they find themselves, the attitudes of administrators, the desires of parents, and the prescribed curriculum.

The Demise of Open Education

As is so often the case, the pendulum of change has swung toward a "back to basics," subject-centered, teacher-centered, highly organized system, and away from a child-centered, activity-centered program characterized by freedom and open education. How long before the pendulum swings back toward concepts embodied in open education remains to be seen. The open education concept was always most popular and successful with preschool educators, perhaps because of a combination of young children's natural ability to work well in an open setting and the fact that preschool teachers are generally comfortable in an informal classroom atmosphere. It seems that the graded concept for older children is difficult to dislodge from the hearts and minds of America's educators. So, once teachers and children enter a graded program, teachers tend to adopt the style and habits associated with the graded approach.

Open education is full of excitement and challenge for teachers who are willing to dedicate themselves to it. The opportunities for an individualized, self-paced program, operated within a context of freedom, respect for children, and relevance, ought to appeal to the teaching profession; however, the failure of open education is attributable to several factors:

1. Many educators never understood the concept of open education or how to implement it.
2. Teachers were not trained for the transition from the graded teaching approach to open education concepts.

Open learning settings give children opportunities to learn through helping other children learn.

3. Many teachers in open education programs did not emphasize or sufficiently explain to parents how the program worked or the progress of their children.
4. Education colleges as a whole did too little or were too late in developing training programs to support open education.

A child-centered form of education will probably regain popularity in the coming years; in fact, it is possible to detect public sentiment for educational practices that are developmentally consistent with young children's needs and maturation. How long it will take for this approach to again become the preferred method for teaching young children will depend to a degree on the advocacy of early childhood educators.

RECURRING THEMES

Certain ingredients are common to good teaching regardless of time or place. Respecting children, attending to individual differences, and getting children interested

Cooperative planning between teacher and child promotes autonomy, responsibility, and self-directed learning.

and involved in their learning are the framework of quality educational programs. Reading about and examining the experiences of great educators helps keep this vision before us. Interestingly, many early educators tended to make schools resemble a family situation, a tendency evident today in some open classrooms where children are grouped as "families," with children of different ages who share responsibilities and arrive at decisions after discussion among family members. Grouping children into families provides not only a structure, but an identity and security in which to learn. In addition, the emphasis on parent involvement underscores the historical importance of the family as a context in which to conduct education.

All great educators have believed in the basic goodness of children; that is, that children by nature tend to behave in socially acceptable ways. They believed it was the role of the teacher to provide the environment for this goodness to manifest itself. The young child learns to behave in a certain way according to how he is treated; the role models he has to emulate; and the environment he has to grow in. The child does not emerge from the womb with a propensity toward badness, but tends to grow and behave as he is treated and taught.

A central point that Luther, Comenius, Pestalozzi, Froebel, Montessori, and Dewey sought to make about our work as educators, no matter in what context—parent, classroom teacher, or child care worker—is that we must do it well and act as though we really care about those whom we have been called to serve. We cannot teach a child how to read unless we care for him.

FURTHER READING

Auleta, Michael. *Foundations of Early Childhood Education: Readings* (New York: Random House, 1969) Historical, social, and psychological background for early childhood education as well as curricular programs and issues.

Day, B. *Open Learning in Early Childhood* (New York: Macmillan, 1975) For teachers and administrators who are developing an open education program, but also useful for parents. Useful activities and learning games for communication/language arts, fine arts, home living, creative dramatics, science, math, movement, and outdoor play; valuable reference for parents of children attending an open education school.

Dewey, John. *Experience and Education* (New York: Collier Books, 1938) Dewey's comparison of traditional and progressive education.

Dropkin, Ruth, and Arthur Tobier, eds. *Roots of Open Education in America: Reminiscences and Reflections* (New York: The City College Workshop Center for Open Education, 1976) Papers that grew out of a 1975 conference at Lillian Weber's Center trace roots of open education back to the Mohawk nation. Settlement houses, one-room schoolhouses, Dewey, and Progressivism are cited for their significant or in some cases overrated contributions.

Howes, V.M. *Informal Teaching in the Open Classroom* (New York: Macmillan, 1974) Helpful hints and ideas about organizing and implementing an open classroom; good section on record keeping.

Ishler, M., and R. Ishler. *Creating the Open Classroom Level* (Buffalo, N.Y.: D.O.K. Publishers, 1974) Handbook for teachers, especially classroom practitioners interested in taking small steps from traditional to child-centered classrooms.

Pratt, Caroline. *I Learn from Children: An Adventure in Progressive Education* (New York: Simon and Schuster, 1948) Pratt believed the path to good teaching was by learning with and from children through self-education; she says in her foreword, "What I know of children, I learned from them. There have been moments when I felt like Columbus discovering a new continent, and conversely, many times when the uncharted world of childhood had presented no clear path by which a mere adult could find her way in it." Excellent account of one pioneer's attempt to put into practice the progressive idea that teachers and children could learn by involvement in play based on children's interests.

Rusk, Robert R. *Doctrines of the Great Educators,* 4th ed. (New York: St. Martin's Press, 1969) Doctrines of fourteen great educators, including Plato, Locke, Rousseau, Pestalozzi, Froebel, and Montessori; selections from original writings provide contrast and comparison of theories.

Sealy, Leonard. *Open Education: A Study of Selected American Elementary Schools* (New Haven, Conn.: Edward W. Hazel Foundation, 1977) Analysis of ten schools in six cities.

Weber, Evelyn. *Ideas Influencing Early Childhood Education: A Theoretical Analysis* (New York: Teachers College Press, 1984) Ideas from Plato to Piaget that have stimulated thought,

TIMELINE—THE HISTORY OF EARLY CHILDHOOD EDUCATION

1524 Martin Luther argued for public support of education for all children in his "Letter to the Mayors and Aldermen of All the Cities of Germany in Behalf of Christian Schools"

1628 John Amos Comenius's *The Great Didactic* proclaimed the value of education for all children according to the laws of nature

1762 Jean Jacques Rousseau wrote *Émile,* explaining that education should take into account the child's natural growth and interests

1780 Robert Raikes initiated the Sunday School movement in England to teach Bible study and religion to children

1801 Johann Pestalozzi wrote *How Gertrude Teaches Her Children,* emphasizing home education and learning by discovery

1816 Robert Owen set up a nursery school in Great Britain at the New Lanark Cotton Mills, believing that early education could counteract bad influences of the home

1817 Thomas Gallaudet founded the first residential school for the deaf in Hartford, Connecticut

1824 The American Sunday School Union was started with the purpose of initiating Sunday schools around the United States

1836 William McGuffey began publishing the *Eclectic Reader* for elementary school children; his writing had a strong impact on moral and literary attitudes in the nineteenth century

1837 Friedrich Froebel, known as the "Father of the Kindergarten," established the first kindergarten in Blankenburgh, Germany

1837 Horace Mann began his job as Secretary of the Massachusetts State Board of Education; he is often called the "Father of the Common Schools" because of the role he played in helping to set up the elementary school system in the United States

1837 Edouard Seguin, influenced by Jean Itard, started the first school for the feeble-minded in France

1855 Mrs. Carl Schurz established the first kindergarten in the United States in Watertown, Wisconsin; the school was founded for children of German immigrants, and the program was conducted in German

1860 Elizabeth Peabody opened a private kindergarten in Boston, Massachusetts, for English-speaking children

1869 The first special education class for the deaf was founded in Boston

1871 The first public kindergarten in North America was started in Ontario, Canada

1873 Susan Blow opened the first public school kindergarten in the United States in St. Louis, Missouri as a cooperative effort with William Harris, Superintendent of Schools

1876 Model kindergarten shown at Philadelphia Centennial Exposition

1880 First teacher-training program for teachers of kindergarten, Oshkosh Normal School, Philadelphia

1884 The American Association of Elementary, Kindergarten, and Nursery School Educators founded to serve in a consulting capacity for other educators

1892 International Kindergarten Union founded

1896 John Dewey started the Laboratory School at the University of Chicago in Illinois, basing his program on child-centered learning with emphasis on life experiences

1905 Sigmund Freud wrote *Three Essays of the Theory of Sexuality* emphasizing the value of a healthy emotional environment during childhood

1907 Maria Montessori started her first preschool in Rome, Italy, called Children's House; her now-famous teaching method was based on the theory that children learn best by themselves in a properly prepared environment

1911 Arnold Gesell, well-known for his research dealing with the importance of the preschool years, began child development study at Yale University

1911 Margaret and Rachel McMillan founded an open-air nursery school in Great Britain, where the class met outdoors and emphasis was on healthy living

1912 Arnold and Beatrice Gesell wrote *The Normal Child and Primary Education*

1915 Eva McLin started the first U.S. Montessori nursery school in New York City

1915 Child Education Foundation of New York City founded a nursery school using Montessori's principles

1918 The first public nursery schools were started in Great Britain

1919 Harriet Johnson started the Nursery School of the Bureau of Educational Experiments, which would later become the Bank Street College of Education

1921 Patty Smith Hill started a progressive, laboratory nursery school at Columbia Teachers College in New York

1921 A.S. Neill founded Summerhill, an experimental school based on the ideas of Rousseau and Dewey

1922 With Edna White as its first director, the Merrill-Palmer Institute Nursery School opened in Detroit, Michigan with the purpose of preparing women in proper child care

1922 Abigail Eliot, influenced by the open-air school in Great Britain and basing her program on personal hygiene and proper behavior, started the Ruggles Street Nursery School in Boston, Massachusetts

TIMELINE—THE HISTORY OF EARLY CHILDHOOD EDUCATION continued

1924 *Childhood Education,* the first professional journal in early childhood education, was published by International Kindergarten Union (IKU)

1926 The National Committee on Nursery Schools was initiated by Patty Smith Hill at Columbia Teachers College in New York; now called the National Association for the Education of Young Children, it provides guidance and consultant services for educators

1926 National Association for Nursery Education (NANE) founded

1930 IKU changed name to Association for Childhood Education

1933 The Work Projects Administration (WPA) provided money to start nursery schools so that unemployed teachers would have jobs

1935 First toy lending library, Toy Loan, was founded in Los Angeles, California

1940 The Lanham Act provided funds for child care during World War II, mainly for day care centers for children whose mothers worked in the war effort

1943 Kaiser Child Care Centers opened in Portland, Oregon, to provide twenty-four-hour child care for children of mothers working in war-related industries

1944 *Young Children* first published by NANE

1946 Dr. Benjamin Spock wrote the *Common Sense Book of Baby and Child Care*

1950 Erik Erikson published his writings on the "eight ages or stages" of personality growth and development and identified "tasks" for each stage of development

1952 Jean Piaget's *The Origins of Intelligence in Children* published in English translation

1955 Rudolph Flesch's *Why Johnny Can't Read* criticized the schools for their methodology in teaching reading and other basic skills

1957 The Soviet Union launched Sputnik, sparking renewed interest in other educational systems and marking the beginning of the "rediscovery" of early childhood education

1958 The National Defense Education Act was passed to provide federal funds for improving education in the sciences, mathematics, and foreign languages

1960 Katharine Whiteside Taylor founded the American Council of Parent Cooperatives for those interested in exchanging ideas in preschool education; it later became Parent Cooperative Preschools International

1960 The Day Care and Child Development Council of America was formed to publicize the need for quality services for children

1964 At the Miami Beach Conference, NANE became NAEYC
1964 The Economic Opportunity Act of 1964 was passed as the beginning of the war on poverty and was the foundation for Head Start
1965 The Elementary and Secondary Education Act was passed to provide federal money for programs for educationally deprived children
1965 The Head Start Program began with federal money allocated for preschool education
1966 Bureau of Education for the Handicapped was established
1967 The Follow Through Program was initiated to extend the Head Start Program into the primary grades
1968 B. F. Skinner wrote *The Technology of Teaching,* which outlines a programmed approach to learning
1968 The federal government established the Handicapped Children's Early Education Program to fund model preschool programs for handicapped children
1970 The White House Conference on Children and Youth
1972 The National Home Start Program began for the purpose of involving parents in their children's education
1975 P.L. 94–142, The Education for All Handicapped Children Act, was passed mandating a free and appropriate education for all handicapped children and extending many rights to parents of handicapped children
1979 International Year of the Child sponsored by the United Nations and designated by Executive Order
1980 The first American LEKOTEK opened its doors in Evanston, Illinois
1980 White House Conference on Families
1981 Head Start Act of 1981 (Omnibus Budget Reconciliation Act of 1981, P.L. 97–35) was passed to extend Head Start and provide for effective delivery of comprehensive services to economically disadvantaged children and their families
1981 Education Consolidation and Improvement Act (ECIA) was passed, consolidating many federal support programs for education
1985 Head Start celebrated its 20th anniversary with a Joint Resolution of the Senate and House "reaffirming congressional support"
1986 The U.S. Secretary of Education proclaimed this the year of the Elementary School, saying, "Let's do all we can this year to remind this nation that the time our children spend in elementary school is crucial to everything they will do for the rest of their lives"

aroused emotions, and shaped ideas of generations of early childhood educators. Enables readers to redefine and reconceptualize views of children and the profession.

Winsor, Charlotte, ed. *Experimental Schools Revisited* (New York: Agathon Press, 1973) Series of bulletins published by Bureau of Educational Experiments, a group of professionals dedicated to cooperative study of children, from 1917 to 1924; document roots of modern education, relate first serious attempts to provide educational programs for toddlers and experiences based on children's maturational levels. Chapters dealing with Play School and Playthings demonstrate philosophical and methodological bases of learning through play.

FURTHER STUDY

1. Compare classrooms you attended as a child to early education classrooms you are now visiting. What are the major similarities and differences? How do you explain these differences?
2. Do you think most teachers are aware of historical influences on their teaching? Is it important for teachers to be aware of these influences? Why or why not?
3. Teaching has been compared to the ministry; according to this view, teaching is a vocation to which one is called. Discuss this concept as a class activity.
4. Many teachers of young children are more Froebelian in their approach to teaching than they realize. Can you find evidence to support this statement?
5. Some critics of education feel that schools have assumed (or have been given) too much responsibility for teaching too many things. Do you think certain subjects or services could be taught or provided through another institution or agency? If so, what are they? Why?
6. Reflect on your experiences in elementary school. What experiences were most meaningful? Why? What teachers do you remember best? Why?
7. Visit a parochial preschool and primary school. How are they similar to and different from public school programs? What strong points did you observe? What weaknesses?
8. Interview the parents of children who attend a parochial school. Find out why they send their children to these schools. Do you agree or disagree with their reasons?
9. Reexamine Comenius's ten basic principles of teaching. Are they applicable today? Which do you agree with most and least?
10. Is it really necessary for children to learn through their senses? Why or why not?
11. To what extent do religious beliefs determine educational practice? Give specific examples from your own experiences and observations to support your answer.
12. Why has society in general and education in particular failed to follow the best educational practices advocated by many great educators?
13. Why is it important that teaching be guided by goals and objectives? Can you cite instances where you observed teaching that was not guided by goals and objectives?
14. Have you observed instances where children were left to their own whims in a laissez-faire school environment? What were the results and why did they occur?
15. Suppose the Russians had not launched a satellite before the United States. Do you think our educational system would be different? If so, how?
16. Educators attach different meanings to openness and open education. Interview teachers, principals, and parents to determine their ideas and definitions of open education, and compare them to those of your classmates. How many different meanings did you find?

17. Visit both a traditional classroom and an open classroom. List activities children participate in. Compare the activities to the models discussed in this chapter.
18. Do you believe open education is a good idea? Why or why not?
19. Besides the recurring themes of the great educators presented in this chapter, are there others you would list? Tell why you selected other themes.
20. List people, agencies, and legislation that are influencing early childhood education. Give specific examples. Do you think the influences will be long-lasting or short-lived?
21. What evidence can you find that Piaget has influenced a program in your area? Cite specific examples.
22. List ways you have been or are being influenced by the ideas and theories of the people and events discussed in this chapter. Do schools make a difference? Or, as Jencks and Mayeske suggest, do families and other institutions make a greater difference? Support your answer.

3

Maria Montessori: The Start of It All

As you read and study:

Explore the circumstances of Maria Montessori's career that influenced her educational methods

Compare the Montessori philosophy and program with those of other early childhood education programs

Examine and critique the basic characteristics of a good Montessori program

Learn the main philosophic and pedagogical principles of the Montessori program

Examine the materials used in a Montessori program

Develop a rationale for criticism or support of the Montessori method

Describe the role of the directress (teacher) in a children's house

Identify and describe features of the prepared environment that are unique to the Montessori method

Describe how the Montessori method does or does not meet children's basic needs

Identify how the Montessori system can be adapted to a regular classroom setting

I f any one person sparked a revival in early childhood education, it was Maria Montessori. From day care centers to PTA meetings, it is usually possible to find someone discussing the pros and cons of her methodology. Nearly every town large enough to support one has a Montessori school. What is so attractive and mesmerizing about the Montessori system? It is intriguing for a number of reasons. First, Montessori education is often identified with the wealthy and upwardly mobile. If parents can afford to give their very young child a preschool education, frequently that education is a Montessori program. Identification with the upwardly mobile gives Montessori education an aura of respectability and elitism. Second, parents who observe in a *good* Montessori program like what they see—orderliness, independent children, self-directed learning, a calm learning environment, and *children* at the center of the learning process. Third, Montessori's philosophy is based on the premise that education begins at birth, and, as we read in Chapter 1, the idea of early learning is popular with parents.

PRINCIPLES OF THE MONTESSORI METHOD

The principles we will discuss by no means constitute all the ideas and practices Montessori stressed. They are based on my synthesis of the system from reading Montessori's writings, working with Montessori teachers, and observing in many Montessori settings.

Respect for the Child

The cornerstone on which all other Montessori principles rest is respect for the child. Montessori said,

> As a rule, however, we do not respect children. We try to force them to follow us without regard to their special needs. We are overbearing with them, and above all, rude; and then we expect them to be submissive and well-behaved, knowing all the time how strong is their instinct of imitation and how touching their faith in and admiration of us. They will imitate us in any case. Let us treat them, therefore, with all the kindness which we would wish to help to develop in them. And by kindness is not meant caresses. Should we not call anyone who embraced us at the first time of meeting rude, vulgar and ill-bred? Kindness consists in interpreting the wishes of others, in conforming one's self to them, and sacrificing, if need be, one's own desire.[1]

Because each child is unique, education should be individualized for each child:

> The educator must be as one inspired by a deep *worship of life,* and must, through this reverence, respect, while he observes with human interest, the *development* of the child life. Now, child life is not an abstraction; *it is the life of individual children.* There exists only one real biological manifestation: the *living individual;* and toward single individuals, one by one observed, education must direct itself.[2]

Children are not miniature adults, and should not be treated as such. Montessori was firm in her belief that a child's life must be recognized as separate and distinct from that of the adult. She attributed most of the responsibility for hampering the education of the young child to adults who imposed their ideas, wishes, and dreams on children, failing to distinguish between the child's life and their own lives.

> In their dealings with children adults do not become egotistic but egocentric. They look upon everything pertaining to a child's soul from their own point of view and, consequently, their misapprehensions are constantly on the increase. Because of this egocentric view, adults look upon the child as *something empty* that is to be filled through their own efforts, as *something inert* and helpless for which they must do everything, as *something lacking an inner guide* and in constant need of direction. In conclusion we may say that the adult looks upon himself as the child's creator and judges the child's actions as good or bad from the viewpoint of his own relations to the child. The adult makes himself the touch stone of what is good and evil in the child. He is infallible, the model upon which the child must be molded. Any deviation on the child's part from adult ways is regarded as an evil which the adult hastens to correct.
>
> An adult who acts in this way, even though he may be convinced that he is filled with zeal, love, and a spirit of sacrifice on behalf of his child, unconsciously suppresses the development of the *child's own personality.*[3]

Some of my students visited a child care center where a Montessori program was being conducted by a Benedictine sister. The sister, seated on the floor next to a new student, had just asked the three-year-old to perform a task. The child screamed that she did not want to do anything and reinforced this uncooperativeness by slapping. The sister calmly repeated the directions and a few minutes later the child stopped screaming and slapping. The sister perceived that an alternative task would be equally appropriate and an activity the child could do. The scene ended with the child participating in this new task. The respect for the child demonstrated in this incident was conspicuously more effective than punishing the child for not listening.

The Absorbent Mind

Montessori believed that no human being is educated by another person; rather, one must *educate oneself.* Montessori states, "It may be said that we acquire knowledge by using our minds; but the child absorbs knowledge directly into his psychic life. Simply by continuing to live, the child learns to speak his native tongue."[4] There are unconscious and conscious stages in the development of the *absorbent mind.* From birth to three years, the *unconscious absorbent mind* develops the senses used for seeing, hearing, tasting, smelling, and touching. The child absorbs everything.

From three to six years, the *conscious absorbent mind* selects sensory impressions from the environment and further develops the senses. In this phase the child is selective in that he refines what he knows. For example, the child in the unconscious stage merely sees and absorbs an array of colors without making distinctions among them; however, from three on, he develops the ability to distinguish, match, and

Maria Montessori emphasized sensory training. Here a child is introduced to letters through seeing, saying, and tracing. The index and middle fingers are used to trace.

grade colors. Montessori challenged the teacher to think through the concept of the absorbent mind:

> How does a child, starting with nothing, orient himself in this complicated world? How does he come to distinguish things, by what marvelous means does he come to learn a language in all its minute details without a teacher but merely by living simply, joyfully, and without fatigue, whereas an adult is in constant need of assistance to orient himself in a new environment to learn a new language, which he finds tedious and which he will never master with the same perfection with which a child acquires his own mother tongue?[5]

Montessori wants us to understand that children cannot help but learn. Simply by living, the child learns from his environment. Jerome Bruner expresses this idea when he says that "learning is involuntary." The child learns because he is a thinking being. What he learns depends greatly on the people in his environment, what they say and do, and how they react to him. In addition, available experiences and materials also help determine the type and quality of learning—and thus the individual.

Sensitive Periods

Montessori believed there were *sensitive periods* when children were more susceptible to certain behaviors and could learn specific skills more easily:

A sensitive period refers to a special sensibility which a creature acquires in its infantile state, while it is still in a process of evolution. It is a transient disposition and limited to the acquisition of a particular trait. Once this trait or characteristic has been acquired, the special sensibility disappears.[6]

A child learns to adjust himself and make acquisitions in his sensitive periods. These are like a beam that lights interiorly or a battery that furnishes energy. It is this sensibility which enables a child to come in contact with the external world in a particularly intense manner. At such a time everything is easy; all is life and enthusiasm. Every effort marks an increase in power. Only when the goal has been obtained does fatigue and the weight of indifference come on.

When one of these psychic passions is exhausted, another area is enkindled. Childhood thus passes from conquest to conquest in a constant rhythm that constitutes its joy and happiness.[7]

The secret of using sensitive periods in teaching is to recognize them when they occur. While all children experience the same sensitive periods—for example, a sensitive period for writing—the time at which a sensitive period occurs is different for each child. Therefore, it becomes the role of the directress (as Montessori teachers are often called) or the parent to detect these times of sensitivity for learning and provide the setting for optimum fulfillment. Observation thus becomes crucial for teachers and parents. Indeed, many educators believe that observation of children's achievement and behavior is more accurate than the use of tests.

The sensitive period for many learnings occurs early in life, during the period of intellectual growth. The experiences necessary for optimum development must be provided at this time. Through observation and practice, Montessori was convinced the sensitive period for development of language was a year or two earlier than originally thought.

Once the sensibility for learning a particular skill occurs, it will never occur again with the same intensity. For example, children will never learn languages as well as when the special sensitivity for language learning occurs. Montessori says, "The child grows up speaking his parent's tongue, yet to grownups the learning of a language is a very great intellectual achievement."[8]

Teachers must do three things: recognize that there are sensitive periods; learn to detect them; and capitalize on them by providing the optimum learning setting to foster their development. Much of what early childhood educators mean by *readiness* is contained in Montessori's concept of sensitive periods.

The Prepared Environment

Montessori believed the child learns best in a *prepared environment.* This environment can be any setting—classroom, a room at home, nursery, or playground. The purpose of the prepared environment is to make the child independent of the adult. It is a place where the child can *do things for himself.* The ideal classrooms Montessori describes are really what educators advocate when they talk about open education; in many respects, Montessori was the precursor of the open classroom movement.

Following a teacher's introduction to the prepared environment, children could come and go according to their desires and needs, deciding for themselves which

The concept of a prepared environment is a critical ingredient in a Montessori classroom. Organization and arrangement determine, in part, how children behave and what they learn.

materials to work with. Montessori removed the typical school desks from the classroom and replaced them with tables and chairs where children could work individually or in small groups.

In a modern Montessori classroom, much of a child's work is done on the floor. Montessori saw no reason for a teacher's desk, since the teacher should be involved with the children where they are doing their work. She also introduced child-sized furniture, lowered chalkboards, and outside areas where children could, at will, take part in gardening and other outdoor activities.

Her concept of a classroom was a place where children could do things for themselves; where they could play with materials placed there for specific purposes; and *where they could educate themselves.* She developed a classroom free of many of the inhibiting elements in some of today's classrooms. An essential characteristic of the prepared environment is freedom. Since children are free, within the environment, to explore materials of their own choosing, they absorb what they find there.

Many adults fear the child will automatically abuse freedom through destructive acts. When a Montessori teacher anticipates destructive acts, she quickly diverts the child's attention to other materials or activities. Although the Montessori teacher believes in freedom for the child and the child's ability to exercise that freedom, the child is not free to make unlimited choices. For example, the child must know how to use materials correctly before he is free to choose those materials. The student is free to choose within the framework of choices provided by the teacher. Choice, however, is a product of discipline and self-control.

Self- or Auto-Education

Montessori called the concept that children are capable of educating themselves *auto-education:*

> The commonest prejudice in ordinary education is that everything can be accomplished by talking (by appealing, that is, to the child's ear), or by holding one's self up as a model to be imitated (a kind of appeal to the eye), while the truth is that the personality can only develop by making use of its own powers.[9]

The child who is actively involved in a prepared environment and exercising freedom of choice literally educates himself. The role freedom plays in self-education is crucial:

> And this freedom is not only an external sign of liberty, but a means of education. If by an awkward movement a child upsets a chair, which falls noisily to the floor, he will have an evident proof of his own incapacity; the same movement had it taken place amidst stationary benches would have passed unnoticed by him. Thus the child has some means by which he can correct himself, and having done so will have before him the actual proof of the power he has gained: the little tables and chairs remain firm and silent each in its own place. It is plainly seen that the *child has learned* to command his movements.[10]

Our universal perception of the teaching-learning act is that the teacher teaches, and because of this, the child learns. We overlook that everyone has learned a great deal through his own efforts. Through the principle of auto-education, Montessori focuses our attention on this human capability. The art of teaching includes preparing the environment so that children, through participation in it, educate themselves. Think of the things you learned by yourself and the conditions and circumstances under which you learned them. This reflection should reveal the self-satisfaction that accompanies self-learning and the power it has to generate further involvement.

Obviously, it is sometimes quicker, more efficient, and more economical to be told or shown what to do and how to do it. Teachers and parents need to understand, however, that auto-education should have a more dominant role in education than we have been willing to give it. In this sense, education should become more child-centered and less teacher-centered.

THE ROLE OF THE TEACHER

The Montessori teacher must have certain qualities to implement the principles of this child-centered approach. The role of the teacher includes:

1. Making the children the center of learning. As Montessori said, "The teacher's task is not to talk, but to prepare and arrange a series of motives for cultural activity in a special environment made for the child."[11]

2. Encouraging children to use the freedom provided for them.
3. Observing children so as to prepare the best possible environment, recognizing sensitive periods, and diverting unacceptable behavior to meaningful tasks.

Montessori believed, "It is necessary for the teacher to *guide* the child without letting him feel her presence too much, so that she may be always ready to supply the desired help, but may never be the obstacle between the child and his experience."[12]

THE MONTESSORI METHOD IN PRACTICE

In a prepared environment, certain materials and activities provide for three basic areas of child involvement: *practical life* or motor education, *sensory materials* for training the senses, and *academic materials* for teaching writing and reading. All these activities are taught according to a prescribed procedure.

Practical Life

The prepared environment emphasizes basic, everyday motor activities, such as walking from place to place in an orderly manner, carrying objects such as trays and chairs, greeting a visitor, walking on a line, and being silent. A new observer to a Montessori classroom is always fascinated by the "dressing frames" designed to perfect the motor skills involved in buttoning, zippering, lacing, buckling, and tying. The philosophy for activities such as these is to make the child independent of the adult and to develop concentration. Water activities play a large role in Montessori methods, and children are taught to scrub, wash, and pour as a means of developing coordination. Practical life exercises also include polishing mirrors and shoes, sweeping the floor, dusting furniture, and peeling vegetables.

Montessorians believe that as the child becomes absorbed in an activity, he gradually lengthens his span of concentration; as he follows a regular sequence of actions, he learns to pay attention to details. They believe that without concentration and involvement through the senses, little learning takes place. Although most people assume that practical life activities are learned incidently, a Montessori teacher shows children how to do these activities through precise details and instructions, with emphasis on sensory materials. Verbal instructions are minimal; the emphasis in the instructional process is on *showing how.*

Montessori also believed children's involvement and concentration in motor activities lengthened their attention span. In a Montessori classroom, it is not uncommon to see a child of four or five polishing his shoes or scrubbing a table for twenty minutes at a time!

Practical life activities are taught in four different types of exercises. *Care of the person* involves such activities as using the dressing frames, polishing shoes, and washing hands. *Care of the environment* includes dusting, polishing a table, and raking leaves. *Social relations* include lessons in grace and courtesy. The fourth type of exercise involves *analysis and control of movement,* and includes locomotor activities such as walking and balancing.

Practical life activities—based on tasks associated with daily living, such as hand washing—are the basis for learning in a Montessori classroom.

Figures 3–1, 3–2, and 3–3 are directions for some of the practical life activities in a Montessori classroom. Notice the procedures and the exactness of presentation.

Sensory Materials

These are materials in a typical Montessori classroom (the learning purpose appears in parenthesis).

- ☐ Pink tower (visual discrimination of dimension)—ten wood cubes of the same shape and texture, all pink, the largest of which is ten centimeters cubed. Each succeeding block is one centimeter smaller. The child builds a tower beginning with the largest block.
- ☐ Brown stairs (visual discrimination of width and height)—ten blocks of wood, all brown, differing in height and width. The child arranges the blocks next to each other from thickest to thinnest so the blocks resemble a staircase.

Material: Tray, rice or corn, two small pitchers (one empty, the other contains rice)

Presentation: The child must be shown how to lift the empty pitcher with the left hand, and with the right raise the pitcher containing rice slightly higher. Grasping the handle, lifting and tilting are practiced. The spout of the full pitcher must be moved to about the center of the empty pitcher before the pouring begins. Set down both pitchers; then change the full one to the right side, to begin the exercise the same way.

 When rice is spilled, the child will set the pitchers down, beside the top of the tray, and pick each grain up, one at a time, with thumb and forefinger.

Purpose: Control of movement.

Point of Interest: Watching the rice.

Control of Error: Hearing the rice drop on the tray.

Age: 2 1/2 years.

Exercise: A container with a smaller diameter, requiring better control of movement. Control the amount of rice for the smaller container.

Note: Set up a similar exercise, using colored popcorn instead of rice.

FIGURE 3–1 Pouring (Source: E.G. Caspari, 1974. All Rights Reserved.)

Material: Apron and basket, green-leafed plant, sheet of white freezer paper, small sponge, caster, bottle of plant polish, orange stick, cotton ball, cup

Presentation:
1. Lay out all the material in order of use from left to right.
2. Bring a plant to the table and place it on the paper.
3. Dampen the sponge at the sink and gently wipe off the top side of the leaf with forward strokes. Hold the leaf on the underside with the other hand. Stroke several leaves to remove the dust.
4. Pour small amount of polish into caster.
5. Wrap a small portion of the cotton ball on the orange stick.
6. Dip the stick in the polish and again stroke gently on the leaf in the same manner as above.

Clean up:
1. Remove cotton from the stick and place it in cup.
2. Empty the soiled cotton into the waste basket.
3. Take the caster and the cup to the sink. Wash and dry them.
4. Wash the sponge and bring it back to the table.
5. Place the material back in the basket.
6. Replace the plant on the shelf.
7. Fold the paper. Replace it with a clean paper only if necessary.
8. Return basket and paper to the shelf.

Purpose: Co-ordination of movement; care of nature's plants

Point of Interest: Seeing the leaf get shiny.

Control of Error: Dull leaves and polish on white paper

Age: 3 years and up

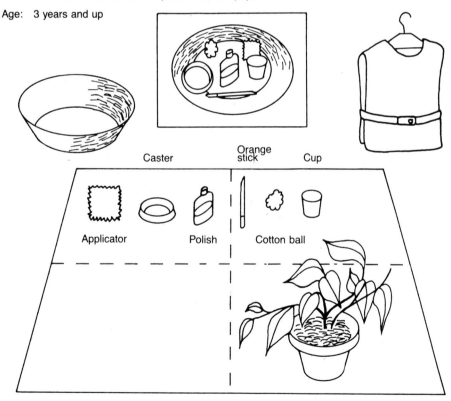

FIGURE 3-2   Plant Shining (Source: © E. G. Caspari, 1974. All Rights Reserved.)

Material: Basket with a duster, soft brush, and feather duster; table to be dusted

Presentation:
Look for the dust, with the eyes at the level of the surface of the table. Start with one half of the table, the one which is immediately in front of you.
Wipe the surface first, as most of the dust will be lying on the top and will give the greatest result.
Always dust away from the body, starting at one end working progressively to the other end, using circular movements.
After the top the sides, after the sides the legs, not forgetting the corners, the inside of the legs, and the underneath of the table. The brush is to be used for the corners.
Shake the duster over the waste basket, or outdoors, if in the country.

Purpose: Coordination of movements, care of the environment, indirect preparation for writing

Point of Interest: The dust to be found in the duster; shaking the dust off the cloth

Control of Error: Any spot of dust left behind

Age: 2 1/2 to 4 1/2 years.

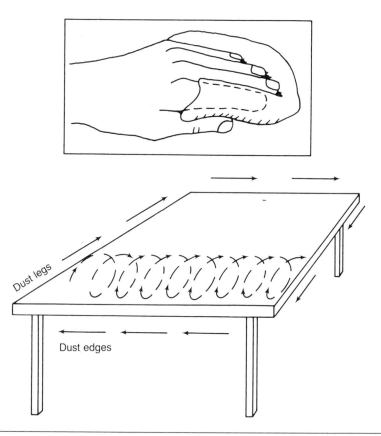

FIGURE 3–3 Dusting (Source: © E. G. Caspari, 1974. All Rights Reserved.)

A prepared environment encourages reading by offering easy access to books.

- [ ] Red rods (visual discrimination of length)—ten rod-shaped pieces of wood, all red, of identical size but differing in lengths from ten centimeters to one meter. The child arranges the rods next to each other from largest to smallest.
- [ ] Cylinder blocks (visual discrimination of size)—four individual wood blocks that have holes of various sizes; one block deals with height, one with diameter, and two with the relationship of both variables. The child removes the cylinders in random order, then matches each cylinder to the correct hole.
- [ ] Smelling jars (olfactory discrimination)—two identical sets of white, opaque glass jars with removable tops through which the child cannot see

but through which odors can pass. The teacher places various substances, such as herbs, in the jars, and the child matches the jars according to the smell of the substance in the jars.

☐ Baric tablets (discrimination of weight)—sets of rectangular pieces of wood which vary according to weight. There are three sets, light, medium, and heavy in weight, which the child matches according to the weight of the tablets.

☐ Color tablets (discrimination of color and education of the chromatic sense)—two identical sets of small, rectangular pieces of wood used for matching color or shading.

☐ Sound boxes (auditory discrimination)—two identical sets of cylinders filled with various materials, such as salt and rice. The child matches the cylinders according to the sound the materials make.

☐ Tonal bells (sound and pitch)—two sets of eight bells, alike in shape and size but different in color; one set is white, the other brown. The child matches the bells according to the tone they make.

☐ Cloth swatches (sense of touch)—the child identifies two identical swatches of cloth according to touch. This activity is performed first without a blindfold, but is later accomplished using a blindfold.

☐ Temperature jugs or thermic bottles (thermic sense and ability to distinguish between temperatures)—small metal jugs filled with water of varying temperatures. The child matches jugs of the same temperature.

Materials for training and developing the senses have these characteristics:

1. Control of error. Materials are designed so that a child can see if he makes a mistake; for example, if he does not build the blocks of the pink tower in their proper order, he does not achieve a tower effect.

2. Isolation of a single quality. Materials are designed so that other variables are held constant except the quality or qualities isolated. Therefore, all blocks of the pink tower are pink because size, not color, is the isolated quality.

3. Active involvement. Materials encourage active involvement rather than the more passive process of looking.

4. Attractiveness. Materials are attractive, with colors and proportions that appeal to children.

Basic Purposes of Sensory Materials

The sensory Montessori materials are often labeled *didactic* (designed to instruct). One of the purposes of Montessori sensory materials is to train the child's senses so he focuses on some obvious, particular quality; for example, with the red rods, the quality is length; with pink tower cubes, size; and with bells, musical pitch. Montessori felt it was necessary to help children discriminate among the many stimuli they receive. Accordingly, the sensory materials help make children more aware of the capacity of their bodies to receive, interpret, and make use of stimuli.

This child is using Montessori's pink tower and brown stairs to learn concepts of seriation and mathematics.

Montessori also thought that perception and the ability to observe details was crucial to reading. She believed children should sharpen their powers of observation and visual discrimination before learning to read.

A third purpose of the sensory materials is to increase the child's ability to think, a process that depends on the ability to distinguish, classify, and organize. Children are constantly faced with decisions concerning the sensory materials: which block comes next, which color matches the other, which shape goes where. These are not decisions the teacher makes, nor are they decisions the child arrives at by guessing; rather, they are decisions made by the intellectual process of observation and selection based upon knowledge gathered through the senses.

Finally, all the sensory activities are not ends unto themselves. Their purpose is to prepare the child for the time when the sensitive periods for writing and reading occur. In this sense, all activities are preliminary steps in the writing-reading process.

In addition, the sensory activities should not be isolated from the real world. If a child is asked to deal with color only when he is working with the color tablets, there is no assurance he will have a meaningful understanding of color. Examples in the classroom should call the child's attention to color. The activity enriches the child's ability to learn only as he uses color as a basis for more learning.

Materials for Writing, Reading, and Mathematics

The third area of Montessori materials is *academic;* specifically, items for writing, reading, and mathematics. Exercises are presented in a sequence that encourages writing before reading. Reading is therefore an outgrowth of writing. Both processes, however, are introduced so gradually that children are never aware they are learning to write and read until one day they realize they are writing and reading. Describing this phenomenon, Montessori said that children "burst spontaneously" into writing and reading.

Montessori believed many children were ready for writing at four years of age. Consequently, a child who enters a Montessori system at age three has done most of the sensory exercises by the time he is four; it is not uncommon to see four- and five-year-old children in a Montessori classroom writing and reading. These are examples of materials for writing and reading:

☐ Ten geometric forms and colored pencils that introduce the child to the co-ordination necessary for writing. After selecting a geometric inset, the child traces it on paper and fills in the outline with a colored pencil of his choosing.

☐ Sandpaper letters, each letter of the alphabet outlined in sandpaper on a card, with vowels in blue and consonants in red. The child sees the shape,

A Montessori environment is characterized by orderliness, with a place for everything and everything in its place. The low shelving gives children ready access and encourages use of the materials.

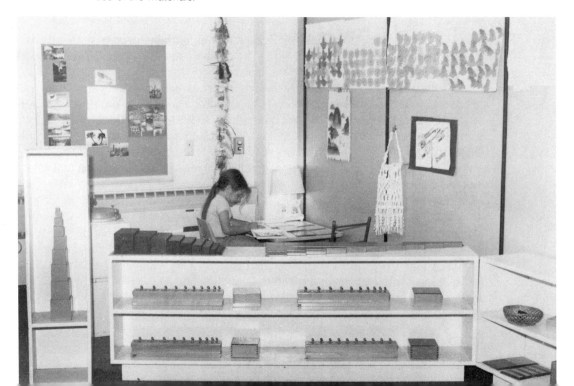

feels the shape, and hears the sound of the letter, which the teacher repeats when introducing it.

☐ Movable alphabet, individual wooden letters. The child learns to put together familiar words.

☐ Command cards, a set of red cards with a single action word printed on each card. The child reads the word on the card and does what the word tells him to do; for example, run, jump.

Examples of materials for mathematics are:

☐ Number rods—a set of red and blue rods varying in length from ten centimeters to one meter, representing the quantities one through ten. With the help of the teacher, the child is introduced to counting.

☐ Sandpaper numerals—each number from one to nine in sandpaper on a card. The child sees, touches, and hears the numbers. He eventually matches number rods and sandpaper numerals. The child also has the opportunity to discover the mathematical facts through the use of these numerals.

☐ Golden beads—a concrete material for the decimal system. The single bead represents one unit. A bar made up of ten units in a row represents a ten; ten of the ten bars form a square representing one hundred; and ten hundred squares form the cube representing one thousand.

Additional Features

Other features of the Montessori system are mixed age grouping and self-pacing. A Montessori classroom always contains children of different ages, usually from two-and-a-half to six years of age. This strategy is becoming more popular in many open classrooms and has long been popular in the British Infant Schools. Advantages of mixed age groups are that children learn from one another; children help each other; a wide range of materials is available for all children; and older children become role models for younger children.

In a Montessori classroom, children are free to learn at their own rate and level of achievement. The child determines which activities he participates in and works at his own pace. Do not assume, however, that the child is allowed to dally at a task. Through observation, the teacher determines when a child has perfected one exercise and is ready to move to a higher level or different exercise. If a child does not perform an activity correctly, the teacher gives him additional help and instruction.

Table 3–1 outlines the basic characteristics of a good Montessori program. Examine it in detail, and use it as a guideline in your observation of Montessori programs. Perhaps you can add other criteria you think make a good program. You will be able to understand further what Montessori education is all about through the vignette of a Day in a Children's House. Keep in mind that while details of educational programs vary from center to center, the basic constructs of the Montessori program do not.

TABLE 3-1 Basic Characteristics of a Montessori Program for Three- to Six-year-old Children

Growth in the Child	Program Organization	Adult Aspects
Independent	Ungraded mix of three-year age span	Professionally educated and certified Montessori educator
Self-directed	Enrollment age between 2.6 and 3.6 years	
Responsible group member	Policy of three-year cycle of attendance	Regularly scheduled staff meetings
Self-disciplined	Five-day week with a minimum daily three-hour session	Ongoing inservice training for auxiliary classroom personnel
Self-accepting	Separate, small groups; specially designed orientation program for new children	Parent education programs
Enjoys learning		
A unique individual	Observational records of the individual child and classroom life	
	Public observation policy	

Source: American Montessori Society. Copyright September 1976. Published in New York, New York.

Criticisms of the Montessori Method

The Montessori system is not without opponents. One criticism deals with the didactic nature of the materials and the program. Critics say the system teaches a narrow spectrum of activities in which concepts are learned in a prescribed manner, following prescribed methods, using a prescribed set of materials.

Critics also maintain the Montessori classroom does not provide for socialization. They cite the lack of group play, games, and other activities normally present in traditional kindergarten programs. This accusation, of course, is no truer for a Montessori setting than for any other classroom. No method or teacher can stop social interaction unless the teacher is a dictator or the children are afraid of her, which could happen in any classroom. Many Montessori activities promote and offer opportunities for task sharing, cooperation, collaboration, and helping. Also, outdoor time and lunchtime (where children eat in pairs, threes, or small groups) afford ample time and opportunity for social interaction.

A related criticism is that children do not have opportunities to participate in dramatics, make-believe, and pretending. Montessori felt that children two-and-one-half to six years of age were not mature enough to handle the demands put on them by a make-believe world, so she did not provide for it in her system. This does not, however, resolve the question of the appropriateness of these activities for young children.

The charge is frequently heard that Montessori schools represent an elitist or middle-class system. This claim very likely stems from the fact that most Montessori schools are private or are operated by individuals for profit or by parochial school

TABLE 3–1   continued

Learning Environment	Program Emphasis	Administrative Support Systems
Full range of sequentially structured developmental aids	Auto-education	Organized as a legally and fiscally responsible entity
Minimum of thirty-five square feet per child indoors, above space for furnishings and storage	Intrinsic motivation	Nondiscriminatory admissions policy
	Process, not product	
	Cooperation, not competition	Regular administrator
Adequate outdoor area	Fostering autonomy in the child	Published educational policies and procedures
Light-weight, proportionate, movable, child-sized furnishings	Fostering competencies based on success	Adherence to state laws and health requirements
Identifiable ground rules	Spontaneous activity	Membership in professional national society
	Peer teaching	
	Sensorimotor preparation for intellectual development	
	Natural social development	
	Biological basis for support of developmental needs	
	Responsible freedom	

systems. While this seems to be the case, there is evidence that Montessori methods are used in some Head Start, day care, and public school programs. The system is not elitist, but the way it is applied may make it seem so.

One reason many parents and teachers feel the Montessori program is rigid is that her ideas and methodologies are so detailed. Another reason is that they have nothing to compare this system to other than the free play programs they are more accustomed to. When parents and teachers compare the Montessori system, which organizes the environment and learning experiences in a specific, precise way, to a free play setting, there is a tendency to view the Montessori setting as rigid. Parents and teachers need to focus instead on the results of the systems.

In some Montessori programs that enroll children with limited language development and skills, teachers must make special efforts to provide for children's language needs. These children will need more language stimulation, experiences and opportunities to engage in adult/child and child/child dialogues than they would probably have if they were involved only in Montessori activities in which teachers demonstrate the use of materials. A good teacher will supplement and enrich whatever program she is using to provide for the children in her care.

SELECTING A MONTESSORI SCHOOL

Parents who want a Montessori program for their preschool children face the problem of finding out if the school that calls itself a Montessori school really is one. Unfortunately, there is no guarantee that the program of studies will be of the kind and

A DAY IN A CHILDREN'S HOUSE[13]

Billy Smith arrives at the Alexander Montessori School at 8:30 a.m. He is left off at the entrance to the school by his mother, who is on her way to work as a secretary at the headquarters of a national airline.

Billy is greeted by one of the classroom aides as he gets out of the car. Billy has gained a great deal of independence in his year and a half at the school, and goes to his classroom by himself. If a child is new to the school, he is escorted to his classroom, or children's house, by an aide until he is able to go by himself.

Billy, who is four years old, has a brother and a sister. He will attend the school until he is six, when he will enter first grade in a Montessori elementary or a local public school.

Billy is greeted by his teacher, Frances Collins, as he enters the classroom. "Good morning, Billy. How are you this morning?" Mrs. Collins greets Billy while shaking his hand. She engages him in a brief conversation about his baby sister.

The previous day, Billy checked out, by himself, a book from the children's house library. This morning, Billy goes to the library card file and finds the card to the book he checked out. He places the card in the book and returns the book to the library. Billy does all the checking out and in of books, including writing his own name, without help. The key to this independence is the arrangement of the library. Mrs. Collins has the library, book cards, and the check-out and check-in systems arranged so the children can do all these things themselves.

In Mrs. Collins's class of thirty-three children, ages range from two-and-a-half to five-and-a-half years. Mrs. Collins has two aides to help her.

Since Billy is the first child to arrive in the children's house this morning, he takes the chairs down from all the tables. He also puts down pieces of carpeting (approximately 2' x 3') on the floor for each child, and places a name card for each child on each piece of carpet. When the children come into the class, they will find their name card, pick it up, and place it on a pile. This is one way Mrs. Collins takes roll and, at the same time, helps the children learn their printed names.

Next, Billy goes to the language area, takes a set of geometric insets to a table (writing is always done on a table), and uses the frame and insets to make a geometric design, of his choice, on a sheet of paper. When his design is finished, he fills in the design with straight lines using colored pencils (see Figure 3–4). Billy uses an ink stamp to stamp lines on the back of his paper, writes his name on the paper, and files his paper in his own file. The materials in his file will be made into a booklet that will be sent home at the end of the week.

Billy is in the sensitive stage for writing, which means his motor skills make him capable of writing on paper, and he is always eager to write. Billy goes to the other side of the language corner to the movable alphabet cabinet and

FIGURE 3–4 Geometric Inserts.

takes a set of word pictures to the carpet. Using the movable alphabet, he constructs a sentence using the picture card and movable alphabet letters. Billy's sentence is: "The king is fat" (see Figure 3–5.) After he has constructed his sentence, Billy takes paper and pencil and goes to a table where he writes this sentence. After he finishes writing, he puts the paper in his file.

At about 10:15 a.m., Billy takes a break for juice. The snack in the Montessori house is on an "as needed" basis, and Billy helps himself, pouring his own drink. Sometimes he and one of his friends take their break together. No attempt is made to force children to take a break or to take it all at once or in groups.

After his snack, Billy goes to the practical life area and polishes a table. This activity takes about fifteen minutes. Billy gets all the materials needed for the activity, completes the task, and puts things away by himself. Through exercises of practical life, Billy develops good work habits and extends his span of concentration. Polishing the table involves him in a gross motor activity which has to be performed in a certain way—setting up the material in a specific sequence (from left to right) and then polishing the table. When he has finished polishing, it is Billy's responsibility to replace the materials and return everything to the shelf.

After polishing the table, Billy goes to the math center. Here he and another student set up the addition strip board and see how many ways they can make "nine." This activity usually takes about ten minutes. After he finishes in the math area, Billy goes to a directed lesson shared by Mrs. Collins and a group of six children. Each child is given a reading booklet (published by a major publishing company), and they discuss the pictures. The children who can, read the story, while those who can't, follow along. Emphasis in this activity is on listening, sequencing, and comprehension. This activity usually lasts from ten to fifteen minutes.

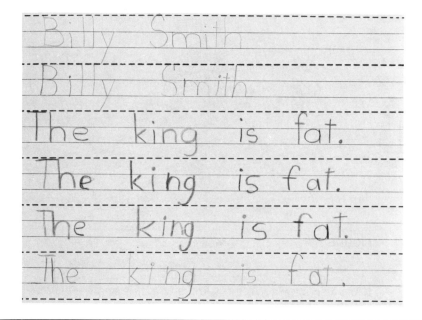

FIGURE 3–5 Writing.

From 11:00 to about 11:20, the children go outside, where they engage in free play for about ten minutes, then have a directed movement lesson consisting of jumping rope, throwing, or catching. In addition to free or directed play, this outdoor time may be used for nature walks and other kinds of field experiences.

When Billy comes in from outdoor play, he joins the other children in a circle activity with Mrs. Collins to learn songs and sing songs previously learned. The songs are usually based on a monthly theme selected by Mrs. Collins. In addition to a song, the children will also do finger plays, recite poems, and use rhythm band instruments. In the circle time (the children sit on a circle or ellipse marked on the floor), Billy holds the flag while the children say the Pledge of Allegiance; another child leads the group in a song about good health habits; and each child is given an opportunity to share an experience that is important to him. Billy tells about his cousin visiting him over the weekend. The circle time also provides an opportunity to talk about matters of interest to the whole group. A child is free to join the circle time as he wishes. The teacher respects the child's personal independence and concentration on the task he is working on, so no one need stop what he is doing just to join the circle time. Because the circle time activities are so interesting, however, children generally want to join. The circle time provides an opportunity for all the children, who have been working at their own pace all morning, to come together.

When circle time is over, usually after about twenty minutes, the children eat their lunch. Each child washes his hands, gets a paper place mat, places it on a table, and sets his lunch pail on it. At Billy's children's house, all the children bring their own lunch. Sometimes a child or several children who did not go outside during the recess time will set the tables.

Billy is responsible for helping clean up the table where he eats. In a children's house, a child does everything he might normally do in his own house: cleaning up, setting the table, getting his own snack. After lunch, he can take part in games and songs. This activity is directed by the teacher. Lunchtime usually lasts about an hour. During lunchtime, the children are also free to visit with each other and use materials of their choice.

After lunch, Billy checks his folder to see if there is any unfinished work. If there is, he finishes it. If there is no work to be finished, the teacher suggests several things for him to do. On this particular day, Billy chooses to work with the geometry cabinet. This activity involves matching a set of cards to their corresponding geometric shapes. This matching activity takes Billy about twenty minutes. After he puts his materials away, Billy chooses easel painting. Again, Billy is responsible for putting on his own apron, getting the paper, putting it on the easel, and painting his own picture. This activity also encourages creativity.

In Billy's children's house, there is no special time for rest. A child rests when he feels a need for it. Even with the two-and-a-half-year-olds, there is no attempt to force a nap time or rest period. The two-and-a-half and three-year-old children go home for the day at noon, so there are only four- and five-year-olds in the school during the afternoon. Billy and his classmates, as a general rule, don't rest.

When his art activity is finished, Billy's teacher offers him a new lesson with the hundred board. Billy is invited to a table and the teacher brings the materials to the table. Part of Billy's task is to pay attention to the directed lesson so he will know how to do the lesson independently. When the teacher feels he is ready, Billy can begin to participate, and he gradually takes over the activity. This does not mean that Billy has entirely absorbed the lesson. If his teacher thinks it is necessary, she will give him another, or a more directed, lesson. This directed activity usually lasts about half an hour.

The last activity of the day is a birthday party for one of the classmates. The day ends at 3:00 p.m. Mrs. Collins says good-bye to Billy and tells him she is looking forward to seeing him tomorrow. Billy goes to the area where the children are picked up by their parents or other caregivers. Billy is picked up by a caregiver.

There is really no such thing as a "typical" day in a children's house. On any particular day, a child may work only in the areas of math and practical life. Also, if a child is undecided about what to do at any time, he will check his work folder to get ideas about what to do, or to see what he needs to finish. He will also confer with his teacher to get direction.

How Billy's Teacher Keeps Her Records

Each child has a work folder with his name on it. Inside are four sheets listing the lessons from each of the four areas or avenues (practical life, sensorial, math, and language) of the Montessori system. Mrs. Collins marks each lesson with a yellow marker when she presents it to the child. When the child has mastered the lesson, she marks it in red, indicating that the child is ready to go to another lesson.

All written work, such as words, sentences, numbers, geometric shapes, and tracing, is kept in the child's work folder. When the child has completed five papers of each activity, Mrs. Collins makes it into a booklet to take home. Reports to parents are made both in conferences and in writing. The Montessori program is explained to the parents before their children are enrolled. Periodic parent programs are also conducted to keep the parents informed and involved.

---

quality advocated by Maria Montessori. Selecting a Montessori preschool is no different from other consumer choices; the customer must beware of being cheated. No truth in advertising law requires operators of a Montessori school to operate a quality program. Because the name has such appeal to parents, some schools call themselves Montessori without either the trained staff or facilities to justify their claim.

Not only do some schools misrepresent themselves, but some teachers as well. There is no requirement that a teacher must have Montessori training of any particular duration or by any prescribed course of instruction. The American Montessori Society (AMS) approves training programs that meet its standards for teacher training, and the Association Montessori Internationale (AMI) approves teacher training programs that meet the standards of the international organization.

To decide whether a Montessori school is a good one, parents should consider these points:

- ☐ Is the school affiliated with a recognized Montessori association (Association Montessori Internationale [AMI] or American Montessori Society [AMS])?
- ☐ Is the teacher a certified Montessori teacher?
- ☐ How many characteristics outlined by the American Montessori Society does the program have?
- ☐ Are practices of the Montessori method part of the program?
- ☐ Contact parents of former students to determine their satisfaction with the program; ask "Would you again send your child to this school? How is your child doing in first grade? How was the Montessori program beneficial to your child?"
- ☐ Compare tuition rates of the Montessori school to other schools. Is any difference in tuition worth it?
- ☐ Ask yourself why you want your child to attend a Montessori school. Is it social status? Prestige? Do you feel your child will achieve more by attending a Montessori school? Visit other preschool programs to determine if a Montessori program is best for your child.
- ☐ Interview the director and staff to learn about the program's philosophy, the curriculum, rules and regulations, and how the program differs from others that are not Montessori.

☐ If you enroll your child, pay attention to his or her progress through visits, written reports, and conferences to be sure the child is learning what will be needed for success in the first grade.

More Information

Information about becoming a Montessori teacher can be obtained by writing to The American Montessori Society, 150 Fifth Avenue, New York, New York 10011. Requests for information about the International Association should be addressed to the Association Montessori Internationale, 780 West End Avenue, New York, New York 10025. Generally, Montessori training takes one year to complete and results in a certificate to teach in Montessori settings. This certification does not generally substitute for public school certification. A bachelor's degree is required for both AMI and AMS training courses.

FURTHER READING

Hainstock, Elizabeth G. *Teaching Montessori in the Home: The Pre-School Years* (New York: Random House, 1971) Makes Montessori ideas understandable to parents and practical for use in the home.

_____. *Teaching Montessori in the Home: The School Years* (New York: Random House, 1971) Companion to *Teaching Montessori in the Home: The Pre-School Years*. Extends concepts of early learning and emphasizes mathematics and language development. Encourages parents to take responsibility for their children's learning, and outlines the three-period lesson.

Kramer, Rita. *Maria Montessori* (New York: G. P. Putnam's Sons, 1976) Well-researched and documented biography.

Lillard, Paula Polk. *Montessori, A Modern Approach* (New York: Schocken Books, 1977) Good account of what happens in the Montessori classroom. Begins with the life of Montessori, concludes with a description of current practices.

Montessori, Maria. *Spontaneous Activity in Education* (New York: Schocken Books, 1965) Continuation of ideas and methodologies begun in *The Montessori Method*. Deals with concepts of attention, intelligence, imagination, and moral development, and discusses provisions for them in a Montessori setting.

Montessori, Mario M., Jr. *Education for Human Development: Understanding Montessori*, Paula Polk Lillard, ed. (New York: Schocken Books, 1976) Written by the grandson of Maria Montessori, essays in this book provide fresh insight into many Montessorian concepts. Addresses some traditional criticisms of the Montessori method and gives a modern approach to the Montessori system. Should be read after one has a knowledge of Montessori and her ideas.

Orem, R. C., ed. *Montessori: Her Method and the Movement* (New York: G. P. Putnam's Sons, 1974) Layman's guide to the Montessori philosophy and method; includes questions and answers.

_____. *Montessori Today* (New York: G. P. Putnam's Sons, 1971) Survey of the philosophies and actual programs of Montessori schools in the United States.

Orem, R. C., and Marjorie Coburn. *Montessori Prescription for Children with Learning Disabilities* (New York: G. P. Putnam's Sons, 1978) Applies and adapts Montessori methods to the needs of the child with learning disabilities. Deals with current trends; gives parents a major role in its program outline.

Standing, E. M. *The Montessori Revolution in Education,* 6th ed. (New York: Schocken Books, 1971) Excellent reference; easy-to-read, understandable description of activities, with illustrations.

Montessori in Perspective, ed. Publications Committee of the National Association for the Education of Young Children, 1966. Collection of articles by educators about the history and method of the Montessori system. Should be read with a knowledge of Montessori and after reading at least one of her own books.

FURTHER STUDY

1. After reading the section in chapter 2 on open education, compare Montessori concepts to those of open education. What are the similarities and differences? Has Montessori influenced open education?

2. Compare Montessori materials to those in other kindergarten and preschool programs. Is it possible for teachers to make Montessori materials? What advantages or disadvantages would there be in making and using these materials?

3. What features of the Montessori program do you like best? Why? What features do you like least? Why? What features are best for children?

4. After visiting a Montessori classroom and talking with teachers, evaluate the criticisms of the system mentioned in the chapter. Are the criticisms valid? Are there any you would add? Why?

5. If a mother of a four-year-old asked your advice about sending her child to a Montessori school, what would you tell her?

6. From your observation of children, give specific examples to support your opinion that there are or are not sensitive periods for learning.

7. Read one of Montessori's books and give an oral report to your class. Include your opinion of the book and its implications for modern education.

8. Interview public and private school teachers about their understanding of the Montessori program. Do they have a good understanding of the program? What are the most critical areas of understanding or misunderstanding? Do you think *all* early childhood teachers should have knowledge of the Montessori program? Why or why not?

9. Do you think the Montessori method will ever be a dominant program in the public school system? Why or why not? Explain why the Montessori program has remained mainly in the private schools. Interview a public school kindergarten or preschool teacher and a Montessori teacher on the topic. Compare their opinions to yours.

10. Review several recent studies that deal with the effect of the Montessori method on preschool children's behavior and achievement. Do the findings differ from what you expected? How? Does this change your opinion of the Montessori method?

4

Jean Piaget: A New Way of Thinking About Thinking

As you read and study:

Critically examine and develop an understanding of Piaget's theory of intellectual development

Learn Piaget's stages of intellectual development and the characteristics of children's thinking in each

Identify the processes Piaget considered critical for intellectual development

Learn the terminology necessary to understand Piaget's theory

Analyze Piaget's stages of intellectual development and understand their relationship to children's development of knowledge

Through observations and practices, identify the characteristics of children's thinking as described by Piaget

Identify the major features and common concepts of educational curricula based on Piaget's theory

Explain the role of autonomy in children's learning

Discuss issues and controversies associated with Piaget's theory

J ean Piaget developed the *cognitive theory* approach to learning. As an epistomologist (one who studies the acquisition of knowledge), Piaget was interested in how humans learn and develop intellectually from birth and continuing through life. He devoted his life to experimentation, observation of children (including his own), and writing about his theory. Piaget enriched our knowledge about children's thinking, and his influence on early childhood education has been significant.

When one hears of or considers intelligence, one often thinks of I.Q.—intelligence quotient—that which is measured on an intelligence test. But I.Q. is not what Piaget means by intelligence. Rather, for him, intelligence is the cognitive or mental process by which knowledge is acquired. Hence, *intelligence* is "to know" and is synonymous with thinking in that it involves the use of mental operations developed as a result of mental and physical interaction with the environment. Basic to Piaget's cognitive theory is children's active involvement with the physical world through direct experiences. A second basic point is that intelligence develops over time, and a third premise is that children are *intrinsically* motivated to develop intelligence.

To adequately understand and appreciate Piaget's cognitive theory, one must understand that his early training as a biologist permeates and influences his thinking and ideas. He conceives of intelligence as having a biological basis—that is, all organisms, including humans, adapt to their environments. You are probably familiar with the process of physical adaptation, whereby an individual, stimulated by environmental factors, reacts and adjusts to that environment; this adjustment results in physical changes. Piaget applies the concept of adaptation to the mental level and uses it to help explain how intellectual development evolves through stages of thinking. Humans mentally adapt to environmental experiences as a result of encounters with people, places, and things; the result is *cognitive development.*

INTELLECTUAL DEVELOPMENT AND ADAPTATION

To Piaget, the adaptive process at the intellectual level operates much the same as at the physical level. He sees the newborn child as lacking intelligence, except that intelligence expressed through reflexive motor actions such as sucking, grasping, head turning, and swallowing. Through the process of adaptation to the environment via these reflexive actions, the intelligence of the young child has its origin and is developed.

> Adaptation is for Piaget, the essence of intellectual functioning, just as it is the essence of biological functioning. It is one of the two basic tendencies inherent in all species; the other is organization, the ability to integrate both physical and psychological structures into coherent systems. Adaptation takes place through organization; the organism discriminates among the myriad stimuli and sensations by which it is bombarded and organizes them into some kind of structure.[1]

Through this interaction with the environment that results in adaptation, the child organizes sensations and experiences. The resulting organization and processes of interaction are what is called *intelligence.* Obviously, therefore, the quality of the environment and the nature of the child's experiences will play a major role in the development of intelligence. For example, the child with various and differing objects available to grasp and suck, and many opportunities for this behavior, will develop differentiated sucking organizations (and therefore an intelligence) quite different from that of the child who has nothing to suck but a pacifier.

The Process of Adaptation

Piaget believed the adaptive process is comprised of two interrelated processes, assimilation and accommodation. On the intellectual level, *assimilation* is the taking in of data through sensory impulses via experiences and impressions and incorporating them into knowledge of people and objects already created as a result of these experiences.

> Every experience we have, whether as infant, child or adult, is taken into the mind and made to fit into the experiences which already exist there. The new experience will need to be changed in some degree in order for it to fit in. Some experiences cannot be taken in because they do not fit. These are rejected. Thus the intellect assimilates new experiences into itself by transforming them to fit the structure which has been built up. This process of acting on the environment in order to build up a model of it in the mind, Piaget calls assimilation.[2]

Accommodation, on the other hand, is the process by which the individual changes his way of thinking, behaving, and believing to come into accord with reality. For example, a child who is familiar with cats because she has several at home may, upon seeing a dog for the first time, call it a cat. She has assimilated dog into her organization of cat. However, she must change (accommodate) her model of what constitutes "catness" to exclude dogs. She does this by starting to construct or build a scheme for dog and thus what "dogness" represents.

> Now with each new experience, the structures which have already been built up will need to modify themselves to accept that new experience, for, as each new experience is fitted in to the old, the structures will be slightly changed. This process by which the intellect continually adjusts its model of the world to fit in each new acquisition, Piaget calls accommodation.[3]

The twin processes of assimilation and accommodation, viewed as an integrated, functioning whole, constitute *adaptation.*

Another term in Piaget's theory of intelligence is *equilibrium.* Equilibrium is a balance between assimilation and accommodation. An individual cannot assimilate new data without changing to some degree his way of thinking or acting to fit those new data. People who always assimilate without much evidence of having changed are characterized as "flying in the face of reality." Yet, an individual cannot always accommodate old ideas to all the information he receives. If this were the case, no beliefs would ever be maintained. A balance is needed between the two. Diagrammed, the process would look something like that in Figure 4–1.

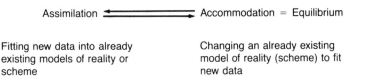

Assimilation $\rightleftharpoons$ Accommodation = Equilibrium

| Fitting new data into already existing models of reality or scheme | Changing an already existing model of reality (scheme) to fit new data |

FIGURE 4–1 The Adaptation Process.

Upon receiving new sensory and experiential data, the child assimilates or fits these data into her already existing knowledge (scheme) of reality and the world. If the new data can be immediately assimilated, then equilibrium occurs. If she is unable to assimilate the data, she tries to accommodate and change her way of thinking, acting, and perceiving to account for the new data and restore equilibrium to the intellectual system. It may well be that she can neither assimilate nor accommodate the new data; if so, she rejects the data entirely.

Instances of rejection are common if what the child is trying to assimilate and accommodate is radically different from her past data and experiences. This partially accounts for Piaget's insistence that all new experiences be planned, so the child has some connection or relationship to previous experiences. A further pedagogical implication of this idea for teachers is the analysis of the child's past experiences through testing, observation, parent conferences, anecdotal records, and student interviews. Present school experiences should build on previous life experiences.

Even more importantly, a teacher must try to assess the cognitive structures of all children and determine the suitability of school tasks in promoting cognitive growth. Before giving a child activities in classification, for example, a teacher must determine the level at which the child is functioning in relation to classification structures. A program such as the Lavatelli Materials can help determine such levels. It is also imperative that the teacher not assign (or demand, as is so frequently done) the child to do tasks for which she lacks the cognitive structure. Undoubtedly, some of the reasons for school failure can be attributed to teachers who insist that children engage in tasks for which they have no experiential background and consequently lack the necessary cognitive structure. For example, it is damaging to a child's mental health to ask her to perform a task that requires her to discriminate between words when she cannot discriminate between the letters of the alphabet.

Schemes

Piaget used the term *scheme* to refer to units of knowledge the child develops through the adaptive process. (In reality, the child develops many schemes.) A newborn has only reflexive actions. By using reflexive actions such as sucking and grasping, the child begins to build her concept and understanding of her world. When the child uses primarily reflexive actions to develop intellectually, she is in what Piaget calls the *sensorimotor stage,* which begins at birth and usually ends between eighteen months and two years. For example, with reflexive actions, she constructs a mental scheme of what is suckable and what is not (what can fit into her mouth and what cannot), and what sensations (warm and cold) occur by sucking. She also uses her grasping reflex in much the same way to build schemes of what can and cannot be grasped.

Why do some children develop or create different schemes? This depends upon the environment in which the child is reared and the quality of the child's experiences in that environment. If the environment establishes perimeters for the development of intelligence, the child who is confined to a crib with no objects to suck or grasp is at a disadvantage in building mental structures through the adaptive process utilizing sensorimotor responses. The child who has a variety of materials has more opportunities to develop alternative schemes. Children who have a variety of materials and a caring adult to help stimulate sensory responses will do even better. By the same token, as the child grows and matures, she will have greater opportunities to develop intellectually in an environment that provides for interaction with people, objects, and things.

In this process of adaptation, Piaget ascribed primary importance to the child's physical activity. Physical activity leads to mental stimulus, which in turn leads to mental activity. Thus it is not possible to draw a clear line between physical activity and mental activity in infancy and early childhood. Settings should enable children to explore their physical environment and to interact with people and objects in this ex-

Through play, children develop mental schemes of the world.

ploration. A child who is confined to a playpen without opportunities for manipulating objects and for social interactions is limited in adaptive opportunities.

Everyone recognizes that children should play, but we have not always recognized the importance of play as the context in which the child constructs mental schemes to form a basis for all other schemes. Play, to Piaget, becomes a powerful process in intellectual development. Parents seem to sense this intuitively in wanting their children to play, particularly with other children. Many kindergarten and first-grade teachers also have an intuitive sense of the importance of play and include many opportunities for play in their curricula.

Constructivism

The constructivist concept is central to understanding Piaget's theory. Children literally construct their knowledge of the world and their level of cognitive functioning. "The more advanced forms of cognition are constructed anew by each individual through a process of 'self-directed' or 'self-regulated activity'."[4] The constructivist process "is defined in terms of the individual's organizing, structuring and restructuring of experience—an ongoing lifelong process—in accordance with existing schemes of thought. In turn, these very schemes become modified and enriched in the course of interaction with the physical and social world."[5] Children continuously organize, structure, and restructure experiences in relation to existing schemes of thought. Experiences provide a basis for constructing schemes.

In explaining the role of constructivism, Constance Kamii, a leading Piaget scholar, states, "Constructivism refers to the fact that knowledge is built by an active child from the inside rather than being transmitted from the outside through the senses."[6]

Maturation

Piaget believed *maturation,* the child's development over time, influenced intellectual development. Factors that influence maturation are (1) genetic characteristics peculiar to the child as an individual, (2) the unique characteristics of the child as a human being, and (3) environmental factors such as nutrition. Maturation helps explain why the thinking of the child is not the same as the thinking of the adult, and why we should not expect a child to think as an adult does. A child who has adults to interact with, as through conversation that solicits and promotes the child's involvement, has the opportunity to develop schemes that differ from those of the child who lacks this opportunity.

Social Transmission

Piaget felt social transmission is important because some information and modes of behavior are best transmitted to the child by people, rather than through other methods such as reading. (When discussing environmental influences, I include people; Piaget considers them a separate factor.) Examples of social transmission include behavior appropriate to certain situations, such as not running in front of speeding cars, not blowing one's nose without a handkerchief, and many curriculum skills involving the 3 Rs. From the cognitive-development viewpoint, however, there is a difference between being told what something is ("the block is large") and understanding what "large" means as a result of playing and experimenting with blocks of different sizes. Telling a child that something is large involves no thinking processes on the child's part; to develop thinking processes one must provide the child with many experiences to perform operations—for example, stacking, sorting, and building with blocks.

STAGES OF DEVELOPMENT

Table 4–1 summarizes Piaget's developmental stages and will help you conceptualize stage-related characteristics. Piaget contended that the developmental stages are the same for all children, including the atypical child, and that all children progress through each stage in the same order. The ages are only approximate and should not be considered fixed. The sequence of growth through the developmental stages does not vary; the ages at which progression occurs do vary.

Sensorimotor Stage

During the period from birth to about two years, children use senses and motor reflexes to begin building knowledge of the world. They use their eyes to view the world, their mouths to suck, and their hands to grasp. Through these innate sensory

TABLE 4–1 Piaget's Stages of Cognitive Development.

Stage	Characteristics
Sensorimotor (Birth–18 months/2 years)	Uses sensorimotor systems of sucking, grasping, and gross body activities to build schemes. Begins to develop object permanency.
	Dependent on concrete representations. Frame of reference is the world of here and now.
Preoperational (2–7 years)	Language development accelerates. Internalizes events. Egocentric in thought and action. Thinks everything has a reason or purpose. Is perceptually bound. Makes judgments primarily on basis of how things look.
Concrete Operations (7–12 years)	Capable of reversal of thought processes. Ability to conserve. Still dependent on how things look for decision making. Less egocentric. Structures time and space. Understanding of number. Beginning of logical thinking.
Formal Operations (12–15 years)	Capable of dealing with verbal and hypothetical problems. Ability to reason scientifically and logically. No longer bound to the concrete. Can think with symbols.

Piaget has prompted early childhood educators to teach children based on their levels of cognitive development. How would teaching differ for each of these children?

and reflexive actions, they continue to develop an increasingly complex, unique, and individualized hierarchy of schemes. What the child is to become both physically and intellectually is related to these sensorimotor functions and interactions. Furth says, "An organism exists only insofar as it functions."[7] This important concept stresses the necessity of an enriched environment for children.

Major characteristics of the sensorimotor period include these:

- ☐ Dependency on and use of innate reflexive actions
- ☐ Initial development of object permanency (the idea that objects can exist without being seen)
- ☐ Egocentricity, whereby the child sees herself as the center of the world and believes events are caused by her
- ☐ Dependence upon concrete representations (things) rather than symbols (words, pictures) for information

By the end of the second year, the child relies less on sensorimotor reflexive actions and begins to use symbols for things that are not present.

Preoperational Stage

The preoperational stage begins at age two and ends at approximately seven years of age. The preoperational child is different from the sensorimotor child in these ways:

- ☐ Language development begins to accelerate rapidly
- ☐ There is less dependence on sensorimotor action
- ☐ There is an increased ability to internalize events, to think by utilizing representational symbols such as words in place of things

The preoperational child continues to share common characteristics with the sensorimotor child, such as egocentricity. At the preoperational level, egocentricity is characterized by being perceptually bound, the outward manifestation of which is making judgments, expressing ideas, and basing perceptions mainly on an interpretation of how things are physically perceived by the senses. How things look to the preoperational child is in turn the foundation for several other stage-related characteristics. First, a child faced with an object that has multiple characteristics, such as a long, round, yellow pencil, will "see" whichever of those qualities first catches her eye. A preoperational child's knowledge is based only on what she is able to see, simply because she does not yet have operational intelligence or the ability to think using mental images.

Second, absence of operations makes it impossible to conserve, or determine that the quantity of an object does not change simply because some transformation occurs in its physical appearance. For example, show a preoperational child two identical rows of matching toy soldiers (see Figure 4–2). Ask the child if there are the same number of toy soldiers in each row. She should answer affirmatively. Next, space out the toy soldiers in one row, and ask the child if the two rows still have the same number of toy soldiers. She may insist that there are more toy soldiers in one row "because it's longer." The child bases her judgment on what she can see, namely, the spatial extension of one row beyond the other row. This is also an example of reversibility. In this case, the child is not capable of reversing thought or action, which would require that she mentally put the row back to its original length.

The preoperational child acts as though everything has a reason or purpose; that is, she believes every act of her mother, her father, and her teacher or every event in nature happens for a specific purpose. This accounts for the child's constant and

All toy soldiers should be equal in size, dimension, and color. When asked if there are the same number of toy soldiers in each row, the preoperational child will answer yes. However, when one row is spread out, so that the correspondence of being exactly opposite from each other is destroyed (below), the preoperational child will say there are more toy soldiers in the bottom row because it is longer.

FIGURE 4–2 Perceptions of a Preoperational Child.

recurring questions about why things happen, how things work, and the correspond-ing exasperation of adults in trying to answer these questions.

Preoperational children also believe everyone thinks as they think and there-fore act as they act for the same reasons. Because the preoperational child is egocen-tric, she cannot put herself in another's place. To ask her to sympathize or empathize with others is asking her to perform an operation beyond her developmental level. This egocentricity also makes it difficult, if not impossible, for her to participate in sharing. The teacher's insistence that a child share in this stage is not only futile for the teacher, but also incomprehensible to the child.

Concrete Operations Stage

Piaget defined *operation* as follows: "First of all, an operation is an action that can be internalized; that is, it can be carried out in thought as well as executed materially. Second, it is a reversible action; that is, can take place in one direction or in the oppo-site direction."[8] Unlike the preoperational child, whose thought goes only in one di-rection (using the body and sensory organs to act on materials), children in the con-crete stage begin to use mental images and symbols during the thinking process and can reverse operations. Although children are very much dependent on the per-ceptual level of how things look to them, development of mental processes can be encouraged and facilitated during this stage through the use of concrete or real ob-jects as opposed to hypothetical situations or places.

Classification and numeration activities help in the development of mental operations.

Telling is not teaching. One should structure the learning setting so the child has experiences at her level with real objects, things, and people. Providing activities at the child's level cannot be overstressed. Teachers often provide activities that are too easy rather than activities that are too difficult. For example, in the toy soldier experiment, the child should have used objects in the practice of one-to-one correspondence.

A characteristic of the concrete operational child is the beginning of the ability to conserve. Unlike the preoperational child, who thinks that because the physical appearance of an object changes it therefore follows that its quality or quantity changes, the concrete operational child begins to develop the ability to understand that change involving physical appearances does not necessarily change quality or quantity (see Figure 4–3).

The child also begins to reverse thought processes, by going back over and "undoing" a mental action she has just accomplished. At the physical level, this relates to

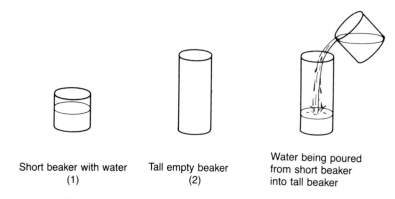

Short beaker with water (1) Tall empty beaker (2) Water being poured from short beaker into tall beaker

The preoperational child cannot conserve or reverse an action even when she observes the action taking place. For example, when a fixed quantity of water (1) is poured from one beaker into a taller beaker (2), the child will say that there is more water in the taller beaker. When asked how this is so, she will answer because it is taller.

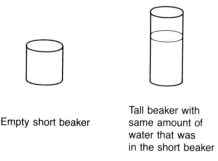

Empty short beaker Tall beaker with same amount of water that was in the short beaker

FIGURE 4–3 Test of Child's Ability to Conserve.

conservation. In the example with two rows of soldiers, the child indicated there were more soldiers in the spread-out row. The child who can reverse an operation can undo it by mentally returning the soldiers to their original position and is then able to determine that there are not more soldiers in the longer row. The concrete operational child begins to manipulate mentally rather than depending only on physical appearances or concrete objects. Whereas the preoperational child cannot "put back" the soldiers mentally, the concrete operational child can. Other mental operations the child is capable of during this stage are:

- ☐ One-to-one correspondence
- ☐ Classification of objects, events, and time according to certain characteristics
- ☐ Classification involving multiple properties of objects
- ☐ Class inclusion operations
- ☐ Complementary classes

The child also structures time and space into logical, coherent, deductive systems. Development for this ability begins, as do all other operations, in the sensorimotor period. During the concrete operations stage, the child is less egocentric. She learns that other people have thoughts and feelings that can differ from her own. One of the more meaningful methods of helping the child develop beyond this innate egocentrism is through interaction with other individuals, especially peers. The teacher's role is not to "teach" children to share or tell them when to apologize for something they've done. It is through involvement with others, interacting and talking about social encounters, that children gradually become less egocentric. This stage does not represent a period into which the child suddenly emerges, after having been a preoperational child. The process of development is not that of Athena stepping from the head of Zeus, but rather a gradual, continual process occurring over a period of time and resulting from maturation and experiences. No simple sets of exercises will cause the child to move up the developmental ladder. Experiences with people and objects result in activities that lead to conceptual understanding.

Formal Operations Stage

The next stage of development, the second part of operational intelligence, is called *formal operations*. It begins at about eleven years of age and extends to about fifteen years. During this period, the child becomes capable of dealing with increasingly complex verbal and hypothetical problems, and less dependent upon concrete objects to solve problems. The child becomes free of the world of "things" as far as mental functioning is concerned. Thinking ranges over a wide time span that includes past, present, and future. The child in this stage develops the ability to reason scientifically and logically, and can think with all the processes and power of an adult. How one thinks is thus pretty well established by the age of fifteen, although the child or adolescent does not stop developing new schemes through assimilation and accommodation.

A GLOSSARY OF PIAGETIAN TERMS

Accommodation   Changing one's ideas, or scheme, of reality to fit the new knowledge one is trying to assimilate.

Adaptation   The processes of assimilation and accommodation.

Assimilation   Fitting or adding new knowledge into already existing schemes of reality.

Concrete Operations   The beginning of operational thought. In concrete operations, the child deals with real things. The operations usually associated with concrete operations are classification, seriation, numerations, and correspondences.

Conservation   Piaget uses this term to describe the judgment that the quantity remains the same after a transformation. When the child is capable of reversing thought processes, he is able to conserve.

Constructivism   The process of continually organizing, structuring, and restructuring experiences into existing schemes of thought.

Egocentric   Centering around the child himself. The young child is literally bound by his own thinking. He understands only one point of view, his own. Also, the child can perceive only one aspect of a situation at a time.

Object Permanency   A child constructs the belief that when something (an object, a parent) disappears from his sight, it doesn't cease to exist, that it has permanency. The young child thinks that when he no longer can see an object, it no longer exists. In the sensorimotor stage, the child begins to learn that when his mother leaves the room she still exists and that when his ball rolls out of sight, it still exists.

Operation   A thought process capable of being reversed and combined with other operations. Operations as conceived by Piaget are also reversible, i.e., $4 - 2 = 2$. The preoperational child is not capable of mentally reversing these operations.

Scheme   A unit of knowledge, an idea. The child begins life with only the reflexive motor actions that develop into schemes. All other thoughts and ideas build on these primitive ones.

EDUCATIONAL CURRICULA BASED ON PIAGET

The High Scope Early Elementary Program: Cognitively Oriented Curriculum

The High Scope Educational Research Foundation is a nonprofit organization that sponsors and supports the cognitively oriented curriculum. The program is based on Piaget's intellectual development theory, and "is an 'open framework' approach that places both the teacher and the child in active, initiating roles. It attempts to blend the virtues of purposeful teaching with open-ended, child-initiated activities."[9]

Since part of the Piagetian theory of intellectual development maintains that children must be actively involved in their own learning through experiences and encounters with people and things, the cognitively oriented curriculum promotes the child's active involvement in his own learning. The program lists these objectives to facilitate the learning process:

☐ An ability to make decisions about what they are going to do and how they are going to do it
☐ An ability to define and solve problems
☐ Self-discipline, ability to identify personal goals, and capacity to pursue and complete self-chosen tasks
☐ An ability to engage with other children and adults in group planning, cooperative effort, and shared leadership
☐ Expressive abilities—to speak, write, dramatize, and graphically represent their experiences, feelings, and ideas
☐ An ability to comprehend other's self-expression through spoken, written, artistic, and graphic representations
☐ An ability to apply classification, seriation, spatial, temporal, and quantitative-mathematical reasoning in diverse life situations
☐ Skills and abilities in the arts, science, and physical movement as vehicles with which to engage their personal talents and energy
☐ Openness to the points of view, values, and behaviors of others
☐ Spirit of inquiry and a personal sense of goals and values
☐ Long-term interests or avocations which can be cultivated both in and outside of school throughout life.[10]

Achievement of these objectives depends on the child's involvement in the key experiences of action, representation, conceptual relations, and curriculum. *Action* includes planning, working, evaluating, and social interactions. *Representation* includes dramatic activity, drawing and painting, speaking, listening, writing, and reading. *Conceptual relations* consist of classification, seriation, number, space, time, causality, and measurement, which includes length, area, weight, volume, and time. *Curriculum content* consists of language arts, mathematics, art, play and drama, construction, sewing and pattern design, music, movement, media, social studies, and science.

The adult's role in the cognitively oriented curriculum encompasses behaviors in three broad areas. Adults must (1) know where the child is starting from; (2) provide an environment where children can become self-initiating, decision makers, and problem solvers; and (3) guide the child. These aspects of the teacher's role are supported by cooperation with adults similarly concerned with children's education.[11] Working in these three areas enables the teacher to come to know each child well. It is important in a cognitively oriented curriculum, as in any other good program, that teachers know at what developmental level each child is functioning. Children benefit most from experiences that match their developmental capacities.

By knowing the developmental stages, teachers can involve the child in appropriate activities. For example, if the child is at the preoperational level, the teacher might use a classification activity involving how objects are similar and different, whereas if the child were at the concrete operational level, a classification activity involving sorting objects into increasingly higher order of classes would be more appropriate. The teacher can thus provide an individualized program for each child. These are ways to identify a child's developmental level:

1. Observe what children are doing, things they make, and pictures they draw
2. Question children about their work, actions, and activities
3. Simulate an activity designed to reveal how the child acts, works, behaves, and interacts

The teacher must also continually encourage and support children's interests and involvement in activities, which occurs in the perimeters of an organized environment and a consistent routine. The teacher must plan what and how children will learn and involve children in planning for their own learning. Teachers plan from key experiences through which children's emerging abilities may be broadened and strengthened. Children generate many of these experiences on their own; others require adult guidance. Many key experiences arise naturally throughout the daily routine. Key experiences are not limited to specific objects or places; they are natural extensions of children's projects and interests. Table 4–2 lists some key experiences that support learning and development.

TABLE 4–2 Key Experiences to Match Developmental Capacities of Children Between Ages Four and Six

Active learning

Exploring actively the attributes and functions of materials with all the senses.
Discovering relations through direct experience.
Manipulating, transforming, and combining materials.
Identifying personal interests by choosing materials, activities, and purposes.
Acquiring skills with tools and equipment.
Using small and large muscles.
Taking care of one's own needs.
Predicting problems and devising ways of solving them.

Speaking and listening to language

Talking with others about personally meaningful experiences.
Describing relations among objects, people, events, and ideas.
Talking with others about needs, interests, ideas, and feelings.
Having one's own spoken language written down by an adult and read back.
Having fun with language: rhyming, making up stories, listening to poems, and stories.
Imitating and describing sounds from the environment.
Listening to others.
Responding to others by asking questions.
Following directions given by others.
Telling stories from pictures and books.
Solving problems or conflicts.

Source: Donna McClelland, Consultant, High Scope Educational Research Foundation.

TABLE 4–2 Continued

Representing experiences and ideas

Recognizing objects by sound, touch, taste, and smell.
Pantomiming actions.
Relating pictures, photographs, and models to real places and things.
Representing personal experiences through: role play, pretending, and dramatic activities; making models out of clay, blocks, etc.; drawing and painting; graphing, mapping, and using objects to make prints.
Sharing and discussing representations.
Interpreting representations of others.

Writing

Dictating, tracing, copying, or writing stories about personally meaningful experiences.
Expressing ideas and feelings by dictating or writing original stories, poems, songs, riddles.
Including descriptive detail in dictation or writing by describing attributes of objects and relations among objects, people, and events.
Using phonics for spelling words.
Writing simple information such as name, address, etc.

Reading

Reading back dictation with an adult.
Matching letters and words that are alike.
Recognizing familiar words such as own name, name of common objects, places, and actions.
Hearing likenesses (rhyming sounds) and differences in words.
Recognizing familiar words such as own name, name of common objects, places, and actions.
Identifying letters in own name and familiar words.
Reading one's own dictated or written story.
Making up words of like sounds including nonsense syllables and words.

Developing logical reasoning

Classification
Investigating and labeling the attributes of things.
Noticing and describing how things are the same and how they are different.
Sorting and matching.
Using and describing something in several different ways.
Describing what characteristics something does not possess or what class it does not belong to.
Holding more than one attribute in mind at a time. (Examples: Can you find something that is red and made of wood?)
Sorting objects and then resorting them using different criteria.
Distinguishing between "some" and "all."

Seriation
Comparing objects using a single criterion: Which one is bigger (smaller), heavier (lighter), rougher (smoother), louder (softer), harder (softer), longer (shorter), wider (narrower), sharper, darker, etc.
Comparing and sorting objects into two groups based on a particular criterion (big/little, tall/short, hard/soft, etc.).

TABLE 4–2 Continued

Arranging several things in order along some dimension and describing the relations (the longest one, the shortest one, etc.).
Arranging things into three groups along some dimension and describing the relations (big, bigger, biggest; long, longer, longest; etc.).

Number concepts
Comparing number and amount: more/less, same amount; more/fewer, same number.
Enumerating (counting) objects, as well as counting by rote.
Identifying and writing numerals to twenty.
Representing number information by talking, drawing, or writing numerals.

Understanding time and space

Spatial Relations
Fitting things together and taking them apart.
Rearranging a set of objects or one object in space (folding, twisting, stretching, stacking, tying) and observing the spatial transformations.
Observing things and places from different spatial viewpoints.
Experiencing and describing the positions of things in relation to each other (e.g., in the middle, on the side of, on, off, on top of, over, above).
Experiencing and describing relative distances among things and locations (close, near, far, next to, apart, together).
Experiencing and representing one's own body: how it is structured, what various body parts can do.
Learning to locate things in the classroom, school, and neighborhood.
Interpreting representations of spatial relations in drawings and pictures.
Distinguishing and describing shapes.
Identifying parts of objects and identifying an object from one of its parts.
Identifying and representing the order of objects in space.
Developing an awareness of symmetry in one's own representations and representations of others.

Time
Planning and completing what one has planned.
Describing and representing past events.
Anticipating future events verbally and by making appropriate preparations.
Starting and stopping an action on signal.
Noticing, describing, and representing the order of events.
Experiencing and describing different rates of movement.
Using conventional time units when talking about past and future events (morning, yesterday, hour, etc.).
Comparing time periods (short, long; new, old; young, old; a little while, a long time).
Observing that clocks and calendars are used to mark the passage of time.
Observing seasonal changes.

Science

Caring for animals.
Planting seeds and caring for growing plants.
Observing, describing, and representing weather changes.
Observing, describing, and representing transformations, i.e., cooking activities (making popcorn, apple sauce, pudding), carving pumpkins, freezing liquids, melting snow, sinking and floating activities.

124

TABLE 4-2 Continued

Exploring the natural environment.
Collecting objects from the natural environment.

Social Studies

Interacting with people of many ages and backgrounds in a variety of situations.
Representing family, school, and community roles and events through socio-dramatic play.
Taking field trips.
Representing field trips by writing experience stories, building models, and drawing pictures.
Utilizing community resources as a basis for classroom activities.

A team teaching concept provides children and adults with greater support, involvement, ideas, attention, help, and expertise. Just as children plan and work in the cognitively oriented classroom, so does the teaching team plan daily for the work of the classroom. The recommended adult-child ratio is ten to one, so a cognitively oriented classroom of thirty children would have three adults—perhaps one teacher, one paid aide, and a volunteer, or one teacher, one assistant teacher, and one aide.

In the cognitively oriented curriculum, the learning process is based on matching children's developing levels of intellectual ability to learning tasks and activities. No effort is made to push children, speed up the learning process, teach for achievement of a developmental level, or teach facts as a substitute for thinking. The children's emerging abilities are "broadened and strengthened" rather than "taught" in the conventional sense. To match learning tasks with developmental levels, children are involved in activities according to their interests, in a framework based partly on ideas from open education (see chapter 2). Open education need not occur in an open space, but can occur in a self-contained classroom. In the open framework, children are involved in decision making, self-direction, and problem solving.

The basic instructional/learning model of the cognitively oriented curriculum is the Plan, Work, Represent and Evaluate model (PWRE). Children plan the activity they will be involved in, work at accomplishing it, represent the activity in some way (write a story or make a model), read their stories or describe their products, and evaluate what they have done. A schedule for a child in a cognitively oriented curriculum might look like this one, described by Richard Lalli:

8:30	Large group time
8:50	Language small group time
9:15	Planning time
9:30	Work time
10:30	Representation time
11:00	Evaluation time
11:20	Lunch and outside
12:00	Large group time (story reading time)
12:30	Math small group time
1:00	Project time
2:15	Circle time (large group time)

A Cognitively Oriented Curriculum in the Okaloosa County (Florida) Public Schools

The Okaloosa County (Florida) Follow Through Program has adapted the Cognitively Oriented Curriculum described by High Scope Foundation in its K–2 classrooms.[12] This model is one of several used in elementary schools throughout the country. The Okaloosa County program uses the Plan, Work, Represent, Evaluate (PWRE) management system model mentioned previously. In addition, many teachers identify and use certain themes as a context or organizing structure for action, representation, conceptual relations, and curriculum content. The themes evolve from the children's interest, social studies, health, and science, and reflect the program's objectives.

Planning

Children plan for the work they will do; for example, a child will plan to plant a cutting she has rooted, her interest aroused by a science unit on plants. Other related activities are also available in the science center. During the planning process, children are asked to think about, communicate verbally or in pictures, and write about these items:

- ☐ The area where one will implement the plan
- ☐ The kind and amount of materials one will need
- ☐ The sequence one will follow in completing the plan
- ☐ The amount of time it will take to complete the plan and the problems one might encounter

The planning format of the PWRE process progresses through several language arts stages as children develop their abilities to communicate. In the oral stage, the teacher writes down what the child says, perhaps as captions or descriptions for the child's drawing of a plan for an activity. In the second stage, the child traces what the teacher has written from the child's dictation. At first, the child might trace only certain words; at a later stage, she may trace sentences. At the third stage, the child copies what the teacher has written. A child now copies words and sentences from left to right, and may also use words found in the classroom (labels) to label parts of the drawing. An extension of this writing activity might be to add words to the plan from word banks—lists of words the child has used in past planning and recognizes as sight words. The word bank leads into individual dictionaries and use of commercial dictionaries (see Figure 4–4). The fourth stage is the children's completely independent writing of the plan, although some may still need help in sounding out and

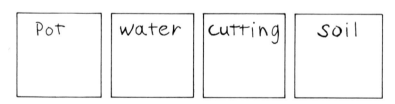

FIGURE 4–4 Word Banks.

spelling words. The child is now becoming independent in the ability to organize ideas and successfully communicate them to others in writing.

Work

Children then carry out the activity in a work format, in this case by planting the cutting, labeling it, and beginning a journal to record the plant's growth.

Representation

The children represent their activities or products however they wish. In the case of the plant, the child writes and tells about her activity of planting the cutting and beginning the journal. The teacher tries to move the child through a hierarchy of thinking levels during the representation stage. Some forms of representation are: taking photographs, making tape recordings; building a model with paper, clay, sticks, or spaghetti, and telling about it; drawing a picture, cartoon, sequence puzzle, or painting; writing stories, books, songs, puppet shows, plays, and journals; and making graphs with real objects, pictures, or symbols. Language is incorporated into all these activities; for example, children are asked to label parts and tell about what they are doing (see Figure 4–5).

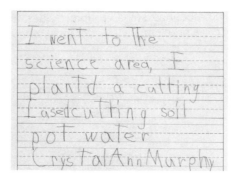

FIGURE 4–5 Representation.

Evaluation

Children then participate in an evaluation of their activities. In small groups, they describe the attributes and details of their products and relate what they have done and how they have done it. The teacher also engages the child in evaluating the activity, asking whether there were any problems to solve, what steps were followed in the representation, what has been the child's commitment to the plan, and what follow up, if any, is planned. Children also have many opportunities to ask questions about other children's projects, so that the children as well as the teacher engage other children in the evaluation process.

Room Arrangement

The organization of materials and equipment in the classroom supports the PWRE process in that the child knows where to find materials and what materials can be used, which encourages development of self-direction and independence. Small group tables are used for seating, independent work space, center time activities, and teacher-directed instruction. Flexibility and versatility contribute to the learning function. The floor plan in Figure 4–6 shows how room arrangement can support and implement the program's philosophy, goals, and objectives, and how a center approach (math, sewing, language arts, construction) provides space for large group activities and meetings, small group activities, and individual work. In a classroom where space is a problem, the teacher must work at making one area serve many dif-

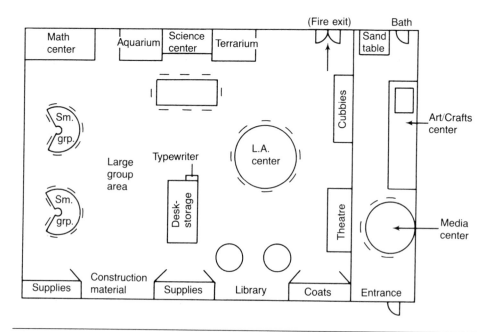

FIGURE 4–6 Floor Plan for PWRE Model.

ferent purposes. The teacher selects the centers and activities to use in the classroom based on several considerations:

☐ Interests of the children (kindergarten children, for example, are interested in blocks, housekeeping, and art)
☐ Opportunities for facilitating active involvement in seriation, number, time relations, classification, spatial relations, and language development
☐ Opportunities for reinforcing needed skills and concepts and functional use of those skills and concepts

Implementing the PWRE model in the classroom depends on:

☐ The teacher's understanding of the cognitively oriented curriculum and the PWRE process
☐ The teacher's knowledge and understanding of child development and intellectual development
☐ The teacher's knowledge of subject areas
☐ Materials available
☐ How the teacher views children
☐ The teacher's personal philosophy of education

Small Group Time

The cognitively oriented curriculum in Okaloosa County balances teacher-initiated and child-initiated activities. During PWRE activities, the teacher and aide make mental (and sometimes written) notes concerning skill needs of individual children. Observed needs are coupled with more formally diagnosed needs in the basic skills areas, and form the basis for planning small group instruction in the communication and mathematics areas.

Small group instruction occurs in the morning, when the children are grouped for both reading and mathematics. The groups rotate between the teacher, who directly instructs each group, and the aide, who directs cooperatively planned follow-up work for each group and independent enriching activities for individual students. (The teacher-directed instruction program is shown in Figure 4–7.) The balance of teacher-initiated and student-initiated activities supports and encourages active involvement at an appropriate instructional level. The success of this approach shows up in test scores and in the enthusiasm of both students and teachers.

THE LAVATELLI PROGRAM

Lavatelli explains a program used both for teacher training and as a curriculum for young children.[13] Lavatelli believed that since Piaget's theory provides a framework for knowing a child's important cognitive developments, it is possible to build a curriculum based on them. Important cognitive developments in early childhood include classification, space and number, and seriation. The program for developing these concepts consists of a detailed teacher's manual and materials designed to involve

A KINDERGARTEN STUDENT IN THE PWRE PROCESS

This account of a kindergarten child, Carol, in a kindergarten that uses the PWRE process, is typical of how a child and teacher interact.[14]

Plan

Carol plans to go to the quiet area to make a train out of unifix cubes (or inch cubes) and count the number of cubes she uses.

Work

Carol makes a train with a long line of cubes. Putting together and counting represent the activity phase of the process. The teacher, Ms. Smith, supports Carol in counting the cubes by removing each cube as Carol counts. The teacher wants to see if Carol can count all the cubes one by one.

Carol successfully counts the 30 cubes in her train. Ms. Smith asks Carol if she knows how to write the number 30. Carol writes 03. Ms. Smith then writes 30 for Carol, and asks Carol to trace the numeral. Then she asks Carol if she can make another train with the same number of cubes. Carol finds more cubes and matches cubes one-to-one until the second train is the same as the first. The teacher asks Carol if her train has an engine. Carol says yes; it has an engine, two boxcars, and a caboose. Ms. Smith asks Carol to show her, using the cubes in the second train, how many cubes are in each car. Carol removes cubes from the train, lines them up in four rows, one below the other, and counts eight for the engine, seven for each of the two boxcars, and eight for the caboose, accounting for all 30 of the cubes.

The teacher writes a label for each car and asks Carol to write after each name the numeral for the number of cubes in each car. Carol is able to do

children. The manual includes actual lesson plans so the novice can get a feel for implementing the program; the goal of each lesson is to present children with an interesting problem to solve at their own rates and in their own ways. The teacher asks questions to determine where the children are in their reasoning and to see if it is possible to produce disequilibrium so that they will assimilate previously neglected variables and begin to accommodate to the new ideas. This is an outline of a lesson from the Lavatelli program:

A. One-to-One Correspondence
   Beads, varying in color, shape, and size
B. Mental Operations
   Identifying properties of objects and matching objects by a one-to-one correspondence of properties.
C. Language Models
   Noun phrases with one or more adjectives (a small, round, red bead).

this. The teacher wants to see if Carol understands that the counted number of cubes in the train (30) remains the same when the cubes have been rearranged into train cars. She asks Carol if she thinks there are still the same number of cubes in her train. Carol counts the cubes to check the number (demonstrating that she does not realize that since she has not added or taken away, the number remains the same). The teacher knows Carol does not fully understand this concept and needs more experience counting objects and comparing amounts.

Representation

Carol represents her activity by drawing the row of cubes on a large piece of graph paper. Ms. Smith asks Carol to count the number of squares for each car of her train and color each car a different color. Carol does this. To give Carol practice writing numerals, Ms. Smith then asks Carol to write the numbers to 30 above her rows of squares, giving each square a number.

Evaluation

When the children are finished representing, they gather in a circle and share their ideas, products, and what they have done. If Ms. Smith's focus is sequencing, she may ask a child what he did first, second, and third. Emphasis may be on different aspects of an activity according to individual needs, interests, or points inherent in the activity or representation. Children are also encouraged to ask questions and make comments. Following the evaluation, the representation can be displayed or taken home. Carol decides to take hers home. Ms. Smith has a clothesline hung low in the classroom so children can display their work at eye level.

Coordinate sentences with directions for more than one action. "Find all the red beads and put them on the string."

Prepositions: *on* the string; *off* the string; *next* to the knot.

D. Directions for Group Sessions: Summary
   1. Distribute sets of equipment to the children and let them explore, discuss, and ask questions about the various pieces.
   2. Find out whether the children know the names for colors, shapes, and sizes by holding up an individual bead and saying, "Tell me about this one. What is it like?" If they don't, teach them the names.
   3. With all the children facing you, string beads varying in size but with color and shape the same. Have the children copy the model. In case of error, ask questions to call attention to the one-to-one correspondence that should exist between the model and the child's copy.
   4. Repeat with the size, color, and number of beads varied.

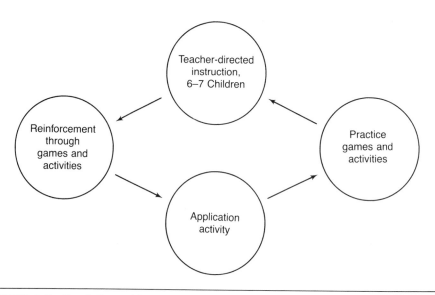

FIGURE 4–7 Small Group Management.

5. Repeat with the size, color, number, and shape varied.
6. In each case, ask the child to justify his choice and supply models of noun phrases when necessary.
7. Have the children draw a picture of your model and explain it.
8. Present the model in a circle instead of a straight line and have the children copy it.

Group sessions are conducted because Lavatelli believed strongly in Piaget's concept that a fundamental process of cognition is *decentration*. Egocentricism is challenged in the group, and the child moves toward an equilibrium between assimilation and accommodation.

Concepts in the classification area include simple sorting, multiplicative classification, all-some relations, class-inclusion relations, discovering intension, combining objects to make up subclasses, recognition of complementary classes, and extension of classes. Space and number include physical correspondence of objects on a one-to-one basis, one-to-one correspondence when physical correspondence is destroyed, conserving the whole when the additive composition of its parts is varied, and conservation of areas and transformation of perspective. Seriation includes ordering objects in a series according to one property, ordering objects in two series inversely related to one another, seriation and visual representation, and transitivity.

Lavatelli's program emphasizes the teacher's role as a model for language usage to develop and establish children's grammatical structures. While Lavatelli agreed with Piaget that language is not necessary for intellectual operations and that logical thinking precedes logical expression of ideas, she did believe that training for logical operations accompanied by training in syntactical structures may aid learning. As a language model, the teacher uses many different kinds of sentences; pro-

Lavatelli materials offer problems for children to solve. This child constructs a tower to match the one at her right, using the rod to measure the height.

vides and encourages teacher-pupil conversation; elicits from students the language structures being modeled; and provides a warm, supportive atmosphere for language development.

The Lavatelli program emphasizes children's finding solutions to problems with their own sets of materials; Lavatelli materials come from a number of sources—Froebel, Binet, Piaget, Montessori, set theory, and creative classroom teachers. Teachers are urged to be supportive and to remember that affective and cognitive development proceed together. Challenging activities that children can solve at their own levels contribute to positive self-image. The structured part of the program occupies only a small portion of the day; Lavatelli advocated organizing the rest of the day around the relatively creative freedom we have come to associate with child-centered education.

THE KAMII AND DEVRIES CURRICULUM

Kamii and DeVries base their curriculum on Piaget's scientific research about the nature of knowledge and its acquisition by children.[15] They emphasize children's doing for themselves through self-initiated activities; the rationale is that the child's initiative motivates involvement in activities, which in turn are the context for learning about the world. This was Dewey's idea also, and we see this concept stressed in open education. The Kamii and DeVries curriculum, therefore, emphasizes the role of play, since it is through play that the child manifests the initiative and interest that motivate further involvement. In the context of play, the child can be encouraged to use her intelligence and develop it further. Kamii and DeVries are critical of educators' attempts to provide artificial motivation for children in learning settings. They feel that by following children's interests, particularly as expressed through spontaneous play, meaningful learning can occur.

Objectives and Principles of Teaching

Based on Piaget's epistemological theory, Kamii and DeVries developed a framework of objectives and principles around which the classroom teacher can formulate an early childhood curriculum. They do not prescribe a specific curriculum of procedures and activities; rather, classroom teachers design their own curriculum using three sources:

- ☐ Activities associated with children's daily lives
- ☐ Curricula from existing child development programs
- ☐ Activities inferred from Piaget's theory and research

For Kamii and DeVries, *autonomy* (the process of governing oneself) is the broad aim of education. Everything in their curriculum, including specific objectives, activities, and teaching principles, flows from this overall aim. Within the framework of autonomy, Kamii and DeVries conceptualize these objectives for early education:

1. In relation to adults, we would like children to develop their autonomy through secure relationships in which adult power is reduced as much as possible.
2. In relation to peers, we would like children to develop their ability to decenter and coordinate different points of view.
3. In relation to learning, we would like children to be alert, curious, critical, and confident in their ability to figure things out and say what they honestly think. We would also like them to have initiative; come up with interesting ideas, problems, and questions; and put things into relationships.[16]

In this period of back-to-basics, educators and parents are apt to look at these goals and wonder why language development, reading, writing, and arithmetic are absent. Early educators may question the absence of social and affective objectives. Kamii and DeVries are well aware of the importance of these areas, but believe that if young children have the qualities outlined in their objectives, then other qualities and skills will follow naturally. As Kamii explains, "Language development independent of social relationships with adults and peers, and independent of children's thinking, is an untenable objective from the Piagetian point of view." Regarding the social and affective objectives, Kamii states that "trust and a positive self-concept are bound to develop if children are respected and their ideas are taken seriously in relationships that

Classroom pets help promote a sense of responsibility and foster attitudes of caring.

foster the development of their autonomy." Likewise, Kamii believes that curious and alert children "are also interested in how many children are present or absent, what the teacher writes on the board when voting takes place, and the list of names that tells whose birthday is coming up next or when their turn will come to be the cook."

Of course, a particular kind of classroom setting is necessary to pursue these objectives—a place where children are encouraged to act independently without fear of coercion, and where right answers to problems are less important than the process of inventing problems and trying to figure them out. There should be opportunities to seek knowledge, raise questions, be curious, and express feelings. Conflicts between children would be worked out through consideration of other points of view. Through these methods, children come to appreciate other people's viewpoints. This kind of interaction also shows children the constructive process.

The Kamii-DeVries curriculum promotes these teaching principles:

☐ Adjusting the source of feedback to allow for the different kinds of knowledge inherent in an activity, such as physical knowledge, logical mathematical knowledge, and social knowledge.

☐ Encouraging social interaction among children because the exchange of viewpoints is essential not only for social and moral development but also for intellectual development.

☐ Respecting and accepting children's answers even though they may be "wrong." "Wrong" answers have to be accepted because they are based on the relationships they can make, which are not the relationships adults can make.

Kamii and DeVries consider daily living activities a rich source of learning opportunities, because the child has opportunities to make decisions, raise questions, compare and contrast, make judgments, try out answers, and explore. All these processes are crucial to intellectual development, and Kamii and DeVries believe good teachers have always encouraged these processes "intuitively," through activities such as sand and water play, cooking, movement exploration, group activities, games, puzzles, stories, gardening, raising plants and animals, block building, and use of playground equipment. For the Piaget-based curriculum, the importance of these traditional activities is their contribution to the child's physical knowledge of the world and structuring of logic-mathematical relationships, such as space and time. They also promote opportunities for language development. Other activities that encourage physical knowledge include ball rolling and throwing; games that involve pushing, pulling, and swinging; and other natural phenomena of mechanics. Activities that encourage reflective thinking about physical relationships include observation of the environment and interaction with environmental objects through pouring water, water play, cooking, and mixing paints. The activities are useless, however, unless children think about the possible effects their actions will produce. The Kamii-DeVries curriculum considers language a process developed by the individual's experience with people and objects. While the majority of preschool and early elementary programs promote language by teaching words for things, Kamii and DeVries believe this method can result in merely learning words without understanding thought relationships. They encourage a program that involves children with people and things; from this active participation, language should develop.

COMMON THEMES OF PIAGET-BASED CURRICULA

Four recurring themes appear in curricula based on Piaget's ideas. One is that a child's thinking is substantially different from that of the adult, and adults must not try to impose their way of thinking on the child. Adults should provide a setting in which the child can think her own ideas and construct her own model of the world. Appropriate teacher behaviors include tolerance, support, acceptance of wrong answers, and encouragement to make hypotheses. A second recurring theme is that children must be actively involved in learning. A child who is a passive recipient of information does not have the proper opportunity to develop intelligence to its fullest. A third theme is that learning should involve concrete objects and experiences with many children and adults, particularly at the sensorimotor and preoperational stages. Children are too often asked to deal with abstractions such as words and numbers when they have no idea what these symbols represent. The fourth common theme of Piagetian programs pertains to the quality and relatedness of experiences. What a child is like at a particular stage is largely a function of past experiences. Good experiences lead to intellectual development. Our job as teachers and parents is to maximize the quality of experiences. In addition, a child's comprehension of an event depends greatly upon the proximity of the event to the concepts involved. If the child has nothing to associate an experience to, it is meaningless. Assimilation and accommodation cannot function unless experiences closely parallel each other.

Issues

Some difficulties associated with Piaget and his theory of intelligence arise from the complexity of his writings, which are hard to read and interpret. As a result, it takes a great deal of time, effort, and energy to determine their implications for education. One is never sure of interpreting Piaget correctly, so individuals must be willing to change their interpretations and constantly improve their understanding and conceptualization of Piaget's theory. Some people think that Piaget's theory of intellectual development is an educational theory, and some educators confuse Piagetian experiments with a Piagetian curriculum. Well-meaning teachers often believe that by having students replicate Piaget experiments, they are "teaching Piaget." The experiments do have merit as a diagnostic process for determining how a child thinks; the results, however, should be used to develop meaningful experiences. As Duckworth points out, "Piaget has no answer to the questions of *what* it is children ought to learn. But once, as educators, we have some sense of what we would like children to learn, then I think that Piaget has a great deal to say about *how* we can go about doing that."[17]

Another issue is the number of early childhood curricula that are developing around Piaget's ideas, incurring the risk of blind acceptance and adoption without thorough knowledge and understanding. To accept a curriculum without understanding its inherent concepts can be as ineffectual as applying a curriculum that has no theory behind it. Last, many people would like to teach more at an earlier age, in the hope of "speeding up" development. (Piaget called this "the American issue.") Piaget's stages should not be considered tasks for mastering as quickly as possible, and efforts to use "direct teaching" are inappropriate.

Programs that seek to implement a Piaget-based curriculum should provide classroom environments rich in materials and opportunities for children to actively participate in learning. Teachers who understand Piaget and who are willing to support and stimulate children in their efforts to construct their own knowledge are also necessary. Piaget's theory has much to offer parents and teachers who believe that children can and are the major players in the process of cognitive development.

FURTHER READING

To someone without a specialized interest in Piaget, reading his works can be somewhat difficult. Undergraduate students will probably have more success in understanding Piaget if his works are read with the help of one of these books.

Brief, Jean-Claude. *Beyond Piaget: A Philosophical Inquiry* (New York: Teachers College Press, 1983) A significant contribution to Piagetian interpretation, this book summarizes Piaget's work in cognitive and genetic psychology and genetic epistemology. Several chapters are geared to helping early childhood educators deal with Piaget's findings about the child's intellectual growth.

Butterworth, George. *Infancy and Epistemology: An Evaluation of Piaget's Theory* (New York: St. Martin's Press, 1982) A current trend is to view babies as competent individuals. This work discusses Piaget's theory of intelligence in relation to child development and the psychology of learning.

Ginsburg, Herbert, and Sylvia Opper. *Piaget's Theory of Intellectual Development*, 2nd ed. (Englewood Cliffs, N.J.: Prentice-Hall, 1979) Written for the student who is beginning a study of Piaget's theory of intellectual development, the objective is to make selected theoretical ideas understandable. A good place to begin reading about Piaget.

Hohmann, Mary, Bernard Banet, and David T. Weikart. *Young Children in Action: A Manual for Preschool Educators* (Ypsilanti, Mich.: The High Scope Press, 1979) Excellent guide to understanding and implementing the Cognitively Oriented Curriculum.

Kamii, Constance. *Number in Preschool and Kindergarten* (Washington, D.C.: National Association for the Education of Young Children, 1982) Excellent, easy-to-read discussion of applying Piaget's theory to teaching numbers by one of the leading Piagetian interpreters. Contains many practical ideas and activities for teaching numerical thinking. The appendix on "Autonomy as the Aim of Education: Implications of Piaget's Theory" should be read by every teacher and parent.

Kamii, Constance, and Georgia DeClark. *Young Children Reinvent Arithmetic* (New York: Teachers College Press, 1985) A must for those who are serious about Piaget's theory and about young children, this book translates Piaget's theory into a program of games and activities.

Kamii, Constance, and Rheta DeVries. *Group Games in Early Educational Implications of Piaget's Theory* (Washington, D.C.: The National Association for the Education of Young Children, 1980) An in-depth look at Piaget's work in Group Games; extensively describes examples of the games and the rationale behind them.

Kamii, Constance, and Rheta DeVries. *Physical Knowledge in Preschool Education: Implications of Piaget's Theory* (Englewood Cliffs, N.J.: Prentice-Hall, 1978) Practical suggestions for applying Piaget's theory of intellectual development through the area of physical knowledge. Chapters on the use of rollers, target ball, inclines, the pendulum, and water play.

Pulaski, Mary Ann Spencer. *Understanding Piaget: An Introduction to Children's Cognitive Development* (New York: Harper and Row, 1980) A comprehensive look at Piaget's numerous works. Includes a Piaget profile and a discussion of learning, education, and children's cognitive development.

Weber, Evelyn. *Ideas Influencing Early Childhood Education: A Theoretical Analysis* (New York: Teachers College, 1984) A theoretical analysis of various theorists, philosphers, and psychologists from Plato to Piaget. Outstanding ideas for new trends that influence early childhood education.

FURTHER STUDY

1. How would you respond to someone who said, "Children can't really learn unless the teacher corrects their wrong answers"?

2. Observe three children at the ages of six months, two years, and four years. Note in each child's activities what you consider typical behavior for that age. Can you find examples of behavior that correspond to one of Piaget's stages?

3. Observe a child between birth and eighteen months. Can you cite any concrete evidence, such as specific actions or incidents, to support the view that the child is developing schemes of the world through sensorimotor actions?

4. Interview early childhood teachers to determine their impressions of how effectively Piaget's theory is applied to early childhood settings. Compare their impressions with yours.

5. Compare the High Scope and Lavatelli programs. Which do you most agree with? Why?

6. Suggest practical ways you might include Piaget's theory in your classroom.

7. Compare Piaget's theory of intellectual development to another theory, such as Montessori's. How are they similar and different?

8. Develop a list of learning activities for young children. Label the activities according to whether they would best suit a sensorimotor or preoperational child.

9. Observe a first-grade classroom. Give specific examples to illustrate that the activities did or did not match the children's levels of intellectual development.

10. Examine textbooks and learning materials for young children. Identify those you feel show the influence of Piaget.

11. List five (5) concepts/ideas about Piaget's theory that you consider most significant for how to teach/rear young children.

12. What concepts/ideas of Piaget's theory do you disagree with? Why?

13. List what you think are the pros and cons of the High Scope, Lavatelli, and Kamii-DeVries curricula.

14. Why does the application of Piaget's theory to education generate so many different options? Why isn't there *one* application of Piaget's theory?

15. Do you think you would like to teach in the Okaloosa County Public Schools and implement Piaget's theory as they do? Why or why not?

16. List all the ways you consider children's thinking to differ from adult thinking.

17. What are the primary differences between Piaget's and Montessori's views of how children develop cognitively?

18. Why are errors and "wrong" answers important in children's learning?

19. List at least six (6) activities teachers can use to promote autonomy in children.

20. If an early childhood teacher said he didn't think it was important to know about Piaget's theory, how would you respond?

5

Child Care: Taking Care of the Nation's Children

As you read and study:

Determine the extent of the need for child care services

Become conversant with the terminology of child care

Evaluate and critique the purposes of child care programs

Develop an understanding of the meaning of child care and how it operates

Determine the nature of child care services and programs in the U.S.

Examine various definitions for child care

Identify the sources and nature of child care funding

Compare and evaluate the effectiveness of child care programs in meeting the needs of children

Examine the reasons for the growing numbers of employer-supported child care programs

Review proprietary child care and the reasons for its increase

Examine and understand the importance of CDA training in early childhood education

Critique state regulations for child care services

Examine issues associated with the care of the nation's children

Consider future trends in child care services and needs

Identify criteria associated with quality child care

POPULARITY OF CHILD CARE

The demand for child care continues to grow. Demand comes primarily from several sources: families in which both parents work, single parents, the mini-baby boom, and changing family patterns. When both parents work, they must find alternate child care in or outside the home. In 1986, 54 percent of mothers with children under six were employed or looking for work, and approximately 8 million children were in need of care. Divorce also creates a greater demand for child care services.

There has been an increase in the birthrate among women between the ages of 30 and 34. Many women who postponed childbearing for careers or because of the need to work now want to have children before it is too late. Changing family patterns also create a need for child care. Both men and women are deciding to become parents—natural or adoptive—without marrying, and the trend toward single parenthood also generates demand for child care arrangements. The implications of these social conditions are clear: children need care by people other than their parents, frequently in places other than their homes. There has been a tremendous growth in *licensed* child care during the past decade; between 1977 and 1985, licensed child care programs increased from 133,000 to 229,000, representing a 72-percent growth![1]

Child care is probably one of the most confusing terms associated with early childhood education because it is often used interchangeably with other terminology such as child welfare, day care, and child services. The concept of child care also differs depending on who uses the term in what context. (The term *child care* is preferred to day care, because children should be the central focus of any program provided for them.) The most common sources for funding and support for child care are these:

- ☐ Parents, who pay all or part of the cost
- ☐ State programs, especially Health and Human Services
- ☐ Federal agencies—Administration for Children, Youth and Families; Social Security Administration; and Child Care Food Program (USDA)
- ☐ Private and charitable foundations, such as United Way or the Easter Seal Society
- ☐ Organizations such as the YMCA, YWCA, YMHA, and religious groups who provide care to members and the public, usually at reduced rates
- ☐ Employers
- ☐ Parent cooperatives

One often-used definition for child care is that of the Child Welfare League of America, as a service provided by the community "because of its concern for children who might otherwise lack the care and protection essential for their healthy development."[2] Two key words in this definition are *care* and *protection*, traditionally interpreted to mean providing for children's physical needs and seeing that they do not harm themselves and are not harmed by others—including their parents. The emphasis of this type of service on physical needs sometimes carries a negative connota-

142

tion. Some regard it as a "holding action," and is typically referred to as "custodial child care." These programs may offer opportunities for free play, but are not usually structured for educational purposes.

The currently accepted concept of child care holds that it is both supplemental and comprehensive. Care is *supplemental* in that parents delegate responsibility to the caregivers for providing care and appropriate experiences in their absence, and *comprehensive* in that, although it includes custodial care such as supervision, food, shelter, and other physical necessities, it goes beyond these to include activities that encourage and facilitate learning and is responsive to children's health, social, and psychological needs. A comprehensive view of child care considers the child to be a whole person; therefore, the major purpose of child care is to facilitate optimum development. Bettye Caldwell notes that *professional child care* is a *comprehensive* service to children and families that functions as a subsystem of the child rearing system and *supplements* the care children receive from their families.[3] More and more programs use the designation *child development* to convey the comprehensive nature of their services. The State of Pennsylvania defines comprehensive services this way:

> Maintaining a safe and healthful environment for the child;
> Implementing an established plan of daily activities and routines for the child;
> Maintaining and updating child records; and
> Providing care which promotes the total development of the child.[4]

Because child care can be provided in many places, by many types of people and agencies, there is a wide variety of care and services. A program may operate twenty-four hours a day, with the center or home open to admit children at any hour. There are also whole-day programs, that usually operate on a 6:30 A.M.–6:00 P.M. schedule to accommodate working parents. Half-day programs, such as those operated in many Head Start centers, usually run from 8:30 or 9:00 A.M. to 1:00 or 2:00 P.M. Parents who work usually supplement this kind of service with a private baby-sitter.

TYPES OF CHILD CARE PROGRAMS

Family Child Care

By far the most popular type of child care is in a family or familylike setting, known as *family day care* or *family child care*. Fifty percent of the children in child care are in such settings. Family child care involves many kinds of arrangements between parents and care providers, and differs from center care, preschool programs, and care provided to children in their own homes. Generally, family child care consists of three types of settings: homes that are unlicensed and unregulated by a state or local agency; homes that are licensed by regulatory agencies; and homes that are licensed and associated with an administrative agency.[5]

Many parents leave their children at homes that are unregulated and unlicensed, and the kind of care a child receives depends on the skill, background, and training of the person who offers it. Some family care providers are motivated to meet state and/or local standards for child care so they can be licensed. Family child

Family child care is the most popular kind, because parents prefer to have their children in a homelike setting, and play is an important part of any child care setting.

care providers may also be associated with a child care agency. They meet state and agency standards for care and, in return, receive assistance, training, and referrals of parents who need child care. The agency usually subsidizes the cost of the children's care when the parents are eligible for subsidies.

Definitions of Family Child Care

In Pennsylvania, a family day care home is defined as "any premise other than the child's own home operated for profit or not for profit, in which child day care is provided at any one time to four, five, or six children, who are not relatives of the caregiver." In Florida, a family day care home is

> An occupied residence in which day-care is regularly provided for no more than five (5) preschool children and elementary school children from more than one unrelated family including preschool children living in the home and preschool children received for day-care who are related to the resident caregiver. Elementary

school siblings of the preschool children received for day-care may also be cared for outside of school hours provided the total number of children including the caregiver's own and those related to her does not exceed ten (10).[6]

FAMILY CHILD CARE PROGRAM

An example of how family child care is sponsored and operated is the program of the Catholic Community Services, Inc. of Dade County Florida (formerly Catholic Service Bureau or Catholic Charities), which provides child care services through center and family programs. Family day care is provided for children ages six weeks to three years old whose parents are working, going to school, or in job training programs. Referrals are also accepted from social service agencies and local court systems, and generally involve cases of child and/or spouse abuse. Referrals also come by word of mouth from friends and relatives.

Parents are served by geographic area, and since Catholic Community Services family child care does not provide transportation, children are placed in family care homes as close to the parents' home as possible.

To be eligible as a family care provider, a person must be over 21, preferably a high school graduate, and have personal characteristics, experience, and skills necessary to work with children, have a first aid certificate and a food handler's permit. A food handler's permit is earned by taking a short course in food preparation and sanitation. To be licensed as a family child care home, a home must have adequate space for indoor play, an outside fenced play area, a smoke detector, fire extinguisher, telephone, and must be organized and clean. Child care homes must also comply with local zoning ordinances (some municipalities do not permit child care services in certain residential areas) and must meet specific building codes. (Zoning and building ordinances differ from city to city and state to state.) Since individual family child care homes are considered private businesses, a certificate of use and an occupation license may also be required.

Local child care licensing units, such as a state or county health and welfare agency, also have standards that must be met. These standards often include age requirements (over 18); absence of a criminal or child abuse record for all family members; surfaces of the home free of toxic materials such as lead-based paint; outside areas free from hazards and litter; at least one toilet and lavatory; an area for isolating sick children; toys and equipment that are safe and can be safely maintained; and ability to provide nutritious meals.

When family child care providers are associated with an agency such as Catholic Community Services, they are generally provided with equipment and supplies that will improve the quality of care. This list is representative of equipment and supplies often found in agency-sponsored homes:

Equipment	Supplies
Portable cribs—children 6 weeks to one year	First Aid Box
Cots (folding nursery)	Crib Sheets
Dressing Table	Cot Sheets
High Chairs	Books
Table 54 x 54—plastic laminated top	Art Supplies
Stack Chairs—10"	Jumbo Peg Board
Potty Chair	Play Gym
Fire Extinguishers	Crib Mobiles
Walkers (as needed)	Busy Box
Play Pen (as needed)	Wooden Building Blocks
Infant Swing (as needed)	Shape Sorter
	Baby's First Blocks
	Rock-A-Stack
	Turn & Learn Activity Center
	Balls/Bowl—Johnson & Johnson
	Spin-A-Sound—Johnson & Johnson
	Peek A-Boo Ball—Johnson & Johnson
	Corn Popper, Push/Pull
	Chatter Telephone
	Poppin Pals
	Tupperware Animal Set
	3–4 piece Puzzles
	Teeter Tot (See-Saw)
	Riding Toys
	Balls, Tricycles

Catholic Community Services also suggests a typical schedule a family child care provider might follow. Any schedule should be flexible, and children's needs should always override the caregiver's need to follow a fixed schedule.

7:00 A.M.	Open to receive children. Health check for fever, diarrhea, untreated colds, rashes, cuts, and bruises.
7:30–8:30 A.M.	Breakfast.
8:30 A.M.	Bathroom. Wash hands and faces and change diapers. Play with toys and family day care provider.
9:30 A.M.	Outside play time.

10:30 A.M.	Play for a short time with children. Use activities provided by child care worker and the family day care provider.
11:30 A.M.–12:30 P.M.	Wash children's hands and serve lunch. Infants: check diapers and feed.
12:45 P.M.	Sponge bathe children if hot and perspiring, powder.
1:00 P.M.	Afternoon nap in cribs or cot (not on floor).
3:00 P.M.	When children wake: bathroom, wash hands, and serve snack. Infants: check diapers.
3:15 P.M.	Play: may be inside or out until children leave.
6:00 P.M.	All children should be picked up. Home is closed.
	Note: For infants—Adjust to the needs of individual feeding and sleeping schedule.
	For toddlers—Adjust to individual needs, but try to follow the schedule.

Good family child care is much more than baby-sitting. There has been a tendency in the past to equate family child care with custodial, but care providers today are becoming more diligent about interacting with and stimulating the children they care for. The quantity and quality of specific services provided in family homes varies from home to home and from agency to agency, of course, but data compiled through the National Day Care Home Study shows that a substantial amount of caregivers' time (almost 50 percent) is spent in direct interaction with children (see Table 5–1). Undoubtedly, one reason parents prefer family child care is that it offers the opportunity for a family atmosphere, especially for younger children. The states usually define family child care, so you should compare the definitions in this chapter to your state's legal definition.

Center Child Care

Care of children in center settings, sometimes also called *center child care* or *group child care*, is conducted in specially designed and constructed centers, in churches, YMCAs and YWCAs, and other such settings. In Pennsylvania, center child care is "a facility in which care is provided for seven or more children, at any one time, where the child care areas are not being used as a family residence. A facility in which care is provided for more than six but less than 12, at any one time, may be licensed/approved as a group day care home if care is provided in a facility where the child care areas are being used as a family residence and the provider meets the requirements of a group day care home."[7] The definition for group or center care in Florida is a little different:

> [To] serve groups of six (6) or more children. It utilizes subgroupings on the basis of age and special need but provides opportunity for experience and learning that

TABLE 5–1 Distribution of Caregiver Time in Family Day Care Homes

Direct Involvement with Children: Ages One to Five	Percentage of Time	Totals
Teach	13.9	
Play	7.8	
Help	8.9	
Direct	3.7	
Converse	3.3	
Control	3.7	
Interaction with babies less than one year old	3.8	
Interaction with school age children	1.0	46.1
Indirect involvement with children:		
Direct/Prepare	16.5	16.5
Noninvolvement with children		
Converse with adults	6.3	
Recreation alone	7.8	
Housekeeping	19.4	
Out of range	1.3	34.8
Miscellaneous		2.6

Source: P. Divine–Hawkins, Family Day Care in the United States. Executive Summary (Washington, D.C.: U.S. Department of Health and Human Services, DHHS Publication No. (OHDS) 80–30287, Sept. 1981), p. 27.

accompanies a mixing of ages. Group day care centers may enroll children under two years of age *only* if special provisions are made for the needs of the infants to be consistently met by one person, rather than a series of people; and which permits the infant to develop a strong, warm relationship with one mother figure. This relationship should approximate the mothering the infant would receive in a family day care home.[8]

In Texas, on the other hand, "A day care center is a child care facility that provides care less than 24 hours a day for more than 12 children under age 14."[9] Center programs are often comprehensive, but many are baby-sitting programs, and some provide less than good custodial care. Just as the quality of public schools varies among districts, so does the quality of day care services vary among settings. This makes it difficult to arrive at a conclusive definition of child care; variations from state to state make it difficult to do anything but generalize.

A DAY IN THE LIFE OF AN INFANT IN A CHILD CARE CENTER

The Jackson/Dade Child Care Center in Miami, Florida, is located about two blocks from the county's largest hospital and the Civic Center. The center is open to anyone, on a first-come, first-served basis, although the majority of the parents are employees of the hospital. Built in 1974 specifically as a child care cen-

The greater numbers of women entering the work force has created demand for good infant care, which includes nurturing caregivers and an enriched environment.

ter, Jackson/Dade is considered a model among day care centers. It is open Monday through Friday from 6 A.M. to midnight. During this time, it serves roughly two groups of children, the first from 6 A.M. to 3:30 P.M. and the second from 3:30 to 11:30 P.M., but other children arrive from 8 to 8:30 in the morning and leave from 4:30 to 5 in the afternoon.

The center serves 136 children. Twenty-two of these slots are funded by Title XX and the remainder are supported by private fees. Parents pay fees from $10 to a maximum of $40 a week. The fee is based on family income, family size, and ability to pay. The staff-child ratio at Jackson/Dade is 1:5 for infants, 1:6 for toddlers, and 1:10 for preschool children. Family incomes range from a low of $6,000 to a high of $37,000; 91 percent of the children are black, 2 percent are Latin, and 7 percent are other categories including white and Jamaican. The families are highly mobile and many are single parents.

Tazale, eight months old, is brought to the center at 7 A.M. by her mother, who works as a court reporter. Her mother tells the caregiver, Margie, about any unusual crankiness, how the child slept, nature of bowel movements, and any special medication needed. If Tazale needs medication, her mother must sign a form indicating the dosage and permission to administer it. When Tazale was enrolled in the center, an infant schedule form was filled out about her. These forms provide valuable information about the child. It is specified on the form precisely who may take the child from the center, which is especially important with divorced and single parents.

This morning, Tazale did not have breakfast. Margie gets a breakfast of scrambled eggs, toast, and milk, prepared by the center cook. Margie makes sure the eggs are finely diced, and gives the toast as a finger food. Tazale has a bottle after breakfast. Margie then puts Tazale on a mat in the center of the care area and gives her a stimulating toy such as a "busy box," stacking toy, a nesting toy, or a puzzle. This exploratory/stimulation time lasts about twenty minutes. During this time, Margie talks to Tazale as a means of role modeling language.

Margie then places Tazale in a feeding table, and places the table in the area with other toddlers so that everyone, infants and toddlers, have their snack together. Today the snack is applesauce, saltine crackers, and water. Tazale eats her applesauce from a small cup and is fed by Margie. The cracker is given as finger food. Margie helps Tazale drink the water from a cup. Margie then reads to Tazale and her three companions from a story book for about ten minutes. About 10:15, Margie takes the children for a walk in the park. The other two children Margie has charge of are able to walk, so two of the children are pushed and two walk. During the walk, Margie talks to the children about what they see.

When they come in from the walk, Margie checks Tazale and her friends to see if they need to be changed. Then Margie takes Tazale and the other three children outside to play in a plastic baby pool. Margie puts toys and cups in the water. She encourages the children to pour and to name objects. After fifteen minutes, Tazale is brought in, diapered, and put in a high chair for lunch.

Since Tazale's mother allows her to have table foods, Margie prepares a lunch of ham, collard greens, corn bread, beans and rice, and milk. This meal is cooked in the center kitchen. Margie chops the ham very fine, mashes the beans and rice, then mixes the ham, rice, and beans together. Margie feeds Tazale the food mixture and allows her to feed herself the corn bread, which is broken into small pieces. The feeding lasts about ten minutes. Margie washes Tazale's face and hands and checks her for diapering. Tazale is then placed in her crib and given a toy to play with until she falls asleep.

Tazale falls asleep at about 11:45 A.M. and sleeps until about 2 P.M. When she wakes, she is completely washed, powdered, and given a fresh change of clothing. She is taken to the feeding table for a snack of graham crackers. Tazale is allowed to eat her cracker by herself. Following the snack, Tazale's hands are washed and she is put in the toddler area to play with the push-pull toys and listen to music. Tazale plays until her mother comes for her at 3:30 P.M.

Margie tells the parent about the day's activities, how and what Tazale ate, the nature of her bowel movements, how long she slept, medication given, and how often she was changed. During the day, Margie writes all of this information down so that if she is not there when the mother comes, another caregiver can tell her.

THE INFANT TODDLER CENTER OF SQUIRREL HILL— PITTSBURGH, PENNSYLVANIA

Cooperation is the hallmark of this nonprofit infant-toddler program, located in the Squirrel Hill Wightman School Community Building. The directors of two child care centers were so deluged with parent requests for infant care, they decided to do something about it. Instead of the typical competitive approach that characterizes many undertakings, they joined forces. The result is the Infant Toddler Center of Squirrel Hill, which opened in the fall of 1981. The Center is sponsored and directed by the directors of the Carnegie Mellon Child Care Center (Carnegie Mellon University) and the Carriage House Children's Center. This cooperative effort, which provides care to children from six weeks to three years old, is unique in several ways:

1. Cooperation forms the basis for program development, and the co-directors share one position in directing the Infant Center.
2. Linking and combining the resources of two well-established child care centers, these two facilities work cooperatively to meet a community need for child care.
3. Responding to and providing services for an articulated community need, this center provides a wholesome and nurturing environment for infants and toddlers.
4. The center provides a unique setting for university students to learn about quality care and educational opportunities designed for this group of clients. Early childhood education settings do not often include a laboratory for infants and toddlers, nor do many universities provide practical on-site experiences. Knowledge about infants is growing at a rapid rate. The present research focus on this age group is unequalled for any other group. The burgeoning amount of information needs to be compiled, disseminated, and continually evaluated.

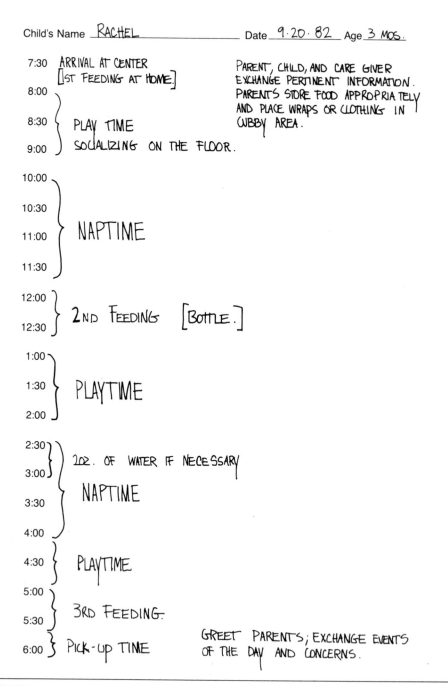

Child's Name RACHEL   Date 9·20·82 Age 3 MOS.

7:30   ARRIVAL AT CENTER   PARENT, CHILD, AND CARE GIVER
       [1ST FEEDING AT HOME.]   EXCHANGE PERTINENT INFORMATION.
8:00   PARENTS STORE FOOD APPROPRIATELY
                                            AND PLACE WRAPS OR CLOTHING IN
8:30   { PLAY TIME   CUBBY AREA.
9:00   SOCIALIZING ON THE FLOOR.

10:00

10:30

11:00 } NAPTIME

11:30

12:00
       } 2ND FEEDING [BOTTLE.]
12:30

1:00
       } PLAYTIME
1:30

2:00

2:30
       } 2OZ. OF WATER IF NECESSARY
3:00
          NAPTIME
3:30

4:00

4:30   { PLAYTIME

5:00
       } 3RD FEEDING.
5:30

6:00   } PICK-UP TIME   GREET PARENTS; EXCHANGE EVENTS
                           OF THE DAY AND CONCERNS.

FIGURE 5–1   Infant-Toddler Center of Squirrel Hill: Individual Daily Schedule

This Infant Toddler Center is open five days a week, from 7:30 A.M. to 6:00 P.M. Tuition is $395.00 per month for full-time care. Part-time or full-time child care arrangements can be made for enrollment in any of the four age-group rooms at the center: the infant room is for six weeks to approximately twelve months; the younger toddler room is for twelve months to approximately eighteen months; the toddler room is for eighteen months to approximately twenty-four months; and the the older toddler room is for twenty-four months to approximately thirty-six months.

The fee does not include children's personal care items, such as sheets, blankets, toys, diapers, formula, baby food, and toiletries. The program provides cribs for the infants, and each parent is responsible for furnishing the infant's crib area. There are 12 infants in the program, and a long waiting list. With their advisory board, the directors are exploring alternative ways to meet the demand for quality care. The ratio of care providers to infants is 1:4 and sometimes 1:3 with the help of students and volunteers. The staff emphasizes interpersonal relationships and caregiver-infant communication and stimulation.

Parents prepare the daily schedules in the infant room. Caregivers refer to these schedules in caring for the children and keep a daily record of eating, sleeping, diapering and play activities on the track sheet (Figure 5–1). The daily schedule that parents prepare is the basis for individual care. The infants' caregivers also try to provide enrichment programming with appropriate activities. Infants are involved in play, language acquisition (both body and verbal), and sensorimotor experiences. The diapering area has a radio, where children hear classical music as they are being changed.

The toddlers are divided into three groups. As they are quickly growing and learning, it is necessary to provide them with opportunities appropriate to their developmental needs. Although parents still provide the center with information concerning each child, the staff implements an appropriate daily schedule, which includes play, art activities, music and movement, and outdoor activities, including walks, to extend their world into the community. Vocabulary and concept development are of primary importance.

Caregivers keep a daily record of each child's habits and behaviors in the areas of eating, sleeping, diapering, general health, and emotional well-being. Hallmarks of this quality program for young children and their families is a loving, warm environment and the desire to promote ongoing communications between parents and staff.

FEDERALLY SUPPORTED CHILD CARE

Child care centers often receive federal funds because they serve low-income families who are eligible for cash assistance under Title XX of the Social Security Act. Title XX was passed by Congress in 1974 and is the major source of federal funds to state-operated child care services. How much a state receives is based on its population; for example, in 1985, Ohio received 24 million dollars through Title XX child care. Table 5–2 shows what families in Ohio paid for Title XX child care. A state may be reimbursed for 75 percent of the cost of day care programs that follow Title XX guidelines. In July of 1982, Title XX became a block grant program. Under Title XX, parents are automatically eligible for day care services on the basis of:

☐ Income Maintenance (the parent receives a public assistance check such as Aid to Families with Dependent Children [AFDC])

☐ Supplemental Security Income (SSI) (the parent is receiving a supplement to Social Security income; for example, a widowed parent of young children is eligible for supplementary Social Security income)

☐ Income Eligible (if the family's gross income is below a figure set by the state, the family is eligible for services; in Florida, the maximum gross income to be eligible for services is $15,303 for a family of four, or $10,070 for a family of two)

☐ Group Eligibility (members of some groups are automatically eligible, such as children of migrant workers; a child who is under the protective care of the state can also qualify for Title XX child care, without regard to income)

Florida admits children to child care supported by Title XX funds according to these priorities:

1. The child is at risk because of abuse or neglect.
2. The parent is involved in a state or federally supported work incentive program (WIN).
3. The parent is income maintenance and/or the child is group eligible.
4. The parent is income eligible.

A second source of federal support comes through the U.S. Department of Agriculture Child Care Food Program (CCFP). The USDA provides monies and commodities (for example, cheese, dry milk, and butter) to child care centers and homes to support their nutritional programs. In lieu of commodities, programs can choose to

TABLE 5–2 What Families Pay for Title XX Child Care Services in Ohio

Family Size	Gross Monthly Income				
2 (no charge under $7,000 annual income)	0–590	591–689	690–787	788–885	886–983
3 (no charge under $8,800 annual income)	0–734	735–855	856–975	976–1095	1096–1215
4 (no charge under $10,500 annual income)	0–875	877–1020	1021–1163	1164–1306	1307–1449
Percent of monthly cost of day care programs paid by family	0%	10%	20%	30%	40%

Chart reads: A family of two with gross monthly earnings between $591 and $689 pays 10 percent of the monthly cost of a day care program. For example, if day care costs $200 a month, this family will pay $20 a month.

Source: Gregory L. Rhodes and Mark Real, *Day Care: Investing in Ohio's Children* (Children's Defense Fund, 1985), p. 47.

receive cash equal to 11¼ cents per child for each lunch or supper served, in addition to the regular reimbursement. Children 12 years of age and younger are eligible for participation. In 1986, the USDA provided approximately $483 million of support through CCFP. A third federal source of support is the child care tax credits for individuals and corporations. The federal tax code provides employers with certain "tax breaks" or benefits for providing child care services to their employees.

Since 1975, parents have been able to itemize the cost of child care as a credit against their federal income taxes. Currently, the amount that can be deducted is based on a sliding scale. From $0 to $10,000 of annual adjusted income, 30 percent of the cost of child care can be deducted. As income increases by $2,000, the percentage decreases by one percent until it reaches 20 percent. The maximum amount that a family can credit is $2,400 for one child and $4,800 for 2 children.

EMPLOYER-SPONSORED CHILD CARE PROGRAMS

As the number of parents in the work force increases, new trends in child care are appearing. Corporate- or employer-sponsored child care—also referred to as *industry* or *industrial child care*—is emerging to meet the need. During the last decade, corporate child care has become one of the more talked about and most frequently implemented child care programs. Although not new (the Stride-Rite Corporation in Boston, Massachusetts, started the first on-site corporate child care program in 1971) there has been a surge in such services. According to a study by the Council on Economic Priorities, the number of corporate-sponsored or supported child care programs increased from 110 in 1972 to 2,500 in 1986. Approximately 150 corporations have child care at the work site. Part of this growth can be attributed to the number of mothers in the work force. A major reason for corporate child care's popularity, however, is the realization that child care is good business. Some feel it raises employee morale, increases productivity, and enhances corporate profits as a result of tax savings. Since 1981, corporations can provide employees child care services tax free. More than 2,000 companies now offer some sort of child care assistance, and tax credits to individuals and corporations total more than $3 billion annually.[10]

While delivery of specific child care services can take many forms, there are two types of employer programs. In one, sometimes called an *employer responsibility* program, the employer assumes the responsibility for child care services, which involves purchasing or providing space, equipment, and personnel, as well as operating the program. In an *employer-assisted* program, the employer helps employees find child care, arranges for child care services, and/or pays for the services in whole or in part. There are a number of ways employers can provide child care services:

1. In corporate-sponsored programs, the corporation provides space, equipment, and child care workers.
2. Corporations can give employees vouchers with which to purchase services at existing child care centers.
3. Corporations can purchase slots at existing child care centers and make them available to employees either free or at reduced rates.

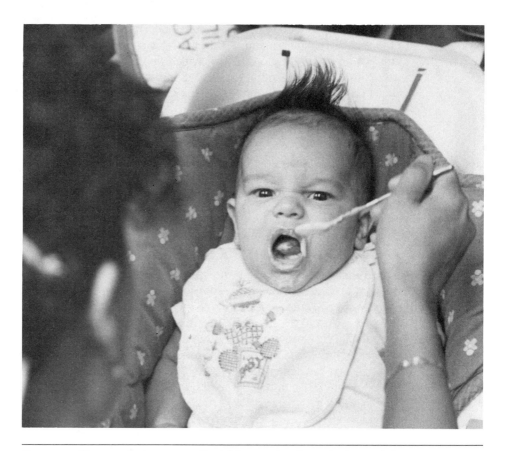

Since over 50 percent of women with children under six are in the work force, corporations are finding the need to provide on-site, supported care. One benefit of on-site care is the chance for parents to visit with their children at mealtimes.

4. A corporation can contract with an agency (as described in the account of the Forbes Metropolitan Health Center).
5. A corporation can contribute to a child care center where many of its employees place their children. The subsidy results in reduced rates for employees and/or priority on a center waiting list.
6. A corporation can provide a paid leave of absence or subsidize a leave of absence for the parent in lieu of specific child care services (paid child care leave).

If they do not provide direct child care benefits, employers can assist in or make child care easier in other ways. They can permit a flexible work schedule, so parents may not need child care, or as much of it. Other possibilities are maternity leave extensions, paternity leaves, and use of sick leave to include absence from work for a sick child.

Advantages of Employer-Sponsored/Supported Child Care

Many advantages accrue to corporations that sponsor/support child care. The presence of a corporate child care program can be an excellent recruiting device—hospitals, in particular, find child care services an added incentive in recruiting personnel. Other claims for corporate-sponsored child care are that it promotes employee morale and reduces absenteeism. A possible side benefit is that the corporation may be eligible for a variety of tax benefits through business expenses, charitable gifts, and depreciation. Knowing they need not worry about child care may motivate employees to stay with a company; in fact, corporate child care can be viewed as a family support system, which tends to encourage positive feelings toward the company and perhaps offset negative feelings about other factors such as pay and working conditions. Employees may also be more inclined to work different shifts when child care is available.

Similarly, there are advantages to employees. Couples who may have decided not to have children because of their careers may reconsider the option of childbearing. Knowing they can bring their child to work may make the difference between having or not having children. Parents can also be more relaxed and confident about their children's care. Many parents can visit their children during breaks or even eat lunch with them. Being near their children is particularly advantageous for nursing mothers. Also, if a child becomes ill, the employee is immediately available. Especially when parents have long commuting distances, parents and children get to spend more time together.

Financial factors include the possibility of deducting the cost of child care from an employee's salary, representing a forced means of budgeting; employers can usually provide high quality care at reasonable cost; and when child care is provided as part of an employee's work benefits package, the cost is not taxable.

EMPLOYER-CONTRACTED CHILD CARE SERVICES AT FORBES METROPOLITAN HEALTH CENTER

Corporations sometimes provide child care services for their employees through private contracts. The Forbes Metropolitan Health Center of Pittsburgh, Pennsylvania, has contracted with The Learning Tree Associates for child care for its more than 300 employees. Forbes provides the site and maintenance services, and the Learning Tree, a private preschool and early learning center, provides the license, equipment, materials, supplies, faculty, and staff for the care of 35 children ranging in age from 6 weeks to 5 years. The child care center is primarily for the benefit of the Forbes staff and their children and is available on a first-come, first-served basis. Parents pay $60.00 per week for infant care and $55.00 for toddler care. The center is open from 6:30 A.M. until 6:00 P.M. five days a week.

At 7:45 A.M., three-year-old Jessica rushes into the elevator at Forbes, stands on her tiptoes, and pushes the button for the second floor. Jessica is anxious to see her friends and teachers at the center, and keeps telling her mom, an x-ray technician, to hurry. Her mom smiles and quickly steps into the elevator. Jessica's mother appears pleased by Jessica's eagerness to get to school. Some change has taken place. Nine months ago, when Jessica's mother started to work, Jessica seemed so attached to her that she screamed when she was left at the center. The professional guidance of the child care staff apparently has solved that problem. When they reach the second floor of the hospital, Jessica is greeted by her teacher (the members of the child care staff, regardless of their job descriptions, are called "teachers" so the children can relate to all of them), and chooses to go to the housekeeping corner, where several of her friends are already playing. At 9:00 A.M., Jessica and the other toddlers gather in groups with their teachers and plan the day's activities. Today Jessica decides to work in the sand and block areas. The group as a whole also decides to visit, after lunch, with several of the elderly patients they haven't seen for a few days. Between these two activities, the children will have a snack of fruit, cheese, and juice. No chocolate or starches are served, and foods with additives are avoided. Snack time is informal, and each child helps himself. The child care center does not provide lunch, as a result of a careful and thoughtful decision by the director of the Learning Tree. Lunch is considered an opportunity to encourage ties between child, home, and parents. Families are encouraged to prepare their sack lunches at home together, and parents employed at the Health Center may take their child to lunch with them in the employee cafeteria.

After lunch, Jessica listens to a story, sings some quiet songs, and does the breathing exercises she has learned as an aid to relaxation. The center staff believes all the children should sleep or rest, but those who appear anxious may move into a separate room where quiet activities are encouraged.

Jessica wakes at 2:30 and, after going to the bathroom, decides she will have another snack. Then she joins the group that has planned an inside walk. When the weather is appropriate, children explore the community that surrounds the Health Center. Children seem to enjoy their "in-house" tours, and the staff uses these walks as a time to teach concepts, encourage social skills, and develop oral communication. After the walk, Jessica engages in free play. Today, Jessica is involved in block building, and when her mother comes to pick her up at 4:30, Jessica tells her to wait until she finishes! Jessica's mom uses this opportunity to talk with one of the staff members regarding Jessica's progress at the center. When Jessica has put the blocks away, her teacher helps her put on her yellow raincoat, gives her a hug and a kiss, and Jessica and her mom walk to the elevator, talking as they leave the room.

Proprietary Child Care

Some day care centers are run by corporations, businesses, and individual proprietors for the purpose of making a profit. Some profit-making centers provide custodial services and preschool and elementary programs as well. Many of these programs emphasize their educational component and appeal to middle-class families who are willing to pay for the promised services. Many centers are also franchised operations—the name and method of operation are sold to an individual who operates the center. Franchising child care is one of the more controversial issues in day care. Critics are quick to make analogies between franchising child care and fast food—apparently it is legitimate to make a profit on the latter, but not on the former! About half of all child care centers in the U.S. are operated for profit, and the number is likely to grow. Child care is a big service industry, with more and more entrepreneurs realizing that there is money to be made in care for the nation's children. Table 5–3 shows the largest national chains operating child care programs.

Foster Child Care

Almost every state uses foster child care. Children are placed in foster care because their parents can't or won't take care of them, or because they have been abused or abandoned. As many as 250,000 children live in foster care homes or foster group homes. Many children in foster care facilities have physical handicaps or some learning problem that makes them less attractive for adoption. A growing phenomenon in America is the number of *hand-me-down children.* Many parents find they cannot afford to raise their children or can no longer discipline them effectively, so they simply turn them over to the juvenile courts, which in turn place them in foster care.

Informal Child Care Arrangements

Many parents make informal child care arrangements with relatives and friends. These arrangements satisfy parents' needs to have their children cared for by people with similar life styles and values. These arrangements sometimes cost less, and compensation can be made in ways other than direct monetary payments. For example, one couple converted part of their house into an efficiency apartment in which an elderly aunt lives rent-free in return for caring for the couple's two-year-old child.

TABLE 5–3 Franchised Child Care Operations

Name of Chain/Headquarters	Centers in Operation (as of 9/1/86)
Kinder-Care Learning Centers (Birmingham, Alabama)	1050
La Petite Academy (Kansas City Missouri)	520
Children's World (Golden, Colorado)	248
Daybridge Learning Centers (Houston, Texas)	178
Gerber Children's Centers (Fremont, Michigan)	109

Source: "How's Business? A Status Report on For-Profit Child Care," *Exchange,* 52 (November 1986): 26.

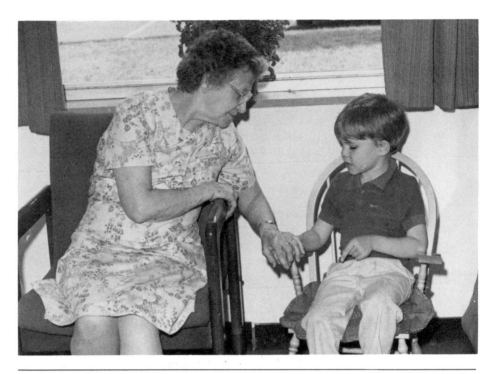

Grandparents and other relatives provide economical and nurturing child care, and many parents feel more comfortable having a relative provide care.

The number of children who are cared for through informal arrangements far exceeds the number in centers or family child care, primarily because of the lack of availability of quality child care programs. When people search for child care, they often turn out of necessity to people who are available and willing to take care of children, but these two criteria are not the best or only criteria people who provide custodial care or baby-sitting services should meet. There is a tremendous difference between placing a child in a quality, comprehensive program as opposed to placing her with an individual who provides primarily custodial care.

Baby-Sitters

Children are their parents' most valuable assets, so parents should not seek the lowest common denominator either in quality or pay when deciding about the kind of person to whom they will entrust their children. These are important qualities for anyone who acts as a baby-sitter:

1. The necessary age and maturity to provide basic care for children. While no particular chronological age makes a person qualified to give basic care, a certain degree of maturity is necessary.

2. Education in providing child care. Training might come through a course offered by a school or service organization, or through caring for younger brothers and sisters. In any case, a sitter should know how to diaper, feed, and interact with children.
3. Basic training in first aid and emergency procedures.
4. Trustworthiness.
5. Child rearing values that agree with those of the parents. Parents must tell baby-sitters how they want certain situations handled, and how they want their children disciplined.
6. Personal qualities of neatness, good grooming, and acceptable verbal skills.
7. Good recommendations and references from others who know and/or have used the sitter.

Drop-in or Casual Child Care

Many parents with part-time jobs or flexible schedules need a place to leave their children. Services that have arisen in response to such needs are in the form of storefront child care centers, child care services in shopping centers, and parents who do occasional baby-sitting in their homes. These services are convenient, but they do have some drawbacks. First, the quality of care may be low simply because the children are transient, and it is difficult to build continuity into a program whose population base is unstable. A second drawback is that sporadic contact with strangers can be stressful to a child.

SICK CHILD CARE

One of a working parent's constant dreads is having a child get sick. Balancing the demands of a job and the obligations of parenthood is manageable as long as children are healthy, but when a child is sick, parents must find someone who will take care of the child or stay home. Fortunately, more and more working parents have flexible employee benefits that enable them to stay home with sick children, but many do not. Also, when children are only mildly ill or do not have a contagious illness, parents feel there should be other options to losing a day's work. Child care providers have begun to respond to parent's needs; some centers provide care for sick children as part of their program, and other providers are opening centers exclusively for the care of ill children.

RAINBOW RETREAT—"R AND R" FOR ILL CHILDREN

Rainbow Retreat in Newport Beach, California, is one of only a few programs that provide care for mildly ill children. Before using its services, parents preregister their children while they are well. Rainbow Retreat provides care for children between the ages of 2 and 12. After they have registered, parents call the center when they need care for their ill children. Gail Gonzalez, director of

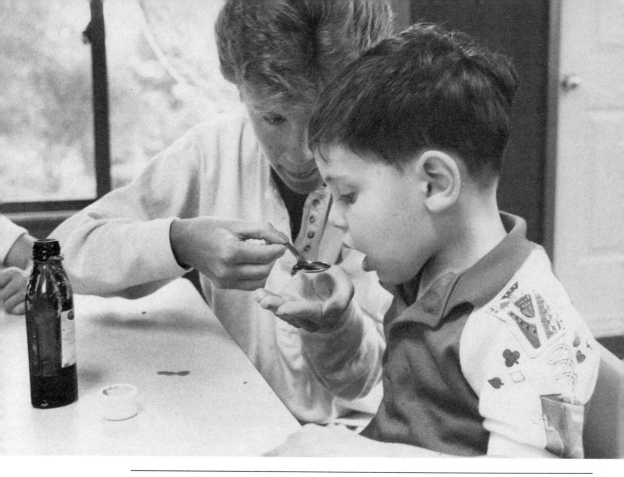

A constant dilemma for many working parents is what to do when a child is ill. Fortunately, more child care programs are offering ill child care.

Rainbow Retreat, or one of her staff members, goes over a check list to determine whether the child can be admitted directly from the home to the center or if he or she must first see a physician. When parents bring their children in, a staff member does a health assessment regarding the nature of the illness and confirms whether they can attend. Care at Rainbow Retreat costs $5.00 an hour with a four-hour minimum stay.

Rainbow Retreat will not admit children with measles, mumps, or chicken pox; otherwise, children with almost any other illness are admitted as long as the child's physician feels he can be in the program. Rainbow Retreat will accept children with fevers, ear infections, vomiting, diarrhea, or colds; it will also accept an asthmatic child who has seen a doctor and whose asthma is under control, postsurgical children who have had, for example, an appendectomy or tonsillectomy, and children in casts who have sprains or fractures.

Although children can stay at Rainbow Retreat for as long as they need ill care, the average stay is two days. Some children stay only one day. Rainbow Retreat can care for 10 children at one time; the daily average is six children. During their stay, children are involved in developmentally appropriate activities that take into consideration their illness and physical condition. This is the daily schedule:

7:00 to 8:30	Admissions
8:30 to 9:00	Circle and planning time
9:00 to 9:30	Snack
9:30 to 10:30	Learning centers
10:30 to 11:30	Small group activity (medicine given)
11:30 to 12:00	Ready for lunch (temperature taken and children observed for change in condition)
12:00 to 12:30	Lunch
12:30 to 3:30	Naptime
3:30 to 4:00	Interaction time (temperatures and assessment)
4:00 to 5:00	Learning centers (medicine given)
5:00 to 6:00	Clean up and discharge

At the end of each day, parents receive a report that includes temperature, diet, output, activity participation, and recommendation for future care.

National Pediatric Support Services is the parent organization of Rainbow Retreat as well as a number of regular child care centers. Rainbow Retreat shares a site with each of the child care centers. In addition to Gail, who is a registered nurse, the staff includes a licensed practical nurse and a teaching assistant. The staff takes special precautions to assure that furniture, equipment, and materials are disinfected daily to control infections, yet at the same time allow children freedom to use the center. As a further precaution to limit the spread of germs, no one wears shoes into Rainbow Retreat.

BEFORE- AND AFTER-SCHOOL CARE

In many respects, the public schools are logical places for before- and after-school care. They have the administrative organization, facilities, and staff to provide care. Some have always felt that school buildings should not sit empty in the afternoons, evenings, holidays, and summers, so using the resources already in place for child care seems to make good sense. So in many communities, public schools are helping to alleviate the need for after-school child care.

The Dade County, Florida, public schools provide after-school care for 10,100 students in 150 of the elementary schools. The school district operates 50 after-school centers with its own personnel; 47 are operated by the YMCA, 20 by the YWCA, and 25 by the Family Christian Association of America. Parents pay from $10.00 to $20.00 per week depending on the per child cost at the individual school. Because the programs are school-based managed, the costs of services vary depending on the nature and cost of each program. Services begin at 1:45 and end at 6:00 P.M. Some schools also provide before-school care, where children can arrive as early as 7:30 A.M. and have breakfast. The curriculum of the child care program includes Boy and Girl Scouts, 4-H, fun activities based on skills and concepts measured by the state assessment tests for grades 3 and 5, drama, and ballet.

In other localities, after-school care may be no more than baby-sitting, with large groups of children supervised by a few adults. The cost of after-school care may be more than parents can afford, and when the child care program follows the school calendar, parents are left to find other care when school is not in session.

Latchkey Children

Every day, many children stay home by themselves until it is time to go to school or return from school to empty houses. Children who care for themselves before and/or after school are referred to as *latchkey* or *self-care* children. Some agencies offer support services to latchkey children, such as training them how to answer the phone or deal with strangers at the door. They also work with parents to help them make the home safer and more secure for the children. Parents also form telephone hot lines so children can call someone if they need help, have questions, or just need to talk to someone. Regardless of the support systems, however, latchkey children deal with many uncertainties when they come home by themselves. Many parents find this arrangement quite satisfactory, however, and feel that it promotes independence, autonomy, and responsibility. Some states have laws against leaving children under a certain age (usually twelve) alone without supervision. Many parents may not be aware of these laws, or may feel they really have no choice.

MILITARY CHILD CARE

The Army, Navy, Air Force, Marine Corps, and Coast Guard operate Child Development Programs at over 450 locations throughout the world and within the U.S. The armed services are the largest providers of employer child care services. The programs provide care of all kinds—hourly, part-day, full day, before and after school, evening, and weekend—to children of military families and other Department of Defense personnel. These programs help family members meet their military responsibilities secure in the knowledge that their children are receiving quality care. Military child care programs are funded through Defense Department appropriations, parent fees, and funds from local programs. Department of Defense funds usually cover the costs of facilities, utilities, supplies, and equipment; parent fees cover the cost of staff salaries.

The Armed Services have also started a program of family child care services. At Presidio, California, for example, the Army operates 55 family child care homes to service about 250 children of military parents. The Army has determined that family child care is a cost-effective way to provide services to parents. Military personnel are discovering that the availability and quality of child care affects job performance.

During times of high civilian unemployment rates, the number of people in the military services tends to grow, creating a greater demand for child care. Military personnel face problems that many civilians do not, such as frequent relocation, sudden mobilization to active duty, and jobs that require irregular shifts. At the same time, problems of military child care are no different from those of civilian: variation in quality of facilities from base to base; the need for more comprehensive as opposed to custodial care; safe facilities; and training for child care personnel.

THE NANNY MOVEMENT

Nannies are the latest rage in child care. More and more parents, especially the upwardly mobile who can afford a nanny (or *manny,* as males are called) are creating a demand for this type of child care. Although an *au pair,* the traditional mother's helper (often from Europe) has always been part of the child care scene, today's parents want someone more highly skilled. A *nanny,* trained in child development, infant care, nutrition, grooming, manners, and family management, meets this need. The intensive training separates the nanny from baby-sitters and *au pairs.* The American Council of Nanny Schools and other agencies are upgrading nanny curricula. In 1986, there were about 18 nanny schools in operation, and many colleges offer two-year training programs.

Nannies' living arrangements, compensation, and duties vary greatly from family to family. Some live and work in the home twenty-four hours a day, while others work an 8- to 10-hour day and have their own homes. Some nannies have responsibility for child care only; others also assume household responsibilities, including meal preparation; others include teaching their charges as part of their responsibilities. In addition to a salary, some nannies receive paid vacations, medical benefits, and use of a car. Besides providing quality child care, a nanny is a constant presence in a child's life, and a trained nanny is a valuable addition to the family and provides more than just child care.

TRAINING AND CERTIFICATION FOR EARLY CHILDHOOD PERSONNEL

A major challenge facing all areas of the early childhood profession is the training and certification of those who care for and teach young children. Training and certification requirements vary from state to state, but more states are tightening standards for child care, preschool, kindergarten, and primary personnel. Many states have mandatory training requirements that an individual must fulfill before being certified as a child care worker. The curriculum of these training programs frequently specifies mandatory inclusion of topics. For example, in Florida, all child care personnel must complete the Department of Health and Rehabilitative Services' 20-hour child care training course. The course is composed of four modules that include

1. State and local rules and regulations governing child care
2. Health, safety, and nutrition
3. Identifying and reporting child abuse and neglect
4. Child growth and development

In addition, all child care personnel must complete an annual 8-hour inservice training program.

Certificate Programs

Many high schools and vocational education programs conduct training leading to an entry-level certificate. This training certifies people to act as child care aides.

Associate Degree Programs

Many community colleges provide training in early childhood education that qualifies recipients to be child care aides, primary child care providers, and assistant teachers.

Baccalaureate Programs

Four-year colleges provide programs that result in teacher certification. The ages and grades to which the certification applies vary from state to state. Some states have separate certification for prekindergarten programs and nursery schools; in other states, these certifications are "add-ons" to elementary (K–6, 1–6, 1–4) certification.

Master's Degree Programs

Depending on the state, individuals may gain initial early childhood certification at the master's level. Many colleges and universities offer master's level programs for people who want to qualify as program directors or assistant directors or who may want to pursue a career in teacher training.

The CDA National Credentialing Program

Fortunately, at the national level, the Child Development Associate (CDA) National Credentialing Program offers early childhood educators the opportunity to develop and demonstrate competencies for meeting the needs of young children. The CDA program began in 1971 and is a major national effort to evaluate and improve the skills of caregivers in center-based, family day care, and home visitor programs. The CDA National Credentialing Program is operated by the Council for Early Childhood Professional Recognition, a subsidiary of the National Association for the Education of Young Children. The Child Development Associate (CDA) is a person who "is able to meet the specific needs of children and who, with parents and other adults, works to nurture children's physical, social, emotional, and intellectual growth in a child development framework."[11]

A candidate for the CDA credential in any of the settings must meet these eligibility requirements:

- ☐ Be 18 years old or older
- ☐ Have access to a center-based program, family day care, or established home-based program
- ☐ Have had, within the past five years, a total of three formal or informal educational experiences in such areas as early childhood education, child development, infant development and care, child nutrition, child health, child

protection, family systems, parent-child relations, or business management

☐ Have had, within the past five years, at least 640 hours of work with children within the ages of each setting requirement and a minimum amount of educational experience (for example, family day care providers must have at least 640 hours of experience working with children and have worked as a family day care provider for at least 10 months within the last five years; a home visitor must have at least 480 hours of experience working with families in a home visitor program with children five years old or younger; and for a center-based program, the candidate must have at least 640 hours of experience working with children aged three through five years in a group setting)

☐ Be able to speak, read, and write well enough to fulfill the responsibilities of a CDA candidate

Candidates for the Bilingual Endorsement must speak, read, and write well enough in both English and Spanish to understand and be understood by both children and adults.

The candidate's competency in the CDA Program is assessed by a local assessment team (LAT) composed of the candidate, the candidate's trainer or advisor, a parent/community representative, and a CDA representative. The assessment is made on the basis of the candidate's performance in the competency areas. Table 5–4 lists the goals and areas for the competencies of caregivers in center-based programs. Over a period of time, the candidate documents his/her competency for each area and compiles a portfolio of the documentation, which includes exhibits, pictures, letters of verification, and other forms of documentation. In addition, the advisor works with the candidate for a minimum of twelve weeks. The parent/community representative observes the candidate and surveys the parents of the children in the candidate's group, and the CDA representative observes and interviews the candidate. There is also judgment-referenced assessment by the Local Assessment Team and

TABLE 5–4 CDA Competency Goals and Functional Areas for Infant/Toddler Caregivers in Center-Based Programs

Competency Goals	Functional Areas
I. To establish and maintain a safe, healthy, learning environment	1. **Safe:** Candidate provides a safe environment to prevent and reduce injuries.
	2. **Healthy:** Candidate promotes good health and nutrition and provides an environment that contributes to the prevention of illness.
	3. **Learning environment:** Candidate uses space, relationships, materials, and routines as resources for constructing an interesting, secure, and enjoyable environment that encourages play, exploration, and learning.

TABLE 5–4 Continued

Competency Goals	Functional Areas
II. To advance physical and intellectual competence	4. **Physical:** Candidate provides a variety of equipment, activities, and opportunities to promote the physical development of children.
	5. **Cognitive:** Candidate provides activities and opportunities that encourage curiosity, exploration, and problem solving appropriate to the developmental levels and learning styles of children.
	6. **Communication:** Candidate actively communicates with children and provides opportunities and support for children to understand, acquire, and use verbal and nonverbal means of communicating thoughts and feelings.
	7. **Creative:** Candidate provides opportunities that stimulate children to play with sound, rhythm, language, materials, space, and ideas in individual ways and to express their creative abilities.
III. To support social and emotional development and provide positive guidance	8. **Self:** Candidate provides physical and emotional development and emotional security for each child and helps each child to know, accept, and take pride in himself or herself and to develop a sense of independence.
	9. **Social:** Candidate helps each child feel accepted in the group, helps children learn to communicate and get along with others, and encourages feelings of empathy and mutual respect among children and adults.
	10. **Guidance:** Candidate provides a supportive environment in which children can begin to learn and practice appropriate and acceptable behaviors as individuals and as a group.
IV. To establish positive and productive relationships with families	11. **Families:** Candidate maintains an open, friendly, and cooperative relationship with each child's family, encourages their involvement in the program, and supports the child's relationship with his or her family.
V. To ensure a well-run, purposeful program responsive to participant needs	12. **Program management:** Candidate is a manager who uses all available resources to ensure an effective operation. The Candidate is a competent organizer, planner, record keeper, communicator, and a cooperative coworker.
VI. To maintain a commitment to professionalism	13. **Professionalism:** Candidate makes decisions based on knowledge of early childhood theories and practices, promotes quality in child care services, and takes advantage of opportunities to improve competence, both for personal and professional growth and for the benefit of children and families.

Source: Child Development Associate Assessment System and Competency Standards, Preschool Caregivers in Center-Based Programs (Washington, D.C.: CDA National Credentialing Program, 1986), pp. 3–4.

verified assessment by the CDA representative, who ascertains that the policies and procedures of the credentialing program have been followed in the assessment process. The assessment process is depicted in Figure 5–2. Thirty-two states and the District of Columbia recognize the CDA credential as one way to fulfill regulations for working with children. The CDA Credential is awarded by the Council for Early Childhood Professional Recognition.

To date, more than 19,000 people have been awarded the CDA credential. The CDA attests to an individual's competence in the specified areas, and many certified teachers complete the credentialing process as a means of furthering their skills for working with young children. (Additional information about CDA can be obtained from the CDA National Credentialing Program, 1718 Connecticut Ave. N.W., Washington, D.C. 20009; the toll-free number is 800-424-4310.)

WHAT CONSTITUTES QUALITY CHILD CARE?

It is easy to say that parents should seek out and insist on good care, but many parents don't know what to look for, and unfortunately, not all care providers know what constitutes quality care. The following guidelines may give parents and professionals a deeper understanding of the indicators of quality care.

Good child care provides for children's needs and interests at each developmental stage. For example, infants need good physical care as well as continuing love and affection, and sensory stimulation. Toddlers need safe surroundings and opportunities to explore. They need caregivers who support and encourage active involvement.

At all age levels, a safe and pleasant physical setting is important, and should include a safe neighborhood free from traffic and environmental hazards; a fenced play area with well-maintained equipment; child-sized equipment and facilities (toilets, sinks); and areas for displaying the children's work, such as finger painting and clay models. The environment should also be attractive and cheerful. The rooms, home, or center should be clean, well lighted, well ventilated, and bright.

The ratio of adults to children should be sufficient to give children the individual care and attention they need. For infants, the ratio of caregivers should be 1:4; for toddlers, the adult-child ratio should be 1:5, and for preschoolers, 1:8 or 1:9, depending on group size. The program should have a written, developmentally based curriculum for meeting children's needs. The curriculum should specify activities for children of all ages that caregivers can use to stimulate infants, provide for the growing independence of toddlers, and address the prereading and writing skills of four- and five-year-olds. The program should go beyond good physical care to include good social, emotional, and cognitive care. It should include a balance of activities, with time for indoor and outdoor play and for learning skills and concepts. There should be parent involvement to help parents learn about the child care setting and their children's growth and development. Parents need to be encouraged to make the child care services part of their lives, so they are not detached from the center, its staff, or what happens to their children.

Whether in a family or center setting, child care providers should be involved in an ongoing program of training and development. The CDA is a good way for staff

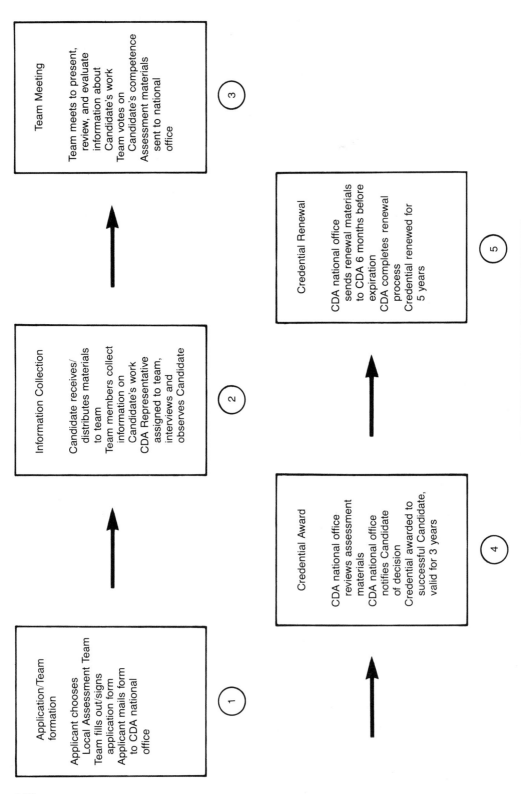

FIGURE 5-2 Stages of the CDA Assessment System (Source: Council for Early Childhood Professional Recognition, CDA Assessment System and Competency Standards for Home Visitors.)

members to become competent and maintain the necessary skills. Program administrators should have a background and training in child development and early childhood education. A director of a child care program or agency should have a bachelor's degree in early childhood education, certification, or, at least, special college work in this area. Knowledge of child growth and development is essential for caregivers. Films, books, training in clinical settings, and experiences with children help caregivers know about development. Caregivers need to be developmentally and child-oriented, rather than self- or center-oriented.

Child care providers, especially those of infants, should be sensitive to the adjustments children make when they come into a child care setting. The environment and the people are new to them. A baby who has been the only child at home and cared for only by his mother or father has a lot to adapt to in a center setting, where there are more infants and more caregivers. Many center infant programs make sure that one care provider takes care of the same infants, to give them the security that comes from familiarity. Likewise, new caregivers must also adjust when they come into the home or center, since every child has a unique personality, preferences, and ways of responding to the world.

Quality in Center Programs

The final report of the National Day Care Study, *Children at the Center,* came to these conclusions about quality in child care centers:

> Qualitatively, these findings imply that smaller groups, especially those supervised by lead care givers with preparation relevant to young children, are marked by activity and harmony. Care givers are warm and stimulating. Children are actively engaged in learning and get along well with others. Presumably as a consequence of this type of day care experience, children also make rapid strides in acquiring the skills and knowledge tapped by standardized tests. Larger groups, especially those supervised by care givers without education or training specifically oriented toward young children, present a contrasting picture. Care givers fall into a passive posture, monitoring activities of many children at once, without active intervention. In such an environment, some children "get lost." Apathy and conflict are somewhat more frequent than in small groups. Gains on standardized tests are less than they might otherwise be in day care settings.[12]

The report also makes some interesting conclusions about class size and the ratio of caregiver to students. Whereas many people have always felt that the smaller the ratio the better, the report concludes that this is not necessarily so, and supports a 1:7 ratio with a group size of 14. This raises some interesting questions about the time-honored 1:5 adult-pupil ratio used in Head Start, but for infants and toddlers, the report supports the 1:5 ratio.

Policy recommendations and the reality of state laws governing child/adult ratios in child care programs are frequently at odds with each other. As Table 5–5 indicates, the ratios vary greatly from state to state and are often higher than child care professionals prefer. The recommendations of NAEYC regarding staff/child ratios are shown in Table 5–6.

TABLE 5–5 How Many Children Can One Adult Care For?
Current Law in the 11 Largest States

State	Infants (birth to 18 mos.)	Toddlers (18 to 36 mos.)	3-year-olds	4-year-olds	5-year-olds
California	4	12	12	12	12
New York	4	6	7	8	9
Texas	5	9	15	18	22
Pennsylvania	4	5	10	10	10
Illinois	4	8	10	10	25
Ohio	8	10	15	15	20
Florida	6	12	15	20	25
Michigan	4	4	10	12	12
New Jersey	4	10	10	15	15
North Carolina	8	12	15	20	25
Massachusetts	3	4	10	10	15

Source: Gregory L. Rhodes and Mark Real, *Day Care: Investing in Ohio's Children* (Children's Defense Fund, 1985), p. 47.

TABLE 5–6 Staff/Child Ratios and Group Size

Age of children*	Group size									
	6	8	10	12	14	16	18	20	22	24
Infants (birth–12 mos.)	1.3	1.4								
Toddlers (12–24 mos.)	1.3	1.4	1.5	1.4						
Two-year-olds (24–36 mos.)		1.4	1.5	1.6**						
Two- and three-year-olds			1.5	1.6	1.7**					
Three-year-olds					1.7	1.8	1.9	1.10**		
Four-year-olds						1.8	1.9	1.10**		
Four- and five-year-olds						1.8	1.9	1.10**		
Five-year-olds						1.8	1.9	1.10		
Six- to eight-year-olds (school age)								1.10	1.11	1.12

*Multi-age grouping is both permissible and desirable. When no infants are included, the staff-child ratio and group size requirements shall be based on the age of the majority of the children in the group. When infants are included, ratios and group size for infants must be maintained.

**Smaller group sizes and lower staff-child ratios are optimal. Larger group sizes and higher staff-child ratios are acceptable only in cases where staff are highly qualified.

Source: *Accreditation Criteria and Procedures of the National Academy of Early Childhood Programs* (Washington, D.C.: National Association for the Education of Young Children, 1984), p. 24.

Quality and Accreditation

Many professional organizations are involved in determining criteria for quality programs. The Southern Association on Children Under Six issued a position statement listing the fundamental needs that must be met in child care:

☐ The child needs to feel that the situation is a safe and comfortable place for him to be
☐ The child needs to learn to feel good about himself
☐ A child needs to be fully employed in activities that are meaningful to him— that support him in his full-time quest to learn

☐ A child needs to develop ability to live comfortably with other children and adults

☐ A child needs to have his physical development supported and be helped to learn health, nutritional, and safety practices

☐ The child in care needs to feel that there is consistency in his life and a shared concern for him among the important people in his life—his parents and his caregivers[13]

In any discussion of quality, the question invariably arises, "Who determines quality?" Fortunately, the National Association for the Education of Young Children has addressed the issue of a standard in its Center Accreditation Project (CAP). The CAP is a national, voluntary accreditation process for child care centers, preschools, and programs that provide before- and after-school care for school-age children. Accreditation is administered through NAEYC's National Academy of Early Childhood Programs. NAEYC cites these benefits of accreditation:

☐ Accredited programs are recognized as quality programs
☐ Parents will seek out accredited programs
☐ The staff learns through the accrediting process

The criteria addressed in the accreditation project are interactions among staff and children, curriculum, staff and parent interactions, administration, staff qualifications and development, staffing patterns, physical environment, health and safety, nutrition and food service, and program evaluation.[14]

FINDING CHILD CARE: INFORMATION AND REFERRAL SYSTEMS

A reality that many parents face when they decide they need child care is locating the care they want. There has never been a systematic way to match parents' needs with the care available. Much of child care, especially family care, is hidden from the public. One solution to this mismatch between consumer demand and existing services is a network of child care information and referral systems that is springing up across the country. These systems, usually computer-based and operated by municipal governments, universities, and nonprofit agencies, are designed to help parents gain access to information about competent, convenient, and affordable care. Information supplied to parents includes names, addresses, and phone numbers of providers and basic information about the services, such as hours of operation, ages of children cared for, and activities provided.

CHILD CARE ISSUES

As in any profession, child care is not without controversies and issues. Some issues that confront child care workers and the profession are who child care is for, whether parents should stay home, whether there should be state and/or national licensing standards, and who should bear the cost.

Who is Child Care For?

One issue concerns whether child care should benefit parents or children. There is a tendency to interpret child care as a service to parents, which critics feel has caused the quality of child care programs to suffer. The needs of children should not be secondary to the needs of parents, and our first concern shoud be to the quality of care children receive. Another aspect of this issue relates to which children should receive services. Ultimately, a system of child care should be available to all parents and their children. Until this is possible, we need priorities. Should child care be aimed at low-income parents who need to work or to engage in work-training programs? Or should priority be given to abused and neglected children? Some questions are not easy to answer.

Should Parents Work or Stay Home?

Another issue is the lack of agreement as to the real need for child care. Some feel the availability of child care encourages women to seek employment rather than stay home to care for their children, which, critics contend, leads in turn to a deterioration of family values and the ultimate breakdown of the family. They also argue that readily available child care erodes traditional values of parenthood and family by giving control of the nation's children to state and federal agencies and encouraging parents to relinquish their parental roles.

On the other hand, others consider child care a right, and women agree that child care helps them gain equal access to the workplace. This growing tension between the advocates of working parents and those who feel that a parent's place—usually the mother's—is at home with her children is likely to continue. Pediatrician T. Berry Brazelton, among others, thinks that women can handle two roles at one time and that it is time for our country to recognize this fact as a national trend.[15] Deborah Fallows, on the other hand, believes children are treated with benign neglect in child care programs and children bear the brunt of being left in the care of others.[16] Burton White maintains that full-time care for children under the age of three is not in their best interest.[17]

In reality, the issue is not whether parents should work; rather, it is what kind of care children receive. The issues of employment and parenthood rest on these factors:

☐ The quality of care children receive in their parents' absence. There is bad care, custodial care, and quality care. Parents who work should make every effort to find and use quality care. On the other hand, society has the obligation to upgrade quality.

☐ Parents' attitudes toward work. Some parents want to work more than they want to rear their children. Some parents cannot provide the emotional and social interchanges that form the basis of effective care. These parents are probably happier working and entrusting their children to quality child care.

Evidence does not support the conclusion that working *per se* is bad for children. As Belsky and Steinberg point out:

> With regard to children's intellectual development, the available evidence indicates, in general, that day care has neither beneficial nor deleterious effects. For children growing up in high risk environments, however, experience in center based care does appear to attenuate the declines in IQ frequently observed in youngsters from economically disadvantaged backgrounds. With regard to emotional development, the weight of evidence indicates that day care is not disruptive of the child's emotional bond with his mother, even when day care is initiated in the first year of life. In addition, there is no indication that exposure to day care decreases the child's preference for his mother in comparison with an alternative familiar caregiver. Finally, with respect to social development, the existing data indicate that day-care reared children, when compared with age-mates reared at home, interact more with peers in both positive and negative ways.[18]

Should There Be National and/or State Standards for Licensing Child Care?

Generally, efforts to establish national or statewide child care standards meet opposition from those who believe that any standards, even minimal, tend to be a bad idea. Wherever there are regulations, there must be a mechanism for enforcement, which costs money. Many believe the money is better spent to improve quality through training and education rather than to create and enforce standards. Opposition to licensing standards usually comes from for-profit child care providers, who feel licensing standards will add to their operating costs, and from religious groups, who feel standards intrude on their freedom of religion.

Should There Be Minimum Standards of Competence for Child Care Workers?

Although many states have minimum requirements, such as age, for child care workers, the requirements are often inadequate. A baker or barber may have to meet higher educational standards than child care workers. The Child Development Associate credential provides a way to enhance professional development and competency training, and this program most nearly resembles a unified national training program.

Improving the Quality of Child Care

One obvious way to improve the quality of child care programs and personnel is through more stringent facility-licensing requirements and increased training requirements. Parents can and should be educated to the need for quality child care. Parents often help perpetuate poor child care by accepting whatever kind of care they can find. If they are properly educated and involved in programs, they can help make child care better for everyone.

The comprehensive nature of good child care programs has to be extended. Many still believe that if a program provides germ-free custodial care, it is a good one. Unfortunately, some of these programs are also sterile in the philosophies and activities they provide to parents and children.

Who Should Pay for Child Care?

Who should pay for child care services is a perennial issue. The federal government's support for child care services has been shrinking over the past decade. This means that the three other available sources for child care support—state agencies, private agencies, and consumers—will, of necessity, have to increase their support. The abilities of states to support child care is, however, a function of their wealth and population. In this sense, the more populous and wealthy the state, the more able it is to support child care. Table 5–7 shows the amount of financial support that ten states give to child care.

As fewer and fewer federal dollars become available, more parents will be called upon to help pay the real cost of their children's care. Yet the fact remains that most parents who have to work probably cannot and will not be able to afford the cost of quality child care programs. Efforts to have child care subsidized by employers, foundations, and charitable groups will have to increase.

How Much Should Child Care Cost?

Traditionally, child care has been a low-cost and low-paying operation. Many programs emphasize keeping costs low so that working and low-income parents will not be overburdened, which has resulted in a very low pay scale for child care workers. Thus, the cost of child care is kept low, and the true cost is subsidized by low-paid workers. Yet, if child care costs rise to provide workers with fairer wages, many families who can hardly afford what they now pay would be priced out of the services. Also, as more public schools offer programs for four-year-olds, many child care work-

TABLE 5–7 Title XX Child Care Spending in 10 States, 1986

State	Child Care Expenditures
1. California	$310,000,000
2. New York	$160,000,000
3. Massachusetts	$ 69,000,000
4. Pennsylvania	$ 65,000,000
5. Illinois	$ 47,000,000
6. Florida	$ 44,000,000
7. New Jersey	$ 34,000,000
8. Texas	$ 32,000,000
9. Ohio	$ 26,000,000
10. North Carolina	$ 24,000,000

Source: *State Child Care Fact Book—1986* (Washington, D.C.: Children's Defense Fund, 1986), pp. 89–90.

ers with degrees will be attracted to these programs by the higher salaries. This shift could tend to lower the quality of child care programs and further decrease salaries. Figure 5–3 depicts the pay of child care workers compared to other occupations and underscores the need to reexamine priorities relating to child care workers' pay and status.

Making Child Care More Humane

Many child care facilities are not good places to leave children; they are sometimes located in dark and dreary basements, and are depressing to both care providers and children. Those who operate child care programs must strive to improve the physical environments of homes and centers. Child care programs can be stifling if children never go anywhere or see anyone besides their caregivers. Good programs take children places and do things with them. They encourage and actively solicit the involvement of grandparents, senior citizens, and other adults so children can be involved with others.

Agreement Between Parents and Care Providers

The number of parents who turn over their children to outside child care providers continues to increase each year. Many parents entrust their children to people they know very little about. They may be reliable and trustworthy, or they may not. Parents are now better informed as to what constitutes quality child care. Although they are becoming more selective, they still leave their children with people who are relative strangers. It is therefore extremely important for quality child care providers to work closely with parents from the time of their initial contact, usually at registration. Caregivers must demonstrate to parents their competence in areas such as child development, nutrition, and an appropriate curriculum. They must also assure parents that they will maintain daily communication about the child's progress.

Parents and caregivers need to agree on discipline matters, and child care providers and social service agencies need to guide parents as to what constitutes good child rearing and appropriate discipline practices.

FUTURE TRENDS IN CHILD CARE

What does the future hold for child care? These are some trends we can anticipate as we approach the 21st century:

- ☐ The number of women who attach themselves in one way or another to the labor force, in full- or part-time capacities, will increase. The rapidity and ease with which this increase occurs will depend in large measure on what child services are available and how parents adjust their work and lives to the need for child care.
- ☐ The number of employer-sponsored or assisted child care programs will increase. The growth of these programs will accelerate because of employees' demands for child care and the obvious advantages to employers. The

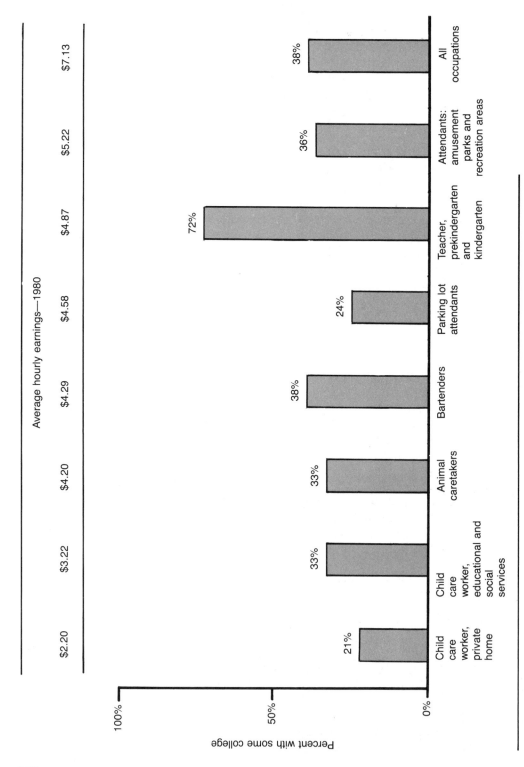

FIGURE 5-3 Earnings and Education of Child Care Workers Compared to Other Occupations (Source: *In Whose Hands? A Demographic Fact Sheet on Child Care Providers* [Washington, D.C.: National Association for the Education of Young Children, 1985], p. 5.)

greater the benefits to the employer, the more likely they will increase their involvement in child care.

☐ Public schools will participate in child care, especially after-school care, at a greater rate. They will also be more inclined, and perhaps even forced, to provide preschool programs.

☐ Good child care, especially the kind provided by many corporations, will have an effect on poor child care. Parents will become more aware of what constitutes good child care and demand it of other programs.

☐ The number of information and referral systems will increase because of the gap between the demand for child care and its availability.

☐ For-profit programs will provide child care services for more families. While these services will not be financially available to all families, those who can will pay what is necessary. Fortunately, the quality of for-profit child care is improving.

☐ There will be a proliferation of child care services sponsored by clubs, religious organizations, and neighborhood groups. Many will not necessarily meet licensing standards, but will satisfy parents' needs.

☐ The federal government's role in child care will become less significant, and the influence of individual states will increase. The federal government will not make comprehensive services available to all children because the expense of a national program of child care would necessitate reordering national budget priorities. The trend in federal support to social service programs is to return monies to the states in the form of block grants, allowing states greater freedom and autonomy in determining how funds are spent. The block grant procedure also reduces direct federal control of state and local programs.

☐ While existing day care services for low-income, disadvantaged families will continue, there will still not be enough services to meet everyone's needs. At the other end of the economic spectrum, services for those who can afford to pay will become more available. Children of the middle class who don't qualify for day care services based on income and whose parents can't afford the fees of profit-making day care programs will remain the forgotten children.

☐ Futuristic thinking about child care must include alternatives to day care, such as adjusted parenting leaves from work and flexible work schedules. It is conceivable, for example, that rather than paying parents to place their children in a child care program, they could be paid to stay at home with them. This strategy could be combined with a program of training parents in child development and child rearing practices.

FURTHER READING

American Academy of Pediatrics. *Tips on Selecting the Right Day Care Facility* (Elk Grove Village, Ill.: American Academy of Pediatrics, 1985) Pamphlet provides ten guidelines to follow in selecting quality child care. An ideal resource to distribute at parent meetings and seminars. Guidelines include nature of the child care worker, kinds of activities, cleanliness, and health services.

Auerbach, Stevanne. *Choosing Child Care: A Guide for Parents* (New York: E. P. Dutton, 1981) Practical, step-by-step advice on finding the right child care services. Many useful checklists for assessing family and center care along with suggestions on selecting babysitters, linking up with other parents, and budgeting for child care expenses.

Blum, Marian. *The Day Care Dilemma* (Lexington, Mass.: Lexington Books, 1983) Blum identifies herself as a strong advocate for women and children. Recommended reading for parents whether or not they face the dilemma of leaving their children in child care programs, as it covers many valuable ideas in child rearing.

Burud, Sandra L., et al. *Employer-Supported Child Care: Investing in Human Resources* (Dover, Mass.: Auburn House, 1984) Provides all the information employers need to establish child care programs that will benefit themselves and their employees, based on data from more than 400 employer-supported programs. Also includes many useful charts and forms.

Clarke-Stewart, Alison. *Daycare* (Cambridge, Mass.: Harvard University Press, 1982) Comprehensive discussion of day care, its history, current status, and future. Good background reading, with a section on child care arrangements in other countries.

Comfort, Randy Lee, and Constance D. Williams. *The Child Care Catalog* (Littleton, Col.: Libraries Unlimited, 1985) Excellent resource guide that includes extensive bibliographies, descriptions of unique programs, names and addresses of people and agencies, and many questions to guide the reader's quest for answers about child care. Also a valuable research tool for anyone who wants a quick overview into the field of child care and a top candidate for inclusion in a parents' resource library.

Endsley, Richard C., and Marilyn R. Bradbard. *Quality Day Care: A Handbook of Choices for Parents and Caregivers* (Englewood Cliffs, N.J.: Prentice-Hall, 1981) Written primarily to help working parents find child care arrangements. Many helpful ideas and sources of information, including results of research.

Fallows, Deborah. *A Mother's Work* (Boston: Houghton Mifflin, 1985) The author's personal experience in choosing between the responsibilities of a career and those of parenting and her extensive research into parents' options for meeting child care needs.

Filstrup, J. M., with D. W. Gross. *Monday Through Friday: Day Care Alternatives* (New York: Teachers College Press, 1982) Examines and explains various child care arrangements. Accounts are interesting and readable because many are told by parents and child care providers.

Gorder, Cheryl. *Home Schools: An Alternative* (Columbus, Ohio: Blue Bird Press, 1985) Gorder wants parents to realize they have choices about where and how their children are educated. Seeks to help parents make choices on the basis of what they believe about their lifestyles, values, and priorities. The author wants parents to be aware of and consider the option of home schooling. Should be read by all preschool and early childhood teachers for its perspective on home schooling and the obstacles parents encounter.

Greenman, James T., and Robert W. Fuqua. *Making Day Care Better* (New York: Teachers College Press, 1984) Outstanding ideas by well-known contributors to improve the day care situation.

Hollingsworth, Jan. *Unspeakable Acts* (New York: Congdon and Weed, 1986) Account of the highly publicized child abuse case in Country Walk, Miami, Florida; should be read by all parents and child care workers. Reviewer Glenn Collins said in the *New York Times*, "In its lurid details, its frustrating complexity and in the agony of the children and families who were victimized, this case would seem to be the paradigm of incidents in Minnesota, California, and elsewhere that have surfaced in recent years. A startling difference, though, is the outcome: the molester was convicted and sentenced to life in prison."

Jaisinghani, Vijay T., and Vivian Gunn Morris. *Child Care in a Family Setting: A Comprehensive Guide to Family Day Care* (Pennsylvania: Family Care Associates, 1986) Outlines most common areas of concern in defining, organizing, and maintaining a quality family day care home. A must for family day care providers as a resource for childproofing your home, keeping accurate records, and the importance of child development.

Johnson, Eric W. *Raising Children To Achieve* (New York: Walker, 1984) Provides specific steps for parents to follow in instilling achievement motivation in their children and themselves. Particularly appealing to people interested in the home education movement.

Lurie, Robert, and Roger Neugebauer, eds. *Caring for Infants and Toddlers: What Works, What Doesn't,* vol. 2. (Redmond, Wash.: Child Care Information Exchange, 1982) Articles from conference proceedings of the third annual conference of the Summit Child Care Center in Summit, N.J. Covers Issues, Curriculum, Health, Parents, Environment, Staff, Administration, and Resources.

Mallucio, A. N., and P. A. Sinaoglu. *The Challenge of Partnership: Working With Parents of Children in Foster Care* (New York: Child Welfare League of America, 1981) Papers dealing with child welfare and providing practical ideas for successful families; focuses on methods for involving parents and foster parents more effectively.

Murphy, Karen. *A House Full of Kids: Running a Successful Day Care Business in Your Own Home* (Boston: Beacon Press, 1984) Good, sensible advice about how to make a profit and run a successful home-based day care program.

National Association for the Education of Young Children. *How to Choose a Good Early Childhood Program* (Washington, D.C.: National Association for the Education of Young Children, 1984) Sound advice to anyone thinking about enrolling a child in an early childhood program. These ideas about what parents should look for can also be used by a staff to assess its program.

Oryx Press. *Directory of Child Care Centers—Volume 1: Northeast* (Phoenix, Ariz.: Oryx Press, 1986) Volume 1 in this series lists child care services in the Northeast: CT, DE, KY, ME, MD, MA, NH, NJ, NY, PA, RI, VT, VA, WV, DC. Other volumes list services for the North Central, Western, and Southern states. Over 12,000 entries in the first volume, giving name of the center, address and telephone number, contact person, capacity, and ages served. This series is valuable for parents who move to a new city and desperately seek child care services.

Resources for Family Development. *How to Jump into Child Care Head First and Land with Your Feet Firmly on the Ground* (Livermore, Calif.: Resources for Family Development, 1985) Excellent, practical, easy-to-read and understand guide for developing a child care program. Squarely addresses business and quality issues. Topics include licensing, landlord-tenant relationships, administration/staffing, programming, health and safety, parent involvement, management, community awareness, and special services.

Rice, Robin D. *The American Nanny* (Washington, D.C.: TAN Press, 1985) Comprehensive guide to finding, assessing, living with, and becoming today's highest quality child care provider.

Scarr, Sandra. *Mother Care/Other Care* (New York: Harper and Row, 1984) Reviews concerns of the working parent as they relate to child care decisions; provides parents with a positive feeling for making informed decisions.

Siegal-Gorelick, Bryna. *The Working Parents' Guide to Child Care: How to Find the Best Care for Your Child.* (Boston: Little, Brown 1983) Interesting and valuable addition to the literature for parents on how to select child care, with three especially noteworthy chapters:

Chapter 1 is devoted to caregivers and day care environments; Chapter 5 advises parents how to assess day care programs; Chapter 7 deals with how parents can help themselves and their children adjust to child care. Fast and worthwhile reading.

Suransky, Valerie P. *The Erosion of Childhood* (Chicago: University of Chicago Press, 1982) Advocates a system of community-based cooperative child care centers. The author believes pay for child care workers should reflect their importance and that parents should spend four to five hours of "commitment time" at a center each week.

Thomas, Carol H., ed. *Current Issues in Day Care: Readings and Resources* (Phoenix, Ariz.: Oryx Press, 1986) Collection of nineteen articles addressing important issues and concerns of parents and caregivers; also guides selection and evaluation of child care programs. In addition, there is information relating to employer-sponsored child care, trends, and environmental and health concerns.

Williamson, Jean, Janis Stevenson, and Jo Sotelo. *Consumer's Guide to Child Care* (St. Meinrad, Ind.: Abbey Press, 1983) Easy-to-use guide to help parents look for the best child-care setting. Provides a wide range of child care options and practical suggestions for assessing settings.

Zigler, E. F., and E. W. Gordon. *Day Care: Scientific and Social Policy Issues* (Boston: Auburn House, 1982) One of the most important books relating to child care, combines recent research on the effects of day care with the implications of this research for delivery of child care services. Should be read by child care workers and parents.

FURTHER STUDY

1. Survey parents in your area to determine how many need child care services. Also, determine what services most parents desire from a child care program. Are most of the parents' child care needs being met?

2. Visit some child care center programs for infants and toddlers. What makes each program unique? Which program would you feel most comfortable working in? Why?

3. Determine the legal requirements for establishing center and home child care programs in your state, city, or locality. What kind of funding is available? What are the similarities and differences of establishing home and center programs? What is your opinion of the guidelines?

4. Invite people from child care programs, welfare departments, and social service areas to speak to your class about child care. Find out who may attend child care programs. Also, find out what qualifications and training are necessary to become a child care employee. How do you feel about training welfare mothers as child care employees?

5. After visiting various child care programs, including center and home programs, discuss similarities and differences. Which of the programs provides the best services? What changes or special provisions need to be made to improve the success of these kinds of programs?

6. Gather information on franchised early childhood programs. What are the similarities and differences? In your opinion, what factors are necessary for the success of these kinds of programs?

7. Design a child care program you feel would meet the needs of children and their parents. How is your program similar to or different from those you visited?

8. Identify five of the most important issues associated with child care. Discuss these with parents, child care teachers, professors, and peers. Which issues are most controversial? How do your opinions differ from those of others?

9. Become familiar with child care definitions and regulations in your state. How do they differ from the information provided in this chapter?
10. Critique the child care of Tazale Benton. What would you change and how would you change it? Explain your changes.
11. Develop a model training program for baby-sitters. What would you include? What competencies would baby-sitters have to demonstrate before they graduate from your program?
12. Develop a manual for baby-sitters that you could use in your baby-sitter training program.
13. Develop a checklist to show parents what to look for in a quality child care program.
14. Some cities operate a hot line for latchkey children to use while they are home alone. List concerns these children might have and how you might alleviate these concerns over a hot line.
15. Interview a group of parents to determine how you could increase their participation in family and child care programs.
16. Visit an employer-sponsored child care program in your area. Describe the program to your classmates, listing pros and cons for parents and employers you found at that particular center.
17. Survey parents to determine the strengths and weaknesses of the child care programs they are using.
18. Conduct a survey to determine the cost of child care services in your area. Arrange your data in a table. What conclusions can you draw?
19. Tell why or why not you would leave your six-week-old infant in center child care, and develop a list of pros and cons for such care. Share this information with your classmates.
20. Do you think politicians always consider the social and personal consequences of their regulations, legislations, and administrative directives? Give specific examples.
21. You have been asked by your state senator to review child care regulations in your state. What suggestions would you make? What are the political and social implications of your suggestions?
22. Compare and contrast child care in Israel, Cuba, and other countries. Compare these systems to your ideas of child care. Could we improve the American system using the ideas of other countries? What determines the type of child care a particular country provides?
23. How will employer-sponsored child care meet the future needs of child care in America? What changes do you feel might result in child care as a result of employer involvement?
24. Is the CDA credential recognized in your state? If yes, find out how many centers are participating in the CDA Program. How many persons have been awarded the CDA Credential?
25. Interview a CDA candidate and gather information about the work one needs to complete for the CDA Credential. How does the candidate feel about the credentialing process? What are his/her goals for completing the CDA program?
26. What are the child care licensing requirements in your state? Do they require training similar to the CDA Program? If yes, how are they alike? How are they different?
27. Write to the Council for Early Childhood Professional Recognition to gather more information on the CDA Program. How do you feel about the CDA Program?

6

Infants and Toddlers: Rediscovering the Early Years

As you read and study:

Identify reasons for the greater number of infant and toddler programs

Understand the physical, motor, cognitive, psychosocial, and language growth and development of infants and toddlers

Understand Piaget's cognitive theory as it relates to infants and toddlers

Examine theories about the process of language development and acquisition

Recognize the developmental differences between infants and toddlers and the need to provide developmentally appropriate programs for each

Analyze and understand the features that contribute to quality infant and toddler programs

Identify what constitutes developmentally appropriate curricula for young children

Understand issues involved in the care and education of infants and toddlers

T
he past decade has seen a great demand for infant and toddler care and education. This demand comes partly from the large numbers of women entering
the labor force, the high divorce rate, and the economic need for both parents
in a family to work. The demand for early education is also fueled by baby-boom parents who want their children to have an "early start" and get off on the "right foot" so
they can have an even better life than their parents. The acceptance of early care and
education can also be attributed to a changing view of the very young and the discovery that babies are remarkably competent individuals. Parents and early childhood
educators are combining forces to give infants and toddlers the care and education
they need without harmfully and needlessly pushing and hurrying them.

PHYSICAL DEVELOPMENT

The infant and toddler years between birth and age three are full of many important
developmental and social events. Infancy, life's first year, includes many firsts—the
first breath, the first smile, first thoughts, first words, and first steps. Many significant
developmental events also occur during toddlerhood, the period between one and
three years. Two events are unassisted walking and rapid language development.
Language and mobility are the cornerstones of autonomy that enable toddlers to become independent. These firsts and unique developmental events are significant in
children's lives and also in the lives of those who care for and teach them. How adults
respond to infants' "firsts" and to toddlers' quest for autonomy helps determine how
they grow and develop and master the life events that await them.

To fully understand their roles as educators and nurturers, caregivers need to understand major features of normal growth and development. To begin, we must recognize that infants and toddlers are not the miniature adults many advertisements picture
them to be. Children need many years to develop fully and become independent. This
period of dependency and caregivers' responses to it are critical for the developing child.
Caregivers must constantly keep in mind that "normal" growth and development are
based on averages, and the "average" is the middle ground of development. (Table 6–1
gives average heights and weights for infants and toddlers.) To assess children's progress, or lack of it, caregivers must know the milestones of different stages of development. At the same time, to assess what is "normal" for each child, they must consider the
whole child. They must look at cultural and family background, including nutritional and
health history, to determine what is normal for that child. Caregivers must also keep in
mind that when children are provided with good nutrition, health care, and a warm, loving
emotional environment, development will tend toward what is "normal" for each of them.

MOTOR DEVELOPMENT

Motor development is an important part of infant and toddler development because
it contributes to intellectual and skill development. Human motor development is
governed by certain basic principles:

Quality programs provide materials and activities for a wide range of interests and abilities. A good program is not limited to the interests and abilities of the "average" infant and toddler.

TABLE 6–1 Height and Weight of Infants and Toddlers

Age	Males		Females	
	Height (inches)	Weight (pounds)	Height (inches)	Weight (pounds)
Birth	19.9	7.2	19.6	7.1
3 months	24.1	13.2	23.4	11.9
6 months	26.7	17.3	25.9	15.9
9 months	28.5	20.2	27.7	18.9
1 year	30.0	22.4	29.3	21.0
1½ years	32.4	25.3	31.9	23.9
2 years	34.5	27.8	34.1	26.2
2½ years	36.3	30.1	35.9	28.5
3 years	38.0	32.4	37.6	30.7

Source: P. V. V. Hamill et al., "Physical Growth: National Center for Health Statistics Percentiles," *The American Journal of Clinical Nutrition,* 32 (1979): 607–629.

TABLE 6–2 Infant/Toddler Motor Milestones

Behavior	Age of Accomplishment for 90% of Infants/Toddlers
Chin up momentarily	3 weeks
Arms-legs move equally	7 weeks
Smiles responsively	2 months
Sits with support	4 months
Reaches for objects	5 months
Smiles spontaneously	5 months
Rolls over	5 months
Crawls	7 months
Creeps	10 months
Pulls self to stand	11 months
Walks holding onto furniture	13 months

Source: William K. Frankenburg, William Sciarillo, and David Burgess, "The Newly Abbreviated and Revised Denver Developmental Screening Test," *The Journal of Pediatrics, 99* (Dec. 1981), pp. 995–999.

☐ Motor development is sequential. (Table 6–2 lists the sequence of development and major developmental milestones.)

☐ Maturation of the motor system proceeds from gross behaviors to fine motor. When learning to reach, for example, an infant sweeps toward an object with the whole arm; as a result of development and experiences, gross reaching gives way to specific reaching and grasping.

☐ Motor development is from the *cephalo* to the *caudal*—from head to foot (tail). The head is the most developed part of the body at birth; infants hold their heads erect before they sit, and sitting precedes walking.

☐ Motor development proceeds from the *proximal* (midline or central part of the body) to the *distal* (extremities). Infants can control their arm movements before they can control finger movements.

Toilet Training

Toilet training is a milestone of the toddler period. This process often causes a great deal of anxiety for parents, caregivers, and toddlers. American parents what to accomplish toilet training as quickly and efficiently as possible, but frustrations arise when they start too early and expect too much of children. Most child rearing experts recommend waiting until children are two years old before beginning toilet training.[1] Although some parents claim that their children are trained as early as one year, it is probably the parent rather than the child who is trained.

The principle of toilet training is that parents and caregivers are helping children develop control over an involuntary response. When an infant's bladder and bowel are full, the urethral and sphincter muscles open. The goal of toilet training is to teach the child to control this involuntary reflex and use the toilet when appropriate. Training involves timing, patience, modeling, preparing the environment, establishing a routine, and developing a partnership between the child and parents/care-

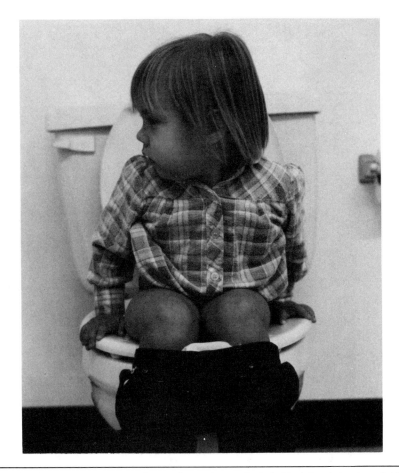

Cooperation between parents and caregivers can make toilet training less stressful for a child than it often is.

givers. Another necessary partnership is between the parents and child care providers who are assisting in the toilet training, especially if parents don't know what to do in toilet training or want to start too soon.

INTELLECTUAL DEVELOPMENT

As we learned in Chapter 4 when we discussed Piaget's theory of intellectual development, the first schemes are *sensorimotor*. According to Piaget, infants do not have "thoughts of the mind." Rather, they come to know their world by acting on it through their senses and motor actions. Infants *construct* (as opposed to absorbing) schemes using sensorimotor reflexive actions. Sucking, an innate sensorimotor scheme, involves turning the head to the source of nourishment, closing the lips around the nipple, sucking, and swallowing. As a result of experiences and maturation, this basic

Caregivers in infant and toddler programs plan developmentally appropriate activities for both groups based on the children's interests and stress involvement.

sensorimotor scheme *adapts* to include anticipatory sucking movements and non-nutritive sucking such as sucking a pacifier or blanket.

New schemes are constructed or created through processes of assimilation and accommodation. Piaget believed children are active constructors of intelligence through assimilation (taking in new experiences) and accommodation (changing existing schemes to fit new information), resulting in *equilibrium*. Piaget said children are constantly in quest of a balance between new experiences and old ideas, between what the world is really like and their view of the world. In this sense, humans are programmed to develop their intelligence through active involvement in the environment.

Sensorimotor schemes promote cognitive development. For example, grasping and sucking are infant sensorimotor schemes. At birth, the grasping reflex consists of closing the fingers around an object placed in the hand. Through experiences and maturation, this basic reflexive grasping action becomes coordinated with looking, opening the hand, retracting the fingers, and grasping. In this sense, the scheme develops from a purely reflexive action to an intentional grasping action. As the infant matures, and in response to experiences, the grasping scheme is combined with a releasing scheme, which leads to a purpose—such as the delightful activity of grasping and releasing things.

Infants begin life with only reflexive motor actions that are used to satisfy biological needs. By using these reflexive actions on the environment, and in response to the specific environmental conditions, however, the reflexive actions are modified through accommodation and adaptation to the environment. Patterns of adaptive behavior are used to initiate more activity, which leads to more adaptive behavior, which in turn leads to more schemes.

Stages of Cognitive Development

Sensorimotor Intelligence

Sensorimotor intellectual development consists of six stages, shown in Table 6–3.

Stage I. During this stage, infants suck and grasp everything. They are literally ruled by reflexive action and are not in control of their behavior. Reflexive responses to objects are undifferentiated, and infants respond the same way to everything. Caregivers and parents should interact with infants and provide objects to encourage interaction. The caregiver is a child's best toy, and there is no substitute for an attentive caregiver. Caregivers must also provide enriched environments so the active child can assimilate and accommodate. Caregivers must also meet infants' basic trust needs, since they accommodate better in an environment they trust.

Stage II. The milestone of this stage is the modification of reflexive actions. New sensorimotor behaviors begin to appear—habitual thumb sucking, indicating hand-mouth coordination; tracking of moving objects with the eyes; and moving the head toward sounds, a sign of the recognition of causality.

Stage III. Piaget called this stage that of "making interesting things last." Infants manipulate objects, demonstrating coordination between vision and tactile senses. They also reproduce events with the purpose of sustaining and repeating acts. The intellectual milestone of this stage is the beginning of *object permanence.* When infants in Stages I and II cannot see an object, it does not exist for them—a case of "out of sight, out of mind." During the later part of Stage III, however, there is a growing awareness that when things are out of sight, they do not cease to exist. *Secondary circular reactions* begin during this stage. This process is characterized by infants' repeating an action with the purpose of getting the same response from an object or person; for example, an infant will repeatedly shake a rattle to repeat the sound. Repetitiveness is a characteristic of all circular reactions. "Secondary" means that the reaction is elicited from a source other than the infant. The infant interacts with people and objects to make interesting sights, sounds, and events last. Given an object, the infant will use all available schemes, such as mouthing, hitting, and banging, and if one of these schemes produces an interesting result, the infant continues to use the scheme to elicit the same response. Imitation becomes increasingly intentional as a means of prolonging an interest.

Stage IV. During this stage, the infant uses means to attain ends. Infants move objects out of the way (means) to get another object (end). They begin to search for hidden objects, although not always in the places they were hidden, indicating a growing understanding of object permanence.

TABLE 6–3   Stages of Sensorimotor Intellectual Development

Stage	Age	Behavior
Stage I: Reflexive action	Birth to 1 month	1. Reflexive actions of sucking, grasping, crying, rooting, swallowing 2. Through experiences, reflexes become more efficient (e.g., amount of sucking required for nourishment) 3. Little or no tolerance for frustration or delayed gratification
Stage II: Primary circular reactions	1 to 4 months	1. Acquired adaptations form 2. Reflexive actions gradually replaced by voluntary actions 3. Circular reactions result in modification of existing schemes
Stage III: Secondary circular reactions	4 to 8 months	1. Increased responses to people and objects 2. Able to initiate activities 3. Beginning of object permanency
Stage IV: Coordination of secondary schemes	8 to 12 months	1. Increased deliberation and purposefulness in responding to people and objects 2. First clear signs of developing intelligence 3. Continuing development of object permanency 4. Actively searches for hidden objects 5. Comprehends meanings of simple words
Stage V: Experimentation (tertiary circular reactions)	12 to 18 months	1. Active experimentation begins through trial and error 2. Spends much time "experimenting" with objects to see what happens; insatiable curiosity 3. Differentiates self from objects 4. Realization that "out of sight" is not "out of reach" or "out of existence" 5. Beginning of understanding of space, time, and causality
Stage VI: Representational intelligence (intention of means)	18 to 24 months	1. Development of cause-effect relationships 2. Representational intelligence begins; can mentally represent objects 3. Engages in symbolic imitative behavior 4. Beginning of sense of time 5. Egocentric in thought and behavior

Through experimentation and interviews, Piaget documented that children construct their own intelligence. It is important for caregivers to provide children with opportunities and materials to actively explore and "experiment."

Stage V. This stage marks the beginning of truly intelligent behavior and is the climax of the sensorimotor period. Physically, it is also the beginning of the toddler stage, with the commencement of walking. Toddlers' physical mobility, combined with their growing ability and desire to "experiment" with objects, makes for fascinating and frustrating child rearing. They are avid explorers, determined to touch, taste, and feel all they can. Although the term "terrible two's" was once used to describe this stage, professionals now recognize that there is nothing terrible about toddlers exploring their environment to develop their intelligence. *Tertiary circular reactions* are characteristic of this stage. Novelty is interesting for its own sake, and toddlers experiment in many different ways with a given object. They use any available items—a wood hammer, a block, a rhythm band instrument—to pound the pegs in a pound-a-peg toy.

Stage VI. This is the stage of transition from sensorimotor to symbolic thought. Toddlers develop the ability to remember, which enables them to try out actions they see others do. During this stage, toddlers can "think" using mental images and memories, enabling them to engage in pretend activities. We need to keep in mind several important concepts about infant and toddler cognitive development:

1. The chronological ages associated with Piaget's stages of cognitive development are approximate. Caregivers should not be preoccupied with children's ages, but should focus on cognitive behavior, which gives a clearer understanding of a child's level of development.
2. Infants and toddlers do not "think" as adults do; they come to know their world by acting on it and need many opportunities for active involvement.
3. Infants and toddlers are actively involved in *constructing* their own intelligence. Children's activity with people and objects stimulates them cognitively and leads to the development of mental schemes.

LANGUAGE DEVELOPMENT

S. I. Hayakawa defines language this way:

> Of all forms of symbolism, language is the most highly developed, most subtle, and most complicated. It has been pointed out that human beings, by agreement, can make anything stand for anything. Now, human beings have agreed, in the course of centuries of mutual dependency, to let the various noises that they can produce with their lungs, throats, tongues, teeth, and lips systematically stand for specified happenings in their nervous systems. We call that system of agreements *language*.[2]

This system of agreements has some basic characteristics. First, it is a set of symbols that stand for certain ideas, thoughts, concepts, things, and feelings. The word *chair* is a written and spoken symbol for that object; the word *love* is a symbol for that emotion. Children do not automatically understand this process of assigning symbols to objects. Second, language is arbitrary, since we can make a symbol stand for anything we wish. By convention and custom, we agree upon certain symbols for certain things. Third, language is constantly changing, in both usage and the constant addition of new words to our vocabulary. Fourth, language involving symbols is a human behavior. While baboons have a repertoire of sounds in their communication system, they have never created a new sound. Fifth, because language is a uniquely human phenomenon, it is also an integral part of human society. It becomes a societal instrument for a wide variety of purposes and functions. Language is a social instrument for inducting children into society. Socialization of children would be difficult without language; thus, parents and schools have a responsibility to provide optimum opportunities for language acquisition.

Communication

We find evidence of communication everywhere in nature. Studies of the communication patterns of bees and dolphins make fascinating reading. Your dog wags her tail, and you interpret it as her communicating to you that she is happy. A baby cries, and his mother immediately interprets it as a sign of distress and changes his diaper. A teacher frowns at a child who is talking, and the child ceases, fearing more tangible punishment. All of these are examples of communication, but none of them involves what we usually think of as language.

Caregivers must recognize that young children are capable of engaging in conversation and give them many opportunities to use the language they are learning.

Effects of Language

Language sets perimeters for cognitive and social achievement. The language a child learns is generally determined by the society or culture into which she is born and, more specifically, by the home and community. The language style of the child's mother (or primary caregiver) also plays a dominant and important role in the language a child learns and in how she learns to communicate. Factors that influence the mother's language are level of education, language style learned as a child, knowledge of child rearing practices, and time and opportunity to use language with her children.

Children have almost no control over the language they learn or how they learn it. A child learns language from the models available at the time of language development. If the language model uses extended conversation and asks questions, the child learns to speak with these qualities. If, on the other hand, the model emphasizes nonverbal communication, then the child learns this style of language.

What and how a child learns affect school achievement and, to a certain extent, self-image. If the child has learned nonstandard English in a nonverbal setting, there will undoubtedly be difficulty with the language of schooling and expectations of the teacher. In the early grades, school achievement is traditionally measured by children's ability to learn to read. Children who do not speak well (generally, standard English is the criterion) often have difficulty learning to write and read, which leads to failure and, in turn, to poor self-image. The roots of school failure and subsequent life failure can often be traced to failure to acquire the vocabulary and language patterns necessary for actively seeking knowledge. Failure to do well in school can often be traced to the language children bring to school.

Renewed interest in early childhood education in general and disadvantaged children in particular has prompted new interest in language development. Recent studies of the effects of poverty have shed new light on the role language plays in the learning processes and have resulted in two sharply contrasting concepts about the language used by poor children, the *language deficit* and *language different* viewpoints.

According to the language deficit theory, any child's language is deficient if it is not middle-class English. According to the language different theory, all language is a means of communication, and the power to communicate renders all languages or dialects equal in effectiveness. From this viewpoint, a child who does not use standard English is not inferior. Rather, the child is using dialect to communicate and, depending on the conversation and the setting, communication occurs with varying degrees of understanding. In this theory, the task of learning to communicate rests with both teacher and child, whereas in the deficit theory, almost all the burden of adjustment is on the child.

Language Acquisition

There are many conflicting theories about how language learning occurs. As is the case in so much of child development and educational methodology, early childhood educators must weigh the evidence and decide upon which belief they will ultimately base their teaching.

Innate Ability

One proponent of the theory that humans are born with the ability to acquire language is Noam Chomsky. He hypothesizes that all children possess a structure or mechanism called a Language Acquisition Device (LAD) which enables them to acquire language. The young child's LAD uses all the language sounds he hears to process many grammatical sentences, even sentences he has never heard before. The child hears a particular language and processes it to form grammatical rules.

Eric Lenneberg has studied innate language acquisition in considerable detail in many different kinds of children, including the deaf. According to Lenneberg:

> All the evidence suggests that the capacities for speech production and related aspects of language acquisition develop according to built-in biological schedules. They appear when the time is ripe and not until then, when a state of what I have called "resonance" exists. The child somehow becomes "excited," in phase with the environment, so that the sounds he hears and has been hearing all along sud-

denly acquire a peculiar prominence. The change is like the establishment of new sensitivities. He becomes aware in a new way, selecting certain parts of the total auditory input for attention, ignoring others.[3]

Lenneberg believes that language development runs a definite course on a definite schedule, although he does not entirely dismiss the role of environment. He offers other reasons to support his contention that language is a "biological propensity":

1. Language development begins at about the same time in children's physical development and follows a fixed sequence;
2. Language is learned by all children, even those who have severe handicaps;
3. Nonhuman forms do not have the capacity for language development;
4. All languages are based on the same principals of syntax, semantics and phonology.[4]

The fact that children generate sentences they have never heard before is often cited as proof of innate ability. What would language be if we were only capable of reproducing the sentences and words we heard? The ability of children in all cultures and social settings to acquire language at a relatively immature age tends to support the thesis that language acquisition and use is more than a product of imitation or direct instruction. Indeed, children learn language without formal instruction.

The idea of a sensitive period for language development makes a great deal of sense and had a particular fascination for Montessori, who believed there were two sensitive periods for language development. The first sensitive period begins at birth and lasts until about three years. During this time, children unconsciously absorb language from the environment. The second period begins at three years and lasts until about eight years. During this time, children are active participants in their language development and learn how to use their power of communication.

Milestones of language development for infants and toddlers are shown in Table 6–4.

Environmental Factors

Theories about a biological basis of language should not be interpreted to mean that children are born with *the* particular language they will speak. While the ability to acquire language has a biological basis, the content of the language—vocabulary—is acquired from the environment, which includes other people as models for language. Therefore, development depends on talk between children and adults, and between children and children. Optimal language development ultimately depends on interaction with the best possible language models. The biological process of language acquisition may be the same for all children, but the content of their language will differ according to environmental factors. A child left to his own devices will not learn the language as well as the child reared in a linguistically rich environment.

A leading proponent of the environmental theory of language development is B. F. Skinner. He believes language learning is mainly a process of reinforcing the child's behavior in certain sounds and sound patterns and not in others. The child's parents reinforce or reward the child when the sounds he makes are a part of the lan-

TABLE 6–4 Language Development in Infants and Toddlers

Age	Language
Birth	Crying
1½ months	Social smile
3 months	Cooing
5 months	Ah, goo
5 months	Razzing
6 months	Babbling
8 months	Da-da/Ma-ma (used inappropriately)
10 months	Da-da/Ma-ma (used appropriately)
11 months	One word
12 months	Two words
14 months	Three words
15 months	Four to six words
18 months	One body part name
21 months	Two-word combinations
24 months	Fifty words
24 months	Two-word sentences (Noun/pronoun and verb used inappropriately)
24 months	Pronouns (I, you, me, etc. used inappropriately)

Source: *Clinical Pediatrics*, 17 (11), (November 1978).

guage, and do not reinforce sound patterns not in the language; in this way, the child learns the language of his parents. This helps explain why adults who learn a second language must train their ears to hear new language sounds. They cannot hear many of the sounds in the new language because these sounds were not reinforced in them when they were children.

The question of innate language acquisition versus language acquisition based on environmental factors is similar to the controversy of nature versus nurture in intellectual development. One cannot reject one viewpoint at the expense of the other. We must consider language acquisition as the product of both innate processes and environmental factors.

Caregivers and Language Learning

People who care for children and who are around them in the early stages of their language learning have a great deal of influence on how and what they learn. Children's language experiences can make the difference in their school success. Many children enter a preschool or child care setting without much experience in talking to other children or adults in different social settings.

Parents and caregivers should focus on the content of language: learning names for things, learning to speak in full sentences, and how to use and understand language. Many of these language activities relate directly to success in kindergarten and first grade. These guidelines are useful in promoting children's language development:

☐ Treat children as partners in the communication process. Many infant behaviors, such as smiling, cooing, and vocalizing, serve to initiate conversation, and caregivers can be responsive to these through conversation.

☐ Conversations are the building blocks of language development. Attentive and caring adults are infants' and toddlers' best stimulators of cognitive and language development. Talk to infants even though they do not "talk" to you.

☐ Use children's names when interacting with them, to personalize the conversation and build self-identity.

☐ Use a variety of means to stimulate and promote language development, including reading stories, singing songs, listening to records, and giving children many opportunities to interact with other adults who can have conversations with them.

☐ Encourage children to converse and share information with other children and adults.

☐ Help children learn to converse in different settings. This requires taking children to different places so they have different places to use their language and different people to use it with. By the same token, going to different places gives children ideas and events for using language.

☐ Have children use language in different ways. Children need to know how to use language to ask questions, explain feelings and emotions, tell what they have done, and to describe things.

☐ Give children experiences in the language of directions and commands. Many children fail in school not because they don't know language, but because they have little or no experience in how language is used for giving and following directions.

☐ Converse with children about what they are doing and how they are doing it. Children learn language through feedback; this includes asking and answering questions and commenting about activities, which shows children that caregivers are paying attention to them and what they are doing.

☐ Talk to children in the full range of adult language, including past and future tenses.

PSYCHOSOCIAL DEVELOPMENT

Erik H. Erikson is noted for his *psychosocial theory* of development. According to Erikson, children's personalities grow and develop in response to social institutions such as families, schools, child care centers and homes, and early childhood programs. Of course, adults are principal components of these environments and therefore play a powerful role in helping or hindering children in their personality development.

Stages of Psychosocial Development

Erikson's theory has eight "stages," which he also classifies as *"ego qualities."* These qualities emerge throughout the human lifespan; four stages apply to children from birth to age eight and are shown in Table 6–5. Stage I, Basic trust vs. Mistrust, begins at birth and ends at about 18 months. During this stage, children learn to trust or mistrust their environments and caregivers. Trust develops when children's needs are met consistently, predictably, and lovingly. Stage II, Autonomy vs. Shame and doubt, begins at 18 months and lasts until about 3 years. This is the stage of independence, when children want to do things for themselves. Lack of opportunities to become autonomous and independent and caregiver overprotection result in self-doubt and poor achievement. Stage III, Initiative vs. Guilt, begins at three years and ends at about five years. During this time children need opportunities to respond with initiative to activities and tasks, which give them a sense of purposefulness and accomplishment. Guilt occurs when children are discouraged or prohibited from initiating activities and are overly restricted in attempts to do things on their own. Stage IV, Industry vs. Inferiority, covers the elementary school years. In this period, children display an industrious attitude and want to be productive. They want recognition for this productivity, and adult response to children's efforts and accomplishments helps develop a positive self-concept. When children are criticized, belittled, or have few opportunities for productivity, the result is a feeling of inferiority.

Characteristics of Caregivers

Regardless of who provides surrogate care for infants and toddlers, caregivers should have certain qualities that will enable them to provide for children's *total* needs on all levels—physical, cognitive, language, and social and emotional. Parents used to think their young were not capable of learning much in the early years, so it didn't make much difference if those who took care of them did much with the children or not, but we now know that it does matter who takes care of and educates the very young. Alice Honig believes that *nurturing* is a necessary quality for all caregivers: "The high-quality infant caregiver is a special kind of nurturing person, with keen observation skills. Flexible, creative, comforting—she or he has a calm style that radiates secure commitment to an infant's well-being."[5]

Quality caregivers really *know* the children they care for. This knowledge, combined with knowledge of child growth and development, enables them to provide care that is appropriate for *each* child. They also *care* about the children. They accept and respect all children and their cultural and socioeconomic backgrounds. Furthermore, quality caregivers *care about themselves*. This self-caring appears in their commitment to the child care profession. It includes learning and developing the skills necessary to be a good care provider. It is further evidenced through good grooming, neatness, cleanliness, and a commitment to good physical and mental health. Quality caregivers understand that they must look and be their best for the children they care for.

Programs for Infants and Toddlers

Infants and toddlers are cared for and educated in many kinds of programs and in many different ways. These include child care centers (some of which specialize in

TABLE 6-5 Erikson's Stages of Psychosocial Development

Stage	Approximate Ages	Developmental Task—Resolution of Psychological Conflict	Role of Early Childhood Educators	Outcome for Child
1. Oral Sensory	Birth to 18 months or 2 years	Basic Trust vs. Mistrust	Meet children's needs with consistency and continuity	Views the world as safe and dependable
2. Muscular-anal	18 months to 3 years	Autonomy vs. Shame	Encourage children to do what they are capable of doing; avoid shaming for any behavior	Learns independence and competence
3. Locomotor Genital	3 to 5 years (to beginning of school)	Initiative vs. Guilt	Encourage children to engage in many activities; provide environment in which children can explore; promote language development	Able to undertake a task, be active and involved
4. Latency	Elementary	Industry vs. Inferiority	Help children win recognition by producing things; recognition results from achievement and success	Feelings of self-worth and industry

Routines are an important and necessary part of any child care program. Caregivers should establish routines and keep parents informed about children's behaviors during the day.

the care of infants), family child care homes, baby-sitting cooperatives, mothers' day-out programs, and people who care for children in their own or the child's home. Regardless of the type of program, a good one requires these basic features:

1. *Quality caregivers.* It is impossible to have a quality program without a quality staff. Those who are responsible for administering and conducting programs for the very young should make every effort to hire a staff that has the characteristics that contribute to high quality.

2. *Good staff/child ratios.* Program directors often say they comply with state guidelines for staff/child ratios and are therefore providing a quality program. However, state guidelines may be too high to enable caregivers and teachers to do their best. The NAEYC guidelines (presented in Chapter 5) suggest ratios every program should strive to achieve.

3. *Responsive environment.* An environment is responsive when it is sensitive to the unique needs of *all* children and is not merely satisfied to meet the needs of the "average" child.

4. *Appropriate curriculum and activities.*

The National Association for the Education of Young Children has developed "Guidelines for Developmentally Appropriate Practice" to help staff plan for activities. These are among the suggestions:

☐ A developmentally appropriate curriculum provides for all areas of children's development—physical, emotional, social, and cognitive—through an integrated approach.

☐ Curriculum planning is based on teachers' observations and recordings of each child's special interests and developmental progress.

☐ Curriculum planning emphasizes an interactive process.

☐ Learning activities and materials should be concrete and real.

☐ Programs should provide for a wider range of developmental interests and abilities than the chronological age range of the group would suggest.

☐ Teachers should offer a variety of activities and materials and increase the difficulty, complexity, and challenge of an activity as children develop understanding and skills.

☐ Adults should provide opportunities for children to choose from among a variety of activities, materials, and equipment and time to explore through active involvement.

☐ The program should offer multicultural and nonsexist experiences, materials, and equipment for children of all ages.

☐ Adults should arrange a balance of rest and active movement for children throughout the program day.

☐ Outdoor experiences should be provided.[6]

CURRICULA FOR INFANTS AND TODDLERS

The curriculum for infants and toddlers consists of all the activities and experiences they are involved in while under the direction of caregivers. Consequently, caregivers and teachers plan for *all* activities and involvements: feeding, washing, diapering/toileting, playing, learning and stimulation interactions, outings, involvements with others, and conversations. Caregivers must plan the curriculum so it is developmentally appropriate. In addition to the ideas that caregivers and teachers can extrapolate from the NAEYC guidelines for a developmentally appropriate curriculum, these concepts can also be included: self-help skills, ability to separate from parents, problem solving, autonomy and independence, and assistance in meeting the developmental milestones associated with physical, cognitive, language, personality, and social development. Table 6–6 is a cognitive activity chart that shows how a curriculum for infants and toddlers can be developed for the cognitive domain.

Childproofing Environments

Infants and toddlers explore the world with their senses. As we have emphasized, young children need opportunities to explore their surroundings. Consequently, caregivers must make many accommodations and adjustments in environments to sup-

TABLE 6–6 Cognitive Activity Chart, Birth to 30 Months

Cognitive Stage	Blocks	Books
Reflexive actions (primary circular reactions) (1–4 months) to suck to get hands to mouth to track and follow movement to provide variety of experiences for modification of reflexive actions	Soft, plastic, bright colors to watch to develop eye muscle to arouse curiosity to motivate movement	Soft, cardboard, bright colors to mouth to grasp with hands to observe contrast in colors and pattern to promote social contact with adult
Secondary circular (4–8 months) to promote eye/hand coordination manipulation to reproduce interesting experiences to initiate activities	Soft, plastic, bright colors to mouth to bang together to coordinate eye and hand movements	Soft cardboard to turn pages to explore with mouth to listen to encourage language
Coordination of secondary schemes (8–12 months) cause/effect object permanence means to ends	Large duplo, square, wooden to stack and knock down to experiment to experience cause and effect	Old magazines, cardboard books to point to label to open and close to take off the shelf to promote language development

	Play		
Music	Mobiles	Sensory Materials	
Caregiver voice, records, radio to listen to range of sounds to locate sounds to be aware of sounds	Homemade or commercial, hands or faces, bright colors to provide visual stimulation to bat at with hands and feet to become aware of self	Lambskin, flannel, silk to provide experiences with different textures to promote reaction to tactile stimulation to soothe emotionally to associate an object with comfort	
	Mirrors	Rattles	Water
Rattles, bells, shaking, clapping to make sounds to cause things to happen to imitate	Floor level, individual to lay in front of to hold look at self look at caregiver to learn about self	Wrist, ankle, commercial to hear a variety of sounds to experience variety of textures to cause things to happen to practice holding to encourage manipulation	Warm and cool to experience water on hands, whole body to use cups for splashing to pour to see what happens if . . .
	Pull Toys	Foods	Peek-A-Boo
Records, instruments to dance to sing to play instruments to bang to shake to encourage simple imitation	With strings to pull and wheels to spin to hear variety of sounds to be able to cause movement	Jello puffed rice yogurt To experience texture and taste	Experience pop 'n pals, to experience surprise jack-in-the-box, to see what happens hiding small toys under a blanket, to learn about the existence of something when not visible

TABLE 6–6   Continued

Cognitive Stage	Blocks	Books

Experimentation (12–18 months)
  to imitate
  to provide for active
    experimentation
	All kinds
	  to build up
	  to knock down
	  to experience cause and
	    effect
	  to integrate fine motor,
	    cognitive, and emotional
	    development (through
	    practice and mastery)
		Nursery rhymes, animals,
		  familiar objects and places
		  to experience the flow and
		    rhythm of language
		  to provide opportunity to
		    imitate sounds
		  to encourage receptive and
		    productive language

Representational intelligence
  (18–24 months)
represent
invent
	All kinds
	  vertical construction
	  horizontal construction
	  to practice construction of spatial
	    relationships with
	    concrete objects
		Nursery rhymes and poems,
		  objects and relationships (in/
		  out/over/under), familiar
		  objects and places
		  to encourage productive
		    language

Preoperational intelligence (24–
  30 months)
  to represent the world
	Large wooden, Lego; use with
	  props (cars, people,
	  animals)
	  to facilitate imagination and
	    language development
		Simple short stories
		  to encourage language
		    production, story telling,
		    and sequencing
		  to encourage the child to
		    relay his or her own story

Source: Developed by Anne DeHaan, St. Joseph Mercy Hospital Learning Center, Pontiac, Michigan, and Harriet Jo Midgett, Americare Systems, Inc., Pontiac, Michigan.

Music	Imitation	Manipulatives	Sensory Materials
Singing nursery rhymes to encourage language production to listen to and produce the rhythm and flow of language	Familiar scenarios; play with dolls, stuffed animals, hats, scarves, purses to reenact caregiving routines to encourage imitation of everyday experiences	Object relationships; play with containers, lids, nesting blocks, buckets and tubs to relate parts to each other and the whole to experiment with objects	Object Properties to explore and use senses through tubs filled with water, puffed cereal to take in new information through the senses
	Imitation	Manipulatives	Sensory Materials
Simple songs and finger plays to encourage language production to practice production of sounds through repetition of rhythm and rhyme	Familiar scenarios; play with stove, sink pots, pans, empty food containers to facilitate imaginative play	Object relationships; play with shape sorter, simple puzzles to integrate fine motor and cognitive skills to relate parts to the whole	Object properties; sensory table or tubs with water, rice, sand to discover properties: sink/float; empty/full; hard/soft; dry/wet
	Imitation	Manipulatives	Sensory Materials
Songs, fingerplays to follow directions to understand spatial concepts, prepositions to practice producing words and sounds	Expanding scenarios; play with dolls and dolls clothes, dress up clothes to experience community roles (fire fighters, doctors, bakers) to expand imitation and imagination through play	Object relationships; play with pegboard (color coding), playdough, with cookie cutter, rolling pins to integrate imagination, fine motor, and language development	Object Properties; cooking activities: to discuss and experience smooth, crunchy, wet, sticky, hot to experience sequencing and transformation to integrate cognitive, fine motor, and language opportunities

port young children's explorations. The following list describes how to childproof homes and child care centers so they enhance young children's developing autonomy:

Home

☐ Remove throw rugs so toddlers don't trip
☐ Put breakable objects out of toddlers' reach
☐ Cover electrical wall outlets with special covers
☐ Remove electrical cords
☐ Install gates in hallways and stairs (make sure gates are federally approved so the toddlers cannot get their heads stuck and strangle)
☐ Take knobs off stoves
☐ Purchase medicines and cleaners that have childproof caps
☐ Store all medicines and cleaning agents out of reach; move all toxic chemicals from low cabinets to high ones (even things like mouthwash should be put in a safe place)
☐ Place safety locks on bathroom doors that can be opened from the outside
☐ Cushion sharp corners of tables and counters with foam rubber and tape or cotton balls
☐ If older children in the home use toys with small parts, beads, etc., have them use these when the toddler is not present or in an area where the toddler can't get them
☐ When cooking, turn all pot handles to the back of the stove
☐ Avoid using cleaning fluids while children are present (because of toxic fumes)
☐ Place guards over hot water faucet in bathrooms so toddlers can't turn them on
☐ Keep wastebaskets on tops of desks
☐ Keep doors to washer and dryer closed at all times
☐ Keep all plastic bags, including garbage bags, stored in a safe place
☐ Shorten cords on draperies; if there are loops on cords, cut them
☐ Immediately wipe up any spilled liquid from the floor

Center

☐ Cover toddler area floors with carpeting or mats
☐ Make sure storage shelves are anchored well and won't tip over; store things so children cannot pull heavy objects off shelves onto themselves
☐ Use only safe equipment and materials, nothing that has sharp edges or is broken
☐ Store all medicines in locked cabinets
☐ Cushion sharp corners with foam rubber and tape
☐ Keep doors closed or install gates
☐ Fence all play areas[7]

Issues in Infant and Toddler Education

Many of the issues we have discussed in earlier chapters relate to the area of infant and toddler education. The first step in the issue of developmental appropriateness is to recognize the need to provide different programs of activities for infants *and* toddlers. To do so, one must get parents and other caregivers to realize that infants, as a group, are different from toddlers and need programs, curricula, and facilities specifically designed for them. Based on this recognition, it is then necessary to design and implement developmentally appropriate curricula. The early childhood profession is leading the way in raising consciousness about the need to match what caregivers do with children to the children's development as individuals. There is a long way to go in this regard, but part of the resolution will come with training caregivers in child development and curriculum planning. Finally, we will want to match caregivers to children of different ages. Not everyone is emotionally or professionally suited to provide care for infants and toddlers. Both groups need adults who can respond to their particular needs and developmental characteristics. As Honig points out, infants need especially nurturing caregivers; toddlers, on the other hand, need adults who can tolerate and allow for their emerging autonomy and independence.

Parent-Child Enrichment Programs

Fifteen-month-old Brian Weisbard has already earned two certificates and is working on a third. The certificates, neatly framed and hung in his bedroom, attest to his accomplishments while attending the Family Center at Nova University's Infant Awareness Program in Ft. Lauderdale, Florida. Brian and his mother, Denise, have been attending parent-child awareness programs for eleven months. Brian's certificates were awarded after participating in activities that involve rocking, spinning, rolling, mirror play, and musical games. Although activities for his third certificate are more demanding, Brian is always excited about going to class, and Denise has no doubt that he will be successful. "Brian is a smart child, and these sessions help me discover just how much he is able to do," Denise says. "He needs these sessions to challenge him and unlock his natural abilities. It's also a good way for him to express himself."

Once a week Brian and Denise, a full-time working mother, spend an hour at the local YWCA. Brian plays and learns in a brightly colored room full of balls, hoops, bolsters, fabric tunnels, and other equipment designed to stimulate young children's physical and intellectual growth. Exploratory play is one of Brian's favorite activities. He giggles, laughs, and frequently screams as he climbs stairs, goes down slides, and jumps in a colorful parachute with twelve other children, all to the strains of "happy music." Brain also likes sensory awareness time, when he gets a chance to help blow soap bubbles. As the bubbles float through the air, he never tires of trying to catch them. Brian hugs and squeezes dolls of different textures. He likes the sticky, slippery feel of cooked spaghetti as he picks up handfuls piled in a big plastic bowl.

Brian's teacher, Marcia Orvieto, provides Denise with parenting information and suggests ways she and Brian can spend "quality time" together. Denise has read and heard a lot about spending quality time with children. "As a working parent I don't have a lot of time to spend with Brian. I'm determined to make the most of it by doing things together that will help nurture and guide him. Some parents think that just spending time with their children is all that matters. I like to think that if I can spend thirty minutes a day with Brian in activities like reading to him, helping him make a collage of various colors and shapes, and playing games, then we have made good use of our time together."

Denise, vice-president of a savings and loan company, wants Brian to socialize with other children and have a chance to learn. This is the major reason she takes him to the parent-child awareness program. Denise's friends sometimes laugh when she tells them Brian goes to school. "But, reading begins at birth," she tells them. "And I want to make sure Brian gets the physical and neurological stimulation necessary for learning." Denise does not believe she is "pushing" Brian; she feels she is building the foundation to get him ready for school and a successful life. "With my work schedule, going to the parent-child center gives us a chance to do things together, and I get a lot of useful child development information, too. I think these programs are great!" Denise is not the only parent who is determined to give her child a good start in life. All over America, parents and their young children are enrolling in record numbers in parent-child programs designed to enhance children's natural learning abilities through play. These programs capitalize on what parents and early childhood educators have known for years: a lot of learning in the early years occurs through play.

But there is more to it than play, as Joan Barnes, founder of Gymboree, points out: "Early childhood educators might describe what we do as sensory motor development. We prefer more informal expressions such as movement education play or growth play. Much of early learning is based on physical activity and play is the child's natural way of being involved in physical activity. Gymboree and other programs provide a place where children can learn by doing." Preschool parent-child enrichment programs are beneficial to parents and children in a number of ways. First, they give parents the opportunity to actively participate in their children's development. Second, many of the programs are planned to combine learning and fun. They integrate ideas from early childhood education, child development, physical education, recreation, physical therapy, and educational psychology into meaningful activities that enhance learning. Third, the programs help parents become better parents. They offer valuable parenting information and insight into child development and behavior. As Karen Anderson, Vice President of Public Affairs for Gymboree says, "Parents tell us that as a result of Gymboree they have become more tolerant and understanding. If they find their child jumping off a sofa onto the coffee table, they understand the child is not trying to be bad, but filling a basic sensory need. He wants to feel a hard surface and a soft surface, he wants to feel what it's like to move through the air. An understanding parent will figure out a way for the child to fulfill that need without getting hurt."

FURTHER READING

Ausberger, Carolyn, et al. *Learning to Talk is Child's Play* (Tucson, Arizona: Communication Skill Builders, 1982) The authors have developed a method of language development called *responsive language teaching*. Its primary ingredients are the caregiver's openness to what a child is trying to say and the ability to provide the language the child needs to hear. Excellent book for showing how to be a child's language learning assistant.

Badger, E. *Infant/Toddler: Introducing Your Child to the Joy of Learning* (New York: Instructo/McGraw-Hill, 1981) New way of looking at stimulation in the development of the infant and the toddler. An introduction to joy in the daily routine of working with young children; encourages the reader to adapt and/or change activities according to the child's specific needs.

Balter, Lawrence, and Anita Shreve. *Dr. Balter's Child Sense: Understanding and Handling the Common Problems of Infancy and Early Childhood* (New York: Poseidon Press, 1985) Covering the period from birth to age five, provides many answers for parents and teachers of young children. Includes responses to problems of the young infant up to concerns of the preschool child, such as another baby, a divorce in the family, and other family considerations.

Biber, Barbara. *Early Education and Psychological Development* (New Haven, Conn.: Yale University Press, 1984) Biber, a leading proponent of the developmental-interaction approach to early childhood education, advocates a "whole child" approach that encourages children to exercise control over their learning with teachers as guides for interactions between students and staff. Valuable insight into the development of the child-centered approach at Bank Street College.

Brutt, Kent Garland, and Karen Kalkstein. *Smart Toys for Babies from Birth to Two* (New York: Harper and Row, 1980) How-to book demonstrating over 70 easy-to-make toys, each designed to stimulate creativity, imagination, and intelligence.

Cataldo, C. *Infant and Toddler Programs: A Guide to Very Early Childhood Education* (Reading, Mass.: Addison-Wesley, 1982) Describes many new infant and toddler programs; hints for those who are looking for an ideal place.

Cazden, Courtney B., Ed. *Language in Early Childhood Education,* Rev. Ed. (Washington, D.C.: National Association for the Education of Young Children, 1981) Help for developing an effective program of language development with practical ideas and suggestions. Most useful topics are developing a total language curriculum, bilingual education, and integration of language and reading.

Dittman, Laura L., Ed. *The Infants We Care For* (Washington, D. C.: National Association for the Education of Young Children, 1984) Members of the NAEYC Commission on the Care and Education of Infants in 1969 identified three goals for care of infants: development of a healthy body, development of an active mind, and development of wholesome feelings. This book raises issues relating to these goals so that caregivers can develop the best possible programs.

Gonzales-Mena, J., and D. Eyer. *Infancy and Caregiving* (Palo Alto, Calif.: Mayfield, 1980) Curriculum guide format with helpful anecdotes and informational charts.

Hagstrom, J. *More Games Babies Play* (New York: Pocket Books, 1981) Good, sensible games to play with babies; follow-up to *Games Babies Play*.

Harmes, Thelma, and Richard M. Clifford. *Early Childhood Environment Rating Scale* (New York: Teachers College Press, 1981) Rating scale for use with all types of child care or early childhood settings.

Hass, Carolyn Buhai. *Look at Me: Activities for Babies and Toddlers* (Glencoe, Ill.: CBH Publishing, 1985) Easy-to-use activities: Toys to Make, Learning Games, Indoor/Outdoor Fun, Books and Reading, Positive Self-Image, Imaginative Play, Arts and Crafts, Easy and Nutritious Recipes, etc.

Honig, Alice S., and Ronald J. Lally. *Infant Caregiving: A Design for Training* (Syracuse, N.Y.: Syracuse University Press, 1981) Comprehensive, easy-to-use guide; focuses on giving care to children three and under, but all caregivers can benefit from concepts, ideas, and suggested activities.

Karnes, Merle B. *Small Wonder!* (Circle Pines, Minn.: American Guidance Service, 1981) Activities emphasizing play and language development of infants.

_____. *You and Your Small Wonder: Activities for Parents and Toddlers on the Go* (Circle Pines, Minn.: American Guidance Service, 1982) 156 activities to help caregivers of toddlers, covering physical, emotional, intellectual growth, and language development. Information on health and safety and child development. Excellent resource for parents and other caregivers.

Leavitt, Robin Lynn, and Brenda Krause Eheart. *Toddler Day Care: A Guide to Responsive Caregiving* (Lexington, Mass.: D.C. Heath, 1985) Practical information in toddler care by operators of the Developmental Child Care Program at the University of Illinois at Urbana-Champaign. Topics from play to assessment are developmentally based. Focuses exclusively on toddler care and education and easy to read and understand.

Lurie, R., and R. Neugebauer. *Caring for Infants and Toddlers: What Works, What Doesn't*, Vol. 2 (Redmond, Wash.: Child Care Information Exchange, 1982) Conference readings from Third Annual Conference "Caring for Infants and Toddlers. . ." sponsored by the Summit Child Care Center.

Maxim, G. *The Sourcebook: Activities to Enrich Programs for Infants and Young Children* (Belmont, Calif.: Wadsworth, 1981) Activities to encourage infants and young children in physical, emotional, motor, and creative development; guidelines for evaluations.

Morrison, George S. *The Education and Development of Infants, Toddlers, and Preschoolers* (Boston: Little, Brown, 1988) Developmental theory and practical applications caregivers need to provide developmentally appropriate curriculum; includes charts and vignettes.

White, Burton, L. *A Parent's Guide to the First Three Years* (Englewood Cliffs, N.J.: Prentice-Hall, 1980) White believes parents should care for children in their homes: "I would not think of putting a child of my own into any substitute-care program on a full-time basis, especially a center-based program." Critics say White fails to consider economic and political realities.

_____. *The First Three Years of Life: The Revised Edition* (New York: Prentice-Hall Press, 1985) White is convinced that parents and caregivers should focus most of their attention on the first three years of life; takes the reader step-by-step through all stages of development during the first three years.

White, Burton, L., Barbara T. Kaban, and Jane S. Attanucci. *The Origins of Human Competence* (Lexington, Mass.: D. C. Heath, 1979) Account of the interactive nature of the relationship between child rearing practices, early experiences, and development of abilities in the first three years of life; authors believe "much of the anxiety, stress, and ill feeling experienced by families raising young children is avoidable."

FURTHER STUDY

1. Visit at least two programs that provide care for infants and toddlers. Observe the curriculum to determine if it is developmentally appropriate. What suggestions would you make for improving the curriculum? Explain what you liked most and least about the program.
2. What five things can caregivers do to promote children's basic trust needs?
3. You have been asked to speak to a group of parents about what they can do to promote their children's language development in the first two years of life. Outline your presentation, and list five specific suggestions you will make to the parents.
4. Observe children between the ages of birth and eighteen months. Identify the six stages of sensorimotor intelligence by describing the behaviors you observed in the children. Cite specific examples of secondary and tertiary reactions. For each of the six stages, list two activities that would be cognitively appropriate.
5. What evidence can you provide to support the theory that language is primarily an innate process?
6. In addition to the caregiver qualities cited in this chapter, list and explain five other qualities you think are important for caregivers of infants and toddlers.
7. Why is motor development important in the early years? What are five things early childhood educators can include in their programs to promote motor development?
8. Most of Sylvia's friends and family members criticized her for sending her 3-week-old baby, Katrina, to a child care center. Sylvia honestly weighed the pros and cons of this decision and believes this was the best one for her and her child. List the positive and negative factors involved in putting a 3-week-old infant in a child care center program. Does the law in your state specify how old a child has to be before enrolled in a child care center? If so, what is this age and what other standards must be followed when providing care for infants?
9. Identify infant/toddler programs in your area. Outline their basic services and curricula. What changes would you recommend and why?
10. Dianne is constantly trying to teach her 18-month-old son Brad how to behave in the house. Basically, she wants him to be good and leave things alone. Yet, as soon as she leaves him alone for a minute, he begins to make a mess of the house. How can Dianne keep Brad from making a mess of the house? What would be reasonable expectations for Brad? Is Brad's behavior expected or unexpected for his age group?
11. Identify customs that are passed down to infants and toddlers as a result of the family's cultural background. How do these customs affect young children's behavior?
12. Visit centers that care for young children of different cultures. List the differences you find. What areas are most similar?
13. Interview parents of young infants from different cultures. What are their five top expectations for their babies? How do expectations differ and how are they alike?
14. Develop a list of recommended items for adults to carry when traveling with young children. How can such a list help parents?

15. Exercising with young babies is a current trend. Express your views on this, and compare your views to those of a mother who attends an infant/parent exercise program.

16. What are signs of a sick infant? Are there signs that indicate serious illness?

17. Develop a set of activities for mothers and their infants to use at home. Try these activities out with parents and infants, and tell what went well and what you would change.

18. Prepare a panel discussion to present the pros and cons of the trend to teach young babies how to read.

19. Every morning, Maria, the caregiver of an infant group, reads a story to the children. But one day, a new parent went storming to see the program director. The parent claimed that Maria's very heavy Spanish accent would negatively affect his son's language development. Do you think the parent was right or wrong? Why? What would you do if you were the program director?

20. Mary insisted that her 14-month-old boy needed to be fed upon demand. The caregivers tried to convince her that they had a set feeding schedule. They argued this issue until the supervisor had to intervene and settle this problem. What method should be used, the child's timetable or the adults' timetable? What would you do as the supervisor? How do programs in your area arrange meal schedules?

7

The Preschool Years: Readiness for Learning

As you read and study:

Trace the history of preschool and nursery education from the McMillan sisters to the present

Understand basic growth and development of preschoolers

Discuss various definitions and purposes of play in preschool education

Consider how play can be used in a program of learning

Examine and critique preschool curricula and schedules

Examine goals and objectives for preschools

Analyze issues related to early schooling and learning

Identify trends in preschool education

B y the end of the toddler period, children are independent in locomotion, and the preschool years begin. This is the time when children benefit most from their independence and locomotion. The preschool years last from age three until children enter a formal school setting at the age of about five or five-and-a-half. There are several reasons we use the term *preschool* to label these years. First, parents and society view this period as the time that children "get ready" for entering kindergarten or first grade, the beginning of what they consider formal schooling. The preschool years are critical; many professionals, such as early childhood teachers, view the events of these years as the cornerstone of later learning. Some parents, however, still think of this preschool period as a time in which children should be unburdened by learning and allowed to play and enjoy life, perhaps, as some feel, for the last time. Looked at this way, the preschool years are noteworthy as the last time, for a period of at least twelve years, in which children's lives will not be dominated and molded by schooling.

Preschools are programs for children before their entry into a formal school setting. For our purposes, preschool means programs for two- to five-year-old children, before kindergarten. We will also discuss what is often thought of as nursery schools, or programs for three- to four-year-old children.

Early childhood educators generally distinguish between preschool and child care. Applying the term *preschool* to a program usually means it has an educational purpose and a curriculum designed to involve children primarily in learning activities. Parents usually enroll their children in preschools because they believe in early learning and want their children to learn. Child care is primarily intended to provide care for children so parents can work. The purposes of child care and preschool are not mutually exclusive, however, and the better programs of either emphasize both quality care and learning. Some preschools have broadened their programs to include child care components. The preschool program may be conducted in the morning, with a child care program in the afternoon; the preschool may have a before-school and afternoon child care program; or child care and preschool programs may be conducted in the same building but as separate programs.

HISTORY OF PRESCHOOL EDUCATION

The history of preschool education is really the history of nursery education, which cannot be separated from the history of kindergarten education. The origin of nursery schools as it affects the United States was in Great Britain. In 1914, Margaret and Rachel McMillan started an open-air nursery with an emphasis on health care and healthy living. They did not ignore cognitive stimulation, and also began a program of visiting homes to work with mothers. Their work led to the passage, in 1918, of the Fisher Act, which provided national support for nursery education. This led to the establishment of the first public nursery schools in Great Britain.

Patty Smith Hill was a champion of the nursery school movement in the U.S. and started a progressive laboratory school at Columbia Teachers College in New

York in 1921. Abigail Eliot, another nursery school pioneer, studied in Great Britain for six months with the McMillan sisters, then started the Ruggles Street Nursery School in Boston in 1922. Meanwhile, also in 1922, the Merrill-Palmer Institute Nursery School opened in Detroit, under the direction of Edna White. The Institute and White were responsible for training many nursery school teachers.

A temporary impetus to nursery education occurred in 1933, when the Federal Works Progress Administration provided funds to hire unemployed teachers in nursery school programs. In 1940, the Lanham Act provided money for child care to mothers employed in defense-related industries. This support ended with the war in 1945. From the 1940s to the present, preschools have been mainly private, sponsored by parent cooperatives, churches, and other agencies. Federal involvement in preschool education has been through Head Start and support for child care programs directed at low-income families and children.

INCREASING POPULARITY OF PRESCHOOLS

We are witnessing an acceleration of a trend that began with the Head Start Program in 1965, namely the entrance of children into preschool programs at earlier ages. Greater numbers of four-year-olds are entering preschools, many operated by public schools. As shown in Table 7–1, the number of three- and four-year-olds in preschools has increased by over 18 percent from 1970 to 1982. When we look at the projections of preschool enrollments for this age group through 1993, the extent of the trend is even more dramatic, as shown in Table 7–2.

Our emphasis throughout this text is on societal changes and their impact and influence on early childhood educational programs. Changing family patterns, increasing numbers of women entering the work force, changing attitudes, and values relating to education and care of children all tend to increase the need for preschool programs. In addition, parents and public policy makers are influenced by the publication of research reports that verify the positive short- and long-term benefits of quality preschool programs to children and society. In general, many parents feel that the place for their children is in a preschool program. Parents not only want their children to receive the benefits of preschool, they also do not want them to be left out or

TABLE 7–1 Preschool Enrollment Rate by Age: 1970 to 1982

Year	Percentage of 3- and 4-Year-Olds in Preschools
1970	20.5%
1972	24.4
1974	28.8
1976	31.3
1978	34.2
1980	36.7
1982	36.4

Source: "The Statistical Trends," *The Principal*, 64 (May 1985), p. 16.

TABLE 7–2 Projected Trends in Preschool Enrollment by Age: 1985 to 1993 (in thousands)

Year	Public Schools			Private Schools		
	3 Yrs.	4 Yrs.	Total	3 Yrs.	4 Yrs.	Total
1985	352	728	1,080	721	1,069	1,790
1986	364	754	1,118	745	1,106	1,851
1987	376	779	1,155	770	1,142	1,912
1988	388	805	1,193	794	1,180	1,974
1989	399	830	1,229	816	1,217	2,033
1990	409	853	1,262	838	1,251	2,089
1991	419	875	1,294	857	1,283	2,140
1992	426	894	1,320	872	1,311	2,183
1993	432	910	1,342	884	1,335	2,219

Source: *The Principal*, 64 (May 1985) p. 16.

left behind. Parents believe enrolling their children in preschool programs is part of their parental duty.

WHO IS THE PRESCHOOLER?

Today's preschooler is not like the four-year-old of previous decades. Many have already attended one, two, or three years of child care or nursery school. Many have traveled widely. Many have experienced the trauma of family divorces, and many have experienced the stress, trauma, and psychological effects of abuse. Both collectively and individually, then, the experiential backgrounds of preschoolers are quite different from those of previous generations. But it is precisely this background of experiences, its impact, and the implications for caregivers that preschool teachers must understand to effectively meet preschoolers' needs.

Physical and Motor Development

A noticeable difference between preschoolers and their infant and toddler counterparts is that preschoolers have lost most of their baby fat and taken on a leaner, lankier look. This "slimming down" enables the preschooler to participate with more confidence in the locomotor activities so vitally necessary during this stage of growth and development. Both girls and boys continue to grow several inches per year throughout the preschool years. At age three, the average boy weighs about 32 pounds and the average girl is about a pound and a half lighter (see Table 7–3).

Preschool children are in an age of rapid motor skill development. They are learning to use and test their bodies. It is a time for learning what they can do and how they can do it as individuals. *Locomotion* plays a large role in motor and skill development and includes activities of moving the body through space—walking, running, hopping, jumping, rolling, dancing, climbing, and leaping. Children use these activities to investigate and explore the relationships between themselves, space, and

Society and parents often demand quality preschools for four-year-olds because the preschool years are considered a valuable time for learning and getting ready for formal schooling.

objects in space. Preschoolers demonstrate the principles of cephalo-caudal and proximo-distal development mentioned in Chapter 6. The cephalo-caudal development enables the preschooler to participate in many physical activities; likewise, the concentration of motor development in the small muscles of the arms and hands enables them to participate in fine motor activities of drawing, coloring, painting, cutting, and pasting. Consequently, preschoolers need programs that provide action, activity, and play, supported by proper nutrition and healthy habits of plentiful rest and good hygiene.

Good education practices also dictate that a preschool curriculum deemphasize activities that require preschoolers to wait or sit for extended periods of time. Al-

TABLE 7–3 Height and Weight of Preschoolers

Age	Males		Females	
	Weight (pounds)	Height (inches)	Weight (pounds)	Height (inches)
3 years	32.4	38.0	30.7	37.6
4 years	36.8	40.5	35.2	40.0
5 years	41.2	43.3	38.9	42.7

Source: Adapted from P.V.V. Hamill et al., "Physical Growth: National Center for Health Statistics Percentiles," *The American Journal of Clinical Nutrition*, 32 (1979), pp. 607–629.

though learning self-control is part of preschoolers' socialization process, developmentally appropriate practices call for activity. It is also important to incorporate health education into programs for four- and five-year-olds. Children should receive information about hygiene and nutrition; because bad habits are almost impossible to break, preschool and elementary curricula should incorporate lifelong goals and objectives for healthy living.

Cognitive Development

Preschoolers are in the preoperational stage of intelligence. As we saw in Chapter 4, these are characteristics of the preoperational stage: (1) children grow in their ability to use symbols, including language; (2) children are not capable of operational thinking (an *operation* is a reversible mental action), which explains why Piaget named this stage preoperational; (3) children center on one thought or idea, often to the exclusion of other thoughts; (4) children are unable to *conserve;* and (5) children are *egocentric.*

     Characteristics during the preoperational stage have particular implications for teachers. Because the preschool child is egocentric, he believes everyone sees what he sees and thinks as he thinks. This egocentrism influences how he responds to things and how he interacts with others. Piaget believed the underlying reason for many of the preoperational child's "errors" of reasoning stemmed from his inability to see viewpoints other than his own. This egocentrism is not selfishness, but, rather, a lack of awareness. Early childhood educators recognize that many children are able to engage in cognitive activities earlier than Piaget thought and that many do not demonstrate a characteristic at the age or to the degree Piaget maintained. For example, Piaget believed that young children are *animistic,* that is, they attribute life to nonliving objects; preoperational children are animistic, but not to the extent Piaget thought they were. Preschool teachers therefore need an understanding of developmental theories that will enable them to match activities to children's cognitive needs and stages.

Language Development

The preschool years are a period of rapid language growth and development. Vocabulary increases, and as children continue to master syntax and grammar, sentence length increases. The first words infants or toddlers use are *holophrases,* one word that conveys the meaning of a sentence. For example, Amy may say "milk" to express "I'd like some more milk, please."

     At one year, the infant knows two or more words; by the age of two, she knows about 275. During the second year of life, the toddler's language proficiency increases to include *telegraphic* speech—combining two- or three-word utterances to act as a sentence. "Amy go," for example, can mean that Amy wants her mother to take her for a walk in the stroller. During the third year of life, children add helping verbs and negatives to their vocabulary, for example, "I don't want milk." Sentences also become longer and more complex. During the fourth and fifth years, children use noun or subject clauses, conjunctions, and prepositions to complete their sentences. During the preschool years, children's language development is diverse, comprehensive, and constitutes a truly impressive range of learning. An even more impressive feature of language acquisition during the preschool years is that children learn intuitively, without a great deal of instruction, the rules of language that apply to words, phrases, and the utterances they use.

Psychosocial Development

During the preschool years, children are in the *initiative vs. guilt* stage of development. They need to initiate activities, and teachers should respond to this need by providing opportunities whereby children can undertake activities that will help them develop a feeling of mastery over themselves and their environment. During this stage, caregivers should avoid harsh criticism and restrictive caregiving and teaching styles. In particular, overprotectiveness promotes hesitancy and fearfulness, which counteract and inhibit children's efforts to initiate.

During the preschool years, children are capable of initiating the majority of their actions and need this initiative to become independent and confident decision makers. Of course, a great deal of risk-taking is involved in this process. Caregivers can support children's initiative and decisions with positive reinforcement. Children can also be encouraged to take risks within a safe environment characterized by limited freedom. This is why an "open" classroom and "free play" activities provide the appropriate environmental support at this stage.

PRESCHOOL PLAY

The notion that children can learn through play begins with Froebel, who built his system of schooling on the educative value of play. As discussed in Chapter 2, he considered play the highest level of child development. Froebel believed that natural unfolding (development) occurred through play. Since that time, most early childhood programs have incorporated play into their curricula, or have made play a major part of the day. Recall also the importance Piaget placed on the contribution of play to intellectual growth.

Play usually occupies a major part of children's lives. Play activities are essential to the environment in which children learn concepts, develop social and physical skills, master life situations, and practice language processes. Children learn through play. Without the opportunity for play and an environment that supports it, a child's learning is limited. Early childhood programs that provide opportunities for play increase and enhance the limits of children's learning.

Play can be thought of as children's work, and the home and preschool as "workplaces" where learning occurs through play. Children engage in play naturally and enjoy it; they do not select play activities because they want to learn. A child does not choose to put blocks in order from small to large because he wants to learn how to seriate, nor does he build an incline because he wants to learn the concept of "down" or the principles of gravity; however, the learning outcomes of his play are ob-

Play offers many opportunities to learn.

vious. Children's play is full of opportunities for learning, but there is no guarantee that, because children play, they will learn.

Karl Groos felt that play prepared children for adult occupations. This may explain why curriculum developers and teachers have always based many activities around adult roles; a frequent justification for a dress-up corner is that it helps children try out adult roles.

Expenditure of surplus energy has been a popular theory about why children play. This theory resembles the cathartic theory, which holds that children use play as a means of relieving frustrations and emotions. Play is certainly an excellent means of relieving stress, and early childhood educators now recognize that play is one antidote to stress.

Piaget believed that play serves an assimilative function; through play, children are able to take in information that assists in the development of schemes. Building on this concept, George Foreman and Fleet Hill believe that play contributes to the constructive process, and coined the term *constructive play* to denote that which "builds on itself to increase the competence of the child."[1] They believe the competence children learn through play makes even more creative acts possible. In other words, competence leads to more and higher levels of competence.

Kinds of Play

Most of a child's play occurs with or in the presence of other children. *Social* play occurs when children play with each other in groups. The most comprehensive description and classification of children's play was applied by Mildred Parten in 1932; her classifications and terminology are still the most common and remain valid today.

- ☐ Unoccupied play—the child does not play with anything or anyone; he merely stands or sits, without doing anything observable
- ☐ Solitary play—although involved in play, the child plays alone, seemingly unaware of other children
- ☐ Onlooker play—the child watches and observes the play of other children; the center of interest is others' play
- ☐ Parallel play—the child plays by himself, but in ways similar to and with toys or materials similar to those of other children
- ☐ Associative play—children interact with each other, perhaps by asking questions or sharing materials, but do not play together
- ☐ Cooperative play—children actively play together, often as a result of organization of the teacher (the least frequently witnessed play in preschools)[2]

Social play allows children to interact with others, enabling them to talk to other children and learn about other points of view. Second, it provides a vehicle for communication. Children have others with whom to practice language and learn from. Third, it helps children learn impulse control; they realize they can't always do whatever they want. And fourth, in giving a child other children with whom to interact, social play negates isolation and helps children learn the interactions so vital to society. In Table 7–4, William Fowler identifies five kinds of play.

Value of Play

Play enhances social interaction and the development of social skills—learning how to share, getting along with others, taking turns, and generally learning how to live in a community. Play promotes physical development and body coordination and develops and refines small and large motor skills. Play helps children discover their bodies: how they function and how they can be used in learning.

Lifetime attitudes toward play develop in early childhood. Children learn motoric skills they will use as adults and learn that play can be restful, therapeutic, and satisfying. If children are taught that play is something one does only after all one's work is finished, or that it takes away from productive work, or is only for special occasions, children will have a negative attitude toward play, feel guilty about participating in it, and have a hard time integrating it into their adult lives.

Play assists in personality and emotional development, since children can try out different roles, release feelings, express themselves in a nonthreatening atmosphere, and consider the roles of others. Play enhances and promotes development in the cognitive, affective, and psychomotor areas. It helps children learn, acquire information, and construct their own intelligence. Through play, children develop schemes, find out how things work (and what won't work), and lay the foundation for

Each type of social play has a function in development. Label each of these pictures according to Parten's classification of play.

TABLE 7–4 Play in Infancy and Early Childhood

Type of Play	Name of Play	Characteristics of Play	Critical Factors of Play	Examples of Play
Type I	Exploratory-Manipulatory (object and pattern play)	Exploration of single objects; sensorimotor enjoyment, responses to environmental stimulation—forms basis for all play	Variety and complexity of toys; adult attention; relation to peers	Looking, listening, touching, feeling, tasting, smelling, moving
Type II	Instrumental (means-ends)	Plays to purposely accomplish things; how objects can be used as tools; object-object manipulation; employing objects to produce effects	Variety of materials; freedom to try things out; adults who encourage children to develop relationships	Puzzle activities, form boards, using objects as instruments
Type III	Construction-Creative	No single set of combinations or organization. Media-materials determine the organization; no predetermined goals; creation of a new form of structure	General learning experiences (a result of adult guidance and child's own activity); specific experiences in creative and building play	Building with blocks, tinker toys, etc.; painting; constructing; using clay
Type IV	Symbolic and Socio-dramatic	Mental play, use of language to symbolize things; visual imagery, use of words and phrases to carry ideas of things through play	Language development; props for play; opportunity to play	Using a tricycle as a truck; dress-up activities; make-believe roles
Type V	Language	Play with language; trying out language: rules of sound, grammar, and how words represent things	Use of language activities—stories, nursery rhymes, etc., with children; literary and conversational stimulation	Play with grammar forms and with meanings (calling a dog a cat)

Source: William Fowler, *Infant and Child Care: A Guide to Education in Group Settings* (Boston: Allyn and Bacon, 1980), pp. 148–58. Used by permission.

cognitive growth. Since play activities are interesting to children, play becomes naturally, or intrinsically, rewarding, and children engage in it for its own value. The interest of the child in his play also leads to a continually lengthened attention span.

The Role of the Teacher in Play

Teachers are the key to whether meaningful play, and therefore learning, occurs in the preschool. What teachers do and the attitudes they have toward play determine the quality of the preschool environment and the events that occur there. Teachers have these responsibilities in a quality play curriculum:

Children learn about and practice adult roles in their play.

1. Planning play experiences—incorporating play into the curriculum, identifying learning outcomes, and integrating specific learning activities with play. Play activities should match children's developmental needs and be free of sex stereotypes.
2. Providing time for play—including it in the schedule as a legitimate activity in its own right.
3. Creating environments for play—structuring indoor and outdoor learning environments to encourage play and support the role of play in learning.
4. Providing materials and equipment—materials and equipment should be appropriate to the children's developmental level and should support a non-sexist and multicultural curriculum.
5. Training assistants and parents in how to promote learning through play.
6. Supervising play activities—by participating in play, teachers help, show, and model when appropriate, and refrain from interfering when appropriate.
7. Observing children's play—teachers can learn how children play and the learning outcomes of play to use in planning classroom activities.

Informal or Free Play

Proponents of learning through spontaneous, informal play activities maintain that learning is best when it occurs in an environment that contains materials and people with whom children can interact. Learning materials may be grouped in centers with similar material and equipment—a kitchen center, a dress-up center, a block center, a music and art center, a water or sand area, and a free play center (usually with equipment such as tricycles, wagons, and wooden slides for promoting large muscle development).

The atmosphere of this kind of preschool setting tends to approximate a home setting, where learning is informal, unstructured, and unpressured. Talk and interactions with adults are spontaneous. Play and learning episodes are generally determined by the interest of the child and, to some extent, that of the teacher, based on what she thinks is best for children. The expected learning outcomes are socialization, emotional development, self-control, and tolerance for a school setting.

Three problems can result from a free play format. One is that many teachers interpret it to mean that children are free to do whatever they wish with whatever materials they want to use. Second, aside from seeing that children have materials to play with, teachers don't plan for special play materials, how they will interact with the materials, or what they are to learn while playing. Third, children are sometimes not held accountable for learnings from free play. Some teachers rarely question children about concepts or point out the nature of the learning. Teachers such as these are seldom part of the process. They act as disinterested bystanders, with their primary goal to see that children don't injure themselves while playing. In a good program of free play indoors and outside, teachers are active participants; sometimes they observe, sometimes they play with the children, sometimes they help the children, but they never intrude or impose.

Dramatic Play

Dramatic play allows children to participate vicariously in a wide range of activities associated with family living, society, and the culture of which they are a part. Dramatic play centers often include areas such as housekeeping, dress-up, occupations, dolls, school, and other situations that follow the children's interests. A skillful teacher can think of many ways to expand their interests. As this happens, she replaces old centers with new ones; for example, after a visit to the police station, a housekeeping center might be replaced by an occupations center.

In the dramatic play area, children have an opportunity to express themselves, assume different roles, and interact with their peers. Dramatic play centers thus act as a nonsexist and multicultured arena in which all children are equal. Teachers can learn a great deal about children by watching and listening to their dramatic play. For example, one teacher heard a child remark to the doll he was feeding that "you better eat all of this 'cause it's all we got in the house." Further investigation resulted in the teacher's linking up the family with a social service agency that helped them with emergency food and money.

Teachers must assume a proactive role in organizing and changing the dramatic play areas. They must set the stage for dramatic play and participate in play with the children. They must also encourage those who "hang back" and are reluctant to play and involve those who may not be particularly popular with the other children. Surprisingly, because of their background and environment, some children have to be taught how to play. In other words, as in all areas of early childhood education, teachers must deal with children's dramatic play in an individual and holistic way.

Medical play allows children to symbolically engage in health care procedures and can help alleviate children's fears of doctors, nurses, other health practitioners, and medical settings.

Medical Play

Medical play is the symbolic reproduction of medical procedures that will be used with a child. Materials include play medical furniture and supplies as well as real medical equipment and supplies. Medical play is used to reduce anxiety, correct misconceptions, teach about medical problems, and provide emotional support. Children use dolls as patients, with real stethoscopes and syringes, and pretend to perform procedures such as listening to the heartbeat and giving injections. This type of play is becoming popular with parents and medical personnel, who see it as an excellent way to meet the special needs that arise from the necessity of medical care.

Outdoor Play

What happens to children outside in a play or recreation area is just as important as what happens inside. However, outdoor play is often considered relatively unimportant, an opportunity for children to let off steam or excess energy. Children do need to relieve stress and tension through play, and outdoor activities do give this opportunity, but we should plan what we allow children to do and the equipment we make available. Outdoor time should not be only a chance for children to run wild.

Outdoor environments and activities promote large and small muscle development and body coordination as well as language development and social interaction. Teachers should plan for a particular child or group of children to move through progressively more difficult levels of running, climbing, and swinging. The outdoor area is a learning environment, and as such, the playground should be structured and designed according to learning objectives.

THE PRESCHOOL CURRICULUM

How do we determine an appropriate curriculum for four-year-olds? Some say society should decide the curriculum according to what it thinks children should learn and do. For example, Western society values knowing how to read and getting along with others; therefore, activities that help children do these things are included in the curriculum. Others say the public schools should guide the curriculum according to what children will have to learn and do in kindergarten and first grade. That kind of preschool curriculum would therefore include many "readiness" activities. (We will discuss readiness in Chapter 8.) Still others say the individual child should determine the curriculum according to what each knows or doesn't know; therefore, the starting place is the needs and interest of children.

Early childhood educators should always start with children and base their curriculum on them. What we teach is and should be based on child development, the needs of children, and what they are like as individuals. If this is done, then the curriculum will be child-centered and developmentally appropriate.

PRESCHOOL GOALS

All programs should have goals to guide activities and on which to base teaching methodologies. Without goals, it is easy to end up teaching just about anything without knowing why. Goals of individual preschools vary, but all programs should have certain essential goals. Simply because programs have goals, however, does not necessarily mean their teaching methods support or achieve those goals. This is a weakness of many preschools—there is a difference between what they say they do and what they actually do. Most good preschools, however, set minimum goals in at least a few of these areas: social and interpersonal skills, self-help and intrapersonal skills, building self-image, academics, thinking, learning readiness, language, and nutrition.

Social and Interpersonal Goals

☐ Helping children learn how to get along with other children, with adults, and how to develop good relationships with teachers
☐ Helping children learn to help others and develop caring attitudes

Self-help Skills/Intrapersonal Goals

☐ Modeling for children how to take care of their personal needs such as dressing (tying, buttoning, zipping) and knowing what clothes to wear
☐ Eating skills (using utensils, napkins, and a cup or glass, setting a table)
☐ Health skills (how to wash and bathe, how to brush their teeth)
☐ Grooming skills (combing hair, cleaning nails)

Self-image Goals

☐ Promoting self-help skills to help children develop good self-image and high self-esteem
☐ Helping a child learn about himself, his family, and his culture
☐ Developing a sense of self-worth by providing experiences for success and competence
☐ Teaching about body parts and their function

Academic Goals

☐ Teaching children to learn their names, addresses and phone numbers
☐ Facilitating children's learning of colors, sizes, shapes and positions such as under, over, and around
☐ Facilitating children's learning of numbers and prewriting skills, shape identification, letter recognition, sounds, and rhyming
☐ Providing for small-muscle development

Thinking Goals

☐ Providing an environment and activities that enable children to develop the skills essential to constructing schemes in a Piagetian sense—classification, seriation, numeration, and knowledge of space and time concepts

Learning Readiness Goals

☐ Facilitating readiness skills related to school success, such as following directions, learning to work by oneself, listening to the teacher, developing an attention span, learning to stay with a task until it is completed, staying in one's seat, and controlling impulses

Language Goals

☐ Providing opportunities for interaction with adults and peers as a means of developing oral language skills
☐ Helping children increase their vocabularies
☐ Helping children learn to converse with other children and adults
☐ Building proficiency in language

Nutrition Goals

☐ Providing experiences that enable children to learn the role of good nutritional practices and habits in their overall development
☐ Providing food preparation experiences
☐ Introducing children to new foods, a balanced menu, and essential nutrients

As of 1985, the Texas curriculum includes prekindergarten elements and sub-elements in five areas: communication development, cognitive development, motor development, fine arts, and social development; these are cognitive elements:

Cognition development, prekindergarten. Cognition development, prekindergarten, shall include the following essential elements:

- *Identifying.* The student shall be provided opportunities to:
  - match objects in a one-to-one correspondence such as a cup to saucer, napkin to plate (mathematics);
  - orally identify the number of objects in a group (mathematics);
  - recognize the empty set (concept of zero: mathematics);
  - discuss ways people can help each other (social studies);
  - know and practice rules of safety at home and school (social studies, science);
  - learn social skills appropriate to group behavior (social studies);
  - identify basic economic wants of people (food, clothing, shelter: social studies);
  - discuss how and why people celebrate special events, including those that are culturally related (birthdays, holidays: social studies);
  - know and observe rules of the home, classroom, and school (social studies);
  - know terms related to direction and location (up/down, near/far, above/below: social studies);
  - identify individuals who help students learn (family members, teachers: social studies);
  - demonstrate awareness of self in terms of name, age, and gender (social studies);
  - discuss what families do together (play, work: social studies);
  - use the senses to gain information about the environment using taste, smell, touch, sight, and sound (science); and
  - describe phenomena in the environment (science).

- *Comparing and contrasting.* The student shall be provided opportunities to:
  - use vocabulary to designate quantities such as more than, less than, equal to, as many as (mathematics);
  - use vocabulary to designate relationships such as under, over, above, below, in front of, far away from (mathematics);
  - learn the vocabulary to compare sets or groups (same as, different from, alike: mathematics);
  - demonstrate concepts of part and whole with manipulative materials (mathematics);
  - use vocabulary to compare objects (taller/shorter, heavier/lighter: social studies, science, mathematics); and

- compare similarities and differences among objects using taste, smell, touch, sight, and sound (science).

- *Classifying.* The student shall be provided opportunities to:
  - form groups by sorting and matching objects according to their attributes (mathematics);
  - combine and separate groups of objects to form new groups (mathematics);
  - identify property as "his/hers/mine/ours" (social studies);
  - classify acceptable/unacceptable behavior at home and school (social studies); and
  - sort objects from the environment according to one or more characteristics (use, composition, location: science).

- *Sequencing and ordering.* The student shall be provided opportunities to:
  - repeat a simple pattern using objects (mathematics);
  - order two or three objects by size (length, height: mathematics);
  - count orally (mathematics);
  - describe sequences in basic family and school routines (social studies); and
  - sequence events in order of their occurrence (science).

- *Predicting cause/effect relationships.* The student shall be provided opportunities to know and discuss the consequences of actions in social relationships (sharing, hitting, disturbing others: social studies).[3]

Developing Independence

Above and beyond the goals of promoting the skill areas, but subsumed in them, are two other goals of the preschool experience—to foster independence and a positive attitude toward learning. In many respects, the major goal of all education from preschool to university is to help students become independent. In addition, they should develop an attitude of liking to learn and wanting to come to school. In a sense, the entire school program should help children do things for themselves, to become autonomous. Some preschools and teachers foster an atmosphere of dependence, helplessness, and reliance on others by doing things for the children instead of helping children learn to do things for themselves. A good rule of thumb for all preschool educators is to avoid doing anything for a child that he can do or learn to do for himself. We can encourage independence by having children take care of their own environment. Children should be responsible for dusting, cleaning, washing, wiping, polishing, emptying waste baskets, vacuuming, and sweeping. Whether programs promote dependency or independence can be ascertained by comparing them to the scale in Table 7–5.

Developing the Whole Child

Preschool educators have always been concerned with the development of the whole child. This concern requires providing activities and experiences that promote growth and development in the physical, emotional, social, and cognitive areas.

TABLE 7–5 Preschool Environment Rating Scale for Independence

Practices that Foster Dependence	Practices that Encourage Independence
1. Teachers put children's wraps on	1. Teachers teach children how to put on their own wraps
2. Adults set table, put out napkins, pour drinks	2. Children set tables, put out napkins, pour own drinks
3. Adults serve children lunch, snack	3. Children serve themselves; preferably eat family style
4. Adults clean up after children	4. Children clean up after themselves
5. Adults feed children	5. Children are taught how to feed themselves
6. Children have to ask adults for materials and equipment	6. Children have reasonably free access to equipment and materials
7. Adults pass out and collect materials	7. Children are responsible for passing out, collecting, and organizing materials

Giving children some responsibility for the care and maintenance of the environment is one way to help them develop independence.

These areas are not separate and mutually exclusive—they are interrelated, and good programs try to balance activities to address these areas.

The Daily Schedule

Although there are various ways to implement a preschool's goals, most preschools operate according to a system of "free play"—self-selection of activities and learning centers. A daily schedule in a preschool program might go like this:

- [ ] *Opening activities:* As children enter, the teacher greets each individually. Daily personal greetings make the child feel important, build a positive attitude toward school, and provide an opportunity to practice language skills. They also give the teacher a chance to check each child's health and emotional status. Children usually don't arrive all at one time, so the first arrivals need something to do while others are arriving. Free selection of activities or letting children self-select from a limited range of quiet activities, such as puzzles, are appropriate. Some teachers further control this procedure by having children use an "Assignment Board" to help them make choices, limit the available choices, and help them practice concepts such as colors, shapes, and recognizing their names. Initially, the teacher can have the board beside her when children come and tell each child what the choices are. She can hand the child's name tag to her and let her put it on the board. Later, children can find their own names and put them up. At the first of the school year, each child's name tag can include his picture (use an instant camera) or a symbol or shape he has selected.
- [ ] *Group meeting/planning:* After all the children arrive, children and teacher plan together and talk about the day ahead. This is also the time for announcements, sharing, and group songs.
- [ ] *Learning centers:* After the group time, children are free to go to one of various learning centers, organized and designed to teach concepts. Table 7–6 lists types of learning centers and the concepts each is intended to teach.
- [ ] *Bathroom/handwashing:* Before any activity in which food is handled, prepared, or eaten, children should wash their hands.
- [ ] *Snacks:* After center activities, a snack is usually served. It should be nutritionally sound, and something the children can serve themselves.
- [ ] *Outdoor activity/play/walk:* Ideally, outside play should be a time for learning new concepts and skills, not just a time to run around aimlessly. Children can practice skills of climbing, jumping, swinging, throwing, and body control. Many walking trips and other events can be incorporated into outdoor play.
- [ ] *Bathroom/toileting:* Bathroom/toileting time provides a chance to teach health, self-help, and intrapersonal skills. Children should also be allowed to use the bathroom whenever necessary.
- [ ] *Lunch:* Lunch should be a relaxing time, and the meal should be served family style, with faculty and children eating together. Children should set

TABLE 7–6 Learning Centers

Center	Concepts
Housekeeping	Classification Language skills Sociodramatic play Functions Processes
Water/Sand	Texture Volume Quantity Measure
Blocks	Size Shape Length Seriation Spatial relations
Books/Language	Verbalization Listening Directions How to use books Colors, size Shapes Names
Puzzles/Perceptual Development	Size Shape Color Whole/part Figure/ground Spatial relations
Woodworking (pinewood; cardboard; styrofoam)	Following directions Functions Planning Whole/part
Art/Crafts/Sewing	Color Size Shape Texture Design Relationships

their own tables and decorate them with place mats and flowers they can make in the arts and crafts center or as a special project. Children should also be involved in cleaning up after meals and snacks.

☐ *Relaxation:* After lunch, children should have a chance to relax, perhaps to the accompaniment of stories, records, and music. This is an ideal time to teach the children breathing exercises and relaxation techniques.

☐ *Naptime:* Children who want or need to should have a chance to rest or sleep. For those who don't need it or can't sleep on a particular day, quiet activities should be available. Under no circumstances should children be "forced" to sleep or lie on a cot or blanket if they cannot sleep or have outgrown their need for an afternoon nap.

☐ *Bathroom/toileting*

☐ *Snack*

☐ *Centers or special projects:* Following naptime is a good time for center activities or special projects. (Special projects can also be conducted in the morning, and some may be more appropriate then, such as cooking something for snack or lunch.) Special projects might be cooking, holidays, collecting, work projects, crafts, and field trips.

☐ *Group time:* The day can end with a group meeting to review the day's activities. This serves the purpose of developing listening and attention skills, promotes oral communication, stresses that learning is important, and helps children evaluate their performance and behavior.

This preschool schedule is for a whole-day program; there are many other program arrangements. Some preschools operate half-day programs five days a week with only a morning session; others operate both a morning and afternoon session; others operate only two or three days a week. In still other programs, parents can choose how many days they will send their children. Creativity and meeting parent needs seem to be hallmarks of preschool programs.

NURSERY SCHOOL AT HERITAGE HOME

Happy Day Nursery School at Heritage Home is a licensed preschool educational program for two-and-a-half-, three- and four-year-old children, located in a nursing care facility.[4] Exposure of the children to nursing home residents is universal, but interaction is on a voluntary basis, and no child is forced to participate in activities in which old and young intermingle. Some children choose to mingle only insofar as they walk through the patients' day-rooms on the way to the playground, while others look forward to warm hugs and handshakes and even wheelchair rides. Most children do, however, become accustomed to the patients and come to see them as friends.

Holidays provide an opportunity for young and old to help each other prepare special treats or seasonal dishes such as apple sauce, cranberry relish, or Christmas cookies, and have parties together, with a patient playing Santa in a wheelchair at Christmas or the friendly treat-distributor on Halloween. Other activities patients and preschoolers share include listening to stories, watching mov-

Programs like that at Heritage Home give children an opportunity to interact with senior citizens and benefit both the young and the old.

ies, bowling with plastic balls and pins, singing, some creative movement, and special crafts projects. Children also visit from room to room, bringing their warmth and vitality to patients along with special holiday or birthday greetings. The experience of sharing time and space has been beneficial for both the children and the patients, and many "barriers" have been broken.

One day, several four-year-olds asked to go to the recreational area of the nursing home. Allegra found a likely audience to listen to her read from her favorite book. Nikki walked over to a woman in a wheelchair and shyly said "hello." The woman reached out her hands and Nikki gave her a warm embrace. Jamie, who had brought a piece of artwork done at home, showed it to a mentally disabled person who was unable to show any response. Elizabeth and Heather went beyond the recreational area and visited bedridden patients. Later in the morning, the entire group of preschoolers brought a birthday cake to a ninety-year-old woman who could not hold back the tears of joy.

The young children exhibit a great deal of compassion as well as curiosity and interest in the world around them. Even though they may not be able to conceptualize age as a life process, they are beginning to acknowledge the physical characteristics associated with it. They can "feel" that people may not all look and sound the same but that a meaningful relationship is still possible despite physical differences.

When they are first introduced to the residents, the children do not visit for very long, and they are often found to be staring—at a face with unfamiliar wrinkles, or at someone whose walk is very labored. After a few days of encouragement, their involvement with the residents begins to be spontaneous.

The children contribute their vitality to the home and interact in an atmosphere that they might otherwise never know. They do not share adults' aversion to a nursing home. They accept the elderly and infirm; they do not seem to be afraid of people with physical or mental disabilities, who may be unattractive or sometimes offensive. In their innocence, they can overlook the distasteful aspects of sickness and focus on qualities they relate to.

The children and residents have been instrumental in helping each other confront and accept death as a natural part of the life cycle. The children's favorite "grandma" often had fruit or candy for them; when she was close to death, the teachers tried to prepare the children. They commented on and asked the children how Mary seemed to them on their daily visits. Adults and children talked openly with Mary about her feelings whenever she or the children introduced the subject. The children saw Mary, their teachers, and their peers laugh, love, and weep, with the freedom to give expression to their feelings. When Mary died, there was anger and sadness, which later gave way to gladness that "Mary doesn't hurt anymore, and she still loves us." The interaction and bonding of old and young proved mutually beneficial.

SELECTING A GOOD EARLY CHILDHOOD PROGRAM

Parents often wonder how to select a good early childhood program. You may want to add to the following guidelines, but these should enable you to help others arrive at an enlightened decision.

☐ What are the physical accommodations? Is the facility pleasant, light, clean, and airy? Is this a physical setting one would want to spend time in? If not, children won't want to, either.

☐ Do the children seem happy and involved or passive? Is television used as a substitute for a good curriculum and good teachers?

☐ What kinds of materials are available for play and learning?

☐ Is the physical setting safe and healthy?

☐ Does the school have a written philosophy and objectives? Does the program philosophy agree with the parents' personal philosophy of how children should be reared and educated?

☐ Does the staff have written plans? Is there a smooth flow of activities or do children wait for long periods "getting ready" for another activity? Does the curriculum provide for skills in self-help, readiness for learning, and cognitive, language, physical, and social-emotional development? Lack of planning indicates lack of direction. Although a program whose faculty doesn't plan is not necessarily poor, planning is one indicator of a good program.

☐ What is the pupil-adult ratio? How much time do teachers spend with children on a one-to-one or small group basis? Do teachers take time to give children individual attention? Do children have an opportunity to be independent and do things for themselves? Are there opportunities for outdoor activities? Are children treated in a nonsexist manner? Are all children encouraged to participate in all activities?

☐ What kind of education or training does the staff have? It should have training in the curriculum and teaching of young children. The director should have a bachelor's degree in childhood education.

☐ How is lunch time handled? Are children allowed to talk while eating? Do staff members eat with the children?

☐ Can the director or a staff member explain the program? Describing a typical day can be helpful.

☐ How does the staff treat adults, including parents?

☐ Is the program affordable? If a program is too expensive for the family budget, parents may be unhappy in the long run; however, parents should inquire about scholarships, reduced fees, fees adjusted to income level, fees paid in monthly installments, and sibling discounts.

☐ Are parents of children enrolled in the program satisfied?

☐ Do the program's hours and services match parents' needs?

☐ How does the staff relate to children? Are the relationships loving and caring?

☐ How do staff members handle typical discipline problems, such as disputes between children? Is there a written discipline philosophy that agrees with the parents' philosophy?

☐ What are the provisions for emergency care and treatment? What other procedures are there for taking care of ill children?

Quality Programs in Public Schools

Among other organizations, the Southern Association on Children Under Six is concerned about the effects of public preschools for four-year-olds and has issued a position statement on quality four-year-old programs in public schools. The statement includes the following quality standards and procedures to avoid:

☐ The administrator or building principal should have a minimum of nine semester hours of early education courses with a focus on developmental characteristics of young children and appropriate programming.

☐ The teacher must hold a valid early childhood certificate; training must have included work with pre-kindergarten children; the training should meet the criteria of the NAEYC guidelines adopted as NCATE Standards for programs in four year institutions.

☐ The child must be age four by the same date identifying eligibility for entrance in kindergarten.

☐ The adult-child ratio should be 1-7, not to exceed 1-10; enrollment that exceeds ten requires the assignment of an additional responsible adult with training in early childhood education/child development.

- ☐ The session for the child should not be less than one half day.
- ☐ The daily schedule must be flexible, include a balance of free-choice and teacher initiated large and small group activities, and reflect the developmental needs of the whole child.
- ☐ The early childhood curriculum must be designed specifically for four year olds and must be appropriate for their developmental level and interests.
- ☐ The learning environment must be arranged in interest centers that provide for individual and group learning experiences.
- ☐ Materials, equipment, and supplies appropriate for a developmental curriculum must be available in sufficient quantities.
- ☐ The classroom must be equipped with movable furniture of correct size, have a water supply available and restroom facilities to accommodate four year old children.
- ☐ The outside play area must be accessible for flexible use; be properly equipped for climbing; riding and gross motor activities; and designed for the safety of the child including fencing.
- ☐ Minimum space requirements should be based on fifty square feet per child inside and one hundred square feet per child outside.
- ☐ The program must include a parent component: education, classroom visitation, and regular conferences to support the child's educational experience.
- ☐ A process must be established to provide communication among the early childhood programs in the school: four year olds, kindergarten, and primary grades.
- ☐ Appropriate developmental evaluation and observations must be conducted periodically to provide information for effective planning for meeting the individual needs of children.

Quality programs should avoid:

- ☐ The reassignment of upper elementary teachers who have no specialized training in early childhood education.
- ☐ The elimination of play and the opportunity for child selected activities.
- ☐ The use of watered down first grade curriculum that includes formal readiness activities, workbooks, and ditto sheets.
- ☐ The placement of children in desks or rows of chairs that inhibit an active learning environment.
- ☐ The accommodation of young children in facilities such as classroom, playground, cafeteria, and bathrooms that are designed for older children.
- ☐ The use of standardized skill tests rather than observations and informal evaluations to assess the needs of the young child.[5]

EFFECTIVENESS OF PRESCHOOL PROGRAMS

The eternal question about early childhood programs is, "Do they do any good?" During the last several years, a number of longitudinal studies were designed to answer this question. The Perry Preschool Study came to this conclusion:

Results to age 19 indicate lasting beneficial effects of preschool education in improving cognitive performance during early childhood; in improving scholastic placement and achievement during the school years; in decreasing delinquency and crime, the use of welfare assistance, and the incidence of teenage pregnancy; and in increasing high school graduation rates and the frequency of enrollment in post-secondary programs and employment.[6]

From an analysis of seven exemplary preschool programs, Schweinhart and Weikart reached this conclusion:

> The documented effects of early childhood education may be organized according to the major outcomes for participants at each period of their lives. These outcomes and the ages at which they occurred are: improved intellectual performance during early childhood; better scholastic placement and improved scholastic achievement during the elementary school years; and, during adolescence, a lower rate of delinquency and higher rates of both graduation from high school and employment at age 19. The best-documented preschool effect is an immediate improvement in intellectual performance as represented by intelligence test scores.[7]

ISSUES OF PRESCHOOL EDUCATION

A major issue of preschool education is whether programs operated by public schools are appropriate or "good." More and more four-year-olds are enrolled in preschool programs operated by the public schools, and many of the programs are academic in nature; the curriculum consists of many activities, concepts, and skills traditionally associated with kindergarten and first grade. Critics of public school programs for four-year-olds think this kind of program puts pressure on children because they aren't developmentally ready. Programs that emphasize academics cause children to experience failure and loss of self-esteem, and even possible depression, burn-out, and learning problems.

A second issue is whether public schools are the appropriate agencies to provide schooling for four-year-olds. Many feel that public school teachers lack the training to meet the unique needs of this age group, and that the public schools are motivated by a desire to gain control of this segment of education rather than to serve the preschoolers' educational needs.

A third issue is the problem of providing quality caregivers and teachers. The growing number of preschools for four-year-olds has created an increasing need for teachers and caregivers. Unfortunately, programs sometimes hire unqualified personnel; each day that brings new revelations of child abuse in centers and programs makes more apparent our inadequacy in screening people who work with children. In our rush to provide programs, we must not cut corners or compromise standards. Professionals have moral, ethical, and legal obligations to protect children and provide them with teachers of the highest quality. Part of this issue involves teacher certification—people who work with or teach preschoolers should have specific training and/or certification for that age group. To allow someone with inappropriate certification to teach preschoolers does an injustice to the concept of a developmentally appropriate curriculum.

Should four-year-olds be in public preschools? This is a fourth issue facing early childhood educators. Despite the trend toward earlier schooling, there is another group that feels school can wait:

Above all, the preschool years are a time for play. Let your child enjoy them. Parents today are being bombarded with advice and suggestions about ways in which, if they just do the right thing, they can make their children smarter and quicker and altogether more effective than they would have been without these special efforts.

"Maybe I don't spend enough time with him," "Maybe I ought to do more about teaching him to read," "Maybe I'm losing time when I just let him grow up naturally," are doubts that worry many young parents today. Even if you don't read the books that tell you how to increase your child's intelligence or how to raise a brighter child, there is a feeling in the air that parents ought to be doing something special about their children's minds.

We assure you, no matter what you read or what anybody tells you, it is not necessary to push your preschooler.[8]

Although enrollment of four-year-old children in public preschools is becoming popular with legislators and professional educators, it is not widely supported by the general public. A Gallup Poll asked, "Some educators have proposed that young children start school a year earlier, at age 4. Does this sound like a good idea or not?" Sixty-four percent of those asked said no. (Interestingly, 55 percent of the nonwhite population favors starting public schooling at age four.)[9]

A fifth issue is how to conduct a preschool program that is developmentally appropriate. Unfortunately, some preschool curricula are more suited to the kindergartener or first grader. Many programs operate under the false assumption that if it is good for kindergarten or first grade, the watered-down version is suitable for preschool. Professional and public organizations are calling the public's attention to the need to match the curriculum and activities of preschool programs to preschoolers' developmental levels, physically, cognitively, socially, and emotionally.

FURTHER READING

Adcock, Don, and Marilyn Segal. *Play and Learning* (Rolling Hills Estates, Calif.: B. L. Winch, 1979) Guide to learning through play for the two-year-old. Provides examples through disciplines and photos. Most of the information was collected through a series of home visits. Useful for both parents and teachers.

Ames, Louise Bates, and Joan Ames Chase. *Don't Push Your Preschooler* (New York: Harper and Row, 1980) Tells parents about the dangers of pushing their children. Points out that children learn to do a great many things without adult interference. Authors advise parents to relax and enjoy their children in the years before school and offer suggestions for helping children become ready for school and life. Explains the practical application of the maturation approach to development.

Beaty, Janice J. *Skills for Preschool Teachers,* 2nd ed. (Columbus, Ohio: Merrill, 1984) Excellent guideline for fulfilling CDA requirements. Helpful to anyone involved with early childhood education.

Brown, Janet F., ed. *Curriculum Planning for Young Children* (Washington, D.C.: National Association for the Education of Young Children, 1982) Collection of articles from *Young Children,* the journal of the National Association for the Education of Young Children. The articles help early childhood educators keep up with research and apply implications of research to everyday practice. Topics included are play, communication, exploring the world, and integrating the arts; final section presents techniques for implementing an effective curriculum.

Burtt, Kent Garland. *Smart Times: A Parent's Guide to Quality Time With Preschoolers* (New York: Harper and Row, 1984) Helps parents and early childhood educators put "quality" into "quality time." Contains over two hundred activities classified into 23 categories, from "Kitchen Companions" to "Skills for Writer-To-Be."

Cowe, Eileen Grace. *Free Play: Organization and Management in the Preschool and Kindergarten* (Springfield, Ill.: Charles C. Thomas, 1982) Informative and practical guide to organizing and managing free play.

Furman, Erna, ed. *What Nursery School Teachers Ask Us About: Psychoanalytic Consultations in Preschools* (Madison, Conn.: International Universities Press, 1986) Deals with questions nursery teachers ask; answers them in straightforward and nonauthoritarian way. The suggestions can be included in daily routines of programs. Chapters are easy to read and free from psychoanalytic jargon. Discussions of "The Roles of Parents and Teachers in the Life of the Young Child," "Separation and Entry to Nursery School," "Stress in the Nursery School," and "Discipline" are particularly interesting and insightful.

Gardner, Howard. *Artful Scribbles: The Significance of Children's Drawings* (New York: Basic Books Publishers, 1980) Interesting and informative insights into children and their art; places the child at the center of the discussion rather the art/product.

Green, Bernard. *Your Child is Bright: Make The Most of It* (New York: St. Martin's Press, 1982) Program for helping parents help their children achieve their best. Chapters on nutrition, communication, and "mind games." A variation on the traditional theme that parents are their children's best teachers.

Griffin, Eleanor Fitch. *Island of Childhood: Education in the Special World of Nursery School* (New York: Teachers College Press, 1982) An alternative to the emphasis of the back-to-basics movement. Author believes achieving relationships and healthy self-concepts are more important than early teaching of reading skills. Presents many ideas popular during the pre-Head Start years, which some feel need to be rediscovered.

Houle, Georgia Bradley. *Learning Centers for Young Children* (West Greenwich, R. I.: Tot-Lot Child Care Products, 1984) Wide variety of usable, practical learning centers for young children, each teacher-created and tested by the author. All utilize existing classroom materials and props. Each description is accompanied by a drawing of the center and the author's ideas of the educational values of the center and materials.

Mahoney, Ellen, and Leah Wilcox. *Ready, Set, Read: Best Books to Prepare Preschoolers* (Metuchen, N. J.: Scarecrow Press, 1985) Based on the principles that readers are made, not born, and that parents are children's first and most important teachers, provides practical and realistic ideas for laying the foundation for reading. Helps parents and others select the best in literature and art to share with children. Suggestions for reading aloud and promoting children's listening skills, art appreciation, and the desire to participate in the reading process. Organized according to developmental levels, beginning with the infant; provides insight into language development.

Sanoff, Henry, and Joan Sanoff. *Learning Environments for Children* (Atlanta, Ga.: Humanics Limited, 1981) From an architect and an educator, guidelines for helping teachers integrate child development with physical environments; many activities to help create learning environments.

Taylor, Katharine Whiteside. *Parents and Children Learn Together*, 3rd ed. (New York: Teachers College Press, 1981) First part deals with parent/parent and parent/child relationships and contemporary concerns such as single parents and parenting and working; second part outlines a plan for establishing parent-cooperative nursery schools.

FURTHER STUDY

1. Visit preschool programs in your area. Determine their philosophies and find out what goes on in a typical day. Which would you send your children to? Why?
2. Many people, including parents and teachers, think all learning occurs in school or schoollike settings. How do out-of-school and home activities contribute to children's learning?
3. Observe children's play to identify the types listed in the chapter.
4. Piaget believed that children construct schemes through play. Observe children's play, and determine what schemes you believe they are constructing.
5. How early do you think children should be enrolled in a preschool program? Interview parents and other educators for their opinions.
6. What do you think should be the basic purposes of a preschool program? Find out what your classmates think. How do your responses differ from theirs?
7. Observe children's play in a preschool program. How would you improve it? What other materials and equipment would you use?
8. Make a chart showing Fowler's five types of play and the six types of social play. Observe in a preschool, and see how many types you can identify.
9. Survey preschool parents to learn what they expect from a preschool program. How do parents' expectations compare to the goals of preschool programs you visited?
10. Tell how you would promote learning through a specific preschool activity. For example, what learning outcomes would you have for a sand/water area? What, specifically, would be your role in helping children learn?
11. Develop goals and objectives for a preschool program. Write a daily schedule that would support your goals.
12. Visit a preschool program and request to see their program goals. How do they compare to those listed in this chapter? What would you change, add, or delete?
13. Outline what you would expect to see in a preschool program based on its program goals. Also list at least five things you would like to see in a typical preschool classroom.
14. Review the information you gathered on your visit to a preschool program and assess how this program is preparing children for their formal school encounter.
15. Compare the philosophies of a day care center, a nursery program, and a preschool program. How are they alike? How are they different?
16. Read articles that define today's trend in establishing quality preschool programs. What are the first three issues discussed? Do you agree with these issues? If not, why?
17. Develop an activity file for a preschool program. Is it easier to find materials for some areas than for others? Why?
18. Gather information both for and against early schooling and learning. Which do you now favor? Why?
19. Interview parents of young children to determine what they look for in a good preschool program. How does what parents look for compare to the guidelines in this chapter?
20. List preschool program resources, including magazines, journals, books, and other materials, that will enrich your future experiences with preschool age children.

8

Kindergarten Education: More Than ABC's

As you read and study:

Trace the history of kindergarten programs from Froebel to the present

Identify and critique goals and objectives for kindergarten programs

Examine the concept of readiness and develop a personal philosophy concerning readiness for learning

Critique the pros and cons of the ages for entrance to kindergarten

Conceptualize and articulate a personal philosophy of kindergarten education

Examine and critique kindergarten programs and schedules

Examine and critique screening programs used in kindergarten programs

Identify and examine issues confronting kindergarten education

KINDERGARTEN EDUCATION: HISTORY AND FUTURE DIRECTION

Froebel's educational concepts and kindergarten program were imported into the United States virtually intact by individuals who believed in his ideas and methods. Froebelian influence remained dominant for almost half a century, until John Dewey and his followers challenged it in the early 1900s. While Froebel's ideas seem perfectly acceptable today, there were not acceptable to those in the mid-eighteenth century who subscribed to the notion of early education. Especially innovative and hard to accept was that learning could be based on play and children's interests—in other words, child-centered. Most European and American schools were subject-oriented and emphasized teaching basic skills. In addition, Froebel was the first to advocate a communal education for young children *outside* the home. Until Froebel, young children were educated in the home, by their mothers. Although Froebel advocated this method too, his ideas for educating children as a group, in a special place outside the home, were revolutionary.

Credit for establishing the first kindergarten in the U.S. is accorded to Margarethe Schurz. After attending lectures on Froebelian principles in Germany, she returned to the U.S. and, in 1855, at Watertown, Wisconsin, opened her kindergarten. Schurz's program was conducted in German, as were many of the new kindergarten programs of the time, since Froebel's ideas of education appealed to many bilingual parents. Schurz also influenced Elizabeth Peabody, the sister-in-law of Horace Mann, when, at the home of a mutual friend, Mrs. Schurz explained the Froebelian system. Peabody was not only fascinated, but converted.

Elizabeth Peabody opened her kindergarten in Boston in 1860. She and her sister, Mary Mann, also published a book, *Kindergarten Guide*. Peabody almost immediately realized that she lacked grounding in the necessary theory to adequately implement Froebel's ideas. She visited kindergartens in Germany, then returned to the U.S. to popularize Froebel's methods. Elizabeth Peabody is generally credited as the main promoter of the kindergarten in the U.S. An event that also helped advance the kindergarten movement was the appearance of appropriate materials. In 1860, Milton Bradley, the toy manufacturer, attended a lecture by Elizabeth Peabody, became a convert to the concept of kindergarten, and began to manufacture Froebel's gifts and occupations.

The first *public* kindergarten was founded in St. Louis, Missouri, in 1873 by Susan E. Blow, with the cooperation of the St. Louis superintendent of schools, William T. Harris. Elizabeth Peabody had corresponded for several years with Harris, and the combination of her prodding and Susan Blow's enthusiasm and knowledge convinced Harris to open a public kindergarten on an experimental basis. Endorsement of the kindergarten program by a public school system did much to increase its popularity and spread the Froebelian influence within early childhood education. In addition, Harris, who later became the U.S. Commissioner of Education, encouraged support for Froebel's ideas and methods.

Training for kindergarten teachers has figured prominently in the development of higher education. The Chicago Kindergarten College was founded in 1886 to teach mothers and train kindergarten teachers. In 1930, the Chicago Kindergarten College became the National College of Education. In 1888, in Boston, Massachusetts, Lucy Wheelock opened a kindergarten training program. Known as the Wheelock School, it became Wheelock College in 1949.

The kindergarten movement in the United States was not without growing pains. Over a period of time, the kindergarten program, at first ahead of its time, became rigid, and methods- and teacher-centered rather than child-centered. By the turn of the century, many kindergarten leaders thought kindergarten programs and training should be open to experimentation and innovation, rather than rigidly follow Froebel's ideas. The chief defender of the Froebelian status quo was Susan Blow. In the more moderate camp was Patty Smith Hill, who thought that, while the kindergarten should remain faithful to Froebel's ideas, it should nevertheless be open to innovation. She believed that to survive, the kindergarten movement would have to move into the twentieth century. She was able to convince many of her colleagues and, more than anyone else, is responsible for the survival of the kindergarten as we know it today.

Patty Smith Hill's influence is evident in the format of many present-day preschools and kindergartens. Free, *creative* play, where children can use materials as they wish, was Hill's idea, and represented a sharp break with Froebelian philosophy. She also introduced large blocks and centers where children could engage in housekeeping, sand and water play, and other activities as they wished, rather than as the teacher dictated.

Many preschool activities have their basis in adult "occupations." Froebel had children engage in building, carpentry, sewing, and sweeping; many Montessori activities (see chapter 3) were conceived for the same purpose. They chose these activities because many adult activities, such as "building" with blocks and carpentry, appeal to children; educators have also long believed that learning materials and activities could be used to introduce children to the world of work. For example, William Harris was interested in the kindergarten because he thought children could be better prepared for industrial society if they had some understanding of adult occupations.

Were Froebel alive today, he would probably not recognize the program he gave his life to developing. Many kindergarten programs are subject-centered rather than child-centered as Froebel envisioned them. Furthermore, Froebel did not see his program as a "school," but as a place where children could develop through play. Although kindergartens are evolving to meet the needs of society and families, we must not forget the philosophy and ideals on which the first kindergartens were based.

WHO IS KINDERGARTEN FOR?

Froebel's kindergarten was for children three to seven years of age; in the U.S., kindergarten has been considered the year before children enter first grade. Since the age at which children enter first grade varies, however, the ages at which they enter kindergarten also vary. People tend to think that kindergarten is for five-year-old children rather than four-year-olds, and most teachers tend to support an older rather than a younger entrance age because they think "older" children are more "ready" for kindergarten and learn better.

The entrance age for kindergarten often creates controversy, usually because parents want an earlier entrance age and teachers want a later entrance age. Some states and districts make exceptions to their age requirements by testing children for early admittance, which creates further controversy over what test to use and what score to use as a cutoff point. Decisions for early entrance are sometimes based on children's behaviors in a kindergarten setting. Children and their parents may attend a special kindergarten day during the summer or early fall, before the beginning of school, so teachers can judge children's readiness for school and learning. Their judgments determine whether children are admitted to kindergarten early.

There is wide public support for tax-supported public kindergartens *and* for making kindergarten attendance compulsory. A Gallup Poll showed that 80 percent of the respondents favored "making kindergarten available for all those who wish it as part of the public school system"; 71 percent favored compulsory kindergarten attendance; and 70 percent think children should start school at ages four or five (29 percent favored age four and 41 percent favored age five).[1] The question today is not so much whether a child will attend kindergarten, but when.

Universal Kindergarten

Kindergarten has rapidly become universal for the majority of the nation's five-year-olds. Today, kindergarten is either a whole or half-day program and within the reach of most of the nation's children, as shown in Table 8–1. As with four-year-olds, the number of five- and six-year-olds projected to attend preschool or kindergarten is dramatic, as shown in Table 8–2.

Yet, much remains to be accomplished. In a survey of early childhood consultants at state departments of education, it was found that:

TABLE 8–1   Preschool Enrollment: 1970 to 1982

Year	Percentage of 5-Year-Olds Enrolled
1970	69.3%
1972	76.1
1974	78.6
1976	81.4
1978	82.1
1980	84.7
1982	83.4

Source: "The Statistical Trends," *The Principal*, 16 (May 1985), p. 16.

TABLE 8–2 Projected Trends in Preschool Enrollment by Age: 1985 to 1993 (in thousands)

	Public Schools (age)		Private Schools (age)	
Year	5 Years	6 Years	5 Years	6 Years
1985	2,490	295	508	41
1986	2,514	299	510	43
1987	2,550	302	512	44
1988	2,580	306	515	44
1989	2,614	309	522	44
1990	2,644	314	529	46
1991	2,667	318	533	46
1992	2,683	321	537	46
1993	2,693	323	538	46

Source: "The Statistical Trends," *The Principal,* 16 (May 1985), p. 16.

Kindergarten has become almost universal for 5- and 6-year-olds. Good kindergartens give children the experiences they need for success in school.

Differences among the states in all categories surveyed are apparent. For example in 44 of the 50 states and the District of Columbia, kindergarten is provided for all students who request it; [in many states, kindergarten is offered on a voluntary basis for children whose parents request it for them;] in 6 states, it is not. In the latter states, five-year-olds are selected for the most part on a lottery basis for admission to kindergarten classes.[2]

There is a big difference between having kindergarten available to parents who request it and a compulsory program for all children. Children who would most benefit are often not enrolled when kindergarten is offered on a voluntary basis.

School Starts in Quandary[3]

The 4- and 5-year-olds working on polliwog badges at neighborhood pools this summer probably aren't giving kindergarten a thought. But some of their parents are.

Johnny might be a good example. He will be 5 on Oct. 16. He's bright, eager, tall for his age. His parents are convinced he belongs in kindergarten this year even though the cutoff date is Sept. 30. After all, Susie down the street, who was 5 in June, is tiny, shy and obviously immature and she's going.

While the majority of children start school as scheduled and no questions asked, every year a few prompt a lot of questions.

In the Pickerington Local School district, for example, school psychologist Tim McManus gets up to 20 calls every summer from parents wanting their 4-year-olds in school.

"People here are achievement oriented," McManus said. When, through testing, he finds a child is eligible, "I try to look ahead" with the parents, he said.

In high school, the early entrant might keep up academically, but what about other areas—will he be big enough for sports; will he be ready for dating; will he be the only one in his class not driving?

Truly gifted children usually cope with those situations, McManus said, because they tend to be well developed in other ways, too. But the questions are enough to make some parents keep their almost-5-year-olds home.

One year, three out of 12 early entry applicants in Pickerington were accepted; another year, one out of 10. But, McManus said he is "not sure what it gets them."

In Columbus last year, only 5 percent of the 120 youngsters applying entered early.

Late starts are even less popular in the two districts. Edward Matthews, head of psychological services for Columbus Public Schools, said he could remember only two requests for testing last year from parents considering holding back their children.

Pickerington officials can remember only one student in the last two years they thought should wait a year.

"If a kid has severe problems, we want him in the educational system so we can start providing for him," McManus said.

But late starts aren't so rare in Worthington. While early entry is being sought for 11 youngsters there this summer, parents of another 23 want their kids held out a year even though they meet the age requirement now, said Bruce Emery, executive director of education.

He expects permission will be granted for as many as 12 of the 23.

Psychologist Bruce Stevenson explained, "There are geographical pockets in Worthington" that strongly believe in either early or late starts.

Some parents don't even ask for school officials' advice before holding their children out an extra year. For example, last fall at Worthington Estates Elementary School, eight kindergartners were a year older than most of their peers.

In Westerville, 25 to 30 kindergarten-age youngsters are held back each year after screening, said Michael Hayfield, elementary curriculum director.

Boys with summer birth dates are most likely to be held back. Educators attribute that to a tendency among boys to develop more slowly than girls at that age. If a child is immature, he is likely to perform that way in preschool, McManus said.

"If there's any question, it's better to have them tested. It costs the parents nothing," said Peggy Blevins, a former special education teacher who is opening Westminster Village Prekindergarten Developmental Class in September.

Some districts screen all entering kindergarten pupils, mainly to acquaint teachers with the level of their pupils' development. Others screen only if parents ask.

Screening tests vary, but typically, pupils are asked their names and telephone numbers; to identify primary colors and pictures of objects; to handle paper and pencil; to define words. The words can range from a simple household word, such as "table," to the more abstract, such as "laziness."

Blevins is convinced a sizable number of 5-year-olds aren't ready for kindergarten and said her program "will be as individualized as possible," with a teacher and aide for each 10 pupils. They'll concentrate on language development and fine and gross motor skills, Blevins said.

SCHOOL READINESS: WHO GETS READY FOR WHOM?

In discussions of preschool programs, no issue generates as much heat as school readiness. Some school districts have raised the entrance ages for admittance to kindergarten and first grade and require that children be five years old by the first of September to be admitted to kindergarten. This decision is based on the reasoning that many children are "not ready," and teachers therefore have difficulty teaching them. There is renewed emphasis on getting children ready for life events and processes such as child care, nursery school, preschool, kindergarten, and first grade. The early childhood education profession is reexamining "readiness," its many interpretations, and the various ways the concept is applied to educational settings.

For most parents and early childhood educators, readiness means the child's ability to participate and succeed in beginning schooling. Readiness includes a child's ability, at a given time, to accomplish activities and engage in processes associated with schooling, whether nursery school, preschool, kindergarten, or first grade. *Readiness* is thus the sum of a child's physical, cognitive, social, and emotional development at a particular time. Readiness does not exist in the abstract—it must relate to something. Increasingly, in today's educational climate, readiness is measured against the process of formal public schooling. By the same token, a child's lack of readiness may be considered a deficit and a detriment, because it indicates a lack of what is needed for success in kindergarten and first grade.

Promoting Readiness

Some early childhood educators and many parents believe that time cures all things, including lack of readiness. They believe that as time passes, a child grows and develops physically and cognitively and, as a result, becomes ready to achieve. This belief is manifested in school admissions policies that advocate children's remaining out of school for a year if they demonstrate lack of readiness as measured by a readiness test. Assuming that the passage of time will bring about readiness is similar to the concept of unfolding, popularized by Froebel. Unfolding implies that development is inevitable and certain and that what a child will be, the optimum degree of development, is determined by heredity and a maturational timetable or biological clock. Froebel likened children to plants and parents and teachers to gardeners whose task is to nurture and care for children so they can mature according to their genetic inheritance and maturational timetable. The concept of unfolding continues to be a powerful force in early childhood education, although many have begun to challenge it as an inadequate and outmoded concept.

The modern popularizer of the concept of unfolding was Arnold Gesell (1880–1961), whose ideas and work continue at the Gesell Institute of Human Development in New Haven, Connecticut. Gesell made fashionable and acceptable the notion of inherent maturation that is *predictable, patterned,* and *orderly.*[4] He also created a number of tests to measure this development, from which he constructed a series of developmental or behavioral norms that specify in detail children's motor, adaptive, language, and personal-social behavior according to chronological age. Gesell also coined the concept of *developmental age* to distinguish children's developmental growth from chronological age; for example, a child who is five years old may have a developmental age of four because he demonstrates the behavioral characteristics of a four-year-old rather than a five-year-old. Gesell believed that parents make their greatest contribution to readiness by providing a climate in which children can grow without interference in their innate timetable and blueprint for development. The popularity of this *maturationist view* has led to a persistent sentiment that children are being hurried to grow up too soon. More critics of early education say that we should let children be children, and not push them into readiness for learning.

Self-education also promotes readiness. The self-education viewpoint stresses the roles children play in their own learning. In most discussions of readiness, people talk as though children play no part in it, giving all the credit to maturation and heredity. All great educators, however, have stressed the role children play in their own development. Froebel talked about unfolding, Maria Montessori advocated auto- or self-education, and Piaget stressed the active involvement of the child in the process of cognitive development. The primary pedagogical implication of self-readiness is that children must be involved in developing their own readiness. Time alone is not sufficient to account for or provide children with the skills they need for school success.

For Froebel, play was the energizer, the process that promotes unfolding. Froebel developed his gifts and occupations to help teachers involve children in play. Montessori believed the prepared environment, with its wealth of sensory materials specifically designed to meet children's interests, is the principle means to help children educate themselves. For Piaget, the physically and mentally active child in an environment that provides for assimilation and accommodation develops the mental schemes necessary for productive learning.

Self-education is child-centered, not subject- or teacher-centered. Children play the star roles in the drama of learning; teachers are the supporting cast. Child-centered readiness programs provide children with enriched environments of material and human resources where they can play and enhance their own development while they construct those cognitive schemes essential for readiness and, ultimately, school success. Concerning self-education, Caroline Pratt said about her famous Play School, "The attempt in the play school has been to place children in an environment through which by experiment with that environment they may become self-educated."[5]

For some children, the home is such an environment; other children lack the enriched environment necessary to fully support their efforts of self-education. Unfortunately, some five-year-olds are denied admission to kindergarten programs because they are not "ready" and spend another year in a sterile home or program environment that has failed to support the growth and development necessary to be ready for the schooling experience.

Providing young children with *quality* preschool programs is another way to promote and assure their readiness. As more and more kindergarten teachers see that children are not ready for basic skills curricula, agencies such as Head Start, child care centers, and public schools have implemented programs for three- and four-year-olds to provide the activities and experiences necessary for kindergarten success. Since 1983, Texas state law mandates that all deprived children attend a public school program for three- and four-year-olds, and Dade County, Florida, received a special $250,000 state grant to begin public school programs for that age group.

What Constitutes Readiness for Learning?

In all the rhetoric associated with readiness, the readiness skills are sometimes overlooked. The areas of readiness skills and behaviors include language, independence, impulse control, interpersonal skills, experiential background, and physical and mental health.

- ☐ Language is the most important readiness skill. Children need language skills for success in school and life. Important language skills include receptive language, such as listening to the teacher and following directions; expressive language, demonstrated in the ability to talk fluently and articulately with teacher and peers, the ability to express oneself in the language of the school, and the ability to communicate needs and ideas; and symbolic language, knowing the names of people, places, and things, words for concepts, and adjectives and prepositions.

- ☐ Independence means the ability to work alone on a task; the ability to take care of oneself; and the ability to initiate projects without always being told what to do. Independence also includes the ability to master and use self-help skills, including but not limited to dressing skills, health skills (toileting, handwashing, using a handkerchief, and brushing teeth), and eating skills (using utensils, napkins, serving oneself, and cleaning up).

- ☐ The ability to control impulses includes a cluster of behaviors that make it possible for children to become meaningfully involved in the learning process. Children who are not able to control their impulses are frequently (and erroneously) labeled hyperactive or learning disabled. Controlling impulses includes working cooperatively with others and not hitting others or interfering with their work; developing an attention span that permits involvement in learning activities for a reasonable length of time; and the ability to sit and stay seated for a period of time.

- ☐ Interpersonal skills are those of getting along with and working with others, including peers and adults. Asked why they want their child to attend a preschool program, parents frequently respond, "To learn how to get along with others." Any child care or preschool program is an experience in group living, and children have the opportunity to interact with others so as to become successful in a group setting. Interpersonal skills include cooperating with others; learning and using basic manners; and most important, learning how to learn from others.

- ☐ Experiential background is important to readiness because experiences are the building blocks of knowledge, the raw materials of cognitive development. They provide the context for mental disequilibrium, which enables children to develop higher levels of thinking. Children must go places—the grocery store, library, zoo—and they must be involved in activities—crafts, building things, painting, coloring, experimenting, and discovering. Children can build only on the background of information they bring to a new experience. If they have had limited experiences, they have little to build on and cannot build well.

- ☐ Children must have the physical and mental health necessary to participate in a full day of learning activities. They must have good nutritional and physical habits that will enable them to fully participate in and profit from any program. They must also have positive and nurturing environments and caregivers so as to develop a self-image for achievement.

These are some other points to keep in mind about readiness:

1. Readiness is a never-ending process. It does not exist only in the preschool years, although we often think of it that way. We are always in need of knowledge, skills, experiences, compassion, and understanding that will help us learn about and participate in the next learning event. We should not think of readiness as something a child does or does not have, but should view it as a constant state—a continuum throughout life.

2. All children are always ready for some kind of learning. Children always need experiences that will promote learning and get them ready for the next step in the process of schooling. As early childhood educators, we should constantly ask "What does the child know? What can I do to help him move to the next level of understanding?"

3. Schools and teachers should get ready for children, not the other way around. Rather than make children get ready for our predetermined curricula and notions of what learning is about, we should rededicate ourselves to the ideal that schools are for children. As it stands, many public schools want children to be ready for predetermined and preconceived programs. In this respect, schools have their priorities reversed. Schools should provide programs based on the needs of children, not on preconceived notions of what children ought to be able to do. Teachers should provide whatever program is necessary for children to learn.

WHAT SHOULD KINDERGARTEN BE LIKE?

To decide what the kindergarten should be like, it is instructive to go back to Froebel:

> The Kindergarten is an institution which treats the child according to its nature; compares it with a flower in a garden; recognizes its threefold relation to God, man and nature; supplies the means for the development of its faculties, for the training of the senses, and for the strengthening of its physical powers. It is the institution where a child plays with children.[6]

But comparing Froebel's vision of the kindergarten to today's kindergartens, we find them light years apart. Today's kindergarten is centered on basic skills, learning objectives, tests, check lists, and state minimum standards. As the public and professional debate goes on over the appropriate purposes and content of kindergarten programs, more organizations and agencies issue statements for refocusing attention on what is best for children. The Nebraska Department of Education offers these suggestions for a good kindergarten program:

☐ Parents and school personnel work cooperatively to build a partnership between home and school that will support the child throughout the school experience . . . . . . not a place where the expectations of the parents and the school are in conflict or where parents feel isolated from their child's experience.

☐ Children experience a planned, child centered environment that encourages learning through exploration and discovery . . . not a sit-down-be-quiet classroom dominated by desks, paper and workbooks.

☐ Children have access to multilevel experiences and activities of varying degrees of complexity. They should be able to use concrete materials which allow for individual differences and natural variations in each one's ability to perform ...

... not a place where all children are expected to perform the same task, reach the same level of performance, and accomplish the same objectives.

☐ Children can make choices and decisions within the limits of the materials provided ...

... not a largely teacher-directed room where children seldom choose.

☐ Children learn there is often more than one right answer. Divergent thinking is developed and encouraged through use of open-ended materials and many informal conversations among the children and with adults ...

... not a place where the day's activities are largely dominated by worksheets and discussions with predetermined answers.

☐ The children's own language, experiences, and stages of development form the basis of reading and writing activities ...

... not the almost universal use of commercial, formal pre-reading and early-reading programs.

☐ Children learn to enjoy books and to appreciate literary language through a daily storytime, creative dramatics and repeated opportunities to hear and learn simple rhymes and other poems ... not a place where the day is too short for storytime and the opportunity to appreciate literature comes only by way of educational television.

☐ Children participate in daily, planned activities fostering both gross and fine motor development, including such activities as running, jumping, bouncing balls, lacing cards, hammering nails, playing with clay, etc. ... not a place where children are expected to sit quietly for long periods of time and perform the motor skills beyond the current ability of many of them.

☐ Children develop mathematical understanding through use of familiar materials such as sand, water, unit blocks and counters ... not a place where children are asked to mark an X on the right answer in a work book.

☐ Children's curiosity about natural, familiar elements forms the basis of scientific observations, experimentation and conclusions. Both planned and spontaneous interaction with plant, animals, rocks, soil, water, etc., is considered to be essential ... not a place where science is included only when time permits or where the books tell outcomes and the teachers do the experiments.

☐ Experimentation, enjoyment and appreciation of varied forms of music are encouraged on a daily basis ... not a place where music is included only when time permits.

☐ Art expression is encouraged through the use of a wide assortment of media integrated within the daily curriculum ... not a place where art usually consists of copying a model, coloring a ditto or cutting and pasting a pattern, and/or where art is delegated to the specialist.

☐ All the activities are planned to promote a positive self-image and attitude toward school and peers ... not a place where the child's worth is measured only by his/her ability to conform to expectations.

☐ Play is respected for its value as an appropriate learning medium for children of this age ... not a place where play is deemphasized because the child "played enough" in preschool and should be ready for "real" learning.[7]

There are specific skills that teachers should help kindergarten children acquire to help them learn better.

Basic Skills Orientation

There is a great deal of tension between those who advocate a readiness-play orientation to kindergarten and those who advocate a basic skills orientation. For example, Florida, the first state to mandate compulsory kindergarten education for all five-year-olds (five by September 1), has a Primary Education Program that requires screening all children within the first six weeks of school for placement into one of three instructional groups: developmental (normal grade level); enrichment (above grade level), and preventative (below grade level). In Dade County, Florida, the nation's fourth largest school district, the kindergarten program operates according to a "balanced curriculum," where basic objectives and minimal instructional times are specified for subject matter areas. These are the objectives for language arts in the specific area of language development:

20. listen and respond to simple oral directions.
21. repeat short sentences in correct order.
22. associate pictures with text read aloud.
23. expand speaking vocabulary using new words correctly.
24. describe in an oral sentence objects, pictures, or events he/she has experienced.
25. demonstrate understanding of positional prepositions, adverbs (i.e., above, below, on, etc.).
26. identify differences between questions and statements and respond appropriately.
27. read simple words.
28. read simple sentences/stories developed in language experience activity.[8]

These are two areas in the Dade County mathematics objectives for kindergarten:

Geometry

1. identify figures: circle, square, triangle, rectangle.
2. compare size, shape: same, different.
3. identify positions: over, under, above, below, between, in the middle of, up, down, bottom, top, on, off, next to, beside, around, in front of, behind, in back of, to the right of, to the left of, inside, outside.

Measurement

4. compare length: longer (est), shorter (est), farther (est), near (est).
5. compare area: more, less, smaller (est), larger (est).
6. compare volume: empty, full, more, less, least, most.
7. compare weight: lighter (est), heavier (est).[9]

This trend toward basic skills teaching in the kindergarten, while much criticized by traditional kindergarten educators and early childhood educators, will likely continue. More and more parents and teachers contend that "kindergarten is no longer a year of milk and cookies; it is the first year of the school experience."

Full- or Half-Day Kindergarten

There are both half-day and full-day kindergarten programs. A school district that operates a half-day program usually offers one session in the morning and one in the afternoon, so that one teacher can teach two classes. Although many kindergartens are half-day programs, there is not general agreement as to whether this system is best. Those who argue for the half-day session say that this is all the schooling the five-year-old child is ready to experience and that it provides an ideal transition to the all-day first grade. Those in favor of full-day sessions generally feel that not only is the child ready for and capable of a program of this length, but that it also allows for a more comprehensive program. We also find other patterns of kindergarten programs, particularly where attendance is not compulsory. Of the various attendance patterns in kindergarten programs, we might find these possibilities in a full-day session:

- ☐ Child attends all day every day.
- ☐ Child attends morning only.
- ☐ Child attends afternoon only.
- ☐ Child attends 1 or more days a week, e.g., Mon/Wed/Fri; or Tues/Thurs; or any other combination.

These are possible attendance patterns for a half-day session:

- ☐ Child attends the A.M. or P.M. session every day.
- ☐ Child attends A.M. or P.M. session one or more days a week in various combinations.
- ☐ Child attends A.M. sessions some days and P.M. sessions some days.

Individualized learning activities focus on specific needs and abilities and allow teachers to continually assess children's achievement. Individualized attention also helps keep children at the center of the teaching/learning process.

Rest in the Kindergarten

Some people think kindergarten-age children tire easily and, especially in an all-day kindergarten, need a chance to rest or sleep. Others believe that most kindergarten children have more energy and stamina than we give them credit for. Besides, the kindergarten curriculum is usually so full that there really isn't time for rest.

There are several ways to handle the issue of rest periods. First, parents can be encouraged to have their children get enough rest at home to be able to participate in a full day's activities. Through newsletters and personal notes, teachers can tell parents how important it is for their children to get eight or more hours of sleep a night, or however much the child needs so as not to be tired during the day. Second, the teacher can explain the importance of rest to the children. Friendly reminders from teachers about the importance of sleep may have more impact than admonishments from parents. Third, every early childhood program should allow time for relaxing with quiet activities. Young children need time to pause and listen to stories, look at books, converse, and refresh themselves. Teachers should build resting-reflective times into their programs. Listening to the teacher read a story is a wonderful way to rest and unwind.

If kindergarten teachers and administrators believe in a rest time, it should be individualized for each child. A child should not be forced to remain on a cot or mat long after it is apparent that he isn't going to sleep. Also, a sensitive and observant kindergarten teacher knows which children need a nap and which do not. If the policy is not to nap, there may be occasions when a particular child needs to sleep and should be allowed to do so. Likewise, if the policy is to nap or rest, children who don't need to should be given alternative activities.

Teachers also need to keep in mind that what is appropriate at the beginning of the school year may not be appropriate later; children who need a nap at the beginning of the school year may quickly outgrow the need. More importantly, teachers must recognize the necessity of providing children with a curriculum and range of activities that incorporates both active and quiet times. Children should also have opportunities to engage in group and individual activities that accommodate their learning styles and temperaments. Individualizing the curriculum addresses many questions about what is appropriate for children, including the need for rest.

Representative Schedules

Table 8–3 shows a sample schedule of a half-day, socially- and cognitively-oriented kindergarten program. Figure 8–1 is a full-day program schedule. Figure 8–2 is the schedule one teacher has worked out for her kindergarten.

TABLE 8–3 Half-Day Kindergarten Schedule

Time	Activity
8:30	Arrival-free time—children select an activity from a group of prearranged activities such as puzzles, games, books, and records which stress cognitive learning.
9:00	Circle time—conversation which emphasizes plans for the day's activities. Can also include discussion of previous day's work.
9:15	Language development program—can be either teacher-designed or a commercial kit, such as Peabody Language Kits, and Alpha-Time.
9:45	Storytime—the children are read stories and discuss them. Children select books from library to take home.
10:15	Activity centers and learning centers—these can deal with any topic, such as science, art, ecology, and writing. All children participate in all the centers, usually on a rotating basis.
10:45	Free choice of games and puzzles selected by teacher for their ability to teach concepts such as size, shape, or number. This period can also be used for outdoor walks in which concepts being developed are extended and reinforced.
11:15	Group discussion—day's activities are reviewed and discussed. The next day's activities are anticipated.
11:45	Dismissal
	Snack, rest, and toilet opportunities may be offered at scheduled times or on an "as needed" basis for each child.

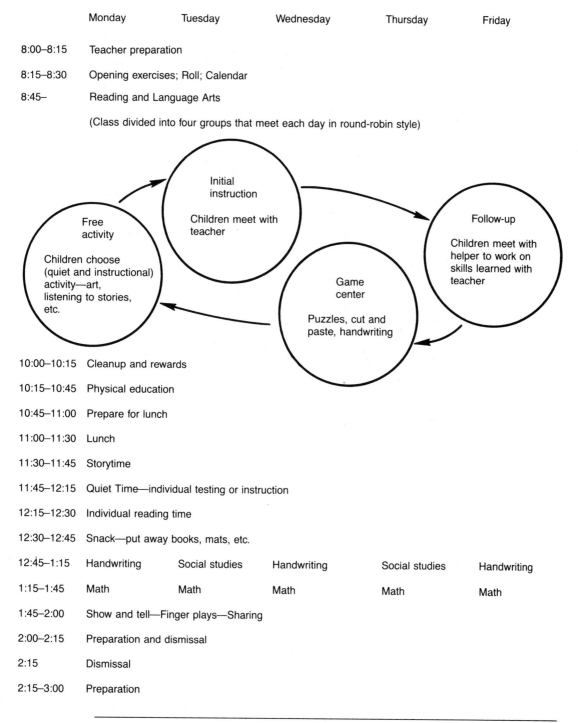

	Monday	Tuesday	Wednesday	Thursday	Friday

8:00–8:15   Teacher preparation

8:15–8:30   Opening exercises; Roll; Calendar

8:45–   Reading and Language Arts

              (Class divided into four groups that meet each day in round-robin style)

Free activity

Children choose (quiet and instructional) activity—art, listening to stories, etc.

Initial instruction

Children meet with teacher

Follow-up

Children meet with helper to work on skills learned with teacher

Game center

Puzzles, cut and paste, handwriting

10:00–10:15   Cleanup and rewards

10:15–10:45   Physical education

10:45–11:00   Prepare for lunch

11:00–11:30   Lunch

11:30–11:45   Storytime

11:45–12:15   Quiet Time—individual testing or instruction

12:15–12:30   Individual reading time

12:30–12:45   Snack—put away books, mats, etc.

| 12:45–1:15 | Handwriting | Social studies | Handwriting | Social studies | Handwriting |
| 1:15–1:45 | Math | Math | Math | Math | Math |

1:45–2:00   Show and tell—Finger plays—Sharing

2:00–2:15   Preparation and dismissal

2:15   Dismissal

2:15–3:00   Preparation

FIGURE 8–1   Full-Day Kindergarten Schedule (Source: Ms. Miriam Mades, Coconut Grove Elementary School, Coconut Grove, Florida)

8:00-8:10 Morning Announcements, Pledge, National Anthem. Take up lunch and snack money.

8:10-9:40 — LANGUAGE ARTS

Morning Routine: Everyone says the following together as I point to pictures or charts on our classroom walls:
- Calendar
- Days of the weeks
- Seasons
- Months of the year
- Colors
- Alphabet Song
- Count by 1's to 100
- Count by 10's to 100
- Count by 5's to 100
- Our Letter People & their Sounds
- Nursery Rhymes
- Shapes

Language Arts Curriculum:
- Alpha Time
- Lippincott Letterbooks
- Getting Ready to Read by Houghton Mifflin
- Developmental Learning Materials (DLM)

Morning Recess 9:40-9:50

9:50-10:50 — MATH

Workbooks: Mathematics Today by H.B.J.

DLM

Thursday: The Children go to the Computer Lab 10:00-10:40

Lunch 10:50-11:30

Storytime 11:30-12:00

P.E. 12:00-12:30

12:30-12:55 — SOCIAL STUDIES & FINE ARTS

Units:
(1) All about Me
(2) Home & Family
(3) Pets
(4) School Helpers
(5) Community Helpers
(6) Fall/Woodland Animals
(7) Farm
(8) Circus/Fair
(9) Columbus Day
(10) Halloween
(11) Early Times
(12) Thanksgiving
(13) Christmas
(14) Transportation
(15) Telephone
(16) Ground Hog Day
(17) Abe Lincoln
(18) Valentine's Day
(19) Washington
(20) Texas
(21) St Patrick's Day
(22) Zoo
(23) Spring
(24) Easter
(25) Plants
(26) Insects
(27) Birds
(28) Sea
(29) Review All Units

Snack Recess 12:55-1:15

1:15-1:35 — HEALTH SAFETY SCIENCE

Monday: Health

Tuesday: Safety

Wednesday: Science

Thursday: Mr McGruff's Elementary School Puppet Program

Friday: Films

1:35-2:20 — MONDAY, TUESDAY & WED. CENTERS

Our centers are:
(1) Home
(2) Sand
(3) Number & Game
(4) Science & Library
(5) Listening
(6) Easel
(7) Art
(8) Flannelboard Bean Bag Toss Puppet
(9) Tree House Puzzles
(10) Blocks
(11) System 80 Language Master Folder Games

Thursday: The children go to the Elem. Library 1:30-2:10

Librarian reads them a story, then they check out a book to take home.

FIGURE 8-2 Brenda McDaniel's Kindergarten Schedule at Evadale Elementary School, Evadale, Texas

A Day in the Kindergarten at Highland Oaks Elementary School

Jennifer Kirk attends kindergarten in the Highland Oaks Elementary School with 911 other children in Grades K–6.[10] The 81 kindergarten children are taught by four teachers, parent volunteers, and a varying number of sixth-grade student helpers. A suite (or pod) is shared by three kindergarten classes and three sixth-grade classes. While each class has its own designated area, no walls separate one area from the other. There are portable screens for arranging a self-contained classroom if the teachers so desire.

The curriculum in the four kindergarten classrooms is the same, using cooperative planning and some team teaching. Each teacher is free to teach in her own way and according to her own teaching style. The management system the four teachers use is the same. Children are grouped randomly at the beginning of the year. Each class consists of three groups, designated the circle group (O), the square group ($\Box$), and the triangle group ($\triangle$), which serve as a basis for reading instruction. The morning is devoted almost entirely to the reading process. While one group is taught a reading lesson by the teacher, the second group does seatwork, and the third group, independent activities.

The program described here occurs in April of the school year, and is a much different program from the kind that would be conducted in September. For example, in September, readiness exercises such as sizes, shapes, and colors would be taught. Before the opening of school, the children are given an orange juice party, at which they meet all the teachers and visit the classroom, while the principal gives their parents school information.

When Jennifer arrives at school at 8:10 A.M. (most of the children come by carpool or walk), she puts her lunch box on a shelf and sits in her designated seat. (At the beginning of the year, the children did not have assigned seats, but could sit wherever they wished; getting to know other children was part of the socialization process.) At 8:30 A.M. the whole school (K–6) participates in opening exercises, announced over the intercom system—the Pledge of Allegiance, the national anthem, school announcements, and birthday announcements. Opening exercises last about twenty minutes.

Jennifer's teacher then conducts a calendar activity with the twenty children sitting on the floor in an arc around her. Days of the week and months of the year are reviewed, and the clock (on the calendar) is set for lunch time. They also talk about what yesterday was and what tomorrow will be. A sharing activity is next. Jennifer brought in a puppet and a book to share. Children are encouraged to share important news, such as the birth of a new brother or sister, going on a trip, a parent's achievement, or a new purchase. They are not allowed to bring toys to share. This time is also used to tell the children about the planned activities for the day. There is always a writing activity on the board. Sometimes this lesson, about which the children will "write" and draw a picture, is written by Jennifer's teacher. The story may be from the basal reader or the children dictate a story or sentence to their teacher.

Jennifer then goes to the reading group. She immediately begins to copy the writing already on the board. When the writing is completed, she will put her paper next to her teacher, who will correct it right away so the children can immediately see their mistakes. Jennifer will then take a SWRL booklet and begin to read silently while she waits for the other children to finish their writing. Reading class lasts about thirty minutes. After reading, Jennifer goes to the seatwork station and draws a picture on the back of the writing paper she previously completed. Afterward, she gets a worksheet, prepared by her teacher, and colors the picture and traces over the letters that make the title for the picture. During this time, Jennifer is free to talk quietly with her friends. When she finishes the writing activity, Jennifer shows the paper to her teacher. The teacher checks quickly to see if it has been completed correctly. If so, Jennifer puts her paper in her folder. Each child has his own folder for his work. By this time of the year, the children are working independently and know the routine of the class, so they know to write their name on all papers, how to fold their papers, and to put them in the folders.

At about 10 A.M., Jennifer goes to the independent activities station, where she can choose from many learning activities. Some of these activities are storybooks, writing with paper and pencil, a cut and paste table, a molding clay table, puzzles, a math table with games, books with numbers, sequence cards, sand box, and housekeeping area and the computer. At about 10:30 A.M., a record is played as the children's signal to clean up. When they have put away the things they were working with, the children sit down quietly at their seats. Jennifer and her classmates go to lunch at 10:40 A.M. While walking to the cafeteria, they sing a song, and hop from stepping-stone to stepping-stone as they go.

Jennifer has a half-hour for lunch. She sits where she wants. This again provides an opportunity for socialization. The children are responsible for cleaning up their eating area. This includes wiping the tables off and picking up papers from the floor. When they are finished, the children line up outside the cafeteria where they are met by their teacher, who also had a thirty-minute lunch period. At 11:15 A.M., Jennifer comes back from lunch. She has about fifteen minutes to go to the restroom, rest, or get a drink of water.

At 11:30 A.M., Jennifer begins math. Today the children are reviewing number words. Jennifer's teacher writes f-o-u-r on the board and Jennifer writes the numeral 4 beside it. This procedure is followed for all of the number words. When this activity is completed, the children are given a teacher-made worksheet on which to match numerals with number words. Following math, at 12:10 P.M., the teacher reads stories to the children. The children usually bring the books from home or check them out of the school library. The children will make a picture about one of the stories, and will also write words to help illustrate or tell about the pictures of their stories. When storytime is over at 12:35 P.M., the children go outside. During this time they have the opportunity to participate in an organized activity conducted by the teacher, or an independent activity such as jumping rope, running races, or reading a book. The children are outside for about half-an-hour. Today Jennifer plays Farmer in the Dell with her teacher and several classmates. At this time the children are also free to get a drink, go to the restroom, and socialize with other children.

At 1 P.M., Jennifer and her classmates come in. They continue their learning of the sign language alphabet and "signing," a special project of the kindergarten class. Learning sign language was begun only after the children had learned the alphabet. This activity began in January with a visit by a staff member of the local association for the deaf, who introduced the children to sign language and signing. This person also acts as a resource person to the class throughout the year. Jennifer's teacher has the group "sign" the writing lesson, and the activity ends by singing and signing the alphabet in sign language.

At about 1:30 P.M., the kindergarten children get ready to go home. There are announcements of interest to the children over the school intercom. Today, the children are reminded about some of the events for the coming week, and are told to have a good weekend. When the announcements are over, the children clean up their classroom. Getting ready to go home includes passing out papers from their folders and putting their chairs on their tables. Jennifer's teacher sings goodby to each of the children with a hand puppet. All the children are given a hug and kiss by the puppet. Many of the children also reach up to hug and kiss their teacher.

In Jennifer's classroom, mobiles, pictures, and collages are hung on the walls and from the ceiling. The hangings are made by the children, and are changed monthly. This is one of the ways Jennifer's teacher makes the classroom appealing.

These are some of the activities throughout the year:

During George Washington Carver week, the children learn about this great American and make peanut butter candy.

Green Jell-o is made for St. Patrick's Day.

Many cooking activities, such as making butter, salads, cinnamon toast, and popcorn, are conducted on a regular basis.

Many activities are conducted around national observances such as Dental Health Week.

Special poems and songs are learned for the holidays.

Regular sniff-look-and-listen walks to emphasize all the senses.

Resource people, many of whom are parents and grandparents, come in to help with projects such as spring baskets, sand painting, and art activities. A father who is a surgeon gave each child a surgical mask and hat to wear while he explained good health practices. A dentist gave the children toothbrushes at the end of her talk.

Many films and filmstrips result in application of specific skills, such as how to use the telephone. Many of these activities help balance the academic orientation of the program.

Independent Social Studies/Science Project. This project is an independent one of the children's choice, to be completed at home. They can, however, enlist family or outside help. Some of the things the children have done are posters, dioramas, and models; anything is acceptable as long as the children explain it to their classmates. The projects are then put on display for a week or so.

A group project undertaken for the local science fair is growing plants for display. This is a culminating activity for a science/health unit.

Campaigning for Office. Jennifer's school has a Junior American Citizen Club (JAC), and each year the children in each grade elect class officers. Every child may run for any office. Jennifer ran for president of her kindergarten class. She, along with the other children who ran for office, made posters and cards to pass out.

Sixth-Grade Student Helpers

Today, one of the helpers in Jennifer's kindergarten is Adam, a sixth-grade student. The fifth- and sixth-grade classes are given an opportunity to help with kindergarten activities during their independent work time. Adam comes to Jennifer's class to read stories, put reading materials in order, and help with other activities. Adam says he likes to work with the kindergarten children because they are nice, easy to work with, and have "good personalities." Adam feels that working with the kindergarten children helps him learn how to work with other people and how to assume responsibility. He also feels it gives him an opportunity to learn things that he doesn't know; for example, during the year, he learned sign language along with the kindergarten children.

Homework

Each child gets one homework assignment each week as part of their reading program. They receive another assignment from their teacher that relates to concepts being taught in class. For example, when studying the sense of touch, a paper on which to attach various textures was sent home for each child. After completion, the paper was returned and displayed in the classroom.

Spanish

Jennifer and her class are taught Spanish for 20 minutes a day, usually right after lunch. (Spanish then takes the place of storytime on the schedule.) A native speaker of Spanish uses only Spanish to speak to the children and the children role play, sing songs, and converse with each other and the teacher. Jennifer learns Spanish quickly, since she is at the sensitive stage for language learning. Her tongue is not stiff, like that of an adult who tries to learn a second language. Jennifer and her classmates are also acquiring an awareness for other people, cultures, and languages.

Computers

The computer curriculum allows children to have fun while learning. Initially, the children are introduced to the parts of the computer through group discussions, matching games, paper-and-pencil activities, and specific computer programs such as *Kids on Keys*. Through individualized instruction, each child learns to load the computer by following simple directions. Commercial software enhances academic skills such as letter and number recognition and reading readiness. Specific programs such as *Kindercomp, Monkey Business,* and *Facemaker* reinforce perceptual skills. The emphasis is on important process areas—visual recognition, memory, sequencing, and reasoning ability. The children's familiarity with and enjoyment of the computer results in self-motivated and computer-literate enthusiasts.

Outstanding Features of Jennifer's Kindergarten

The emphasis in Jennifer's kindergarten is on learning the basic skills of reading, writing, and arithmetic. Teaching and learning occur in an academic atmo-

FIGURE 8–3 Me and My Mommy

FIGURE 8–4 My Family

sphere full of fun and joy. The teachers plan for and teach their program well, knowing what they want to accomplish and how they want to accomplish it.

One of the outstanding features of Jennifer's kindergarten program is the great amount of affection and caring shown by teachers and staff for the children in the program. Their caring attitude is reflected in the high level of concern for children's achievement and well-being. Caring shown to the children is in turn reflected in the kindness, courtesy, and affection children show for each other. Such a high-quality, affective climate provides a humane balance to the basic skills orientation of the program.

The classrooms in which teachers and children live and learn are pleasant to be in, because the teachers and children make them so. Walls and bulletin boards are attractively filled with children's work. The teachers encourage high-quality work for the children, and the children are proud to display their achievements. One of the children's work is shown in Figures 8–3 and 8–4.

TESTING IN THE KINDERGARTEN

Because of federal mandates and state laws, school districts usually evaluate children in some way before or at the time of their entrance into school. Also, some type of screening occurs at the time of kindergarten entrance to evaluate learning readiness. Unfortunately, children are often classified on the basis of how well they perform on these screenings, but when testing is appropriate and when the results are used as a basis for teaching children what they need to learn, it is valuable and worthwhile. There are basically seven purposes of readiness tests:

1. To identify what children know
2. To identify special needs
3. To assist in referral decisions
4. To determine appropriate placement
5. To help develop lesson plans and programs
6. To identify behavioral as opposed to chronological level
7. To inform parents about their children's developmental progress

Screening Processes

Screening measures give school personnel a broad picture of what children know, are able to do, and their physical and emotional status. As gross indicators of children's abilities, screening procedures provide information for use in decisions about placement for initial instruction, referral to other agencies, and additional testing that may be necessary to pinpoint a learning or health problem. Many school districts conduct a comprehensive screening program in the spring for children who will enter in the fall. Screening can involve:

☐ Gathering parent information about health, learning patterns, learning achievements, personal habits, and special problems
☐ Health screening, including a physical examination, health history, and a blood sample for analysis
☐ Vision, hearing, and speech screening
☐ Collecting and analyzing data from former programs and teachers, such as preschools and child care programs
☐ Administering a cognitive and/or behavioral screening instrument

Comprehensive screening programs can be conducted in one day or over several days. Data for each child are usually evaluated by a team of professionals who make instructional placement recommendations and, when appropriate, referrals and recommendations for additional testing and to other agencies for assistance.

Screening Instruments

Many screening instruments provide information for grouping and for planning instructional strategies. Most screening instruments can be administered by people who do not have specialized training in test administration. Parent volunteers can often help administer screening instruments, many of which can be administered in fifteen or twenty minutes.

BRIGANCE® K and 1 Screen

The BRIGANCE® K and 1 Screen is an evaluation instrument for use in kindergarten and grade 1. The Kindergarten Pupil Data Sheet for the BRIGANCE® K and 1 Screen is shown in Figure 8–5. This sheet shows the skills, behaviors and concepts evaluated in the kindergarten portion of the screening instrument. Samples of test items and directions for administration are shown in Figures 8–6 and 8–7.

DIAL-R

The DIAL-R (Developmental Indicators for the Assessment of Learning) is a screening instrument for use with prekindergarten children. It is team-administered and involves individual observation for motor skills, concepts, and language skills. The DIAL-R requires approximately 25–30 minutes to administer. The DIAL-R scoresheet is shown in Figure 8–8. The DIAL-R is designed for screening large numbers of children. The screening team consists of a coordinator, an operator for each of the skills areas being screened, and aides or volunteers to register parents and children.

Computers in the Kindergarten

Children often come to kindergarten computer-literate, and many are more knowledgeable than their teachers. There is no longer a question of whether we should provide computer-literacy activities in the kindergarten; it is a question of how much and what kind. While some early childhood educators argue that kindergarten children are not developmentally ready for the skills and processes required for computer use, others think just the opposite. Three researchers examined how computer use in the home and kindergarten affected children's readiness skills. The kindergartners in the program received one hour a week of instruction in the areas of reading readiness, mathematics, Piagetian cognitive operations, and keyboard skills. The researchers found large gains in reading readiness and keyboard skills, but little gain in math readiness and Piagetian operations. The findings were somewhat affected by the greater availability of software in reading readiness and keyboard skills than in the other two areas. Also, children who had use of computers in their homes and school did better than those who had use of computers only in school. The researchers concluded: "We found no indication that computing experiences interfere with the normal cognitive development of preschoolers."[11]

Two basic goals for computer literacy in the kindergarten should be to have children learn what computers are and to learn to use them. Objectives of a kindergarten computer literacy program should include the following:

1. Naming the different parts of a computer
2. Telling what a computer does and what it can be used for
3. Loading and running a basic software program
4. Using the computer keyboard to operate a software program
5. Typing words and a simple story using a word-processor software program

A.

				Year	Month	Day	
Student's Name	Colin Killoran		Date of Screening	81	6	15	School/Program Vinal School
Parents/Guardian	Kristin and Edmund Killoran		Birthdate	76	1	10	Teacher Leslie Feingold
Address	310 Locke Street		Age	5	5	5	Assessor Dennis Dowd

B. BASIC SCREENING ASSESSMENTS

Page	Assessment Number	Skill (Circle the skill for each correct response and make notes as appropriate.)	Number of Correct Responses	Point Value	Student's Score
2	1	**Personal Data Response:** Verbally gives: ① first name ② full name ③ age 4. address (street or mail) 5. birthdate (month and day)	3 ×	2 points each	6/10
3	2	**Color Recognition:** Identifies and names the colors: ① red ② blue ③ green ④ yellow ⑤ orange 6. purple ⑦ brown ⑧ black ⑨ pink 10. gray	8 ×	1 point each	8/10
5	3	**Picture Vocabulary:** Recognizes and names picture of: ① dog ② cat ③ key ④ girl ⑤ boy ⑥ airplane ⑦ apple 8. leaf ⑨ cup 10. car	8 ×	1 point each	8/10
6	4A	**Visual Discrimination:** Visually discriminates which one of four symbols is different: ① ○ ② ○ ③ ○ ④ ⑤ ○ ⑥ ○ 7.1 ⑧ P 9. V 10. X ① ○ ② – ③ + ④ □ 5. △	7 ×	1 point each	7/10
			4 ×	2 pts. ea.	8/10
8	5	**Visual-Motor Skills:** Copies: ① ○ ②	③ + ④ □ 5. △			
9	6	**Gross Motor Skills:** ① Hops 2 hops on one foot. ② Hops 2 hops on either foot. ③ Stands on one foot momentarily. ④ Stands on either foot momentarily. ⑤ Stands on one foot for 5 seconds. ⑥ Stands on either foot for 5 secs. ⑦ Walks forward heel toe and heel toe and heel 4 steps. 8. Walks backward toe and heel 4 steps. ⑨ Stands on one foot momentarily with eyes closed. 10. Stands on either foot momentarily with eyes closed.	8 ×	1 point each	8/10
12	8	**Rote Counting:** Counts by rote to: (Circle all numerals prior to the first error.) ① ② ③ ④ ⑤ ⑥ 7 8 9 10	6 ×	.5 point each	3/5
13	9	**Identification of Body Parts:** Identifies by pointing or touching: ① chin ② fingernails ③ heel ④ elbow ⑤ ankle ⑥ shoulder ⑦ jaw 8. hips ⑨ wrist 10. waist	8 ×	.5 point each	4/5
15	11	**Follows Verbal Directions:** Listens to, remembers, and follows: ① one verbal direction 2. two verbal directions	1 ×	2.5 points each	2.5/5
17	12	**Numeral Comprehension:** Matches quantity with numerals: ② ① ④ ③ 5	4 ×	2 pts. ea.	8/10
21	15	**Prints Personal Data:** ① Prints first name Reversals: Yes ___ No ✓	1 ×	5 points	5/5
22	16	**Syntax and Fluency:** ① Speech is understandable. ② Speaks in complete sentences.	2 ×	5 pts. ea.	10/10

Total Score 77.5/100

D. OBSERVATIONS:
1. Handedness: Right ✓ Left ___ Uncertain ___
2. Pencil grasp: Correct ✓ Incorrect ___
3. Maintained paper in the proper position when writing: Yes ___ No ✓
4. Record other observations below or on the back.

Cooperative had difficulty attending to verbal directions and relied on manual clues

E. SUMMARY: (Compared to other students included in this screening)

1. this student scored:	___ Higher	Average ✓	___ Lower
2. this student's age is:	___ Older	Average ✓	___ Younger
3. the teacher rates this student:	___ Higher	Average ✓	___ Lower
4. the assessor rates this student:	___ Higher	Average ✓	___ Lower

F. RECOMMENDATIONS: Place in: ___ Preschool ___ Low Kindergarten ___ Average Kindergarten ✓ High Kindergarten

Other (Indicate.) _____

Refer for: (Indicate if needed.) Ask nurse to check hearing

FIGURE 8–5 BRIGANCE® Pupil Data Sheet (© 1982, Curriculum Associates, Inc., reproduced by permission of the publisher)

275

FIGURE 8-6 BRIGANCE® Picture Vocabulary Screening Instrument (© 1982, Curriculum Associates, Inc., reproduced by permission of the publisher)

SKILL: Recognizes and names pictures commonly used in readiness material.

1. dog 2. cat 3. key 4. girl 5. boy
6. airplane 7. apple 8. leaf 9. cup 10. car

PUPIL DATA SHEETS: Kindergarten and First Grade.

ASSESSMENT METHOD: Student performance—individual oral response.

MATERIAL: S-5.

DISCONTINUE: After two consecutive errors.

TIME: Your discretion. Five seconds per picture is recommended.

ACCURACY: Give credit for each correct response.

POINT VALUES: Kindergarten: 1 point each.
First grade: .5 point each.

NOTES:
1. **Possible Observations:** As the student names the pictures, you may wish to observe for the following:
   a. *Articulation Problems:* Are any sounds omitted, substituted, or distorted? See "Articulation of Sounds" on pages S-27 and 27.
   b. *Focusing Difficulties:* Does the student appear to have difficulty focusing on one picture because of being distracted by the other pictures? See **NOTE #5.**
   c. *Interest:* Does the student appear to have an interest in looking at and talking about the pictures? Does the student want to talk about a particular picture?
   d. *Syntax and Fluency:* Is the student's speech understandable and are some of the responses in sentences? See "Syntax and Fluency" on page 22.

2. **Supplemental Assessments:** The pictures may be used to informally assess the student's comprehension and language development. This may be accomplished by asking questions such as the following:
   a. Which two are pets?
   b. Which two are people?
   c. Which two grow on trees?
   d. Which two can we ride in?
   e. Which two have four legs?
   f. Which two can talk?
   g. Why do we have keys? airplanes? cars? cups?
   h. Which ones do you have at home?

DIRECTIONS: This assessment is made by pointing to each picture on S-5 and asking the student to name it.

Point to each picture and

Ask: **What is this?** or **What do you call it?**

Give encouragement if needed.

3. **Assessing the Student with Limited Speech or Who Is Reluctant to Respond Verbally:** If there is difficulty in getting the student to respond verbally, you may wish to ask the student to point to each picture as you name it.

4. **Referencing:** The objects used in this assessment are common to the reading readiness materials of the following publishers:
   Addison-Wesley Reading Program. Reading, Mass.: Addison-Wesley Publishing Company, Inc., 1979.
   HBJ Bookmark Reading. New York: Harcourt Brace Jovanovich, Inc., 1979.
   The Houghton Mifflin Reading Series. Boston: Houghton Mifflin Company, 1979.
   Pathfinder. Boston: Allyn and Bacon, Inc., 1979.
   Reading 720 Rainbow Edition. Lexington, Mass.: Ginn and Company, 1979.
   Scott, Foresman Reading. Glenview, Ill.: Scott, Foresman and Company, 1981.
   Series r. New York: Macmillan Publishing Company, 1980.
   Young American Basic Series. Skokie, Ill.: Rand McNally and Company, 1978.

5. **Screen if Needed:** If it appears that the student is having difficulty focusing on one item at a time because of the visual stimuli of the entire page, you should cover the other items on the page by using blank sheets of paper.

6. **Advanced Skills:** The "Response to Picture" assessment on page 26 in the Advanced Section assesses more advanced skills. You may wish to use it to informally assess the skill level of the more capable student.

FIGURE 8–7 BRIGANCE® Picture Vocabulary Screening Instrument (© 1982, Curriculum Associates, Inc., reproduced by permission of the publisher)

DIAL-R
SCORESHEET

Child's Name _____ LAST ___ FIRST ___ NICKNAME

Address _____ STREET ___ CITY/STATE/ZIP

Phone Number (___) AREA CODE ___ NUMBER ___ Language ___

Parents' Names ___ MOTHER ___ FATHER
1 2 3

School _____
Class _____

Today's Date _____
Birth Date _____
C.A. _____

YEAR   MONTH   DAY

Hearing + −
Vision + −

Boy ___   Girl ___

MOTOR (red)

	under 2 yrs.	2-3 yrs.	3-4 yrs.	4-5 yrs.	5-6 yrs.	OBSERVATIONS
	0	1	2	3	4	1 2 3 4 5 6 7 8
1. Catching	0	−	1	2	3	
2. Jumping, Hopping, and Skipping	0	1-2	3-8	9-12	13-16	
jumps: 0 1						
+ hops: (right) 0 1 2 3 4 5 6						
(left) 0 1 2 3 4 5 6						
+ skip:						
0-any 1-slide 2-step/hop 3-skip						
3. Building	0	1	2	3	4	
4. Touching Fingers	0	1	2	3	4	
5. Cutting	0-1	1-7	8-9	10-11	12	
6. Matching	0	1-7	8-11	12-18	19-24	
7. Copying	0					
I 0 1 2 E 0 1 2						
O 0 1 2 N 0 1 2						
+ 0 1 2 D 0 1 2						
□ 0 1 2 S 0 1 2						
△ 0 1 2						
◇ 0 1 2						
8. Writing Name	0	−	−	1	2	

TOTAL (Max.=31)

CONCEPTS (green)

	under 2 yrs.	2-3 yrs.	3-4 yrs.	4-5 yrs.	5-6 yrs.	OBSERVATIONS
	0	1	2	3	4	1 2 3 4 5 6 7 8
1. Naming Colors	0	1-7	8-15	16-18		
R O W G BL Y B BR P						
2. Identifying Body Parts	0	1-9	10-12	13-15	16-18	
nose neck chin ankle						
hair stomach shoulder hip						
ear knee chest waist						
teeth thumb heel						
tongue elbow wrist						
3. Counting (Rote)	0-2	3-4	5-8	9-10	11	
4. Counting (Meaningful)	0	1	3	5-7	9	
1 3 5 7 9						
5. Positioning	0	1-2	3	4	5	
on under corner between middle						
6. Identifying Concepts	0	1-14	15-20	21-26	27-28	
biggest big						
hot empty						
night long						
longest more						
most fast						
fastest little						
littlest cold						
full day						
shortest short						
least less						
slowest slow						
7. Naming Letters	0	−	−	1-10	11-16	
O B P E R W Y G						
8. Sorting Chips	0	−	−	1-4	5-8	
by color: R B Y						
by size: big little						
by shape: ○ □ △						

TOTAL (Max.=31)

LANGUAGE (purple)

	under 2 yrs.	2-3 yrs.	3-4 yrs.	4-5 yrs.	5-6 yrs.	OBSERVATIONS
	0	1	2	3	4	1 2 3 4 5 6 7 8
1. Articulating	0	1-14	15-26	27-29		
pin rabbit truck						
bed chair dress						
cup knife sandwich						
towel leg thumb						
hand fish mouth/teeth						
2. Giving Personal Data	0	1-3	4	5	6-7	
first name street phone #						
last name sex						
age city/state						
3. Remembering	0	1-3	4-5	6-7	8-9	
clapping A B C						
numbers A B C						
sentences A B C						
4. Naming Nouns	0	1-15	16	17	18	
cat phone comb						
plane TV pencil						
car clock ambulance						
5. Naming Verbs	0	1-9	10-14	15-16	17-18	
sleep call comb						
fly watch write						
drive time go to hospital						
6. Classifying Foods	0	1-2	3-4	5-6	7-8	
Tally ___						
7. Problem Solving	0	1	2-3	4-5	6-8	
hungry 0 1 2						
dark room 0 1 2						
rain 0 1 2						
broken 0 1 2						
8. Sentence Length	0	1-2	3	4	5-8	

TOTAL (Max.=31)

Motor score _____
Concepts score _____   (see page 58 for Cut-off Points by Area Scores)
Language score _____
Total score _____   (see page 15 for Cut-off Points by Total Score)
# of Observations _____   (see page 50 for Cut-off Points by Observations)

DECISION _____

CHILDCRAFT
EDUCATION CORP.

FIGURE 8-8 DIAL-R Scoresheet (Carol Mardell-Czudnowski and Dorothea S. Goldenberg, DIAL-R Scoresheet. Edison, N.J.: ChildCraft Corp., 1983. Reproduced by permission.)

These objectives should be integrated with normal classroom activities. For example, children can listen to stories about computers, take a field trip to a business that uses computers, make a computer model in the art center, cut out letters from magazines and make a computer keyboard, and use a typewriter to write their names.

Turtle in the Kindergarten[12]

Five-year-old Jane has just finished an activity-time lesson during which she has drawn a picture of something she likes to climb—she has made a picture of the climbing bar. Then she goes to a corner of the room called "The Turtle's Corner" where there is a computer and a large chart displaying the commands for operating the computer program. She is going to draw her picture on the computer.

Since the beginning of the school year, Jane has been using an Apple II-E computer and a series of commands to make a small white triangle, called a turtle, move forward and right on the computer screen. She has been using a Logo program called Instant to draw squares, half-circles, and rectangles. Her teacher has programmed the system so Jane and her classmates can make the turtle execute one of these commands simply by pressing one key. Today she is ready to start to draw on the computer screen a picture she has drawn by hand of the same subject.

Jane has in front of her the Instant chart that gives all the commands for the computer program. If Jane makes a mistake as she draws her picture, she presses the "U" key, a command that erases the entire picture and redraws it except for the mistaken last step. Jane finishes in about fifteen minutes. Her teacher saves the picture on a disk and will print it for Jane to use as an illustration in a book she is writing about what she does in the classroom.

Each of the twenty-three children in the kindergarten gets a turn to use the computer before anyone can have a second turn. In this way, everyone has equal access to this powerful teaching and learning tool.

Jane's teacher has chosen Logo for the computer program because it allows the children to be in control. They draw the pictures and graphics they want to draw. Logo is an excellent way to teach computer skills. Jane's teacher also feels she can learn a lot about the children's learning styles and how they solve problems by how they approach drawing their pictures.

Reading in the Kindergarten

Most elementary schools and many kindergartens focus on reading readiness and teaching reading. Students and teachers spend much of their time and energy in this process and related activities. Methods of organizing the classroom, such as grouping and scheduling, are frequently based on reading, and social patterns are often established according to membership in reading groups.

Learning to read in the primary grades is not an unreasonable expectation, and children look forward to it. Parents assume that when their children enter school, they will be taught to read. Learning to read is not only a social dictate, it is an academic necessity; how well a child reads often determines how successful he is in school. But with the greater emphasis on early schooling and basic skills, the teaching of reading is being pushed down to the kindergarten. Many parents and early childhood educators question a number of factors associated with early reading: first, its appropriateness and advisability; second, the teaching methods; and third, the pressure on children and the consequent stress it can cause.

Effective Approaches

As a first step in teaching, teachers should demystify the reading process. Many teachers do a good job of teaching reading through processes and procedures that are easy to understand and implement, and which can lead to a child's almost spontaneous ability to read. It would be beneficial to all teachers and children for the profession to examine, identify, and promote the conditions under which some children have learned to read without overemphasis on direct instruction or strict adherence to a basal approach. Teachers should realize that simply spending more time on formal reading instruction will not make children learn to read better or more quickly. Activities that interest children can be a means for teaching them to read. Performances, storytelling, writing, conversations with peers and adults, and field trips provide a natural approach that can be *supplemented* by reading instruction. Reading is, after all, an *extension* of oral language and writing.

We must also stop making nonreaders of children by asking them to perform reading tasks and activities they are not capable of. A child does not suddenly develop a reading problem in the kindergarten or first grade; reading problems occur when children come to school and are confronted with tasks that they are not developmentally ready for. The Texas Association for the Education of Young Children has issued descriptions of developmentally *appropriate* and *inappropriate* kindergarten reading programs. These are the recommendations for an appropriate program:

1. Young children learn through experiences that provide for all of the developmental needs—physical, socio-emotional, as well as intellectual.
2. Young children learn through self-selected activities while participating in a variety of centers which are interesting and meaningful to them. (Learning Centers include: socio-dramatic, block, science, math, manipulatives, listening, reading, writing, art, music, and construction.)
3. Young children are encouraged to talk about their experiences with other children and adults in the classroom.
4. Young children are involved in a variety of psychomotor experiences, including music, rhythms, movement, large and small motor manipulatives and outdoor activity.
5. Young children are provided with many opportunities to interact in meaningful print contexts: listening to stories, participating in shared book experiences, making language experience stories and books, developing key word vocabularies, reading classroom labels, and using print in the various learning centers.

And this is the description of an inappropriate program:

1. Formal kindergarten reading programs usually focus upon whole group instruction in visual-motor and phonics lessons with commercially prepared workbooks and ditto sheets.
2. Formal kindergarten reading programs usually include reading instruction in a basal reading series. This process frequently involves the learning of *rules* with emphasis upon the *form* rather than the *meaning* of written language.
3. A formal kindergarten reading program often requires children to sit for inappropriately long blocks of time in teacher directed activities with overemphasis upon table work and fine motor skills.
4. A formal kindergarten reading program focuses upon isolated skill oriented experiences which include repetition and memorization.[13]

BILINGUAL EDUCATION

For most people, *bilingual education* means that children (or adults, or both) will be taught a second language. Some people interpret this to mean that the child's native language, whether English, Spanish, Urdu, or any of the other 125 languages in which bilingual programs are conducted, will tend to be suppressed. For other people, bilingual means the child will become proficient in a second language. Title 11 of Public Law 98-511, the Bilingual Education Act, sets forth the federal government's policy of bilingual education:

> The Congress declares it to be the policy of the United States, in order to establish equal educational opportunity for all children and to promote educational excellence (A) to encourage the establishment and operation, where appropriate, of educational programs using bilingual educational practices, techniques, and methods, (B) to encourage the establishment of special alternative instructional programs for students of limited English proficiency in school districts where the establishment of bilingual education programs is not practicable or for other appropriate reasons, and (C) for those purposes, to provide financial assistance to local educational agencies.[14]

Diversity is a positive aspect of American society. Ethnic pride and identity have caused renewed interest in languages and a more conscious effort to preserve children's native languages. Sixty years ago, foreign-born Americans and their children wanted to camouflage their ethnicity and unlearn their language because it seemed unpatriotic or un-American; today, however, we hold the opposite viewpoint.

Another reason for interest in bilingual education is the emphasis on civil rights. Indeed, much of the concept of providing children an opportunity to know, value, and use their heritage and language stems from people's recognition that they have a right to them.

Types of Programs

Schools have several potential responses to a child's linguistic deficiency. They can hope the child will learn English merely by exposure to it in the classroom. Second, they can provide a program of *Teaching English to Speakers of Other Languages*

Bilingual and multicultural education helps children develop to their fullest potential.

(TESOL), which emphasizes teaching the child English as quickly as possible so as to conduct the program of schooling in English. A third response is to provide a *transitional* program, in which the child studies in the native language until he becomes proficient in the second language. The goal in this type of program is to help the child acquire concepts and skills through his native language while he is becoming proficient in English. English is still the dominant language of the United States, although some cities that have a large number of speakers of other languages are officially bilingual.

P.L. 98–511 defines a program of *transitional bilingual education*—most of the bilingual programs are transitional—this way:

> The term 'program of transitional bilingual education' means a program of instruction, designed for children of limited English proficiency in elementary or secondary schools, which provides, with respect to the years of study to which such

program is applicable, structured English language instruction, and, to the extent necessary to allow a child to achieve competence in the English langauge, instruction in the child's native language. Such instruction shall incorporate the cultural heritage of such children and of other children in American society. Such instruction shall, to the extent necessary, be in all courses or subjects of study which will allow a child to meet grade-promotion and graduation standards.[15]

Bilingual-Multicultural Preschool Curriculum Models

In 1975, the Administration for Children, Youth and Families authorized development and implementation of bilingual and multicultural programs at the preschool level. The goal of these programs is to develop bilingual/multicultural early childhood curriculum approaches that provide instruction in two languages, foster children's cognitive and social growth through multicultural references, and to provide for individualization of instruction based upon children's linguistic needs. The four models and descriptive information about them is shown in Table 8–4.

HELPING CHILDREN MAKE TRANSITIONS

A child faces a transition whenever there is a change in environment, in how schooling is conducted, and in the people with whom they will interact. The preschool and kindergarten years are full of transitions. A major transition is leaving kindergarten to enter first grade. This transition may not be too difficult for children housed in the same school as the primary grades. For others, for whom the kindergarten is separate from the primary program or for children who have not attended kindergarten, the experience can be unsettling, traumatic, or joyful and rewarding. It can influence, positively or negatively, the child's attitude toward schooling. Children with special needs who are making a transition from a special program to a mainstreamed classroom need extra attention and support, as we will discuss in Chapter 11. These are guidelines for teachers, caregivers, parents, and others to lessen the stress of any transition:

- ☐ Alert and educate children ahead of time to the new situation. For example, children can visit, for a short time or for a day or two, the first grade they will be entering, and they can practice doing things in their kindergarten the way they are conducted in the primary grades.
- ☐ Work with parents to educate them to the new setting and the expectations regarding dress, behavior, achievement, and parent/teacher relationships. A parent handbook is useful for this purpose.
- ☐ Educate parents to the curriculum their children will use by showing them books and conducting sample lessons with them; this helps them understand what their children will learn.
- ☐ Work with parents of children with special needs to help them become familiar with and understand the new program. In particular, bilingual parents and parents with handicapped children will need extra transitional support.

TABLE 8-4 Bilingual Models

Curriculum Models	Characteristics	Language Strategies
ALERTA (Drawn from child development, socio-linguistic and anthropological theory) Alerta Institute for Urban and Minority Education Columbia University New York, NY 10027	Child centered Bilinqualism for two linguistic groups Education that is multicultural Team approach—all staff involved in all aspects of implementation	Small teacher directed language clusters for 1st & 2nd language development Child-initiated use of language reinforced by teachers throughout the day
AMANECER (Drawn from collected early childhood program descriptions) 5835 Callaghan, Suite 350-111 San Antonio, TX 78285	Teacher Action Program Color coded packets that form an organized system or model Use of classroom management system Focus on unit planning	1st & 2nd language Circle Times Teacher designed units to develop cognitive and communication skills
NUEVAS FRONTERAS (Drawn from studies of Ramirez and Castaneda) Pergamos Press, Inc. Fairview Park Elmsford, NY 10523	Use of cognitive styles and learning behaviors of children 13 unit guides Detailed lesson plans already developed	Language grouping First & Second language Teaching Plans Simultaneous translations
UN MARCO ABIERTO (Drawn from Piaget's development theory) High/Scope Educational Research Foundation 600 North River Street Ypsilanti, MI 48197	Cognitively oriented curriculum Open framework for planning Teachers develop classroom activities based on "Key Experiences"	1st & 2nd language development expected through natural conversation Use of simultaneous translation and code switching Children and adults serve as language resources

Source: Soledad Arenas, Education Specialist, Head Start Bureau/ACYF (Conference of the National Association of Bilingual Education, 1984).

TABLE 8–4

Culture in Program	Record Keeping	Requirements for Successful Implementation
Culture is defined as all that a child experiences—past traditions, present environment Parents and staff in classroom and center activities Use of community environment Culture reflected in materials and total center environment	Daily Lesson Plan Weekly Lesson Plan Survey of Children's Culture Survey of the Community Classroom & Material Survey Guide for grouping children for language clusters Daily written observations Assessment of children's progress	Half teaching staff fully bilingual Team approach—staff & parents must be actively involved in implementation Daily written observations by adults Daily, Weekly Team Planning Time Positive intergroup relations across components
Emphasis on family life experiences of individual children Use of community members in the classroom Chidren's culture reflected in classroom	Keeping Up With Folders Language Profile Master Checklist Daily Lesson Cards Weekly Planning Guides Teacher Checklist	At least half teaching staff fully bilingual Ongoing purchase of consumables Planning Time Consistent Record Keeping Teaching Teams must plan together
Culture integrated into curriculum units Focus on historical roots, traditions, holidays Parent & community participation Cultural democracy based on respect for differences	Daily Lesson Plan Weekly Classroom Plan Language Assessment Form Early Learning Behavior Checklist Progress Report Individual Learning Plan	Half teaching staff fully bilingual Ongoing purchase of consumables Planning Time for the teaching team
Use of parents as cultural resources Use of culturally relevant objects from home and community	Daily Planning & Evaluation Form Bilingual/Bicultural Child Observation Record Preschool Teacher Training Profile Bilingual bicultural parent Interview & Assessment Schedule Teacher Checklist	Teachers, paraprofessionals & parents work together in the classroom as a teaching team Daily planning time for teaching team Half teaching team fully bilingual

- [ ] Teachers can work with, train, and orient each other as to what they do in each program. Visiting each other's classrooms for a day gives teachers insight into the programs they receive children from and those they send children to.
- [ ] Teachers and coordinators can coordinate curriculum between programs so that what children do in kindergarten relates to what they will do in first grade.
- [ ] Establish a "Transition Committee" of teachers and parents to help identify activities and processes for facilitating transitions.

The nature, extent, creativity, and effectiveness of transitional experiences for children, parents and staff will be limited only by the commitment of all involved. If we are interested in providing good preschools, kindergartens, and primary schools, then we will include transitional experiences in the curricula of all the programs.

WHAT LIES AHEAD?

The trend in kindergarten education is toward full-day, cognitive-based programs. Kindergartens give public schools an opportunity to provide children with the help they need for later success in school and life. Children come to kindergarten programs knowing more than their counterparts of twenty years ago. Children with different abilities and a society with different needs require that kindergarten programs change accordingly.

FURTHER READING

Balaban, Nancy. *Starting School* (New York: Teachers College Press, 1985) Sensitive and practical suggestions to help teachers and caregivers ease the separation process for young children starting their early childhood program experiences.

Fishman, Joshua, and Gary D. Keller, eds. *Bilingual Education for Hispanic Students in the United States* (New York: Teachers College Press, 1982) Chapters on "Defining the Goals of Bilingual Education," "Attitudes Toward Spanish and Bilingual Education," and "How Young Children Become Bilingual" help the reader focus on the Hispanic dimension of bilingual education.

Hakuta, Kenji. *Mirror of Language: The Debate on Bilingualism* (New York: Basic Books, 1986) Controversies in bilingualism, second-language literacy, and the teaching of second languages.

Lambert, Wallace E. *Bilingual Education Series 10: Faces and Facets of Bilingualism* (Washington, D.C.: The Center for Applied Linguistics, and Rossly, Va.: Inter-America Research Associates, 1981) Helpful articles about first- and second-language learning; addresses cultural and social aspects of bilingualism.

Ramsey, Marjorie E., and Kathleen M. Bayless. *Kindergarten Programs and Early Schooling*, 2nd ed. (Englewood Cliffs, N.J.: Prentice-Hall, 1984) Emphasis on kindergarten areas, with a particularly good chapter on block building and woodworking.

Spodek, Bernard, ed. *Today's Kindergarten: Exploring the Knowledge Base, Expanding the Curriculum* (New York: Teachers College Press, 1986) Collection of topics from bilingual education to socialization; focuses on concepts, ideas, and issues relating to young children.

Trelease, Jim. *The Read-Aloud Handbook* (New York: Penguin Books, 1982) Introduction to developing children's interest in reading by having parents and teachers read aloud to them. Chapters deal with a rationale for reading aloud; how to read aloud; and do's and don'ts. Also includes lists of books that are good for reading aloud.

FURTHER STUDY

1. Interview parents to determine what they think children should learn in kindergarten. How do their ideas compare to the ideas in this chapter?
2. Critique the kindergarten skills objectives of the Dade County Public Schools. What would you add or delete? Why?
3. Do you think you would be a cognitive-skills oriented teacher or a social-emotional-play-oriented teacher? Explain your reasons, and compare your response to those of your classmates.
4. List what you think should be the goals of a kindergarten program. Explain your reasons.
5. Draw a floor plan for a kindergarten program and develop a daily schedule to support your teaching goals.
6. As a teacher, would you support an earlier or later entrance age to kindergarten? If your local legislator wanted specific reasons, what would you tell him or her? Ask other teachers, and compare their viewpoints.
7. How might the country in which a child is reared affect what should be taught in kindergarten?
8. Give examples from your observations of kindergarten programs to support one of these opinions: Society is pushing kindergarten children, or many kindergartens are not teaching children enough.
9. List special services school districts provide to kindergarten children.
10. Compare the curriculum of a private kindergarten, a private for-profit kindergarten, a parochial school kindergarten, and a public school kindergarten. What are the similarities and/or differences? Which would you send your child to? Why?
11. Do you think kindergarten should be mandatory for all children? At what age should it be mandatory?
12. Should the results of a readiness test be the final word on whether a child is admitted to kindergarten? Explain your answer.
13. Criticize the State of Nebraska statements as to what constitutes a good kindergarten. What would you add or change? Why?
14. What are reasons for the current interest in helping children make transitions from one setting or agency to another? What are other transitions that early childhood educators should help children make, besides those mentioned in this chapter?
15. Visit a kindergarten that uses one of the bilingual models mentioned in this chapter. Determine what the teachers think are the strengths and weaknesses of the program. How do the children like the program? Would you use the program? Why or why not?
16. Do you think the schools should teach programs of bilingual education? Why?
17. You have been asked to speak to a parent's group about the pros and cons of teaching reading in kindergarten. What major topics would you include?
18. How would you advise parents to promote literacy in the home?
19. List five reasons children should be computer-literate.
20. What are the issues facing kindergarten education?

9

The Primary Years: The Process of Schooling

As you read and study:

Compare and contrast the differences between preschool and kindergarten children and children in the primary grades

Explain the physical, cognitive, language, psychosocial, and moral characteristics of primary children

Be aware of the academic nature of the primary grades

Identify and discuss basic skills and basic skills tests

Cite ways the basic skills curricula influence primary children and their teaching and learning

Identify issues relating to primary education

Analyze computer curricula for the primary grades and understand their essential features

Speculate about the future of primary education

I n contrast to the renewed interest in infants, one might almost say that the years from six to eight are the forgotten years of early childhood, and primary children are frequently overlooked in terms of early childhood education. Although the profession defines early childhood education as from birth to age eight, children from birth through kindergarten receive most of the attention; primary grade children are more often thought of as belonging to the elementary years. Indeed, the years from six to twelve are often referred to as the *middle years* or *middle childhood*, the years between early childhood and adolescence.

WHAT ARE PRIMARY CHILDREN LIKE?

Physical Development

Two words describe the physical growth of the primary age child—*slow* and *steady*. Children at this age do not make the rapid and obvious height and weight gains of the infant, toddler, and preschool years. This is instead a time of continual growth during which children develop increasing control over their bodies and explore the things they are able to do. Boys continue to be taller and heavier than girls during this period; average height and weight gains are two-and-a-half inches and five pounds per year. Wide variations appear not only in individual rates of growth and development, however, but also among the sizes of children in each classroom. The wide differences in physical appearances result from genetic and cultural factors, nutritional intake and habits, health care, and experiential background.

Someone who had not been around primary children for many years might notice of a first grade class "how much bigger the children are today!" The perception that children today are larger than children of 50 years ago is accurate; children today *are* bigger than they were in the past. This comparison is a *secular trend* that occurs in industrialized, developed countries with high standards of health care and nutrition. This secular trend does not continue indefinitely, because there are genetic determinants beyond which humans as a species cannot develop. In fact, the secular trend in the U.S. has diminished, but is just beginning in some developing countries. Figure 9–1 shows that five-year-old boys and girls in the U.S. in 1965 were about two inches taller than five-year-olds in 1905, and nine-year-olds in 1965 were three inches taller than children in 1905.

Motor Development

The primary child is adept at many motor skills. The six-year-old is in the *initiative* stage of psychosocial development; seven- and eight-year-old children are in the *industry* stage. Not only are children intuitively driven to initiate activities, they are also learning to be competent and productive individuals. The primary years are thus a time to use and test developing motor skills. Children at this age should be actively involved in projects and creative activities that enable them to use their bodies to learn

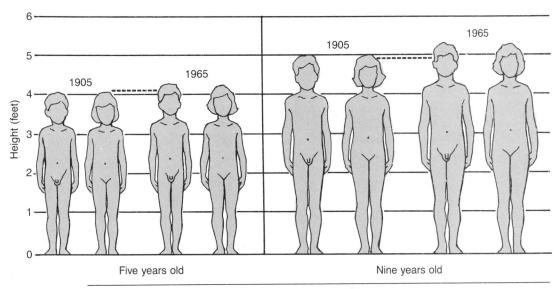

FIGURE 9–1 Early Maturation (From J. M. Tanner, "Earlier Maturation in Man," *Scientific American*, 218, 1 [January 1968]: 21)

and to develop feelings of purpose and competence. Their growing competence and confidence in their physical skills is reflected in their using them in games of running, chasing, and kicking. A nearly universal characteristic of children in this period is their almost constant physical involvement.

Differences between boys' and girls' motor skills during the primary years are minimal; their abilities are about equal. One implication for teachers is that they should not try to limit either boys' or girls' involvements in activities based on gender. Also, children should not be organized into leagues and activities that require physical and motor skills beyond their abilities or that are too competitive. We see evidence of the continuing refinement of fine motor skills in the primary years in children's abilities to do many of the tasks they were previously unable to do or could do only with difficulty. They are now able to dress themselves relatively easily and attend to most of their personal needs, such as using utensils, combing their hair, and brushing their teeth. They are also more proficient at school tasks that require fine motor skills, such as writing, artwork, and use of computers.

Cognitive Development

Children's cognitive development during the elementary school years enables them to do things as fifth and sixth graders that they could not do as first and second graders. A major difference between these two age groups is that the older child's thinking has become less egocentric and more logical. The cognitive milestone that enables children between seven and eleven to think and act as they do is *concrete operational thought*; their reasoning, however, is still tied to the concrete. Logical operations are possible with concrete objects and referents in the here and now. Abstract reasoning comes later, in the *formal operation stage* during adolescence.

Moral Development

The leading proponents of a developmental concept of children's moral growth are Jean Piaget and Lawrence Kohlberg. Piaget identified the two stages of moral thinking typical of children in the elementary grades as the stage of *heteronomy*—being governed by others regarding right and wrong—and the stage of *autonomy*—being governed by oneself regarding right and wrong.

> The analysis of the child's moral judgments has led us perforce to the discussion of the great problem of the relations of social life to the rational consciousness. The conclusion we came to was that the morality prescribed for the individual by society is not homogeneous because society itself is not just one thing. Society is the sum of social relations, and among these relations we can distinguish two extreme types: relations of constraint, whose characteristic is to impose upon the individual from outside a system of rules with obligatory content, and relations of cooperation whose characteristic is to create within people's minds the consciousness of ideal norms at the back of all rules. Arising from the ties of authority and unilateral respect, the relations of constraint therefore characterize most of the features of society as it exists, and in particular the relations of the child to its adult surrounding. Defined by equality and mutual respect, the relations of cooperation, on the contrary, constitute an equiliberal limit rather than a static system.[1]

The stage of heteronomy is characterized by "relations of constraint." In this stage, the child's concept of good and bad and right and wrong is determined by the judgments pronounced by adults. An act is "wrong" because one's parents or teacher say it is wrong. The child's understanding of morality is based upon the authority of adults and those values which "constrain" her.

Gradually, as the child matures and has opportunities for experiences with peers and adults, moral thinking may change to "relations of cooperation." This stage of personal morality is characterized by exchange of viewpoints between children and between children and adults as to what is right, wrong, good, or bad. This level of moral development is not achieved by authority, but rather by social experiences within which one has opportunities to try out different ideas and discuss moral situations. Autonomous behavior does not mean that children agree with other children or adults, but that autonomous people exchange opinions and try to negotiate solutions.

The stage of relations of constraint is characteristic of children up through first and second grades, while the stage of relations of cooperation is characteristic for children in the middle and upper elementary grades. The real criterion for determining which developmental stage a child is operating in, however, is how she is thinking, not how old she is.

Lawrence Kohlberg, a follower of Piaget, also believes children's moral thinking occurs in developmental levels. The levels and substages of moral growth as conceptualized by Kohlberg are preconventional, conventional, and postconventional.[2]

Level I, Preconventional Level (Ages 4–10)

Morality is basically a matter of good or bad, based on a system of punishments and rewards as administered by adults in authority positions. In Stage 1, the punishment-and-obedience orientation, the child operates within and responds to physical consequences of behavior. Good and bad are based upon the rewards they bring, and the child bases judgments on whether an action will bring pleasure. In Stage 2, the instrumental-relativist orientation, the child's actions are motivated by satisfaction of needs. Consequently, interpersonal relations have their basis in arrangements of mutual convenience based on need satisfaction. ("You scratch my back; I'll scratch yours.")

Level II, Conventional Level (Ages 10–13)

Morality is doing what is socially accepted, desired, and approved. The child conforms to, supports, and justifies the order of society. Stage 3 is the interpersonal concordance or "good boy—nice girl" orientation. Emphasis is on what a "good boy" or "nice girl" would do. The child conforms to images of what good behavior is. In Stage 4, the "law-and-order" orientation, emphasis is on respect for authority and doing one's duty under the law.

Level III, Postconventional Level (Age 13 and Beyond)

Morality consists of principles beyond a particular group or authority structure. The individual develops a moral system that reflects universal considerations and rights.

Stage 5 is the social-contract legalistic orientation. Right action consists of the individual rights agreed upon by all society. In addition to democratic and constitutional considerations, what is right is relative to personal values. At Stage 6, the universal-ethical-principle orientation, what is right is determined by universal principles of justice, reciprocity, and equality. The actions of the individual are based on a combination of conscience and these ethical principles.

Just as Piaget's cognitive stages are fixed and invariant for all children, so too are Kohlberg's moral levels. All individuals move through the process of moral development beginning at Level I and progress through each level. No level can be skipped, nor does an individual necessarily achieve every level. Just as intellectual development may become fixed at a particular level of development, so may an individual become fixed at any one of the moral levels.

Implications for Classrooms

What implications do the theories of Piaget, Kohlberg, and programs for promoting affective education have for classroom practice? First, the teacher must like and respect children. Second, the classroom climate must be accepting of individual values. Respect for children means respect for and acceptance of the value system the child brings to school. It is easy to accept an individual with a value system similar to one's own; it takes more self-discipline and maturity to accept an individual with a different value system. Third, teachers and schools must be willing to deal with issues, morals, and value systems other than those they promote for convenience, such as obedience and docility. Fourth, Kohlberg maintains that a sense of justice must prevail in the schools, instead of the injustice that arises from imposing arbitrary institutional values. Fifth, children must have opportunities to interact with peers and different age groups of children and adults to enable them to move to the higher levels of moral functioning. Sixth, students must have opportunities to make decisions and discuss the results of decision making. Developing a value system cannot occur through telling or through a solitary opportunity at decision making.

SIGNIFICANCE OF THE PRIMARY YEARS

The primary years of early childhood education are significant because children are inducted into the process of formal schooling. The preschool experience is often viewed as preparation for school; with first grade, the process of schooling begins. How this induction goes will, to a large extent, determine whether children like or dislike the process of schooling. Children's attitudes toward themselves and their lives are determined at this time. The degree of success now will set limits on life-long success as well as school success. Preparation for dealing with, engaging in, and successfully completing school tasks begins long before the primary grades, but it is during the primary grades that children encounter failure, grade retention, and negative attitudes. Negative experiences during this period have a profound effect on their efforts to develop positive self-image. Primary children are in Erikson's *industry vs. inferiority* stage. They want and need to be competent; faced with school failure, they can develop feelings of inferiority and a feeling that they will never be able to do anything well.

In the primary years, children encounter the academic-oriented, basic-skills-based, achievement-test-centered, accountability-conscious, pressure-filled process that characterizes modern schooling. Many states prescribe minimum basic skills for grades one, two, and three, with achievement measured by state examinations. In Florida, a student can be retained twice in the primary grades for failure to achieve; results of a third grade achievement examination given at the *beginning* of the school year are used to make decisions regarding promotion to the fourth grade.

REASONS FOR THE BACK-TO-BASICS MOVEMENT

Schooling in the elementary years has become a serious enterprise for which it is possible to identify political, social, and economic reasons. First, educators, parents and politicians are realizing that solutions to illiteracy, a poorly prepared work force, and many social problems begin in the first years of school, not after the problems have gone beyond correction. A second reason is that the public will not tolerate further decline in educational standards. The public wants the schools to do a better job teaching the basic skills because of declining SAT scores, the need for remedial reading courses for college freshmen, the high rate of adult illiteracy, and the inability of many high school graduates to fill out a job application. Third, parents and the general public believe a return to "old fashioned" schooling that emphasizes basic skills and discipline will alleviate and perhaps cure the apparent decline of traditional American values.

The emphasis on testing has affected children and influenced curriculum both positively and negatively.

Basic Skills and Teaching Methodology

The back-to-basics movement is more than a return to the "three R's." It affects the methodology of teaching and the classroom environment. We see its effects several ways:

1. Emphasis on drill, memorization, and a teacher-directed and controlled learning environment
2. More homework as an aid to learning. We now take it for granted that children will have homework in the primary grades; some school districts prescribe a certain amount of homework for each subject and grade level. Parents support the emphasis on homework because they see it as a way to keep children involved in the learning process.
3. Renewal of the teacher's role as disciplinarian. Teachers are rediscovering their role in managing and guiding behavior (see Chapter 12), and parents and the public expect teachers to maintain an atmosphere of no-nonsense learning.
4. Higher standards for grade promotion. Promotion is often tied to or based on results of achievement test scores, and promotion standards based on age and level of socialization are coming under tighter public scrutiny.
5. Redefining the curriculum of the primary grades by state legislatures, which specify minimum basic skills for each grade level.
6. Use of tests to measure student achievement, determine promotions, judge teacher performance, and measure the quality of schools.

CURRICULUM FOR THE PRIMARY GRADES

Whether or not we approve of the basic skills emphasis in the primary grades, the fact remains that the present curriculum centers around reading, writing, and arithmetic. The curricular emphasis in the primary grades *is* the basic skills. Other content areas—science, social studies, art/music, health and physical education—are often included only when and if their is time, which means that in actual practice, they may not be taught at all.

With the emphasis on basic skills and teaching/learning accountability, many states specify minimum basic skills that form the basis for the primary curriculum. Many of these states also produce assessment instruments to test student achievement of these skills. Figure 9–2 shows a sample assessment item for mathematics at the beginning of grade three. These are sample assessment items for reading for grade three:

DIRECTIONS: Read the story and choose the sentence that best tells the main idea, or what the story is about.

> The baby has a basket of toys. He has a toy duck. He has a doll. He has a train and a truck. He likes his duck.

1. Which sentence best tells the main idea?
   A. ☐ He likes his duck.
   B. ☐ He has a doll.
   C. ☐ He has a train and a truck.
   D. ☐ The baby has a basket of toys.

> The children at school had a picnic. They played games. They ran in the grass. They went up a hill. They had good things to eat.

2. Which sentence best tells the main idea?
   A. ☐ The children at school had a picnic.
   B. ☐ They ran in the grass.
   C. ☐ They went up a hill.
   D. ☐ They had good things to eat.[3]

Figure 9–3 is an example of the Dade County writing assessment, and Figure 9–4 shows a reading objective and test item for grade 1 that is part of the Texas assessment of skills.

Special Primary Curricula

Despite the preoccupation with basic skills, from time to time other curricula receive attention for possible inclusion in the primary grades. There is, for example, a growing feeling among early childhood educators that solutions to many societal prob-

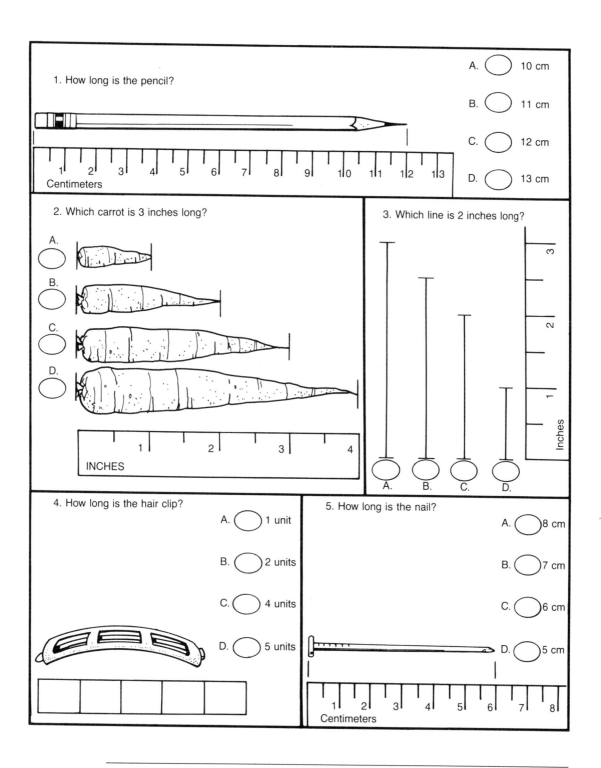

FIGURE 9–2 Sample Assessment Items: Mathematics, Grade 3 (From the School Board of Dade County, Florida)

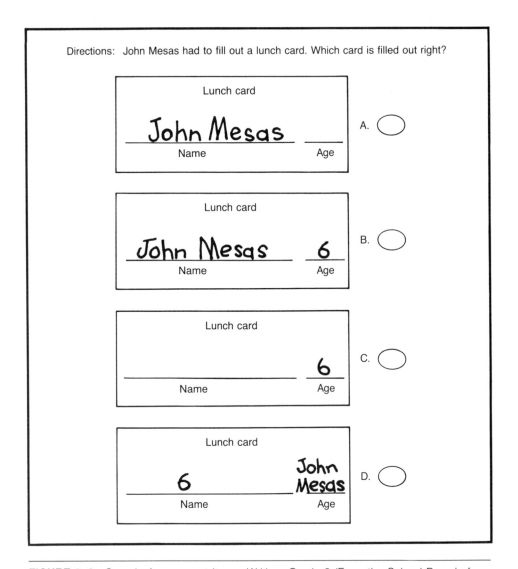

FIGURE 9–3 Sample Assessment Items: Writing, Grade 3 (From the School Board of Dade County, Florida)

lems, including war and conflict, should begin in the primary and preschool years. Consequently, there is emphasis on *prosocial behaviors*—teaching children the fundamentals of peaceful living, kindness, helpfulness, and cooperation. Teachers can do several things to foster development of prosocial skills in the classroom.

☐ Be a good role model for children. Teachers must demonstrate in their own lives and relationships with children and other adults the behaviors of cooperation and kindness that they want to encourage in children.

Teacher says: Read the word in the box to yourself. Find the picture of this word. Fill in the space under the picture of this word.

Find the picture of this word.

doghouse

(correct)   (incomplete)   (irrelevant)

FIGURE 9–4 Sample Assessment Item for Reading, Grade 1 (From Texas Education Agency, *Texas Education Assessment of Minimum Skills: Reading Objectives and Measurement Specifications, 1986–1990, Grade 1,* 1986, pp. 10–11.)

☐ Provide positive feedback and reinforcement when children perform pro-social behaviors. When children are rewarded for appropriate behavior, they tend to repeat that behavior.

☐ Provide opportunities for children to help and show kindness to others. Co-operative programs between primary children and nursing and retirement homes are excellent opportunities to practice helping and kind behaviors.

☐ Conduct classroom routines and activities so they are as free as possible of conflict. At the same time, teachers can provide many opportunities for children to work together and practice skills for cooperative living. Learning centers and activities can be designed for children to share and work cooperatively.

☐ Provide practice in conflict resolution skills when real conflicts occur. These skills include: taking turns, apologizing, compromising, and talking through problems. Teachers can also help children by redirecting their behavior and attention to other activities.

☐ Conduct classroom activities based on multicultural principles (see Chapter 11) and free from stereotyping and sexist behaviors (see Chapter 14).

☐ Read stories to children and provide literature for them to read that exemplify prosocial behaviors.

☐ Counsel and work with parents to encourage them to limit their children's television viewing, especially of programs that are violent.

☐ Help children feel good about themselves, build strong self-images, and be competent individuals. Children who are happy, confident, and competent feel good about themselves and behave positively toward others.

Computers in the Primary Grades

Surprisingly, many people, including early childhood educators, still think computers are a fad that will disappear if we ignore them long enough. But computers are an integral part of society, and they are here to stay. Three problems confront early childhood teachers in their search to implement an effective program of computer instruction: their personal acceptance of computers; decisions about how to use computers in the classroom; and assuring themselves that computers do not have a negative influence on children. Teachers cannot afford to decide *not* to use computers; in fact, they must promote access to computers and come up with creative ways to involve students.

Computer literacy is imperative for today's children.

Children and their teachers need to be computer-literate, and this goal should drive and direct the computer program of the primary grades. You can develop an effective program of computer literacy with the following guidelines:

1. Computer literacy must be defined comprehensively, including two general areas: learning *with* computers and learning *about* computers.
2. However, decisions concerning what children learn about computers should be made not by asking "What can we teach kids about computers?" but by asking "What understandings about computers, their impact on our world, and their uses are *developmentally appropriate* for, and *educationally relevant* to, young children." This implies that lectures on the history of computers or rote memorization of computer components terminology should not be included in the curriculum. Only when meaningful concepts can be actively learned should they be considered for inclusion.
3. For both general areas, educators should (a) decide first how and when to use computers to accomplish the goals of early education, and (b) integrate these uses into the curriculum, while (c) remaining consistent with the beliefs, principles, and practices of the program. These guidelines have several important ramifications. For example, they imply that (a) the development of the "whole child" will be given first and primary consideration; (b) there will not be a "computers" unit that is separate from work in social studies, science, language arts, and so on; and (c) *individual children will have different needs, interests, and abilities and, therefore, will learn different things about computers and will use them in different ways.* This should be welcomed as well as accepted; no effort should be made to force all children to "master" all aspects of computer literacy. Instead of one definition of computer literacy for all, teachers should determine what computers can do to help a particular child reach a particular goal.[4]

A suggested scope and sequence of topics and skills for preschool, kindergarten, and the primary grades is outlined in Table 9–1.

CHARACTERISTICS OF A GOOD PRIMARY TEACHER

When all is said and done, it is the teacher who sets the tone and direction for classroom instruction and learning. Without a quality teacher, there will not be a quality program. A quality primary teacher must possess all the personal qualities of a humane, loving, caring person. In addition, the teacher must be capable of dealing with young children who are full of energy. Unlike upper elementary children, who are more goal- and self-directed, primary children need help in developing the skills and personal habits that will enable them to be self-directed and independent learners. To help them develop these skills and habits should be the primary teacher's foremost goal. These guidelines will help implement that goal:

1. Plan for instruction. Planning is the basis for the vision of what a teacher wants for herself and for the children. Teachers who try to operate without a plan are like builders without a blueprint. Although planning takes time, it saves time in the long run, and it provides direction for instruction.
2. Be the classroom leader. A quality teacher *leads* the classroom. Some teachers forget this, and although children at all ages are capable of performing

TABLE 9–1 Teaching Young Children *About* Computers: A Suggested Outline

	Preschool	Kindergarten	1	2	3
I. Hardware, Software, Outerwear, and Underwear: What Should Young Children Understand?					
A. What is a computer? How does a computer work?	I	I	I	D	D
1. Models for understanding hardware and software	I	I	D	D	D
2. Computers need instructions	I	D	D	D	D
3. Computers can do many jobs	I	D	D	D	D
4. Computers work with letters, words, numbers, sound, and pictures					
B. What are the parts of a computer? What do they do?					
1. Computer systems and components (parts)		I	D	D	D
2. Models for understanding parts of a computer and what they do		I	D	D	D
C. What different kinds of computers are there?					I
1. History					
2. Types of computers		I	I	D	D
D. Capabilities and limitations					
1. What computers can and cannot do	I	I	D	D	D
2. Artificial intelligence			I	I	D
II. How Are Computers Used in the Neighborhood?					
A. Local applications of computers		I	D	D	D
B. Impact of computers		I	D	D	D
III. How Can *We* Use Computers?					
A. Getting started: using computers, typing, and problem solving	I	I	D	D	D
B. Computer programming: now we teach the computer	I	D	D	D	D
C. Using computers as tools: learning what is in the curriculum with computers	I	D	D	D	D

I = Incidental, Informal, Introduction

D = Directed activities, Discussions

Source: Douglas H. Clements, *Computers in Early and Primary Education* (Englewood Cliffs, N.J.: Prentice-Hall, 1985), p. 54.

leadership responsibilities, it is the teacher who sets the tone, direction, and guidelines within which effective instruction occurs. Without strong leadership—not overbearing or dictatorial leadership—classrooms don't operate well. Planning for instruction helps a teacher lead.

3. Involve children in meaningful learning tasks. To learn, children need to be *involved*. To learn to read they must read; to learn to write, they must write. Although these guidelines may seem self-evident, they aren't always implemented. To learn, children need to spend time on learning tasks.

4. Provide individualized instruction. In a classroom of 25 to 30 or more children, there is a wide range of differences. The teacher must provide for these ranges in abilities and interests if children are going to learn to their fullest. There is a difference between *individual* and *individualized* instruction; it is impossible to provide individual attention to all children all the time, but providing for children at their individual levels is possible and necessary. Educators are often accused of teaching to the average, boring the more able, and leaving the less able behind. This criticism can be addressed with individualized instruction.

Good teachers keep their teaching child-centered.

ISSUES IN PRIMARY EDUCATION

Testing

Much of the primary school child's life is influenced by testing. What children study, how they study it, and the length of time they study it are all determined by testing. Decisions about promotion are also made from test results. With so much emphasis on tests, it is understandable that the issue raises many concerns. Critics maintain that the testing movement reduces teaching and learning to the lowest common denominator—teaching children what they need to know to get the right answers.

Promotion

It should not be surprising that a central issue of the back-to-basics movement is whether a child should be promoted if he doesn't demonstrate competence in the skills specified for his grade. Retention as a cure for poor or nonachievement is popular, especially with the public pressure for tougher standards and greater accountability. Despite the use of retention as a panacea for poor achievement, "the evidence to date suggests that achievement-based promotion does not deal effectively with the problem of low achievement."[5] Better and more helpful approaches to student achievement include strategies such as these:

- ☐ Promotion combined with remedial instruction
- ☐ Promotion to a transition class in which students receive help to master the skills they don't know
- ☐ Use of after-school and summer programs to help students master skills
- ☐ Providing children specific and individualized help in mastery of skills
- ☐ Working with parents to teach them how to help their children work on mastery skills
- ☐ Identifying children who may need help before they enter first grade so that remedial services can be provided early

Any effort to improve student achievement must emphasize helping children rather than practices that threaten to detract from their self-image and which make them solely responsible for their failure.

Homework

Many parents and teachers consider homework essential to the back-to-basics movement and the redefinition of primary education. Unfortunately, however, homework is often assigned on the assumption that it will help children, and the more homework, the better. When assigning homework, teachers should keep in mind the purpose of the homework, the child's ability to do the assigned work, and the relation of the homework to curriculum goals. These additional guidelines will also prove helpful:

1. What happens in the classroom is the real ballgame. That is where achievement test scores are going to go up or down. Homework can enhance the game, but doesn't really change it.

2. More isn't better. Increasing the quantity of homework without addressing curriculum issues will produce minimal results. The homework curriculum must be carefully planned so that it is integral to the classroom learning.
3. Good teaching. Reinforcement is an essential element in motivating and instructing students. A teacher who gives homework should also give reinforcement. Feedback must be a part of the homework scheme.
4. School isn't everything. Both the quantity and timing of homework must be considered in light of the student's total life.[6]

Child-Centered Teaching and Learning

There has always been a tension between subject-centered teaching and child-centered teaching. Whenever subject matter becomes the center of focus in an educational system, as is presently the case, there is a danger that children's needs and developmental characteristics will be moved to the background. Educators must constantly remind themselves and the public that schools are for children, and their best interests must have priority. It makes little sense for a school to raise the average of its achievement tests scores at the cost of lowering children's self-esteem and intrinsic self-worth.

HOME SCHOOLING

One hundred and fifty years ago, home schooling was rather widespread. With the advent of compulsory public schooling in 1836, home schooling went into decline. During the last decade, however, there has been a remarkable increase in the number of parents who are taking their children out of school to teach them at home. It is difficult to determine exactly how many parents are using home schooling, but Susannah Sheffer of Holt Associates, a support agency to the home schooling movement in Boston, Massachusetts, estimates that 20,000 families are educating 50,000 children at home.

John Holt (1923–1985) was a leading proponent of home schooling and an early popularizer and supporter of the open education movement. In his books *How Children Learn* and *How Children Fail*, he stressed the need for children to learn in environments that were free from undue pressure and where they could control their own learning. As Holt became increasingly disenchanted with the public schools as places that are conducive to children's best interests, he championed home schooling as an option for parents who wanted to provide an optimal education for their children. These are some of the motivations for parents' educating their children at home:

1. Some parents like being home with their children. They think a parent's place—preferably the mother's place—is at home. They also believe that having children living and learning in the home enhances family cohesiveness and unity. Proponents of strengthening the family unit see home schooling as a contributor to family stability.

Thea and Nathan Wheeling: Learning at Home

Thea Wheeling of Franklin, Pennsylvania, has home-schooled her seven-year-old son, Nathan, for the past three years. Thea is not happy about the age at which children go off to school for formal learning. As she explains, "All the reading I was doing indicated that children are not ready for formal learning until between the ages of eight to ten. I wanted to delay Nathan's formal learning until that time. I didn't want him to enter a public school setting where he would be forced to learn. In a public school there is too much competition and aggression. These are the kinds of things that affect a child's self-esteem. My husband, Greg, and I wanted the best for Nathan and we believe I am providing the best for him at home."

Although some people perceive of home schooling as children's sitting all day at the kitchen or dining room table, this is certainly not true for Thea and Nathan. "We don't have typical days," says Thea. "We usually begin by doing math—Nathan's favorite—and writing and language activities for about half an hour or so. We also read a lot. I read to Nathan and he reads to me. He also really enjoys reading to his baby sister Leslie, who is two years old." Nathan says the best part of his home school days are the times he and his mother read to each other.

Thea believes that good learning and teaching are integrated with real-life activities. Nathan, who is quite advanced in math, helps Thea pay her monthly bills, helps balance the checkbook, and addresses and mails family correspondence. Many of Nathan's learning experiences occur outside the home in the community. "We do a lot of things with nature, so we are always going on walks and field trips. Nathan is a member of the Junior Naturalist Club, and he learns a lot by participating in it."

Once a week, Nathan visits and stays overnight with his great-grandmother, who is 82. He helps her with household chores and yard work. According to Thea, "This is the kind of activity Nathan wouldn't be able to do if he were in school. I believe he has learned many prosocial skills by being involved with a wide range of other adults. As a result, he has learned a lot about helping others, sharing, and human interactions."

Thea believes that home schooling gives Nathan opportunities to learn in natural, unhurried ways, free from pressure to learn and achieve. "We can wait for certain kinds of learning to occur. When he made his P backward, I didn't worry about it. He didn't have to do it like everyone else in the class. We went on and read stories and wrote poetry. He soon learned how to make a P the right way, and I didn't have to scold or nag him to do it."

Thea and Greg plan to enter Nathan in public school beginning with third grade. "He has a good foundation," says Thea. "Scholastically, he is ahead of where he should be for his grade level. He also knows how to learn on his own. His vision and hearing have had more time to develop and he has reached the age of cause-and-effect reasoning. Now he is ready for formal learning. I don't think he will have any problems adjusting to public schooling."

2. Some parents don't want to give up the educating of their children to other people or agencies. As one parent expresses it, "Why should I let someone else have all the fun and joy of teaching my children?"

3. Some parents believe children learn best when they decide themselves what they will learn, and when and how they will learn it. With evidence of the "hurried child" and the current push in preschool and primary grades for basic education, some parents think home schooling is a natural alternative to the pressures of public schooling.

4. Some parents prefer home schooling as an appropriate way to inculcate religious values of their choice, since the public schools, of course, must steer away from religion.

5. Some parents believe that before the age of eight or ten, children are not physically or cognitively ready for the pressures and demands of formal, public schooling.

Issues of Home Schooling

Socialization

Almost without exception, the first issue raised in regard to children schooled at home is whether they are being properly socialized. Most people believe one of the primary functions of preschools, public schools, and play groups is to socialize young children; consequently, they think that if children don't go to school, they will miss opportunities for socialization. Thea Wheeling, however, believes that young children's socialization occurs best in the family setting. "We can provide for Nathan's socialization better than the public schools. In the public schools, there are 20 to 30 children all the same age with only one adult, the teacher. This is not a real situation nor a natural way to socialize. Opportunities for socialization are limited in a public school classroom. In the real world, children interact with adults of all ages who live by different rules and have different relationships. The best socialization occurs in a family setting. As a family, we interact with other families, the church, community agencies, other adults, the elderly, and with children of all ages. Nathan has more opportunities for real socialization than children who stay in a classroom all day with one adult. We don't prevent him from socializing with other children and adults; on the other hand, in a school setting children are frequently prevented from interacting with others."

Lack of Learning

The public—especially the segment that believes true learning occurs only in a school setting—wonders if children really learn anything at home. The Wheelings submit a learning/teaching plan to the school district each year. The plan includes specific learning goals and objectives for all the curriculum areas Nathan's peers will cover.

Many home schoolers use prepackaged curricula available from commercial publishers. Others use a combination of commercial materials and materials loaned by the public schools. Many public school principals and teachers are supportive of home schoolers' efforts and provide material and advice and encourage children and their families to participate in special activities and events. Thea, on the other hand, prefers to base Nathan's learning activities on the events and activities of daily living, although she is careful to ensure that Nathan learns the information and skills he needs for the end-of-year achievement tests he takes each year at the school. "So far he has done very well," says Thea. "He scores at or above his age level in many areas." She also has frequent conferences with the public school teachers to be sure she is providing Nathan with equivalent instruction in her home schooling program.

Teacher Certification

Critics of the home school movement question whether people who are not certified teachers can do a good job of teaching their children at home. Some think home schooling should be taught by a certified teacher. Thea responds to such criticism by saying, "I am a literate person. I read a lot in books and professional journals, seek advice from others, attend meetings with other home school parents and follow the curriculum of the public school. I agree with those who say that a parent is the child's first and best teacher."

Parent Rights

There is a tension between parents who believe they have the right to provide an alternative but equivalent education for their children and those who believe strongly in compulsory public school attendance. Critics think the home school movement undermines the traditional role of the public schools. It is unlikely that the issues of home schooling will ever be resolved to everyone's satisfaction; at the same time, home schooling is a reality for a growing number of children whose parents believe they have the right and ability to teach their children at home and that learning occurs best at home.

THE FUTURE OF PRIMARY EDUCATION

The educational system is slow to meet the demands and dictates of society, so it is unlikely that there will be dramatic changes over the decade. The direction will be determined by continual reassessment of the purpose of education and attempts to match the needs of society to the goals of the schools. Drug use, child abuse, the breakup of the family, and illiteracy are some of the societal problems the schools are being asked to address in significant ways. At the same time, national leaders are articulating their visions for America's elementary schools, and they provide useful information about what the future may hold. One notable example is the 1986 report by William Bennett, Secretary of Education. In this first study of the nation's elementary schools in three decades, Bennett said the schools were doing a good job, but could do a better job by implementing some of these suggestions:

- ☐ There should be greater parent involvement, with parents taking a central role in educating their children

☐ All adults must accept responsibility for educating children.
☐ Teachers should be more involved in curriculum decisions
☐ The elementary curriculum should be "unified" or integrated so that one subject area reinforces another
☐ Elementary schools need more time to devote to learning, perhaps with a 12-month school year
☐ Corporations should provide money to elementary schools to help them achieve their goals
☐ All elementary schools should have a disciplinary code
☐ Elementary schools must help save children from drugs
☐ Elementary children should be promoted on the basis of mastery of skills rather than according to a "chronological lockstep"
☐ Curricular reforms should include the "sublime and most solemn responsibility" of all elementary schools—to teach children to read; emphasis on writing; hands-on experiences in science; emphasis on problem solving in math; social studies that encompasses geography, history, and civics as well as the habits of life in a democratic society; arts programs; computer literacy; and every school should have a library, and every child should have a library card.[7]

These suggestions are worthy of consideration, although they raise questions about implementation, costs, and their influence on children and the educational process.

FURTHER READING

Clements, Douglas H. *Computers in Early and Primary Education* (Englewood Cliffs, N.J.: Prentice-Hall, 1985) Practical guide to computers and their use; shows how to integrate computers into the various curriculum areas.

Kepner, Harry S. (ed.) *Computers in the Classroom* (Washington, D.C.: National Education Association, 1982) Comprehensive compilation of articles about computers and their application; focuses on instructional use of computers and guidelines for selection and use of software.

FURTHER STUDY

1. Interview parents and teachers to determine their views pro and con of nonpromotion in the primary grades. Summarize your findings. What are your opinions on retention?
2. Visit elementary schools to determine their computer literacy curricula. Do you think the schools are doing as much as they can to promote computer literacy in the primary grades?
3. Are you computer literate? Could you implement a program of computer literacy in a first grade? Why or why not?
4. Survey children in a first, second, and third grade to determine how many have computers in the home. Find out what software is most popular, whether the children like working on computers, and what suggestions they would make for using computers in the school. List five implications of your findings for you as an early childhood teacher.

5. List at least six reasons that early childhood teachers should know about child growth and development.
6. Critique Bennett's recommendations for the public schools. Which recommendations do you agree and disagree with?
7. Do you think the public and the public schools are too caught up in the back-to-basics movement? Why or why not?
8. List five things primary teachers can do to minimize the negative effects of the testing movement on young children.
9. In addition to the characteristics of primary teachers listed in this chapter, what others do you think are desirable? Recall your own primary teachers. What characteristics did they have that had the greatest influence on you?
10. You have been asked to submit ten recommendations for changing and improving primary education in the U.S. Offer a rationale for each of your recommendations.
11. What other issues of primary education would you add to those mentioned in this chapter? How would you suggest dealing with them?
12. Do you think the primary grades are the neglected years of early childhood education? Why or why not?
13. Identify five contemporary issues or concerns facing society, and tell how teachers and primary schools could address each of them.
14. Why do many educators and parents think assigning homework is one way to improve the process of education and children's achievement? Do you agree?
15. Survey the homework practices and policies of school districts and teachers in your area. What conclusions can you draw? What recommendations would you make?
16. Explain how first grade children's cognitive and physical differences would make a difference in how they were taught. Give specific examples.
17. Of the three primary grades, decide which you would most like to teach, and explain your reasons.
18. What do you think are the most important subjects of the primary grades? Why? What would you say to a parent who thought any subjects besides reading, writing, and arithmetic were a waste of time?
19. Give your views pro and con for "social" promotion. What would you say to a state legislator who said that all children should be failed until they learned what they were supposed to in each grade?
20. Write about primary education in the year 2010. Tell what schools will be like, what children will learn, and how teaching will occur. Explain how you will prepare yourself for this future.

10

The Federal Government and Early Childhood Education: Helping Children Win

As you read and study:

Examine the objectives of Head Start, Follow Through, and other federal programs

Describe and understand the full range of services that Head Start provides to children and their families

Describe the nature and purposes of the Home Base program

Discuss the purposes and function of the Head Start Measures Project

Analyze and understand the Head Start Migrant program

Clarify your personal values regarding involvement of the federal government in educational programs

Analyze the impact of Head Start on children and families

Examine the results of federally supported programs for children and their families

Examine current attitudes toward federal support for early childhood programs

E vidence from many sources indicates that when parents' incomes are inadequate to meet social and educational needs, children are impaired in their ability to become contributing members of society. One of the most damaging consequences of poverty, however, is the effect of that lack of opportunity on self-image.

It is estimated that about thirty million children live in poverty, meaning that their families' incomes are below the poverty guidelines set by the U.S. government. The effects of poverty are debilitating for both children and families. Being poor means more than being eligible for a free school lunch. It means these children as a group are less healthy, live in inadequate housing, and do not have the opportunities for activities and experiences their wealthier counterparts have. Divorce brings economic consequences as well as social ones. A child in a household headed by a single female has a greater chance of being poor; the majority of low-income families are headed by females. Poverty, in a sense, has become feminized.

One purpose of Head Start and other early intervention programs is to help children overcome the effects of a poor environment.

TABLE 10-1 1986 Family Income Guidelines for All States Except Alaska and Hawaii

Size of Family Unit*	Income
1	$ 5,360
2	$ 7,240
3	$ 9,120
4	$11,000
5	$12,880
6	$14,760
7	$16,640
8	$18,520

*For family units with more than 8 members, add $1,880 for each additional member.

By federal definition, being poor means that you and your family do not have an income that allows you to purchase adequate health care, housing, food, clothing, and educational services. As of 1985, the federal government used the income levels in Table 10-1 (adjusted to family size and farm or nonfarm residence) to define the poverty level. (These figures change constantly because of inflation and the rising cost of living.)

HEAD START: HISTORY AND OPERATING PRINCIPLES

To help overcome the negative effects of poverty on the lives of adults and children, the federal government, in 1964, passed the Economic Opportunity Act. One of the main purposes of this act was to break intergenerational cycles of poverty by providing educational and social opportunities for children from low-income families. The Economic Opportunity Act created the Office of Economic Opportunity, and from this office Project Head Start was developed and administered. Head Start was implemented during the summer of 1965, and approximately 550,000 children in 2,500 child-development centers were enrolled in the program. Today, the National Head Start program has a budget of $1,075,059,000, and serves 452,080 children or about 20 percent of those eligible. There are 1,305 Head Start programs, including 106 Indian and 24 Migrant programs for a total 24,123 classrooms at an average cost per child of $2,377 annually. A total of 9,597,070 children have been served by Head Start since it began.[1] Table 10-2 shows the racial and ethnic composition of Head Start

TABLE 10-2 Racial and Ethnic Composition of Head Start

Racial/Ethnic Group	Percentage of Enrollment
American Indian	4%
Hispanic	21%
Black	40%
White	32%
Asian	3%

Source: Administration for Children, Youth and Families, "Project Head Start Statistical Fact Sheet" (Washington, D.C.: Dec. 1985), p. 1.

TABLE 10–3   Ages of Children Served by Head Start

Age	Percentage of Enrollment
6-year-olds	1%
5-year-olds	14%
4-year-olds	58%
3-year-olds	25%
Under 3 years of age	2%

Source: Administration for Children, Youth and Families, "Project Head Start Statistical Fact Sheet" (Washington, D.C.: Dec. 1985), p. 2.

programs; Table 10–3 shows the ages of children served. Head Start was established and operates according to the following premises.

1. Children who come from low-income families often have not received the cognitive, social, and physical experiences normally associated with success in first grade.
2. Many programs created by poverty can be alleviated or compensated for if children receive these experiences before they start school.
3. Intergenerational poverty cycles can be broken by providing educational and social opportunities for children early in their lives.

The Head Start programs provide children with experiences to promote development in all areas: physical, social, emotional, and cognitive.

The Economic Opportunity Act required communities to create community action agencies to coordinate programs and money for Project Head Start. The act further specified that any nonprofit organization could apply for operational money, develop a program, and operate a Head Start center; thus, organizations such as churches, parent groups, and public schools could design a Head Start program and apply to the community action agency for funds. It was also possible for an agency to apply directly to the federal offices of Project Head Start for financing rather than to the community action agency. Many organizations currently receive their money this way and are therefore known as single-purpose agencies. While many Head Start programs were initially established by public school systems, most operated for only six to eight weeks during the summer. Presently, at the federal level, funding for Head Start comes through the Administration for Children, Youth and Families (ACYF). Figure 10–1 shows the organizational structure that governs the operation of Head Start programs.

Head Start is intended to provide a comprehensive developmental program for preschool children from low-income families. The project is also committed to helping children achieve a positive outlook on life through success in school and daily life activities. The overall general goal is to promote social competence by providing children with opportunities to achieve their potential in cognitive, language, socioemotional, and physical development.

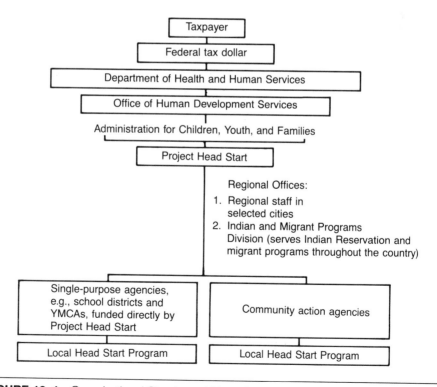

FIGURE 10–1 Organizational Structure of Head Start

Agencies are permitted and encouraged to consider several program models and select the option best-suited to the needs of the children and the capabilities and resources of the program staff. Available program options are the standard Head Start model, variations in center attendance, double sessions, home-based models, and locally designed variations.

The overall goal of Head Start is to bring about a greater degree of social competence in disadvantaged children. By social competence is meant the child's everyday effectiveness in dealing with his environment and later responsibilities in school and life. Social competence takes into account the interrelatedness of cognitive and intellectual development, physical and mental health, nutritional needs, and other factors that enable a child to function optimally. Head Start is a comprehensive developmental approach to helping achieve social competence. To this end, Head Start goals provide for:

A. The improvement of the child's health and physical abilities.
B. The encouragement of self-confidence, spontaneity, curiosity, and self-discipline which will assist in the development of the child's social and emotional health.
C. The enhancement of the child's mental processes and skills with particular attention to conceptual and verbal skills.
D. The establishment of patterns and expectations of success for the child, which will create a climate of confidence for his present and future learning efforts and overall development.
E. An increase in the ability of the child and his family to relate to each other and to others in a loving and supporting manner.
F. The enhancement of the sense of dignity and self-worth within the child and his family.

Head Start's approach is based on the philosophy that: (1) a child can benefit most from a comprehensive, interdisciplinary program to foster his development and remedy his problems, and (2) the child's entire family, as well as the community, must be involved.[2]

Implementation of these objectives occurs through Head Start child development centers, which provide a wide range of social, economic, educative, and physical services for children and their families.

HEAD START COMPONENTS

Head Start has the following program components: education, parent involvement, health service (including psychological services, nutrition, and mental health), social service, and career development for staff, parents, and administration.

Education

Objectives

The educational program of Head Start is guided by the following objectives:

1. Provide children with a learning environment and the varied experiences which will help them develop socially, intellectually, physically, and emotionally in a manner appropriate to their age and state of development toward the overall goal of social competence.
2. Integrate the educational aspects of the various Head Start components in the daily program of activities.
3. Involve parents in educational activities of the program to enhance their role as the principal influence on the child's education and development.
4. Assist parents to increase knowledge, understanding, skills and experience in child growth and development.
5. Identify and reinforce experiences which occur in the home that parents can utilize as educational activities for their children.[3]

These educational objectives guide local programs in developing their own programs that are unique and responsive to the children, families, and communities they serve. Thus, there is really no national Head Start curriculum, although some people mistakenly believe there is. Many Head Start centers stress activities generally typical of nursery school-kindergarten programs and include activities associated with success in school, such as taking and following directions, listening, and becoming accustomed to the routines and materials of learning, such as books.

Programmatic Direction

One problem many Head Start centers have with the educational component of their programs is translating the national goals into meaningful local goals. This in turn results in uncertainty about the kind of program the center will conduct, making it difficult for teachers to select appropriate activities. Head Start's educational objectives are sufficiently comprehensive to permit a center to conduct just about any kind of educational program it considers appropriate; however, herein lies the problem. If a center director has adequate preparation and is able to conceptualize what a good program should include, then working within the guidelines of the Head Start educational objectives can be a strength. If directors do not have adequate preparation, the program may be full of directionless activities.

The Administration for Children, Youth and Families defines a part-day Head Start Program as one in which children attend less than six hours a day. Full-day programs are those in which children attend six or more hours a day. Keep in mind that local programs are free to develop their own programs within Head Start guidelines. This is a schedule for a relatively unstructured, full-day program (activities in parentheses should be scheduled according to the children's needs):

Teachers and assistant teachers arrive
   (plan for day)
   (set up room for day)
Children arrive, greeted individually, health inspection
Early morning activities
Breakfast
Brush teeth

(Group time)
Free choice of activities in learning areas (1 hour)
  art, building, dramatic, reading, manipulative
(Group time)
(Snack)
Outdoor activities (1 hour)
  organized games and exercises
(Group time)
Lunch
Brush teeth
Nap time (30 minutes–1 hour)
(Snack)
(Outdoor activities)
Children leave
(Teachers and assistant teachers evaluate and plan)
  Assistant teachers leave
  Teacher leaves
  Home visits[4]

This schedule is typical of a more structured program:

7:30 Arrival, individual activities
8:00 Breakfast, toothbrushing, toileting
8:45 Planning time (individually as children complete health needs)
9:00 Work time
9:40 Clean-up, toileting
10:00 Recall time and snack (children assist with snack)
10:25 Small group time
10:40 Circle time (health activities, songs and games—planned experiences in either health, safety, or nutrition *must* be provided on a weekly basis, as a part of the daily routine activities, i.e., small group time, circle time)
11:00 Outside activity time
11:30 Preparation for lunch (handwashing, table setting)
12:00 Lunchtime
12:30 Circle time (stories, finger plays, nursery rhymes—opportunities must be provided for children to engage in a fifteen-minute activity prior to napping)
12:45 Rest time, teacher breaks (removal of children's shoes is required at rest time)
1:45 Snack
2:00 Dismissal, individual activities
2:30 Team planning[5]

Performance Standards

Since 1973, Head Start programs have had performance standards or requirements that must be met to continue receiving federal funds. For example, according to the standards, educational objectives must be written to incorporate activities and services for meeting the needs of all children in the Head Start center. Each objective in all the component areas has a corresponding performance standard. Linking objectives to minimum standards of performance represents an admirable attempt by Head Start to strengthen its program of services.

Coordination with Public Schools

The attitude among Head Start personnel has been that whatever the public schools included in their programs, Head Start would not. Unfortunately, the crucial issues of personalizing instruction and doing what is best for children may have been overlooked. Head Start is now beginning to adopt the position that it will provide what the child needs and rely on the public school to extend and go beyond this. Obviously, this philosophy calls for more coordination and liaison between Head Start and the public schools.

Educational Skills Project

To strengthen its educational component, the Administration for Children, Youth and Families in 1978 launched its Basic Educational Skills Program to place greater emphasis on teaching basic skills. As a pilot project, the program looked for effective ways to teach Head Start children communication and problem-solving skills and to help them acquire positive attitudes toward learning. It sought to link basic skills instruction in Head Start and elementary programs, through collaborative efforts with public schools, to ensure the outcomes would be beneficial to Head Start children in the center programs and in the elementary schools they later attended. The Basic Educational Skills Program concluded in 1982.

Parent Involvement

From the outset, Head Start has been committed to the philosophy that if children's lives are to improve, corresponding changes must be made in the lives of parents. One cannot hope to change children's lives without involving parents, so part of the Head Start thrust is directed toward that end. Objectives for this program are to:

1. Provide a planned program of experiences and activities which support and enhance the parental role as the principal influence in their child's education and development.
2. Provide a program that recognizes the parents as:
   A. Responsible guardians of their children's well-being.
   B. Prime educators of their children.
   C. Contributors to the Head Start Program and to their communities.
3. Provide the following kinds of opportunities for parent participation:
   A. Direct involvement in decision making in program planning and operations.
   B. Participation in classroom and other program activities as paid employees, volunteers or observers.
   C. Activities for parents which they have helped to develop.
   D. Working with their own children in cooperation with Head Start staff.[6]

Modeling

It is not uncommon to find parents employed as aides and teachers in Head Start. The belief is that by helping parents learn, you also help their children learn. For example, parents who learn in the Head Start center that mealtime is a time for conversation are more likely to model this behavior by talking to their children at home. In this respect, there is a great deal of emphasis on the Head Start teacher's modeling appropriate behavior for parents so that parents will tend to model for their children.

Increasing Parent Income, Responsibility, and Pride

Employing parents in Head Start centers is also a way to increase family incomes. Many parent volunteers have later been hired as bus drivers, cooks, and aides. As a result of seminars and training programs, some parents have gained the skills necessary to assume positions of increased responsibility, such as assistant teacher, teacher, and program director. To make this process a reality, each Head Start center must create and implement a career development ladder, whereby employees and volunteers, through training and involvement, can move from one position to another with increased responsibility and pay. Jobs in Head Start are not viewed as dead-end positions. Of course, pay and responsibility are not the only benefits; self-image, an important factor in personal life, is also enhanced.

Policy Council

Every Head Start program operates under policies established by a council that includes parents. If an agency receives money to operate three Head Start centers, each local center has a *parent committee,* and representatives from the parent committees serve on the Policy Council for the three programs. Half the Policy Council members are selected from among parents with children in the program, and half from interested community agencies (day care, family services) and parents who have previously had children in Head Start. Policies established by the Council include determining the attendance area for the center, determining the basis on which children should be recruited, helping develop and oversee the program budget, and acting as a personnel and grievance committee.

The philosophy inherent in involving parents in a Policy Council is twofold. First, in many instances the people for whom programs are developed are the last to be consulted about the programs. The Policy Council system ensures that parents will have a voice in decisions. The second rationale for the Policy Council is to give parents an opportunity to develop skills for operating programs and meetings. A basic concept of Head Start is to place people who lack certain skills in positions where they can develop these skills. This helps them learn skills they can transfer to other settings and promotes self-confidence. Those who question the disadvantaged parent's ability to make Head Start decisions must remember that lack of formal education does not mean one cannot make good decisions, and also that the Policy Council does not operate in a vacuum—it has the advice and guidance of the center director as well as educational consultants and the center teachers.

Generally, Head Start teachers attend policy advisory committee meetings and offer comments, recommendations, and opinions, but do not vote. Not all Head Start policy comes directly from the Policy Council. The Administration for Children, Youth and Families requires centers to observe its performance standards and guidelines. In this sense, the Policy Council works within a framework designed by child development and educational experts. While teachers make certain recommendations to the council about policy and procedures, the ultimate decisions as to how the program will operate, within the framework of the performance standards, is the responsibility of the Policy Council. Consequently, the council does not necessarily do anything it wishes; rather, a group of people learn responsible action through making decisions about things that affect them.

Positive View of Education

Through involvement, parents who have previously had a poor concept of education come to appreciate the power and value of education in their lives and their children's. This changed attitude toward education is reflected in parental attitudes and interaction with children, and research shows that the attitude of the child's parents toward education plays a major role in determining the child's attitude.

Health Services

Head Start's health services component delivers a comprehensive developmental program of medical, dental, mental health, and nutrition services to the child. Objectives for the medical and dental components are to:

1. Provide a comprehensive developmental health services program which includes a broad range of medical, dental, mental health, and nutrition services to preschool children, including handicapped children, to assist the child in his physical, emotional, cognitive, and social development toward the overall goal of social competence.
2. Promote preventive health services and early intervention.
3. Provide the child's family with the necessary skills and insight and otherwise attempt to link the family to an ongoing health care system to ensure that the child continues to receive comprehensive developmental health care even after he leaves the Head Start program.[7]

Direct Service

Child health services in public school settings usually consist of examinations and reports to the parent; corrective and remedial care are often left to the discretion of the parent. Head Start, however, assumes a much more active role. The child's current health status is monitored and reported to the parent and, in cooperation with the parent, corrective and preventive procedures are undertaken. For example, if the child needs glasses, corrective orthopedic surgery, or dental care, services may be provided through the Head Start budget. However, the program usually works with social service agencies to provide services or money for health needs.

Regardless of the procedure, the parents' role in providing health care for the child is never bypassed. Although Head Start employees may take the child to the doctor or dentist, every effort is made to see that the parent receives support and assistance for securing appropriate services. For example, the community worker for the Head Start program might provide transportation for the parent, of if the parent has difficulty arranging an appointment with a specialist, the community worker might make arrangements. The philosophy inherent in this process supports the right of the parent as the primary caregiver; an associated rationale is that through involvement in providing health services, parents learn how to provide for future needs.

Daily Health Education

In addition to arranging medical examinations and care, each Head Start program also teaches children how to care for their health, including the importance of eating proper foods and care of their teeth.

Mental Health Objectives

The mental health portion of the Head Start health services component has these objectives:

1. Assist all children participating in the program in emotional, cognitive and social development toward the overall goal of social competence in coordination with the education program and other related component activities.
2. Provide handicapped children and children with special needs with the necessary mental health services which will ensure that the child and his family achieve the full benefits of participation in the program.
3. Provide staff and parents with an understanding of child growth and development, and appreciation of individual differences, and the need for a supportive environment.
4. Provide for prevention, early identification and early intervention in problems that interfere with a child's development.
5. Develop a positive attitude toward mental health services and a recognition of the contribution of psychology, medicine, social services, education and others to the mental health program.
6. Mobilize community resources to serve children with problems that prevent them from coping with their environment.[8]

Reading the objectives, we see that the Head Start concept of mental health focuses on early detection and prevention. Since detecting problems depends upon the abilities of Head Start staff members, training programs are initiated for that purpose. A Head Start program might hire a psychologist to help design and implement a diagnostic program through observation. The staff and parents would be trained to detect children's problems, and the psychologist would help the staff develop a set of prescriptions for dealing with particular behaviors. Thus, for example, a program to modify the behavior of an overly aggressive child would be developed and implemented under expert guidance. In addition, follow-up activities for use with the child in the center and home would also be developed.

Head Start programs also seek to direct children and parents to existing mental health delivery systems such as community health centers. It is not the intent of Head Start programs to duplicate existing services, but to help its clientele become aware of and utilize available services.

Social Services

The social services worker (or family services coordinator) also works with families to analyze and find solutions to problems. The purpose of the social services component is to help families find the services that will enable them to lead full and meaningful lives. Solutions generally come through liaison with existing agencies, such as welfare departments, health agencies, and school systems. For example, if a family is not receiving its full welfare benefits, or if it could benefit from family counseling, the social services worker would handle these problems through linkage with an appropriate public agency. Objectives for the social services component are to:

1. Establish and maintain an outreach and recruitment process which systematically insures enrollment of eligible children.
2. Provide enrollment of eligible children regardless of race, sex, creed, color, national origin, or handicapping condition.
3. Achieve parent participation in the center and home program and related activities.
4. Assist the family in its own efforts to improve the condition and quality of family life.
5. Make parents aware of community services and resources and facilitate their use.[9]

Eligibility

It is also the function of the social services component to enroll those who are eligible for Head Start. After eligibility has been determined, the children must be enrolled. The basic criterion for admission to Head Start is family income level. Ninety percent of the children enrolled in a Head Start program must come from families that meet poverty guidelines; 10 percent may come from higher income families.

Nutrition

Head Start provides nutritious meals as well as nutrition education for children and their families. Objectives for the nutrition component are to:

1. Help provide food which will help meet the child's daily nutritional needs in the child's home or in another clean and pleasant environment recognizing individual differences and cultural patterns and thereby promote sound physical, social, and emotional growth and development.
2. Provide an environment for nutritional services which will support and promote the use of the feeding situation as an opportunity for learning.
3. Help staff, child and family to understand the relationship of nutrition to health, factors which influence food practices, variety of ways to provide for

nutritional needs and to apply this knowledge in the development of sound food habits even after leaving the Head Start program.

4. Demonstrate the interrelationships of nutrition to other activities of the Head Start program and its contribution to the overall child development goals.

5. Involve all staff, parents and other community agencies as appropriate in meeting the child's nutritional needs so that nutritional care provided by Head Start complements and supplements that of the home and community.[10]

A basic premise of Head Start is that children must be properly fed to have the strength and energy to learn. This philosophy also calls for teaching children good nutrition habits that will carry over for the rest of their lives and be passed on to their children. In addition, mothers are given basic nutritional education so they, in turn, can continue the nutritional program of the Head Start center. Nutrition education for parents includes seminars on buying food and reading and comparing grocery advertisements. One Head Start program in consumer education for parents and staff emphasized can sizes, number of servings per can, comparison of prices, nutritional value, and specific foods that can maximize dollar value.

Nutrition programs consist of a breakfast, snack, and lunch at the center. The menus are not traditional school cafeteria fare, but include food children like as well as foods indigenous to their ethnic background. Table 10–4 illustrates a typical weekly Head Start menu. Generally, Head Start centers serve food family style—the food is served in bowls and children help themselves whenever possible. Of course, there are variations from center to center, but whatever the style, a meal is a vehicle for teaching skills and knowledge.

TABLE 10–4 A Typical Weekly Menu for a Head Start Program (breakfast, lunch, and snack)

Monday	Tuesday	Wednesday	Thursday	Friday
cinnamon toast fruit milk	hot biscuits with butter scrambled eggs juice milk	french toast applesauce milk	cheese omelette toast with butter juice milk	farina with raisins milk
hot dog baked beans coleslaw muffin with butter pears milk	fried chicken yams broccoli cranberry sauce milk brown/serve rolls butter	spaghetti with meatballs celery & carrot stick french bread with butter milk apple	tuna/noodles casserole peas & carrots raisin cup milk bread & butter	roast beef mashed potatoes lima beans choc. sundae milk hot biscuits
melba toast boiled egg juice	dried cereal milk	pineapple chunks milk pretzels	mini-cheesecake milk	variety snack corn-rice-wheat chex party snack milk

Source: Tri-County Head Start, Hughesville, Maryland. Used with permission.

Staff Development

Staff development is one of the major program goals of Head Start, and remains a part of the project that involves parents. Many teachers and aides in Head Start centers have no previous college training, and many are parents. Much of the parent training in child development and educational practices occurs through staff development programs. Generally, before center employees begin teaching, they receive intensive training with on-the-job experiences as a volunteer, aide, bus driver, or cook. They have contact with children, know about the program and are familiar with its goals and objectives, and have an experience base for training. Inservice training is usually conducted by professionals hired at the local level or by representatives of the Head Start regional offices whose duties include assistance in designing training programs. Head Start programs also provide CDA training for their staffs (see Chapter 5).

Administration

The Head Start administration component is designed to help local programs strengthen their administrative and management capabilities to bring about effective delivery of services. This component covers five major areas: program planning and management; personnel management; financial management; procurement and property management; and eligibility and enrollment.

HEAD START IMPROVEMENTS AND INNOVATIONS

Traditionally, Head Start services have been delivered in five half- or whole-day programs, but there is a trend toward local options in service delivery. Under this approach, local Head Start programs are encouraged to plan, develop, and implement alternative ways to deliver services to children and parents. Centers can, for example, have children attend centers on an "as needed" basis, instead of five days a week; a child might attend only one or two days a week depending upon his needs, capacities, and abilities.

All Head Start programs are encouraged to explore ways to deliver services directly to the child in the home. This approach is based on the premise that the parent is the most important person in the child's life and the home the optimum place for growth and development. In brief, the local option encourages Head Start Centers to plan programs that fit their needs and the needs of children and parents, while also taking into consideration the characteristics of the community they serve.

Home-Based Option

Home-based programs are a Head Start option that local agencies may choose as a means of delivering Head Start services. Home-based programs began in 1972 with the three-year Home Start Demonstration Project. Skilled home visitors assist parents in providing developmental activities and support services that children would normally receive in a center-based program. Presently, 3,000 home visitors provide

Meals and snacks are opportunities to learn about nutrition and for social interaction and decision making.

services to over 35,000 children and their families by working through 500 Head Start programs. The primary difference between a center-based program and a home-based option is that the home-based option focuses on the parent and child in the home setting. The home-based option is augmented by group socialization activities conducted at the center, in one of the family's homes, or somewhere else, such as a community center. The home-based option has these strengths:

1. Parent involvement is the very keystone of the program.
2. Geographically isolated families have an invaluable opportunity to be part of a comprehensive child and family program.
3. The individualized family plan is based on both a child and family assessment.
4. The family plan is facilitated by a home visitor who is an adult educator with knowledge and training related to all Head Start components.
5. The program includes the entire family.[11]

The Bear River Head Start Program in Logan, Utah, has developed a training manual to help home visitors work with parents. This is an excerpt for the fourth week of the program:

Small muscle development means the use of hands and fingers. It is important to eye-hand coordination. A child must first see a target then be able to hit it. An example of this would be pouring milk into a glass. When your child enters school, he needs small muscle skills.

1. Encourage your child to dress himself and fasten his clothes.
2. Let your child spread his bread or pour milk from a small pitcher or bottle.
3. Make your own puzzles. Use magazine pictures and cardboard. Be careful not to make them too hard. Beginning puzzles may only have three or four pieces.
4. Let your child practice lacing shoes.
5. Play a game of dropping clothes pins into a jar or can.
6. *Above all, have patience.* Learning these skills takes time.[12]

The manual includes a song and finger play to accompany the unit on small muscle development, as shown in Figure 10–2. According to Glenna Markey of the Bear River Head Start, there are several keys to making a home-based program work:

☐ The home visitor must work with the parent, *not* the child. When *parents* work with their children, we achieve the intended results of the Home Base program.
☐ The home visitor must help the parent become a "child development specialist," ultimately benefiting the parents' children and grandchildren.
☐ The home visitor must try to do such a good job that the parent can do without her. In this sense, the home visitors put themselves out of a job!

Another model for working with parents and children was the Child and Family Resource Program (CFRP). The Child and Family Resource Program was a national Head Start demonstration program. It was funded in June 1973, and funding ceased in 1984. The program was a child-centered program designed to provide family support services that are crucial for, and directly related to, the sustained healthy growth and development of children from the prenatal period through age eight. Head Start

EENSY, WEENSY SPIDER

Traditional   Traditional

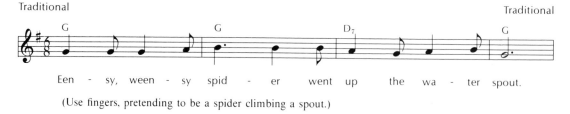

Een - sy, ween - sy spid - er went up the wa - ter spout.

(Use fingers, pretending to be a spider climbing a spout.)

Down came the rain and washed the spid - er out.

(Let hands fall, palms down.)   (With palms out, sweep arms upward.)

Out came the sun and dried up all the rain, And the

(Use arms to form a circle overhead with fingers touching.)

een - sy, ween - sy spid - er went up the spout a - gain.

(Let arms fall downward, and fingers climb spout again.)

FIGURE 10–2   Eensy, Weensy Spider—A Song and Finger Play

programs normally enroll three- to five-year-old children of low-income families and provide them with education, parent involvement, health services, and social services, whereas a Head Start that was part of the CFRP enrolled families. It promoted child development and met children's needs by working through the family as a unit. The CFRP provided the same services as Head Start and additional services tailored to the needs of each family.[13]

A five-year longitudinal evaluation of CFRP that began in 1977 indicated that the program was effective in meeting its program objectives. Specifically, CFRP improved families' prospects for economic self-sufficiency, improved access to community services, improved preventive health care, strengthened parental coping skills, increased parents' awareness of their role as educators of their own children, and was effective in enrolling children in Head Start.[14]

Follow Through

Follow Through is a federally funded program for promoting the overall development of children from low-income families who are enrolled in kindergarten through third grade and for extending the educational gains made in Head Start and other preschool programs. Follow Through was originally funded in 1967 under the Economic Opportunity Act of 1964 to provide assistance to children from low-income families served by Head Start; it is currently funded through 1990 under the Human Services Reauthorization Act of 1986. Current federal funding is about $7,500,000. A study of Follow Through produced these findings:

> Finding 1: The effectiveness of each Follow Through model varied substantially from site group to site group; overall model averages varied little in comparison.
> Finding 2: Models that emphasize basic skills succeeded better than other models in helping children gain these skills.
> Finding 3: Where models have put their primary emphasis elsewhere than on the basic skills, the children they served have tended to score lower on tests of these skills than they would have done without Follow Through.
> Finding 4: No type of model was notably more successful than the others in raising scores on cognitive conceptual skills.
> Finding 5: Models that emphasize basic skills produced better results on tests of self-concept than did other models.
> Finding 6: Model comparisons in New York and Philadelphia yield results which are similar to those found in overall comparisons.[15]

We can expect these findings to be heavily debated and discussed, since decisions about specific models and amounts of federal grants will be based on the data.

Project Developmental Continuity

Project Developmental Continuity (PDC) was a national Head Start demonstration program begun in 1974 and funded by the Administration for Children, Youth and Families. Funding concluded in 1981. The basic purpose of the PDC program was to establish ways for promoting greater continuity between Head Start programs and schools the Head Start children later attend. Specifically, the goals were:

> To assure continuity of experience for children from Head Start through the early primary years by stimulating intellectual (including language), social-emotional and physical development, thereby promoting educational gains for children through the development of social competence.
> To develop models for developmental continuity that can be implemented on a wide scale in Head Start and other child development programs and school systems.[16]

These notions were the conceptual basis for the project:

> Growth and learning occur as gradual and continuous processes;
> Development is enhanced when programs are planned according to each child's needs, flow out of previous experience in and out of the home, and offer an orderly sequence of increasing complexity;

The education of the child begins with the family and, therefore, the family's influence, stake and role in a child's development must be explicitly acknowledged in any early childhood education program.[17]

Health Care Program

Health Care, an innovative program initiated in 1970, explores methods for increasing medical services to disadvantaged children, increasing the number of children receiving health services, and promoting better utilization of existing facilities and services.

The Head Start Measures Project

The Head Start Measures Project is a federally funded program to help local Head Start programs assess and match curricular activities, instruction, and services to children's individual needs. The project was developed and is conducted by the College of Education at the University of Arizona. The project began in the 1984–85 program year in 179 Head Start programs and now has more than 220 centers, representing 22,000 children, participating.

A central feature of the Measures Project is the *Head Start Measures Battery* (HSMB), designed for assessment and planning with Head Start preschool children in the areas of language, math, nature and science, perception, reading, and social development. The areas of prereading and fine and gross motor skills are presently under development. Children are assessed at the beginning and end of the program year. The assessment results provide teachers with information about each child's fall and spring developmental levels, developmental growth throughout the year, what skills they learned, and the extent to which educational goals were met.

The measures approach views each child as progressing along an individual *developmental path* and focuses on what children are able to do as opposed to what they cannot do. Using the results of the Measures Battery, teachers match learning and teaching episodes to children's skills and developmental levels. Assessment and activity planning are linked through the use of *path referencing.* Information is provided for each child's developmental path in each of the six areas. The teacher knows what skills the child has mastered and can plan activities he is ready to learn on his path of development. The HSMB provides a developmental level score for each child, the child's performance or mastery level on each skill, and a teaching level score, indicating the level of skills taught to the child. Results of the HSMB are provided to individual programs in three ways: developmental profiles for the class and for each child, developmental profiles in conjunction with a planning guide to assist in developing plans for learning activities, and skill level progress reports showing the child's improvement in each skill area.

Using the HSMB assessment and planning system, teachers are able to *assess* children's developmental levels; *screen* children to locate those who need special attention; *plan,* using the HSMB planning guide, to identify what skills children are ready to learn; *update* plans as children learn; *communicate* to parents what their children can do and what they are ready to learn; and *document* each child's progress. Research findings for the first year of implementation for the Measures Project (1984–85) indicate that "Children show improvement in Developmental Level (DL) over what would be expected from maturation alone; that children who participated in the planning portion of the system showed more improvement than those who did not; that children improved more if teachers had more accurate knowledge of the children's Developmental Levels; and that an analysis of the overall results of the HSMB assessment in the Head Start program shows evidence that teachers are individualizing activities for their children."[18]

A test item from the Head Start Measures Battery is shown in Figure 10–3. The HSMB Classroom Activity Guide was developed for Head Start by Child Inc. with the cooperation of the University of Arizona. The purpose of the Classroom Activity Guide is to assure effective use of the information from the HSMB. Figure 10–4 shows a learning activity for the reading skill of matching upper and lower case letters with the same form.

Services to Handicapped Children

Since at least 10 percent of Head Start enrollment consists of handicapped children, there may be some handicapped children in each classroom. Head Start defines handicapped children as "mentally retarded, hard of hearing, deaf, speech impaired, visually handicapped, seriously emotionally disturbed, crippled, or other health-impaired children, who by reason thereof require special education and related services."[19] To provide adequately for these children, staff and parents receive training in methods and procedures related to the particular disabilities. Head Start also provides staff training in identification, treatment, and prevention of child abuse and neglect. (See Chapter 11 for more information on educating the handicapped.)

HEAD START ISSUES

Funding

Each year, Head Start program staff grow apprehensive until Congress decides their fiscal fate, but Head Start is one of the most resilient programs and has always been able to resist threats of budget cuts or elimination. First, and probably foremost, Head Start is a popular program with the public and with those it serves. It is considered one of the federal programs that really helps people and has gained a wide following and constituency. Second, Head Start has made a difference in the lives of those it serves, and it is difficult to cut a successful program. Thus Head Start has not only remained in operation, its budget has increased each funding period.

Influences on Family Life

A second issue is the charge that Head Start weakens the family. Many critics of early childhood education see any attempt to provide services (educational or care) for children outside their homes as a threat to the family. In fact, Head Start, with its em-

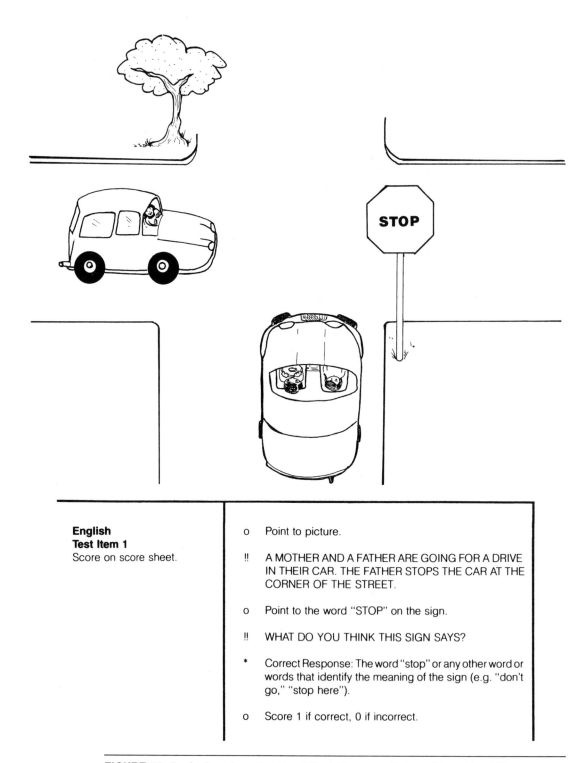

English
Test Item 1
Score on score sheet.

o   Point to picture.

‼   A MOTHER AND A FATHER ARE GOING FOR A DRIVE IN THEIR CAR. THE FATHER STOPS THE CAR AT THE CORNER OF THE STREET.

o   Point to the word "STOP" on the sign.

‼   WHAT DO YOU THINK THIS SIGN SAYS?

*   Correct Response: The word "stop" or any other word or words that identify the meaning of the sign (e.g. "don't go," "stop here").

o   Score 1 if correct, 0 if incorrect.

FIGURE 10–3   An Item from the Head Start Measures Battery (From *Head Start Measures Battery,* University of Arizona)

HSMB READING SKILL #18: Match upper and lower case letters with the same form.

LEARNING GOALS: The child will be learning:

1. The letters of the alphabet.

2. That all letters have two forms, upper case ("capitals"), and lower case ("small letters").

3. To match identical letters, capitals to capitals and lower case to lower case.

4. To match capital and small letters, when their shapes are identical except for size. (Shown an <u>O</u>, child chooses an <u>o</u> from a group of letters, etc.)

EDUCATIONAL OBJECTIVE: intellectual (recognizing symbols for letters)

GROUP SIZE: 2 - 3   LEARNING CENTER: table games or circle

MATERIALS: 2 different colored circles or rings 12" in diameter, 4 sets of alphabet cards, 2" x 2": 2 sets of upper case letters and 2 sets of lower case letters, 1 letter per card; small box or basket for each player.

NOTE TO TEACHER: A quick review of the names of the letters, using your set of alphabet cards, will help the children be more successful. After they have learned how to play this game, it can be left in the table games learning center for the children to use independently.

LEARNING ACTIVITY: To play this game, sit on the floor with the two colored circles in front of you. Keep two sets of alphabet cards (1 upper case and 1 lower case) for yourself and divide the other set among the children (how many cards per child will depend on the number playing). Put each player's cards in a box or basket. "Stir" your cards to mix them up, chanting as you stir: "Stir your cards, stir your cards, mix them if you please." Choose a card from your box, and say: "Match me, match me, match me if you can. I'm an upper case letter, a capital _!" Place the card on the circle for capital letters. "Who can match the capital _?" The child with the matching _ takes it from her box and places it next to your card on the circle. Both of you say together: "Capital _ matches capital _!" Continue the game by choosing another card from your set. If it is a lower case letter, say: "Match me, match me, match me if you can. I'm a lower case letter, a small letter _!" etc.

TEACHER'S COMMENTS:

FIGURE 10–4 Reading Scale—Matching and Identifying Letters (From *Head Start Measures Battery Classroom Activity Guide, 1986–87,* Child Incorporated, Lamar, Texas)

Ten percent of Head Start enrollment must include children with special needs.

phasis on parent involvement and its Home Base program, encourages and supports family life.

Continuity

When a child leaves a Head Start program and begins formal schooling, he no longer receives any of its services. Head Start is now challenged to seek ways to continue services to children throughout their school careers. Head Start must expand its work with parents to provide them with the means to extend Head Start practices in the home. One of the program's major strengths has been its credibility with parents.

Continuity between the program and school represents another major challenge. Head Start must be concerned not only with how to extend Follow Through services into the elementary school, but how to make them a permanent part of the school setting. This task may be difficult, since public schools are reluctant to assume responsibility for much more than instructional programs, and because the back-to-basics movement forces public schools to concentrate on raising achievement test scores. Furthermore, as pointed out in a recent evaluation of Follow Through,

It is difficult to implement change in the functioning of institutions by means of intervention from the outside. Efforts to innovate in schools, even spearheaded by well-placed insiders, are often frustrated by the overt or covert unwillingness of teachers, parents, pupils, administrators and others to change accustomed ways of carrying out the business of education. Abundant anecdotal evidence attests to the wide variety of problems that the sponsors have faced in trying to implement their models in the sites. Any extensions of Follow Through to other districts, however, would probably encounter analogous circumstances, and so we are confident that our findings reflect the outcomes one might expect from a broader Follow Through program.[20]

The back-to-basics movement, with its emphasis on basic skill learning and test scores, may pose a threat to many of the good things Head Start does. If the public believes the primary purpose of programs such as Head Start should be to raise children's achievement test scores in first grade and beyond, then the comprehensive nature of Head Start services will be in danger.

Public School Involvement

Should the public schools become involved in Head Start and day care? Not everyone agrees that they should; however, there appears to be a large-scale effort on the part of the public schools and national teachers' organizations to gain control of existing social service agencies, day care, and Head Start programs. There is growing recognition that the number of families who need Head Start programs is much greater than the number of families served. The ability of social service organizations to meet the needs of families is limited, and the demand for services greater than currently available resources. Therefore, many professionals and legislators feel that, since public schools already exist in every community, it makes sense to give them the responsibility for delivering services to preschool children and their families.

The rationale for public school involvement is further advanced with the argument that, when the schools are by-passed, their functions are duplicated, and this is a waste of money and effort. Also, many school districts have unused classrooms and buildings because the declining birthrate has reduced the school age population. Many educators feel it does not make sense to close these buildings because of declining enrollment and at the same time build new buildings for preschool programs.

There are many strong arguments against public school involvement in social services. One is that public schools are not doing a good job in their traditional role of teaching the basic skills of reading, writing, and arithmetic. Critics cite the dropout rate, illiteracy figures, and declining achievement test scores as evidence that the schools have failed. Therefore, the argument continues, if the schools are already failing, how can we expect them to succeed at another job? Second, critics of public school involvement in preschool and family affairs point to the historic reluctance of the schools to take responsibility for this area of education. Many teachers, administrators, and taxpayers feel that preschool and family education does not represent the legitimate function of the public schools. This argument will probably be the most persuasive in determining whether public schools will become more involved than they already are. The third argument against public school involvement is that teachers and administrators are not trained to assume responsibilities for working with preschool children and their families because colleges of education have not trained teachers for this role. On the other hand, the colleges respond that they could initiate retraining programs for teachers and design new training programs. Fourth, if greater numbers of certified teachers were employed in early childhood programs, there would be fewer positions for people without college degrees. This would have a negative effect on people already employed in these programs, some of whom are parents. One of the reasons many child care agencies and Head Start centers are in operation is to provide low-income parents with an opportunity to earn money. Many of the employment opportunities available in early childhood programs that do not require certification should be filled by individuals without the four-year degree.

Does Head Start Make A Difference?

No question in early childhood education has been debated, discussed, considered, and examined more than whether Head Start makes a difference in the lives of children. The most conclusive evidence that serves to answer this question comes from the report of the Consortium for Longitudinal Studies (often referred to as the Lazar study) which analyzed studies of low-income children who participated in experimental infant and preschool programs in the 1960s.[21]

The Lazar study found that early education programs significantly reduced the number of children assigned to special education; significantly reduced the number of children retained in grade; and significantly increased children's scores on fourth grade mathematics achievement tests with a suggestive trend toward increased scores on fourth grade reading tests. In addition, low-income children who attended preschools surpassed their controls on the Stanford-Binet I.Q. test for up to three years after the program ended. Also, children who attended preschool were more likely than control children to give reasons of achievement for being proud of themselves.

Further evidence for the positive effects of preschool education comes from the Perry Preschool Project, "a longitudinal experiment designed to reveal the effects of early educational intervention on disadvantaged young people." Describing the causes and effects of this project, the authors comment:

> The pattern of causes and effects was as follows. The children in the sample
> started out in a condition of poverty and appeared to have low cognitive ability. Pre-
> school education provided the experimental group with cognitive stimulation so
> that their cognitive ability was higher upon school entry then it would have been
> otherwise. From this initial position, they began to experience and demonstrate
> greater success in school: greater commitment to schooling, higher school achieve-
> ment, and reinforcement of a more success-oriented role by teachers, parents,
> and peers. Being more strongly bound to school success, they engaged in deviant
> behavior less frequently, first in the classroom and later in the community. Our
> prediction is that they will reap the rewards of greater school success: higher educa-
> tional attainment, higher occupational status, and higher income.[22]

Head Start programs give children a chance to achieve their full potential.

To the question, "What do we know so far about Head Start?" Schweinhart and Weikart respond:

1. Short-, mid-, and long-term positive effects are available.
2. Adequately funded Head Start programs run by well-trained, competent teachers can achieve the level of quality operation that will lead to positive effects.
3. Equal educational opportunity for all people is a fundamental goal of the great American experiment and good Head Start programs can make a sound contribution to the achievement of the goal.[23]

HEAD START'S FUTURE

On the occasion of Head Start's fifteenth anniversary in 1980, President Carter convened a panel to suggest a blueprint for the future. The Committee called for steps to protect Head Start and measures to contribute to its controlled expansion. Specifically, the committee had these recommendations and conclusions:

Follow Through helps Head Start children receive educational and social services through the primary grades.

    A. Protect program quality
      1. Protect against inflation
      2. Incorporate more trained caregivers; begin to raise caregiver wages
      3. Increase program and managerial resources
      4. Legislate Head Start's permanent status in ACYF
    B. New Directions
      1. Plan for future expansion in enrollment (2% per year—the equivalent of 36,000 children per year)
      2. Build on Family-Centered Programs: Head Start as a family resource program—extend services to children under three; provide more assistance to children of working parents; develop self-help approaches; expand preventive health measures, e.g., nutrition and accident prevention; strengthen continuity with schools; broaden pool of volunteers, e.g., include more family members.

*   *   *

Head Start is a social program which has been proven to be effective. The program has earned the trust of the poor and the respect of a broad range of Americans. Head Start in many ways represents what is best about this nation—the joining together of diverse peoples in a common effort to help those less well-off. In this age of economic retrenchment, when it is tempting to write off the poor as a casualty of inflation, Head Start is more important than ever. The program's record of achievement reminds us that, yes, it is possible to give children from low-income families a better and healthier start on life, and that this early assistance has long lasting benefits.[24]

Some people believe that for Head Start to remain effective, it must respond to and address the problems that result from changes in families, poverty and the feminization of poverty, teenage pregnancy and parenting, and working women. They make these suggestions for Head Start:

1. Strengthen its focus on parental employability and preparation to enter the workforce
2. Present both boys and girls with positive male images
3. Promote positive family relationships
4. Focus on adult male-female relationships
5. Adapt effective sex education models to the parent involvement component
6. Influence the quality of social services
7. Seek to increase parental knowledge about child rearing and parenting skills
8. Develop leadership potential among low-income families
9. Extend hours and services to accommodate the need for full-day care for infants, toddlers, preschool and school-age children
10. Increase support to children's transportation to accommodate employed mothers
11. Restructure the parent involvement component to accommodate working parents' schedules
12. Increase its focus on children's affective and social development
13. Place greater emphasis on maintaining a stable staff
14. Develop a program to help families conserve their resources and raise their standard of living
15. Emphasize human resource development programs for parents to improve their employability[25]

On the other hand, others think these suggestions are "dangerous" because there are not enough funds available to support them and the original Head Start objectives as well. One Head Start staffer makes these proposals for Head Start:

1. Additional support
2. Avoid adding objectives unless specific funds are made available
3. Employ staff for 12 months
4. Demand knowledgeable and insightful national and regional leadership
5. Work closely with schools interested in programs for four-year-olds
6. Arrange training for parents and staff in skills that pay well
7. Provide full-day care for working parents and parents in training

8. Reduce bureaucracy
9. Stress social competence and motor skill development while counteracting the push to basics[26]

MIGRANT EDUCATION

In 1965, Congress authorized Title I of the Elementary and Secondary Education Act (ESEA) to provide public school programs for disadvantaged children. These funds, however, did not provide adequate services for the children of migrant workers; consequently, in 1966, ESEA Title I was amended by P.L. 89–750 to provide money specifically for education of migrant children:

> "Currently migratory child" means a child (a) whose parent or guardian is a migratory agricultural worker or migratory fisherman; and (b) who has within the past twelve months moved from one school district into another (or, in a state comprising a single school district has moved from one school administrative area into another) in order to enable the child, the child's guardian, or a member of the child's immediate family to obtain temporary or seasonal employment in an agricultural or fishing activity.[27]

Historically, the migrant child has suffered educationally because his family seldom lives in one place for any length of time; public schools have not always been willing to give migrant children the special attention they need; and migrant children have had to work to supplement their families' incomes. Without an education, migrant children are caught in the trap of illiteracy and inadequate job skills that prevents their escaping the cycle of poverty.

Because migratory work results in short-term residency, many migrant children have little chance to go to school. In the past, school districts were not always aware of the migrant child as a potential student because he stayed in the district only a short time. To help locate migrant children, some states, in cooperation with the U.S. Office of Education, have established the Migrant Education Identification and Recruitment Program (MEIRP). The purpose of the MEIRP program is to identify migrant children and enroll them in the Migrant Student Record Transfer System and in a local education program such as a public school, Head Start, or child care program.

Because migrant children move so often, and are frequently enrolled in a school for only weeks at a time, there is a need to have information about them as quickly as possible. The *Migrant Student Record Transfer System* (MSRTS) is a national computerized communications network designed to compile, store, and transmit migrant children's education and health records. Located in Little Rock, Arkansas, and funded by the federal government, this high-speed data system records, maintains, and transmits information on more than 750,000 migrant children. MSRTS serves more than 20,000 schools in the U.S., including Washington, D.C., and Puerto Rico. The system

☐ Enables teachers who receive a migrant child to have almost immediate access to achievement and health records. Ideally, because of MSRTS, a

TABLE 10-5 Top Ten Migrant States/Territories

State or Territory	Total Number Identified	Percent of Total Identified
1. California	142,055	27%
2. Texas	129,874	24%
3. Florida	56,244	11%
4. Washington	21,218	4%
5. Michigan	18,591	4%
6. Arkansas	17,041	3%
7. Arizona	15,718	3%
8. Louisiana	12,570	2%
9. Oregon	12,200	2%
10. New York	9,705	2%
11. All other states/territories	95,640	18%
Grand Total	530,856	

Source: Florida Department of Education.

teacher can begin immediately to provide instruction according to a child's achievement level. Teachers can thus concentrate on meeting children's needs rather than identifying them.

☐ Eliminates the need for multiple testing, physical examinations, and repeated inoculations.

☐ Allows quick and accurate placement of children and indicates where help is needed.

The MSRTS works this way: (1) a school official or migrant recruiter identifies a potential migrant child; (2) the child is "certified" as a migrant according to federal guidelines and regulations; (3) a staff worker gathers personal, educational, and health histories; (4) data is then entered into the computer and transmitted to Little Rock (if the child has no existing record, a file is created; if the child has a file, it is updated); (5) the child's file is transmitted from Little Rock to the enrolling school.

A DAY IN THE LIFE OF A CHILD IN THE MIGRANT PRESCHOOL EDUCATION PROGRAM IN MABTON, WASHINGTON

Carlos Trevino, age four, migrates with his parents, five brothers, and a younger sister from Texas to Washington in April. His family comes to the Yakima Valley to cut asparagus. The labor camp where he lives is provided by the asparagus growers.

Carlos's family gets up at 3 A.M. and gets Carlos and his younger sister ready for their day at the Mabton Child Development Center. The bus arrives for Carlos at 3:30, and he is transported to the Mabton Child Development Center, supported with funds from Chapter 1, Migrant, Washington State Title XX Day Care, and the United States Department of Agriculture (for meals and snacks). Carlos lives six miles from the center and arrives at 4:15 A.M. Upon his arrival he is immediately put to bed by a Title XX worker. Carlos goes right to sleep and wakes at 7 A.M., when all the children are awakened. Carlos washes his face and hands, combs his hair, and gets ready for breakfast. Today, his breakfast consists of migas (corn tortilla with egg), milk, and a quarter of an orange.

The menu for breakfast and other meals is approved by the U.S. Department of Agriculture and is culturally related to the Mexican-American children in the Mabton program. After eating breakfast, he helps clean up the table. Today it is his job to wipe the table. He then brushes his teeth.

There are twenty children in Carlos's class, taught by one teacher and two assistants. Today, Carlos begins his day with a free choice of activities. He can select from one of the following learning areas: kitchen area, block area, art, or manipulative area.

Carlos chooses the manipulative area, where there are materials and games that will help him learn to tie his shoes. Other materials such as puzzles will help with visual memory, pegboards will help him learn colors, and other materials are designed to promote readiness for learning to read and write. During this free choice time, one of the teachers will help Carlos to make sure he is learning basic concepts identified by the center. The lacing cards will help him gain the manual dexterity he will need to learn to tie his shoes, hold a pencil, and perform other tasks requiring manual dexterity and fine motor control.

At 9 A.M., Carlos goes outside, where he can swing, slide, play in the sand, and use a tricycle. His teacher encourages him to play in the sand. She believes the sandbox toys will help him with his manual dexterity. At 9:30, Carlos has a snack of milk and banana. This snack is served by the children themselves. They prepare the tables, pour their own milk, peel their own bananas, and clean up. At 9:45 A.M., Carlos goes into his classroom, where he receives instruction in the individualized bilingual education curriculum. During this lesson, the room is arranged so there are three tables with six to seven children at each table. Each teacher teaches a group lesson lasting from ten to fifteen minutes. Each group rotates from one table to another, so they receive a total of thirty or forty-five minutes of language instruction. At 10:30 A.M., Carlos again has a free choice activity, and chooses to go to the block area. At 11 A.M., he goes outside and plays on the swings. At 11:15, Carlos goes inside and washes his hands and face and combs his hair before lunch. He has been taught to do these acts of personal hygiene for himself by the staff. Then he helps set the table.

When the tables are set, the children seat themselves, and the food is placed on the table in bowls for the children to pass and serve themselves. Mealtimes help the children learn manners, the use of eating utensils, and decision making. The teachers eat with the children.

After lunch, Carlos has a play period outside before his nap at 12:45 P.M. While the children are sleeping, the teachers plan the next day's activities.

Carlos wakes from his nap at 3 P.M. and has a snack of guacamole con tortilla (avocado with tortilla) and milk. Carlos helps clean up from the snack time, then chooses to take part in a planned art activity, making a collage. Each child's collage is hung on the bulletin board. At 3:45, the bus arrives and Carlos goes home.

Carlos's older brother Roberto, who is in the third grade, also gets up at 3 A.M., but he prepares for the daily cutting of asparagus rather than school. Asparagus harvesting begins about April 1 and ends about June 25 every year. At 4 A.M., after a breakfast of eggs, chorizo (ground beef and sausage), tortillas, and milk, Roberto goes with his father to the asparagus fields. He cuts about eighty pounds of asparagus from 4:15 until 10:00 A.M. Roberto's family is paid seven cents a pound for the asparagus. What Roberto earns will be paid to his father. By state law, Roberto is allowed to miss one hour of school per day, with his parents' permission, to cut asparagus. Since the family needs the money Roberto is able to earn, they readily give their permission. Someone from Roberto's family takes him from the fields to the labor camp where one of the other migrant workers takes him and other children to school. This way, only one worker has to lose time in the fields.

Roberto arrives at school at about 10:30 A.M. Classes have already begun, and he continues with the regular curriculum and schedule until after lunch. During the afternoon, Roberto spends up to two hours in a migrant resource room. Here his teacher has developed an individual skills program based on information she received from the Migrant Student Record Transfer System and the schools' own testing program. Roberto receives a complete program in mathematics, reading, and oral language. Skills learned in this program should bring him up to grade level with other students in the school.

National Issues of Migrant Education

How much money should we spend on migrant education? Among those who advocate cutting federal spending in general, there are those who would like to see monies for migrant education reduced. On the other hand, the plight of migrants and their children inspires others to suggest increasing federal spending for their education. Again, the issue of funding migrant programs is no different from funding crises in other federal social services agencies: it is primarily a question of national priorities, and unfortunately, the poor and disadvantaged are not the top priority. Another concern is determining the best formula for dividing federal funds for migrant education among the states; for example, should funding be based on migrant population at a particular time, or on the level and quality of services provided to migrants? There is also concern as to what individual states should be required to do for their portion of federal dollars. Some say there should be specific federal guidelines; others say the states should have wide latitude in determining the kinds of services migrants in their state should receive.

A frequent question about migrant education is "Who is eligible?" The answer is based partly on a definition of migrancy—and this raises the issue of who should be considered a migrant child. Many claim that the definition based on moving from one school district to another is inadequate and fails to address the needs of migrant children.

MIGRANT HOME PRESCHOOL PROGRAM OF THE MARION EDUCATION SERVICE DISTRICT IN MARION COUNTY, OREGON

This program serves migrant children and families of Willamette Valley in Marion County, Oregon. The project is designed to provide preschoolers ages four to five with basic concepts they will need when they enter first grade or kindergarten. The program also involves parents in the educational process through participation and observation. Approximately 130 families and 150 children of Spanish and Russian background have taken part in the program since it began in 1977. These are some of the goals of the program:

To provide a preschool experience for migrant children

To involve parents in the educational process

To familiarize parents with certain concepts they can teach their children and that will help the children in school

To teach basic skills and concepts in the child's native language and, when the child is ready, to transfer those skills and concepts into English

To make a smoother transition from home to public school

Each day, a group of six to eight children are picked up at their homes and transported in minibuses to the home of one of the children in the group. There are over one hundred children in the program, in a total of twelve groups. Six are morning groups and six are afternoon groups. A calendar schedule which shows the date and home each group will be taught in is developed each month in cooperation with the parents in the program. Children are assigned to their groups by geographic area, age, and home language. The program operates in a radius of about ten miles. It takes about half an hour to pick up each group. Part of the enrollment procedure is a commitment from each family that its home can be used as a teaching center. If a parent does not want his home used, the family is usually not enrolled in the program.

Karen Aumick, teacher and director of the program, teaches a morning group every day. Before driving the bus to pick up her children, Karen packs a box of learning materials and a snack for the children. Karen teaches the group of children in the home for two hours each morning. Since Karen is the teacher-director, she teaches only a morning group. Her afternoons are spent in planning the program and in supervision of the other six aides in the program. Part of Karen's planning includes writing a master lesson plan, which the teacher-aides individualize for their own groups.

Each of the six teacher-aides (four Spanish-speaking and two Russian-speaking) has two groups, a morning and an afternoon group. The program is conducted bilingually. For example, the names for colors are taught in the child's native language. When the children have mastered the words in their native language, they are taught the names in English.

As with any program, there are certain challenges. For instance, some homes are so small that it is difficult to accommodate a group of children. When this is the case, the teachers seek ways to compensate for the size of the home. Some homes may not have a table around which the whole group can gather, so lesson plans have to be written to reflect the uniqueness of each home. Television and other children in the home make it necessary to plan around these and other unique situations.

Many positive features of the preschool program make it beneficial to both children and parents. By conducting a program in the home, a positive relationship is developed with the parents. Migrant parents get to know what American education is like and what to expect when their children do enter school. Because the program is bilingual, parents are able to participate in the activities. This participation, in turn, helps parents know what to teach their younger children. The program also introduces the children to the education process in a comfortable home setting, without the shock of abrupt transition from home to school that many migrant children experience. This comfortable transition is particularly important when a child does not know the language of the school.

Cultural differences are accounted for in the program and care is taken to assure that nothing is done that could be culturally offensive. For example, on a fast day, when there is a restricted diet for the Russian Old Believers, a child would not be given cookies for a snack, since fat or milk products might be contained in the cookies. Instead, carrots, celery, and apples would be offered.

EDUCATION CONSOLIDATION AND IMPROVEMENT ACT (CHAPTER 1)

Chapter 1 of the Education Consolidation and Improvement Act of 1981 serves about five million children in about 30 percent of the nation's public schools; in fiscal year 1987–88, it had a budget of 3.5 billion dollars. Two-thirds of the participating children are in grades K–6. The purpose of this program is to meet the special needs of educationally deprived elementary and secondary school children in low-income areas. Each project design should be of sufficient size, scope, and quality to give promise of substantial progress toward meeting children's educational needs. Chapter 1 funds provide remedial instruction in reading and mathematics to upgrade the achievement levels of children who are below grade level in these subjects. The local educational agency provides the program design and determines the criteria by which children are eligible, so the criteria vary from state to state and district to district. Additional teachers and teachers' aides are funded to provide more individualized instruction for eligible children. Chapter 1 funds support about 164,000 full-time equivalent staff positions, as well as inservice training, teaching supplies, and audiovisual materials and equipment. Regular classroom teachers and Chapter 1 teachers must work together to meet the children's needs.

The program is to be supplemental to the regular educational program provided by the local educational agency. In this sense, Chapter 1 is a "pull out" program, in which children are taken out of their rooms for a certain amount of time, usually an hour a day, for remedial instruction in the basic skills. No part of the regular program is to be supplanted by the Chapter 1 program. Each school is responsible for planning its program to meet the needs of the children it serves. The local program is monitored to make sure it meets federal and state guidelines. A parent advisory committee is required at every target school, to be composed of parents, school staff, and community members. At least 51 percent of the committee must be parents of Chapter 1 children. The committee is responsible for helping to formulate plans for the school's Chapter 1 program and for seeing that the plans are carried through.

THE FEDERAL GOVERNMENT AND EDUCATIONAL INVOLVEMENT

Because it was not reserved or specified as a federal function in the Constitution, education is a state function. Today, all fifty states have regulations for and control over the education process. Historically, however, the federal government has been very much involved in early childhood education. Its influence comes basically from three sources. The first source is the preamble to the Constitution, which states that the government must *promote the general welfare;* the government uses this phrase as justification for its support of educational programs. On this basis, Congress has passed many statutes that provide money, services, and support to education. The second source of federal support and control over education comes from specific provisions in the Constitution, such as the Fourteenth Amendment, which provides for "due process." Many court cases have been decided in favor of groups, such as the handicapped, who have been denied opportunities for an education. The third source of federal involvement is through funding provided by specific legislation. If state and local educational agencies want to receive and use federal money, they must comply with federal regulations and laws. When the federal government furnishes money, it controls how that money will be used.

Pros and Cons

Not everyone supports the federal presence in education. Some believe it is too large and dominating. A few school districts refuse to accept federal aid under the conditions the federal government imposes. It is unlikely, however, that there will be widespread rejection of federal aid to education. Many federal programs, such as Head Start, Chapter 1, and migrant programs were funded for specific purposes, and are referred to as a *category programs,* designed to deliver services to a specific category of recipients. The current trend is to consolidate category grants into "block grants," whereby a number of programs are funded under one grant, with three results: the sum of the block grant is less than the total of the category grants it consolidates, with the reduced funding justified on the basis of reduced administrative costs; second, target groups in the category programs are no longer specified, eliminating or reducing many federal restrictions on use of the money and allowing states to set their own priorities; and third, as implied, federal control of education programs is reduced. Reduced funding and fewer federal programs appear to be the trend for the immediate future.

Privatization is a word politicians use to express their wish to have private groups, agencies, and individuals increase their support of educational programs. They believe the federal government should reduce its support because it should not be in the education or welfare business to the extent that it is. The private sector is seen as the source of replacement of these funds. *Volunteerism* is also urged as a way to provide human resources support and reduce reliance on federal dollars.

FURTHER READING

Beaty, Janice J. *Skills for Preschool Teachers,* 3rd ed. (Columbus, Ohio: Merrill, 1988) Designed specifically for the Head Start, day care, and kindergarten worker, content parallels the Child Development Associate Competencies; helpful for anyone contemplating this training program.

Lang, F., and H. Vojna. *Advocacy in Head Start* (College Park, Md.: Head Start Resource and Training Center, University of Maryland, nd.) Step-by-step manual for Head Start program staff and parents on how to work with their agency, community organizations, and the legislative process.

Living and Teaching Nutrition (College Park, Md.: Head Start Resource and Training Center, University of Maryland, 1983) Inservice training guide featuring nine workshops; chapters include: What's New in Nutrition? How's Your Diet? Economical Nutrition; Fresh Fruits and Vegetables; Dental Health and Sugar; Planning Menus and Planning Snacks; Family-Style Eating; Cooking Experiences for Young Children; Nutrition Activities for Young Children.

Morrison, George S. *Parent Involvement in the Home, School and Community* (Columbus, Ohio: Merrill, 1978) Practical approach to involving parents; reality-based and full of useful information.

U.S. Department of Health, Education, and Welfare, Office of Human Development Services, Administration for Children, Youth, and Family, Head Start Bureau. *Partners and Parents: The Home Start Experience with Preschoolers and Their Families.* Publication No. DHEW (OHDS) 78-31106 (Washington, D.C.: U.S. Government Printing Office, 1977) Comprehensive discussion and review of the Home Start experience with a description of all the original Home Start programs.

U.S. Department of Health, Education, and Welfare, Office of Child Development. *Project Head Start—A Guide for Head Start—A Guide for Head Start Personnel* (Washington, D.C.: U.S. Government Printing Office) Series of thirteen booklets called the *Rainbow Series* (because the cover of each booklet is a different color) that provides excellent information about Head Start and its programs. Designed primarily for Head Start personnel, the booklets are devoted to practical ideas, suggestions, and rationale.

Vojna, H. *The Family Needs Assessment Process* (College Park, Md.: Head Start Resource and Training Center, University of Maryland, nd.) Resource tool for social service workers to assess how families manage their lives, identifying strengths and problem areas. Includes chapters on How to Analyze Family Needs and Services Data; Family Needs Assessment Forms; Family Action Plans.

Walton, J. *Logical Mathematical Thinking and the Preschool Classroom* (College Park, Md.: Head Start Resource and Training Center, University of Maryland, nd.) Includes games and activities for use with small groups; activities use materials teachers can make or assemble. Includes diagrams, directions, and short discussion of the activities' theoretical basis (Piaget).

FURTHER STUDY

1. Accompany a Head Start worker when she visits homes. How do you think qualities of the homes you visited affect the children's learning ability?
2. Discuss the range of cultural differences in your community. Give an example of a classroom problem that may result from cultural variations.
3. Interview parents of Head Start children to find out what they feel has been the impact of Head Start on their family.
4. Visit a local school district and gather information about its federally supported programs. What kind of federal education programs does the district have? How is the money spent? Do you approve or disapprove of what you saw?
5. Visit several Head Start centers and compare and contrast their programs. How are they similar and different? How do you account for this?
6. After reviewing current literature and interviewing children, parents, and Head Start personnel, briefly state your opinion concerning the success or failure of the present Head Start program. Give reasons for your comments and discuss with your peers.
7. Interview Head Start workers to determine their opinions about the future of the program. What changes do they suggest?
8. Examine the latest poverty income guidelines published by the federal government. Do you feel these incomes are sufficient for rearing a family? Why or why not? What solutions would you propose to the problem of substandard incomes for a large number of American families?
9. Compare the schedule of a Head Start center in this chapter with a Head Start center in your community. Also compare the Head Start schedules to those of preschools. What would you change? Be specific, and include your reasons.
10. Develop a list of pros and cons for involving parents in early childhood programs. What implications does this list have for teachers of young children? For Head Start programs? How do you feel about parent involvement in early childhood programs?
11. Develop a questionnaire you could give to parents to find out their needs and ideas about home-based and center-based early childhood programs. Which do they prefer?
12. Collect magazine articles about working with parents. Save only those that give specific ideas and tips. What is their major emphasis? Could parents use them?
13. Develop a set of criteria for deciding which families would be eligible for a home-based education program.
14. Conduct a poll of parents to find out how they think early childhood programs and schools can help them in educating their children; how they think they can be involved in

early childhood programs; what specific help they feel they need in child rearing and educating; and what activities they would like in a home visitation program.

15. Survey parents to determine their views and beliefs about federal cutbacks to social programs and early childhood programs. Analyze their opinions as they correlate to income level, cultural background, and educational level.

16. What effects have federal cuts in social services had on particular families and children in your area? Give specific examples.

17. Contact the migrant education office in your area. What are the occupations of migrant parents? What are the major problems faced by the children and families? What services are being provided for them? Do you think the services to migrants are as effective and comprehensive as they should be?

18. Write a position paper supporting or rejecting federal support to early childhood programs.

19. Interview the director of the Follow Through program in your school district. After this interview, visit a Follow Through classroom. Do you support the purposes of Follow Through? Why? What three things impressed you most and least about the program?

20. Would you want to teach in a Head Start/Follow Through program? Why or why not?

21. Visit a government-subsidized child care program and inquire about their policies and regulations; compare them to those of a private facility.

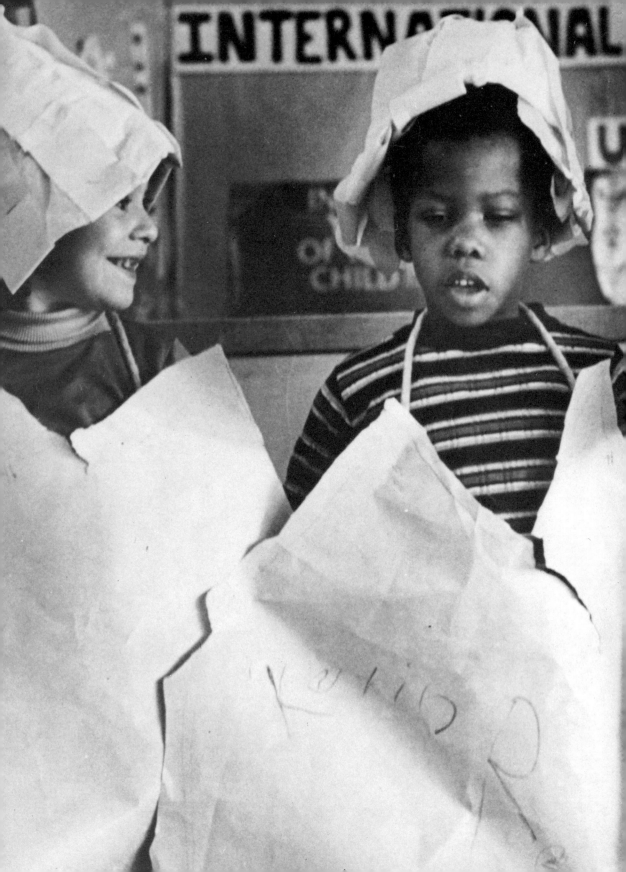

11

Teaching Children with Special Needs: Developing Awareness

As you read and study:

Identify and learn the terminology and legal definitions of children with special needs

Assess the legal, political, moral, and social bases for mainstreaming children in early childhood programs

Develop and evaluate a personal philosophy about teaching in the mainstream

Identify reasons for current interest in special needs children

Develop an understanding of the major provisions of P.L. 94–142 and P.L. 99–457

Determine the implications of P.L. 94–142 and P.L. 99–457 for children and families

Identify and evaluate issues relating to mainstreaming and teaching handicapped children

Examine and critique programs for the gifted

Develop methods for involving parents of special needs children in educational programs

Examine and review what is involved in an Individual Education Program

Develop an understanding of multicultural education

Develop a philosophy of teaching for multicultural awareness and understanding

SPECIAL NEEDS CHILDREN

Educators and the public are very much involved in providing all children with an education appropriate to their physical, mental, social, and emotional abilities. In particular, there is a great deal of emphasis on educating children who have needs that other children do not. There are special needs children in every classroom of every school in the United States. These children are handicapped, gifted, and children with multicultural heritages. They require teaching strategies and approaches designed to meet their special needs.

Handicapped Children

To understand about programs for the handicapped, it is important to know the federal government's definition of handicapped children; the definition is further refined in definitions of each of the specified handicapping categories:

> The term "handicapped children" means those children evaluated . . . as being mentally retarded, hard of hearing, deaf, speech impaired, visually handicapped, seriously emotionally disturbed, orthopedically impaired, other health impaired, deaf-blind, multi-handicapped, or as having specific learning disabilities, who because of those impairments need special education and related services.[1]

Several facets of the government's definition differ from the public's general conception of the handicapped. First, the federal definition is more comprehensive. Second, the public generally thinks of handicaps as mainly physical disabilities and not so much in terms of the emotionally or orthopedically impaired. Table 11–1 shows the number of handicapped children in the various categories; about 10 to 12 percent of the nation's children are handicapped.

Gifted Children

There is not universal agreement as to the definition of "gifted," but the most generally accepted is the description in P.L. 95–561, the Gifted and Talented Act of 1978:

> The term *gifted and talented children* means children and, whenever applicable, youth who are identified at the preschool, elementary, or secondary level as possessing demonstrated or potential abilities that give evidence of high performance capabilities in areas such as intellectual, creative, specific academic, or leadership ability, or in the performing and visual arts, and who by reason thereof, require services or activities not ordinarily provided by the school.

This definition distinguishes between *giftedness*, characterized by above-average intellectual ability, and *talented*, referring to individuals who excel in such areas as drama, art, music, athletics, and leadership. Students can have these abilities separately or in combination. A talented five-year-old may be learning disabled, and an orthopedically handicapped student may be gifted.

TABLE 11–1   Handicapped Children and Youth Served Under P.L. 94-142 and P.L. 89-313, 1985–1986

Type of Handicap	Total Served, Ages 0–21, U.S. and Insular Areas
Mentally Retarded	686,077
Hard of Hearing and Deaf	68,413
Speech Impaired	1,128,471
Visually Handicapped	29,026
Emotionally Disturbed	376,943
Orthopedically Impaired	59,000
Deaf-Blind	2,133
Multi-handicapped	89,701
Learning Disabled	1,872,339
Other Health Impaired	58,141
Total for year	4,370,244

Source: Office of Special Education and Rehabilitative Services, U.S. Dept. of Education, National Summary of Handicapped Children Receiving Education and Related Services under P.L. 94-142 and P.L. 89-313, 1985–1986.

Multicultural Children

Multicultural students are those whose home culture differs from that of the general population and/or school. These children are members of minority cultures such as Asian American, Native American, black American, or Hispanic. Multicultural children may or may not have special learning needs; quite often, however, they have special language needs. Other children may need help because of differences in behavior based on cultural customs and values. All children in every classroom, regardless of their cultural background, need teachers who are multiculturally aware and who promote multicultural understanding.

TEACHING IN THE MAINSTREAM

Many children are taught in the mainstream when they enter the public schools. *Mainstreaming* is the social and educational integration of special needs children into the general instructional process, usually the regular classroom. This practice implies that such children will be identified and that the services of special educators and other professionals as well as regular teachers will be utilized. Mainstreaming means the special needs child will be educated in the regular school classroom for part or all of the school day. Removal from the regular classroom should occur only if the regular classroom cannot offer appropriate instruction; then instruction is usually provided by a special educator such as a resource teacher.

Mainstreaming can be interpreted to mean that children with special needs will be a part of the system of education that has traditionally meant "normal" children and regular classrooms. In another sense, mainstreaming means the schools are returning special needs children to the system from which they have been excluded for over three-quarters of a century. Until recently, it was acceptable, and thought to be educationally sound, legal, and humane, to provide separate (but not always equal) education for special needs children outside the regular classroom. It is no longer justifiable to do so if the child can benefit from an educational program in the regular classroom. In mainstreaming, emphasis is on the concept of *normalcy*. This means that children will be treated normally and educated as normally as possible. These are guidelines for preparing to teach in a mainstreamed classroom:

☐ Have a well thought-out philosophy of education. This is important no matter what kind of children you teach; however, it is absolutely necessary to think through your attitudes toward the handicapped.

☐ Know the nature of the handicapped children you will be teaching. Just as it is important to know normal childhood growth and development, it is essential for you to know about the different handicaps and how to account for them in the teaching-learning process.

Mainstreaming integrates the handicapped child into the least restrictive environment, often the regular classroom. Special needs children also include those of different cultures, and multicultural activities should be part of every early childhood classroom.

☐ Since P.L. 94–142 requires individualized education for the handicapped child, it is important to know how to do this. While developing a program for the individual child is not the same as individualized instruction, knowing the differences between the two and how to conduct both processes makes sense pedagogically.

☐ Methods and techniques of diagnostic and prescriptive teaching are essential as a basis for writing and implementing the Individualized Educational Program.

☐ Working with parents is an absolute must for every classroom teacher. You should learn all you can about parent conferences and communication, parent involvement, and parents as volunteers and aides. In a sense, P.L. 94–142 and P.L. 99–457 mainstream parents as well as children.

☐ Working with paraprofessionals offers a unique opportunity for the classroom teacher to individualize instruction. Since it is obvious that the regular classroom teacher needs help in individualizing instruction, it makes sense to use paraprofessionals in this process. You should become knowledgeable about and adept in working with paraprofessionals.

☐ As more individual education becomes a reality, teachers will need skills in assessing student behavior. Therefore, training in tests and measurements and observational skills are a necessity.

☐ Teachers must know how to identify sources of, and how to order and use, a broad range of instructional materials, including media. One cannot hope to individualize without a full range of materials and media. The learning modalities teachers must regularly be concerned with are visual, auditory, and tactile/kinesthetic. Some children in a classroom may learn best through one mode; other children may learn best through another. The classroom teacher can utilize media, in particular, to help make teaching styles congruent with children's learning modalities.

☐ Every teacher in a mainstreamed classroom (and even those who are not) should be familiar with P.L. 94–142 and P.L. 99–457 and their implications.

INTEREST IN SPECIAL NEEDS CHILDREN

There are several reasons for the present interest in education of special needs children. First, court cases and legal decisions have extended to special needs children the rights and privileges enjoyed by everyone. To ensure that these rights and privileges are accorded to their children, parent involvement is a necessity. In some instances, court decisions have encouraged or ordered this involvement. In the absence of the special needs child's ability to be his own advocate, the courts, agencies, and parents are assuming that function.

Legislation enacted at the state and federal levels has specified that handicapped children must receive a free and appropriate education. In essence, this legislation promotes and encourages development of programs for education of the handicapped. This legislation also provides for parent involvement. Thus, educators are involving parents of handicapped children because they must.

Second, there is federal money available to create programs for special needs children, and greater social consciousness toward children with special needs. People recognize that the handicapped have often been treated as second-class citizens and have been victims of oppression and degradation, so there is an effort to make reparations for past behavior and attitudes.

Third, many young people see teaching special needs children as a rewarding profession, with unlimited opportunities to contribute. These young people feel they can best serve society, children, and themselves by teaching, and many preservice professionals feel that most children will learn on their own, but the special needs child needs help and training. Consequently, many bright, young educators are devoting their lives to helping these children.

Fourth, American education emphasizes meeting the needs of individual children, and special needs children require special attention and accommodation.

Public Law 94–142

The landmark legislation providing for the needs of the handicapped is P.L. 94–142. Section 3 of this law states:

> It is the purpose of this Act to assure that all handicapped children have available to them, within the time periods specified in section 612(2)(B), a free appropriate public education which emphasizes special education and related services designed to meet their unique needs, to assure that the rights of handicapped children and their parents or guardians are protected, to assist States and localities to provide for the education of all handicapped children, and to assess and assure the effectiveness of efforts to educate handicapped children.[2]

P.L. 94–142 provides for a free and appropriate education (FAPE) for all persons between the ages of three and twenty-one. The operative word is *appropriate;* the child must receive an education suited to his age, maturity, handicapping condition, past achievements, and parental expectations. The common practice was to diagnose children as handicapped and then put them in an existing program, whether or not that program was specifically appropriate; now, the educational program has to be appropriate to the child, which means that a plan must be developed for each child.

The child's education must occur within the least restrictive educational environment. *Least restrictive* means that environment in which the child will be able to receive a program that meets his specific needs—the regular classroom, if that is the environment in which the child can learn best. The least restrictive educational environment is not always the regular classroom; however, this law provides more opportunity to be with regular children.

The law requires *individualization of instruction* and *diagnosis.* Not only must the child's education be appropriate, it must also be individualized, taking into consideration his specific needs, handicapping conditions, and preferences, as well as those of his parents. The key to the individualization process is another feature of the law that requires development of an individual educational plan (IEP) for each child. This plan must specify what will be done for the child, and how and when it will be done. The plan must be in writing. In developing this educational plan, a person trained in diagnosing handicapping conditions, such as a school psychologist, must be involved, as well as a classroom teacher, the parent, and, where appropriate, the child himself.

There are several implications associated with this educational plan. One is that for the first time, on a formal basis, parents and children are involved in the educational determination of what will happen to the child. Second, the child must have a plan tailor-made or individualized for him. This individualization assures accurate diagnosis and realistic goal setting, as well as responsible implementation of the program. This brings an element of personalization to the process, and increases the possibility that the teaching-learning process will be more humane.

The legislation specifies that parents and child will have a role in diagnosis, placement, and development of the individualized educational plan. Parents can state their desires for the child, and information parents have about the child's learning style, interests, and abilities can be considered in developing the educational plan. This process was not always possible or even considered necessary before passage of P.L. 94–142.

The law also provides for parents to initiate a hearing if they do not agree with the diagnosis, placement, or educational plan. This provision gives the parent "clout" in encouraging public school personnel to provide a free and appropriate education for the child.

Implications for Parents

While the implications of P.L. 94–142 are far-reaching for children and adults with handicaps, its implications for involving parents in the educational process are especially important. To receive money under the provisions of the law or to continue receiving federal money for other programs, school districts must involve parents in the development of the educational program of their handicapped child. Involvement becomes the right of every parent of a handicapped child. The second implication of this act is that parents' knowledge of the child must be included in the development of the educational plan. Third, parents are assured of continued involvement in their child's education because the plan has to be reviewed and revised at least annually, and because of the law's due process features, which stipulate that if the parents are not satisfied with the child's placement or with the educational plan, they have the right to appeal to higher authorities in the schools and, ultimately, to the courts. child advocate organizations, organizations for handicapped citizens, and civil rights groups advise parents of their rights and responsibilities under the provisions of this act.

Parents' Rights

Under the provisions of P.L. 94–142, parents have these rights regarding their child's education:

1. The parent must give consent for evaluation of the child.
2. The parent has the right to "examine all relevant records with respect to the identification, evaluation, and educational placement of the child."

3. The parent must be given written prior notice whenever a change in "the identification, evaluation or educational placement of the child" occurs.
4. This written notice must be in the parent's native tongue.
5. The parent has an "opportunity to present complaints with respect to any matter relating to the identification, evaluation, or educational placement of the child."
6. The parent has the right to a due process hearing in relation to any complaint.
7. The parent has the right to participate in development of the individual educational program for the child.
8. Meetings to develop the IEP must be conducted in the parent's native tongue.
9. Meetings to develop the IEP must be held at a time and place agreeable to the parent.

P.L. 94–142's most obvious benefit is to give the handicapped child access to the regular classroom. As mainstreaming continues, there will be more peer interaction among the handicapped and nonhandicapped. The concept of *least restrictive environment* offers a great deal of opportunity for handicapped children, assuring that the child will be educated and cared for in the environment that best meets his needs. Figure 11–1 illustrates the process of establishing a least restrictive environment.

Child Find

Public Law 94–142 provides for Child Find agencies to facilitate identification of handicapped children. Child Find programs are operated by state and local agencies, including school districts. The major purposes of Child Find are to:

☐ Locate and identify handicapped children and youth
☐ Conduct screening and assessment tests
☐ Recommend educational and therapeutic services
☐ Refer parents to appropriate social service agencies

PUBLIC LAW 99–457

Congress passed P.L. 99–457, landmark legislation relating to handicapped infants, toddlers and preschoolers, in 1986. P.L. 99–457 authorizes two new programs, a Federal Preschool Program and and Early Intervention Program. The Federal Preschool Program extends to handicapped children between the ages of three and five the rights extended to the handicapped under P.L. 94–142. By the 1990–91 school year, states applying for P.L. 94–142 funds will have to assure that they are providing a free and appropriate public education to all handicapped children ages three to five. This age group was included in P.L. 94–142, but often did not receive public school services because states had discretion as to whether to provide services to this age group. Beginning with the 1990–91 school year the states can no longer choose not to provide services if they want to continue to receive funding under P.L. 94–142.

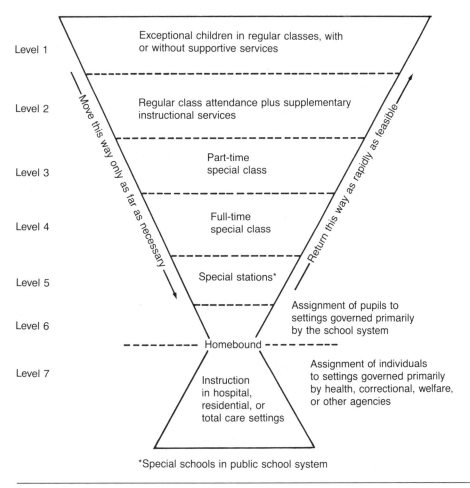

Level 1 — Exceptional children in regular classes, with or without supportive services

Level 2 — Regular class attendance plus supplementary instructional services

Level 3 — Part-time special class

Level 4 — Full-time special class

Level 5 — Special stations*

Level 6 — Homebound

Level 7 — Instruction in hospital, residential, or total care settings

Move this way only as far as necessary

Return this way as rapidly as feasible

Assignment of pupils to settings governed primarily by the school system

Assignment of individuals to settings governed primarily by health, correctional, welfare, or other agencies

*Special schools in public school system

FIGURE 11–1 The Cascade System of Educational Placement (From "Proposed CEC Policy Statement on the Organization and Administration of Special Education," *Exceptional Children*, 1973, *39*, 495. Copyright by the Council for Exceptional Children. Reprinted with permission.)

The legislation recognizes that families play a large role in delivery of services to preschool handicapped children; consequently, P.L. 99–457 provides that, whenever appropriate and to the extent desired by parents, the preschooler's individualized IEP will include instruction for parents. The legislation also recognizes the desirability of variations in program options to provide services to handicapped preschoolers. Variations may be part-day, home-based, and part- or full-day center-based.

The Early Intervention Program authorized by P.L. 99–457 establishes a state grant program for handicapped infants and toddlers from birth to two years who: (1) are experiencing developmental delays in one or more of the following areas: cogni-

Public Law 99-457 recognizes the needs of handicapped infants and toddlers. When appropriate, parents also receive help and instruction for providing services to their handicapped child.

tive, physical, language and speech, psychosocial, or self-help skills; or (2) have a physical or mental condition that has a high probability of resulting in delay (e.g., Down syndrome, cerebral palsy; and (3) are at risk medically or environmentally for substantial developmental delays if early intervention is not provided. This program provides for early intervention for all eligible children. The law provides a five-year implementation period; during the fifth year of implementation, participating states must make early intervention services available to all handicapped infants and toddlers. Early intervention services provided under 99–457 include:

☐ A multidisciplinary assessment and a written Individualized Family Services Plan (IFSP) developed by a multidisciplinary team and the parents.

Services must meet developmental needs and can include special education, speech and language pathology and audiology, occupational therapy, physical therapy, psychological services, parent and family training and counseling services, transition services, medical diagnostic services, and health services

☐ An Individualized Family Service Plan, which must contain a statement of the child's present levels of development; a statement of the family's strengths and needs in regard to enhancing the child's development; a statement of major expected outcomes for the child and family; the criteria, procedures, and timeliness for determining progress; the specific early intervention services necessary to meet the unique needs of the child and family; the projected dates for initiation of services; the name of the case manager; and transition procedures from the early intervention program into a preschool program

FUNCTION OF THE IEP

The use of an individualized educational program with all children, not just the handicapped, is gaining acceptance with teachers. Individualizing objectives, methodology, and teaching can ensure that the teaching process will become more accurate and accountable. Figure 11–2 shows an IEP form developed by Dade County, Florida. The format of the IEP may be different in each state, but all plans must include annual goals and instructional objectives.

The IEP has several purposes. First, it protects the child and parent by assuring that planning will occur. Second, the IEP assures that the child will have a plan tailored to his individual strengths, weaknesses, and learning styles. Third, the IEP helps teachers and other instructional and administrative personnel focus their teaching and resources on the child's specific needs, and promotes the best use of everyone's time, efforts, and talents.

Fourth, teachers can be more confident in their teaching because they have planned what and how they will teach. Parents can be confident that the instructional processes for their child have been planned in advance and that individual differences and needs have been considered. Fifth, the IEP assures that the handicapped child will receive a broad range of services from other agencies. The plan must not only include an educational component, but must also specify how the child's total needs will be met. If the child can benefit from physical therapy, for example, it must be written into the IEP. This provision is beneficial not only for the child, but for the classroom teacher as well, because it broadens her perspective of the educational function. Sixth, the IEP helps to clarify and refine decisions as to what is best for the child—where he should be placed, how he should be taught and helped. It also assures that the child will not be categorized or labeled without discussion of his unique needs. Seventh, review of the IEP at least annually forces educators to consider how and what the child has learned, whether what was prescribed is effective, and to prescribe new or modified learning strategies.

DADE COUNTY PUBLIC SCHOOLS   EXCEPTIONAL STUDENT EDUCATION
INDIVIDUALIZED EDUCATION PLAN (IEP) AND AUTHORIZATION FOR PLACEMENT

NAME_____ BIRTHDATE_____ SCHOOL_____CONFERENCE DATE_____

ADDRESS_____

Present Levels of Educational Performance | Special Education Placement
and Related Services; Persons Responsible_____

Annual Goals	Instructional Objectives/Evaluation Criteria	+ or −	Date

Projected: Date of Initiation_____Anticipated Duration _____

Extent of participation in regular program:_____ MIS-12075 (05-78)

TEAM CHAIRPERSON:_____ LEA REPRESENTATIVE:_____

Ethnic Origin—*Circle One*

Committee Members   Title

1. White
2. Black
3. Hispanic
4. Asian
5. Indian, American

1._____
2._____
3._____
4._____
5._____
6._____

Language Proficiency—*Circle One*

Parent Involvement: YES ☐   NO ☐
Notification Dates: _____ _____ _____
Notification Method: _____ _____ _____
Date of Annual Review: _____

A. Monolingual - No English
B. Intermediate - Some English
C. Bilingual - Both English & another
      language equally well
D. Independent - Mostly English
E. Monolingual - English exclusively

Recommendation for Placement for _____ *(Year)*

☐ Terminate Special Class Placement (refer to Placement Committee)

Comment: _____

Additional Information/Comments:

☐ Continue Special Class Placement

Parent signed <u>New</u> IEP: YES ☐   NO ☐

DADE COUNTY PUBLIC SCHOOLS
EXCEPTIONAL STUDENT EDUCATION

STUDENT'S WEEKLY CALENDAR

Student Name _____

I.D.# _____

	Monday	Tuesday	Wednesday	Thursday	Friday
7:30					
8:00					
8:30					
9:00					
9:30					
10:00					
10:30					
11:00					
11:30					
12:00					
12:30					
1:00					
1:30					
2:00					
2:30					
3:00					
3:30					
4:00					
4:30					

R = Regular Education
E = Exceptional Education

ADDITIONAL NOTES:

____ % Exceptional Education Time plus
____ % Regular Education Time =
100% Program Time

A current calendar must be maintained to account for all program aspects (100% total) of the child's school time, including regular education.

Signature_____
Exceptional Education Classroom Teacher

_____ _____
Program   Date of this Calendar

. LEA Representative _____

.Position _____

FIGURE 11–2 Individualized Educational Plan or IEP (From the Dade County, Florida, Public Schools)

TEACHING THE HANDICAPPED

As an early childhood educator, you will have children with special needs in your classroom. Learning disabled students constitute the majority of handicapped children. These are some of the general types of handicaps you will encounter in your classroom:

☐ Visual impairment—loss of visual function sufficient to restrict the learning process

☐ Hearing impairment—slightly to severely defective hearing

☐ Physical handicap—a condition that impedes normal development of gross or fine motor abilities

☐ Speech impairment or communication disorder—disorders of expressive or receptive language; stuttering, chronic voice disorders, or serious articulation problems affecting social, emotional, and educational achievement

☐ Health impairment—illnesses of a chronic and prolonged nature such as epilepsy, hemophilia, asthma, cardiac conditions, severe allergies, blood disorders, diabetes, and neurological disorders

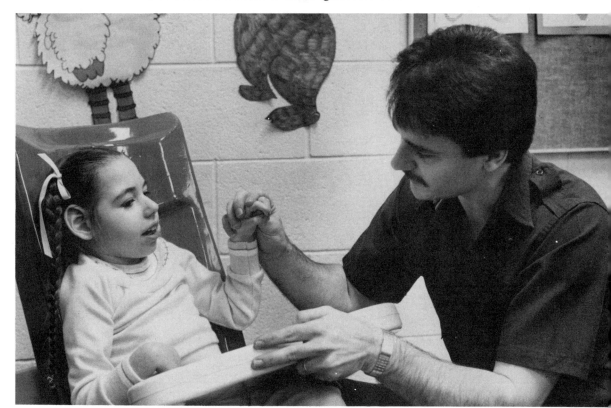

To integrate special needs children into a regular classroom, schools must make adjustments in human and educational resources.

☐ Serious emotional disturbances—dangerous aggressiveness, self-destructiveness, severe withdrawal and uncommunicative, hyperactive to the extent that it affects adaptive behavior, severely anxious, depressed, psychotic, or autistic

☐ Specific learning disabilities—disorder in one or more of the basic psychological processes involved in understanding or using language, spoken or written, that may manifest itself in imperfect ability to listen, think, speak, read, write, spell, or perform mathematical calculations

Resource Room

One method of providing for the handicapped child in a mainstreamed setting is the *resource room*. As the name implies, this classroom is an instructional setting that provides resources for handicapped students and their teachers. A student who participates in the resource program is enrolled in the regular educational program and goes to the resource room on a regular basis for special support, usually of an academic nature. The regular classroom teachers of the exceptional student receive support from materials and ideas shared by the resource teacher. In this way, teachers discover different approaches or alternative methods for dealing with the student's problem. The *resource teacher* has training in special education and experience in teaching handicapped students. The resource teacher shares ideas with the other faculty members to promote positive attitudes toward exceptional learners.

The Transdisciplinary Team

The *transdisciplinary team approach* to special needs children consists of *interdisciplinary* involvement across and among various health and social services disciplines. Members of the team can include any of these professionals: early childhood educator, physical therapist, occupational therapist, speech therapist, psychologist, social worker, and pediatrician. The rationale for the transdisciplinary approach is that a unified and holistic approach is the most effective way to provide resources and deliver services to children and their families. Members of the transdisciplinary team diagnose, prescribe, share information, and work cooperatively to meet children's needs. One of the members, usually the early childhood educator, heads the team, and other members act as consultants. The team leader carries out the instructions of the other team members. A variation of this model is to have members of the team, such as the physical therapist, work directly with the child at specified times (for example, twice a week) and provide activities and suggestions for the early childhood educator to implement at other times.

MATCHING CHILDREN'S CHARACTERISTICS TO SETTING RESOURCES

Mary Wilson has developed a Match-Up Matrix to help educators make decisions about necessary human and materials resources, facilities, and special arrangements for integrating the handicapped into regular classroom settings.[3]

Adam

Two-and-a-half-year-old Adam has diplegia (involvement of the lower extremities) and a seizure disorder resulting from a head injury he received in a car accident at 18 months of age. Shortly after the accident, Adam received physical therapy through the hospital's outpatient services. On the recommendation of his therapist, Adam's parents are seeking to enroll him in a preschool.

Adam uses a walker to maneuver in his environment. Though he is able to do many things with minimal effort, he often asks for help. His language and cognitive skills have been assessed at or above age level; however, self-help skills have been affected by his gross motor delays. Though seizures occurred frequently after the accident, with daily medication there has been no recurrence except with a high fever. Adam relates well to adults, though he sometimes appears unnecessarily dependent upon them. Adam has limited opportunities to interact with children his own age. He has a teenage brother, both parents work, and a housekeeper/baby-sitter sees to his needs. Both parents are concerned about Adam's care and want him "to be happy."

In the Match-Up Matrix of Adam's needs and the preschool's resources, we see a match in nearly every area; nevertheless, a few adjustments are necessary (Table 11–2). The greatest concern involves motor and, secondarily, self-help skills. The walker in a busy classroom requires attention to traffic patterns, seating, and mobility into and out of areas, especially the small bathroom. The hospital's physical therapist has offered to visit the school and share suggestions for Adam's independence. As with many young children who have not attended school, Adam will need help to learn independent play skills and interactive social skills. A final concern is Adam's seizure disorder. Though the staff members have been assured that they are unlikely to observe a seizure at school, the team feels it is important to know what to expect and what to do.

His parents decide to enroll Adam in the Sunshine Preschool. When they visit the program after the first two months, they are amazed by how much Adam can do for himself. As a result, they are beginning to demand more independence in daily routines at home. His therapist reports an increase in his progress and, particularly, in his motivation since he started school.

Sally

Sally is a 3-year-old girl with cerebral palsy described as "spastic quadriparesis," which indicates involvement in all extremities. She is learning to use an adapted wheelchair with help. She reaches for objects, but is often inaccurate. She controls her head and trunk, but requires support for sitting. Sally seems to understand all that is said to her; however, her motor impairment affects the intelligibility of her speech and her ability to demonstrate what she knows. Though she can make her immediate needs known through simple words and gestures, the use of a picture board helps her to express concepts. Sally smiles, laughs, and approaches adults and children, but her participation is limited. She needs help to dress, undress, and feed herself. Sally may throw tantrums to control certain situations, particularly at home. Sally's parents are eager to get services for their daughter. She has not

TABLE 11–2 Match-Up Matrix for Adam at Sunshine Preschool

Setting	Training	Specialists	Equipment and Materials	Appropriate Peers	Aide/ Helper	Action
Motor	− Traffic Seating Mobility	+ Therapist from hospital	+	− Not independent	N.A.	*1
Language	+	N.A.	N.A.	+	N.A.	
Cognitive	+	N.A.	N.A.	+	N.A.	
Social	− Sharing Independent play	N.A.	N.A.	+	N.A.	*3
Self-help	− Independent dressing, toileting	N.A.	− Traffic	+	N.A.	*2
Behavior	+	N.A.	N.A.	+	N.A.	
Medical	− Information on seizures	+ Family doctor/ neurologist	N.A.	N.A.	N.A.	*4
Home	+ Teenage brother	N.A.	N.A.	N.A.	N.A.	

Note: A + indicates a child's needs can be met with current setting resources; a − indicates a setting resource need followed by action/ resource need. The numbers in the action column indicate priority; #1 is what staff will do first.

been in school before, though her mother now feels she is "ready." Her parents believe Sally's strengths are in social and cognitive skills and feel that any classroom could easily handle their daughter's needs. Nevertheless, Sally's mother has offered to volunteer several days per week at lunch to help her daughter at that time.

Sally's matrix presents a complex situation. Motor is the area of most concern, but the extent of the handicap affects several areas. The team has also identified language as an area lacking a match. Though Sally has strengths in

TABLE 11–3 Match-Up Matrix for Sally at Rainbow Preschool

Setting	Training	Specialists	Equipment and Materials	Appropriate Peers	Aide/ Helper	Action
Motor	− Handling Positioning	− Hospital therapist? Doctor refers?	− Wheelchair Toys Utensils	− Independent mobility	− Mother volunteers peers? para?	*1
Language	− Poor speech Use of picture board	+ School consultant/ parents	− Pictures of school activity/ needs	− Need training	− Needs help with board	*2
Cognitive	+	N.A.	− Adaptive toys, tools	+	N.A.	*4
Social	+	N.A.	N.A.	− Help peers understand	− Help child participate, interact	*5
Self-help	− Dressing Toileting Feeding	− Hospital therapist? Doctor refers?	− Clothing Potty chair Utensils	− Have peers help	+ Mother volunteers	*3
Behavior	+	N.A.	− Program for tantrum at home and school	+	+ Trained para- professionals	*6
Medical	+	N.A.	N.A.	N.A.	N.A.	
Home	− Understands child needs	− Social worker? Parent support group	− Information on cerebral palsy	N.A.	+ Mother volunteers	*7

Note: * indicates order of priorities.

cognitive and social areas, equipment or an adult presence would be required to facilitate Sally's participation. Sally's behavior and the lack of experience in school settings suggest the need for consistent, individualized programming.

Through the Match-Up Matrix, the parents and school agreed that the Sunshine Preschool was not the appropriate program to serve Sally's needs at that time (Table 11–3). However, the matrix allowed the team to identify what services were required and made an informed referral. The team was also able to identify what resources or skills would enable successful enrollment at Sunshine Preschool in the future.

Sally's parents decided to enroll her at Rainbow Preschool, an interdisciplinary program for eight multihandicapped youngsters of all cognitive levels. Located in an elementary school, the preschool and the kindergarten classes have frequent contact. Sally's parents participate in the parent group which provides information, training, and support to its members. Sally's parents have indicated interest in reapplying to Sunshine next year. The team looks forward to that application, confident that Sally will have made progress and may indeed be "ready" for their school, and the school for her.

Handicapped Children in Head Start Programs

Head Start services to handicapped children consist of the following:

1. *Outreach and recruitment.* This effort is directed toward locating, identifying and recruiting handicapped children into Head Start. The most common sources for outreach are parents, public health departments, school systems, and newspapers articles.
2. *Diagnosis and assessment of handicapped children.* Head Start staff members work with private diagnostic consultants to achieve this service.
3. *Mainstreaming and special services.* Special services include individualized instruction, parent counseling, and psychological and physical therapy.
4. *Teaching and technical assistance.* This includes working with staff and parents to provide training for working with handicapped children.
5. *Coordination with other agencies.* Head Start staff work closely with other agencies to identify, recruit, and provide services to handicapped children and their families.
6. *Summer Head Start.* Many Head Start children who would otherwise probably not receive services before entering public school are served in summer programs.

Guidelines for Teaching the Handicapped

Teachers of the handicapped can improve their teaching by emphasizing children's abilities rather than focusing on their handicapping conditions. Handicapped children have many talents and abilities and are capable of a wide range of achievements, and teachers can help them fulfill their potentials as they would any other child. Teaching methods that are effective with the nonhandicapped may be equally effective with the handicapped. Conversely, many instructional activities that special educators use with the handicapped work just as well with the nonhandicapped. Teachers first need to diagnose what children are able to do. Diagnosis can occur informally, through observation, examination of work samples, teacher-made tests, discussions with parents, examination of cumulative records, and discussions with other teachers.

Use of concrete examples and materials and multisensory approaches to learning are also important in teaching the handicapped. And, as with the nonhandicapped, it is important to involve children in learning activities. The teacher must also model what children are to do, rather than just tell them what to do. A good procedure is to tell children what they are to do; model a behavior or have a child who has already mastered a skill model it for others; have children perform the skill or task under supervision and give them corrective feedback; let children practice or perform the behavior; and involve the children in evaluating their performance. Make learning interesting. Dolls, for example, can help teach concepts of body parts and hygiene. Make the learning environment a pleasant and rewarding place to be. A dependable classroom schedule is easier for handicapped children because it gives them a sense of security and consistency.

Parent involvement is one of the most effective ways to increase student achievement. Parents can help with the instructional process both at home and in school. The teacher also needs to make a special effort to involve all children in all classroom activities. With a few modifications, most activities conducted in early childhood programs can be made appropriate for the handicapped. In addition, a goal of every early childhood program should be to have children become independent of others, especially teachers and parents. Table 11–4 offers specific procedures for adapting teaching methods to handicapped children's special needs.

INTEGRATION OF NONHANDICAPPED WITH HANDICAPPED CHILDREN IN EARLY CHILDHOOD PROGRAMS

Integration of handicapped and nonhandicapped children is becoming more popular as a way of providing better education and support services. Special education programs use two kinds of integration. The first is a type of *reverse mainstreaming,* in which nonhandicapped children are placed in programs for the handicapped. In this model, the handicapped are the majority of children in the program. Usually, a group of two-thirds handicapped children and one-third nonhandicapped works well, but the optimum ratio for any program varies. The other type of integration occurs when the handicapped are *mainstreamed,* or placed in a program for nonhandicapped children, so that the nonhandicapped constitute the majority of the class.

Reverse mainstreaming is receiving a lot of attention in early childhood education today, and a number of assumptions are implicit in any model of reverse mainstreaming: (1) the instructional program and activities will be appropriate for both handicapped and nonhandicapped; (2) integration will have a positive rather than negative effect on both groups; (3) the program is pedagogically and administratively manageable. These are issues to consider in a program of reverse mainstreaming:

☐ Recruitment, identification, and selection of children to participate in the program

TABLE 11–4 Adapting to the Child with Special Needs

Impairment	Characteristics	Specific Teaching Approaches
Any disability		Accept the child
		Create real experiences to develop the sense of touch, taste, hearing, sight, or smell
		Adapt environment to accommodate needs
		Model appropriate behavior and language
		Encourage independence
		Allow ample time to complete tasks
		Facilitate participation in all class activities
		Remove hazards
		Apply same standards of behavior for all children, when possible
		Capitalize on children's talents, skills, interests
		Practice emergency procedures
		Confer frequently with child's therapist/physician/ parents
		Maintain accurate records of progress or observed changes
		Respond appropriately to other children's fears or questions about the disability
Language/ speech	Use of single words and/or gestures	Describe ongoing activities
		Use phrases and short sentences
	Severe articulation problems, making it difficult to understand the child	Restate rather than correct
		Provide abundant opportunities to talk
	Difficulty following directions	Listen and respond to content of language
		Show interest; maintain eye contact
		Use speech rather than gestures
		Provide daily oral experience in singing and regular language activities
Mental	Few communication skills	Provide consistent, brief directions
	Poor motor skills	Plan for much repetition
	Lack of self-help skills	Reinforce successful efforts
	Learning at slower rate	Praise appropriate social behavior and participation
	Short attention span	Use multisensory experiences
		Break tasks into small components if necessary

TABLE 11–4 Continued

Impairment	Characteristics	Specific Teaching Approaches
Hearing	Limited communication skills (usually) Inability to understand others' speech and language May be learning hand signs in addition to speech reading and use of residual hearing	Learn child's hearing capacity Use child's name when directing speech to her/him Articulate clearly with moderate speed; avoid exaggeration, loud voice, or mumbling Seat child for good visibility of activity, teacher, or other children Learn to change hearing aid battery and/or cord (See language/speech section for additional suggestions)
Visual	Some children may see shadow forms, colors, or even large pictures Peripheral vision may be best (turned-away face does not indicate inattentiveness)	Orient child to classroom layout and materials locations Give directions related to child's body and orientation Describe objects and activities completely Give notice of change in activity Encourage other children to identify themselves and describe what is happening Acknowledge child when she/he enters room Provide activities to develop motor skills, listening skills, moving about, and use of senses
Physical	May use crutches or wheelchair Poor fine and/or large motor control and coordination May have speech delay Tenseness or stress may increase spasticity	Change child's position frequently (20–30 min.) Allow space for movement Keep change of clothing available Determine child's most comfortable floor sitting position

Source: Dorothy Morgan and May Elizabeth York, "Ideas for Mainstreaming Young Children," *Young Children*, 36, no. 2 (January, 1981), pp. 22–23.

☐ Working with all parents, especially parents of the nonhandicapped, to assure them that their children are receiving a good—even an above-average educational experience

☐ Identification of services, equipment, materials, and necessary special training

The principal advantages of integrating a classroom that was previously for only the handicapped are that the nonhandicapped provide role models for behavior and skill development and the teacher is able to maintain perspective on normal growth and development.

MAKING TRANSITIONS

Transitional experiences from one setting to another are a must for the special needs child, especially for children who have attended preschool in a special setting or in a separate public school facility from the elementary school. To help the special needs child make a transition from one setting to another, the staffs of the sending agency and the receiving agency must cooperate in arrangements, activities, and plans; for example:

- ☐ Try to approximate certain features of the receiving environment. If the new classroom has a larger ratio of children to adults, gradually get the child used to working and functioning in larger groups.
- ☐ Help the child become accustomed to social skills appropriate to the new environment. If the child has been using a restroom inside the classroom but will have to go outside the classroom in the new school, help her practice this new routine.
- ☐ Use materials and activities as the child will encounter them in the new setting. Get a set of textbooks the child will use and familiarize her with the format and activities.
- ☐ Approximate the kind and length of instructional activities the child will be expected to participate in and complete.
- ☐ Visit the new school with the child and her parents.
- ☐ Communicate with the receiving teacher to share information about the child.
- ☐ Structure a social setting in the receiving classroom. Arrange a "buddy system" with a child in the new classroom.
- ☐ After the child has made the transition, visit the classroom to demonstrate a supportive, caring attitude to the receiving teacher, parents, and child.
- ☐ The receiving teacher has reciprocal responsibilities to make the transition as stress-free and rewarding as possible. Successful transitions involve all concerned: parents, children, teachers, administrators, and support personnel. (Other suggestions for transitional experiences are described in Chapter 8.)

GIFTED CHILDREN

Practitioners Ann and Elizabeth Lupkowski believe young gifted children may display the following behaviors:

- ☐ **Long attention span.** The attention span of gifted children is often longer than that of their peers.... Some young gifted children are able to work on projects for blocks of time as long as 45 minutes to 2½ hours.
- ☐ **Creativity and imagination.** Gifted children may have unique and innovative ideas for the use of common materials or unique names for possessions.... These

children may also design unusual dramatic play situations, such as astronauts landing on the moon, and they often have imaginary friends or companions.

☐ **Social relationships.** All children have varied social skills, and gifted children are no exception. They may be leaders of other children, with advanced social skills for their age, or they may prefer to be alone to work on their own interests. . . . Some gifted children may find innovative ways to settle disputes. Also, young gifted children may prefer to interact with older children and adults rather than with their same-age peers.

☐ **Number concepts.** Some gifted children seem to be fascinated with numbers before they begin formal schooling.

☐ **Verbal skills.** Gifted preschoolers may recognize letters early and show an early interest in printed matter. They may be interested in foreign languages and also exhibit correct pronunciation and sentence structure in their native language. Young gifted children may show an advanced vocabulary and may begin reading before they start school, although the significance of early reading as an indicator of giftedness has not been established.

☐ **Memory.** Gifted children may show exceptional memories.

☐ **Specific interests.** The young gifted child may show an in-depth interest in one or more areas and spend a great deal of time developing a collection of a class of objects, such as rocks or plastic animals.

☐ **Attention to detail.** Gifted children often notice "insignificant" details in pictures and situations. They also enjoy making things more complex—elaborating on rules for games, for example.

☐ **High energy level.** Some gifted children have been called hyperactive because of the high level of energy they show. These children also seem to need little sleep.

☐ **Reasoning ability.** The ability to form analogies at a young age and to justify those responses may be another indicator of giftedness. . . . Perhaps the ability to successfully complete and justify this type of task is an indicator of advanced cognitive development.

☐ **Insight ability.** Exceptional insight ability has been postulated as another characteristic of the intellectually gifted. They may be superior in insight ability because of the ability to sift out relevant information, blend those pieces of information, and add new information to appropriate information acquired in the past. These children have the ability to find solutions to complex problems.[4]

Pediatrician Michael Lewis has found four signs that most—but not all—gifted young children display during the first year of life:

1. **Sleep Problems.** These children either don't go to sleep easily, they wake up early, or they don't sleep long amounts of time. Any or all of these patterns may be present.

    While these kids give the impression that they are having some problems with sleeping, we don't think this is actually the case. Evidently, these children are exhibiting individual differences in sleep patterns: the only *problem* is that the parents don't get enough sleep.

2. **Alertness and Attentiveness.** One of the outstanding signs that parents report is that these children always look interested in what is going on around them. They are usually alert—their eyes are open, scanning the field, and they listen attentively. Indeed, they give you the feeling there is an inquisitive mind at work, even though it is is the mind of a five-week-old.

Gifted children need differentiated programs and activities, and teachers must extend and enrich learning activities.

3. **Early Stranger Fear or Recognition.** Normally, by eight months of age, children are smart enough to remember who they know and who they don't know. When they see a stranger they can compare the image of that person against the images of people they know. When it doesn't match anyone familiar, they become inhibited. Some of these children (about 70 percent) go on to become frightened and upset, a reaction we call stranger anxiety. This pattern normally shows itself in babies at about eight or nine months. In a large proportion of gifted children, we are seeing stranger anxiety showing itself in the third to fourth month of life.

   Not all gifted children we have seen show fearfulness; some just show interest. But, one way or another, all show early *recognition* that they see a stranger.

4. **Early Language Usage.** Many children speak what seem to be intelligent sounds—"mama," "dada" and other words such as these—somewhere in the last quarter of the first year. However, we don't really consider them true words or true noun usage. It is the most complicated words, such as "boat" or "tree" or "dog" that we consider true noun usage. We have noticed that many gifted children start to produce these terms in the last quarter of the first year, when most children are still saying "mama," "dada," "cup," or other simple words.[5]

Gifted children may not display all these signs, but the presence of several of them can alert parents and early childhood teachers to make appropriate instructional, environmental, and social adjustments.

Mainstreaming the Gifted

There is a tendency among professional educators to provide special classes and programs and sometimes schools for the gifted and talented, which would seem to be a move away from providing for these children in regular classrooms. Regular classroom teachers can provide for the gifted in their classrooms through enrichment and acceleration. Enrichment provides an opportunity for children to pursue topics in greater depth and in different ways than they normally might. Acceleration permits children to progress academically at their own pace. Many schools have resource rooms for the gifted and talented, where children can spend a half-day or more every week working with a teacher who is interested and trained in working with the gifted. There are seven ways to provide for the needs of gifted and talented children; of the seven, the *resource room-pullout* is the most popular and common method.

☐ *Enrichment classroom.* The classroom teacher conducts a differentiated program of study without the help of outside personnel.

☐ *Consultant teacher.* A program of differentiated instruction is conducted in the regular classroom with the assistance of a specially trained consultant.

☐ *Resource room-pullout.* Gifted students leave the classroom for a short period of time to receive instruction from a specially trained teacher.

☐ *Community mentor.* Gifted students interact with an adult from the community who has special knowledge in the area of interest.

☐ *Independent study.* Students select projects and work on them under the supervision of a qualified teacher.

☐ *Special class.* Gifted students are grouped together during most of the class time and are instructed by a specially trained teacher.

☐ *Special schools.* Gifted students receive differentiated instruction at a special school with a specially trained staff.[6]

In the regular classroom, a teacher can encourage children to pursue special interests, as a means of extending and enriching classroom learning. She can use parents and resource people to tutor and work in special ways with the gifted and talented children, and provide opportunities for the children to assume leadership responsibilities. They may be interested in tutoring other students who need extra practice or help. Tutoring can cut across grade and age levels. Students can also help explain directions and procedures to the class. The teacher can encourage them to use their talents and abilities outside the classroom by becoming involved with other people and agencies, and encourage creativity through classroom activities that require divergent thinking (for example, "Let's think of all the different uses for a paper clip"). The teacher must challenge children to think through the use of higher-order questions that encourage them to explain, apply, analyze, rearrange, and judge.

CHILDREN WITH MULTICULTURAL HERITAGES

Backgrounds and languages reflect society's cultural pluralism. Children are influenced in many ways by the cultures in which they are reared. They learn distinctive ways of communicating, both verbal and nonverbal; develop a preference for certain foods; dress in certain kinds of clothing; develop ways of interacting with others, and subscribe to a particular value system. Children need to learn about each other's cultural differences.

As an early childhood educator you will want to promote multicultural awareness in your classroom. In its simplest form, *multicultural awareness* is the appreciation and understanding of other people and their cultures, as well as one's own culture. The terms and concepts for describing multicultural awareness are not as important as the methods, procedures, and activities for developing a meaningful program. Educators and the public often assume they are promoting multicultural awareness when they are actually presenting only a fragment of the concept. Multicultural awareness in the classroom is not the presentation of other cultures to the exclusion of the cultures represented by children in the class. Rather, a multicultural awareness program should focus on other cultures while at the same time making children aware of the content, nature, and richness of their own. Learning about other cultures concurrently with their own enables children to integrate commonalities and appreciate differences without inferring inferiority or superiority of one or the other.

Ideas and Activities for Multicultural Awareness in Early Childhood Programs

- ☐ One's own culture—children study their own cultural background, and are able to understand others' cultures as they come to know more about their own.
- ☐ People puzzles—paste pictures of children and adults of different cultures from magazines and old books on cardboard and cut them up to make puzzles
- ☐ Puppets—have students make puppets in ethnic dress and put on class plays
- ☐ Stamp and postcard collections—have students compile stamps and postcards of different nations and display them in the classroom after discussions
- ☐ Family trees—begin with students' own family trees; also, make a "family tree" of the class members
- ☐ Artifact collection—have students collect items of interest that depict different cultures, including the American; discuss the items, and analyze and compare to each other
- ☐ Easy food recipes—supervise the students in making foods from different cultures
- ☐ Arts and crafts—make jewelry, mosaics, or headdresses of other lands

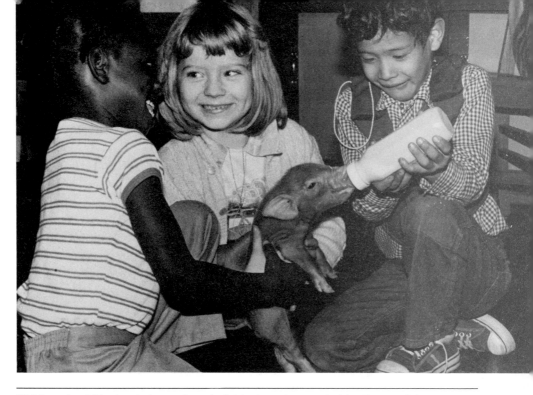

Children should be treated as unique individuals and respected for the special contributions they can make to the classroom. Early childhood teachers should be familiar with the backgrounds of all children they teach.

☐ Songs and dances—have students learn easy songs and dances of other cultures
☐ Clothing—collect old pieces of fabric that students can make into ethnic clothing; they can paint, color, or embroider old sheets
☐ Maps—make a large, simplified world map and pin students' names to show where they or their families originated; colored strings from the various places may all lead to your city
☐ Class mural—toward the end of the year, have all students contribute their drawings and interpretations of the cultures they study throughout the year; display the mural in the classroom or hallway
☐ Special events—celebrate a special holiday or event as it is done in a particular culture; a UNICEF calendar is a good source of ideas
☐ Human resources—invite a member of the community to present and discuss a particular aspect of his or her native culture
☐ Games—have students learn games children play in another part of the world
☐ Parents—parents can come to the school or center to share customs, crafts, and foods
☐ Field trips—children can visit other schools or centers and take field trips to ethnic neighborhoods or stores

- ☐ Multicultural learning center—a learning center can be devoted to books, magazines, media, and cultural objects
- ☐ Role playing—role playing can help students get a feel for another culture
- ☐ National, state, and local resources—many agencies offer materials and assistance in multicultural instruction; an excellent source is the U.S. Committee for UNICEF, United Nations Children's Fund, 331 East 38th Street, New York, NY 10016

The Role of the Teacher in Multicultural Education

The teacher is the key to a multicultural classroom. These guidelines can help teachers become more effective in teaching multiculturalism:

- ☐ Treat the children in your class as unique individuals, each with something special to contribute
- ☐ Promote uniqueness as a positive attribute; use the word "unique" often
- ☐ Become familiar with the cultural backgrounds of the children you teach; ask their parents about special family customs and holidays, and if possible, visit their neighborhoods
- ☐ Use the above information in your lesson planning; through the language arts, music, art, and classroom cooking, you can include a number of different cultural customs in your curriculum, calling special attention to the class members who celebrate these events in their homes
- ☐ Share your own heritage with your class; tell them old family stories, and show them old photographs
- ☐ Be aware of what you say and what you do regarding other cultures and cultural groups
- ☐ Exhibit accepting and respectful behavior toward visitors and volunteers in your classroom
- ☐ Familiarize yourself with the ethnic resources in your center/school and community; another teacher may have a child whose parent would be willing to share his cultural heritage with your class as well
- ☐ Attend multicultural events in your community—international festivals, ethnic fairs, or holiday parties related to one cultural group, such as Oktoberfest[7]

INVOLVING SPECIAL NEEDS FAMILIES

Many of the procedures for involving parents can also be used with parents of children with special needs; however, teachers must consider the entire context of family life. The family's total needs must be met, and educational, social, and medical problems addressed. It is important to work cooperatively with community agencies that can assist in delivery of these services. Parents of children with special needs frequently lack the support systems necessary for dealing with their and their children's needs. It is up to educators to be supportive, to help create support systems, and provide linkage to support systems.

Parents Need Help

Parents of special needs children need help, not sympathy, and help is often best when it is *self-help.* One barrier to self-help is the feeling of the handicapped child's parent toward his child, himself, and society. Hopelessness and helplessness may prevail. Parents may feel guilty, fearing they did something to cause the handicap. They need support to escape from and deal realistically with their feelings of guilt. Sometimes parents feel ashamed of their child and themselves and react to this feeling by withdrawing from society, consciously or unconsciously attempting to protect themselves and the child from attention. Parents need help to see that there is nothing "wrong" with their children and that they are unique and interesting.

Mainstreaming has helped not only handicapped children and their parents, but all parents and all children. By extending certain basic rights and processes to the handicapped, all special needs children will be assured of these rights. It will not be long before every child will have an IEP written for him.

FURTHER READING

Adams, Barbara. *Like It Is: Facts and Feelings About Handicaps from Kids You Know* (New York: Walker, 1979) Realistic and honest presentation by handicapped children and youth who tell about their various handicaps, special needs, and desire to be treated like everyone else. Chapters deal with hearing and speech impairment, visual impairment, orthopedic handicaps, developmental disabilities/mental retardation, learning disabilities, and behavior disorders. Excellent first-person vignettes.

Allen, K. E. *Mainstreaming in Early Childhood Education* (Albany, N.Y.: Delmar, 1980) Describes and outlines different methods for integrating handicapped children into preschool programs; provides current ideas on six major areas of special education and early childhood education needs; covers the importance of the home-school relationship.

Buscaglia, Leo. *The Disabled and Their Parents: A Counseling Challenge* (New York: Holt, Rinehart, and Winston, 1983) Buscaglia believes the disabled and their families need reality-based guidance, and challenges professionals to provide better information on the nature and implications of each disability and the complex problems of day-to-day living.

Brown, Tricia, and Fran Ortiz. *Someone Special Just Like You* (New York: Holt, Rinehart, and Winston, 1984) Picture book with supporting text shows special needs children engaged in activities that all children like to do. Helps children, teachers, and parents understand that handicaps need not separate children from the experiences that are vital to growing and a happy life. Underlying theme is normalcy—being accepted and having opportunities to participate in all of life's enriching activities.

De Ruiter, James A., and W. L. Wansart. *Psychology of Learning Disabilities: Applications and Educational Practices* (Rockville, Md.: Aspen, 1982) Thorough research and interpretation based on teachers' observations, feedback, and different teaching approaches for children with learning disabilities. Structural models explain assessment and teaching practices.

Escobedo, Theresa H., ed. *Early Childhood Bilingual Education: A Hispanic Perspective* (New York: Teachers College Press, 1983) Collection of articles focusing on bilingual education, with emphasis on early childhood education. Discusses patterns of language acquisition, skill development, etc.

Fantine, Mario D., and Rene Cardenas. *Parenting in a Multicultural Society* (New York: Longman, 1980) Focuses on nonprofessional status of motherhood and our nation's lack of support for families. Contributors describe the mythical American family and how the system needs to change to link societal and family ties in a multicultural society.

Featherstone, Helen. *A Difference in the Family: Life With a Disabled Child* (New York: Basic Books, 1980) Written by the parent of a seriously disabled child, this book deals with problems and pleasures of rearing the handicapped.

Haring, Norris, G., ed. *Exceptional Children and Youth* (Columbus, Ohio: Merrill, 1982) Detailed guide to educating children with special needs; pictures augment important points. Includes profiles of special needs children.

Kendall, Frances E. *Diversity in the Classroom* (New York: Teachers College Press, 1983) Outlines resources and multicultural approaches to teaching and learning; also gives ideas for setting up a multicultural classroom environment.

Lewis, Rena B., and Donald H. Doorlag. *Teaching Special Students in the Mainstream* (Columbus, Ohio: Merrill, 1983) Clear and informative account of providing for children with special needs; tips and practical advice.

McGuinness, Diane. *When Children Don't Learn: Understanding the Biology and Psychology of Learning Disabilities* (New York: Basic Books, 1985) Challenges educators to examine how individual children learn and to develop programs, not labels, to help them reach their potential; also prompts reexamination of traditional assumptions about sex differences in learning and their implications for classroom learning.

McNeill, Earldene, Velma Schmidt, and Judy Allen. *Cultural Awareness for Young Children* (Dallas, Texas: Learning Tree Press, 1981) Product of the Learning Tree School and its efforts to help children develop awareness of six American cultures: Asian, Black, Cowboy, Eskimo, Mexican, and Native-American. Presents many activities touching lifestyles, foods, and customs.

Mitchell, Joyce Slayton. *Taking on the World: Empowering Strategies for Parents of Children with Disabilities* (New York: Harcourt Brace Jovanovich, 1982) Action-filled manual with step-by-step directions and practical advice on advocating for children with disabilities. Part One deals with how to take on family, medicine, school, church, work, and bureaucracy; part Two deals with empowering strategies and advises how to stabilize, mobilize, and activate.

National Center for Clinical Infant Programs. *Equals in This Partnership: Parents of Disabled and At-Risk Infants and Toddlers Speak to Professionals* (Washington, D.C.: National Center for Clinical Infant Programs, 1984) In 1984, a conference on "Comprehensive Approaches to Disabled and At-Risk Infants and Toddlers" was held in Washington, D.C. This booklet contains proceedings of that conference. Premise is that parents and families, not professionals and consultants, have to be in charge of education and care of their handicapped children.

Osman, Betty B., and Henriette Blinder. *No One to Play With: The Social Side of Learning Disabilities* (New York: Random House, 1982) Focuses on learning disabilities as a major educational concern and a source of social problems in daily life; authors call this "living disabilities," and provide techniques to help children become more successful socially and academically.

Pasanella, Anne Langstaff, and Cara B. Volkmar. *Coming Back or Never Leaving—Instructional Programming for Handicapped Students in the Mainstream* (Columbus, Ohio: Merrill, 1981) Deals with assessing the handicapped student in the classroom by careful observation of normal classroom routines; includes samples of evaluations and assessment along with various games to test motor coordination, language, and speech.

Pelton, Leroy, H., ed. *The Social Context of Child Abuse and Neglect* (New York: Human Sciences Press, 1985) Pelton believes child abuse has been overly "psychologized," meaning that in their orientation to abuse, too many professionals adopt the medical model of "disease, treatment, and cure." Instead, Pelton says caregivers must examine social and economic reasons for abuse and the need for social services to address the situational context of abuse. Focuses on the role of poverty in abuse.

Peterson, Nancy L. *Early Intervention for Handicapped and At-Risk Children: An Introduction to Early Childhood-Special Education* (Denver, Col.: Love, 1987) Comprehensive and readable introduction to the field; good descriptions of children with special needs and programs for providing services.

Piazza, Robert, and Rosaline Rothman. *Pre-School Education for the Handicapped* (Guilford, Conn.: Special Learning Corp. 1982) Touches upon most crucial aspects of early identification of handicaps; considers value of having parents, educational programs, and teachers work together toward the same goals.

Ramsey, Patricia G. *Children's Understanding of Diversity: Multicultural Perspectives in Early Childhood Education* (New York: Teachers College Press, 1986) How early childhood education can help minimize prejudice; provides actual classroom practice experiences.

Roedell, Wendy C., Nancy E. Jackson, and Holbert B. Robinson. *Gifted Young Children* (New York: Teachers College Press, 1980) Describes physical, social, emotional, and intellectual attributes of the gifted; detailed examination of standardized and informal methods of assessing young children's abilities. Many practical ideas for teaching the gifted.

Ross, Robert T., et al. *Lives of the Mentally Retarded: A Forty-Year Follow-up Study* (Stanford, Calif.: Stanford University Press, 1985) Reports findings of a study to determine status of San Francisco school children forty years after they were identified as "educable mentally retarded." One surprising conclusion of the study was that: "Most of the subjects are little different from persons of "normal" intelligence who share their social class status. Their work histories were acceptable, marital relationships fairly stable, child rearing practices appropriate. . . . They appeared to be productive, law-abiding citizens of the community." Authors conclude that "except in their school years and except for their place in the school system, they had no identity as retarded persons."

Townley, Roderick. *Safe and Sound: A Parent's Guide to Child Protection* (New York: Simon and Schuster, 1985) For parents with children of all ages; useful information on physical abuse, choosing a day care center, and what to do if your child disappears; also a section on topics such as punishment versus rehabilitation for offenders.

Webb, James T., Elizabeth A. Meckstroth, and Stephanie S. Tolan. *Guiding The Gifted Child: A Practical Source for Parents and Teachers* (Columbus, Ohio: Ohio Psychology Publishing Company, 1982) Authors believe helping parents help their gifted children is critical, especially where schools or other programs don't provide services for gifted children. Sections on resources for developing skills in guiding gifted children and organizations that work with parents.

FURTHER STUDY

1. Visit parents of a handicapped child. What problems do the parents have to deal with? Are they dealing with them adequately? What suggestions would you make for helping these parents with their problems?
2. Visit several public schools to see how they are providing individualized and appropriate programs for handicapped children. What efforts are being made to involve parents?

3. By visiting agencies, interviewing parents, and reading, determine the number of specific ways in which a handicapped condition can occur.
4. Interview parents of handicapped children. What do they feel are parents' greatest problems? What do they consider the greatest needs for their children? List specific ways they have been involved in educational agencies. How have educational agencies avoided or resisted providing for their or their children's needs?
5. What are some assets that many handicapped children possess?
6. Visit and spend some time in a mainstreamed classroom. What specific skills would you need to become a good teacher in such a setting?
7. Visit a resource room. How is this setting different from a regular classroom? Would you want to teach in a resource room? Why or why not?
8. List the pros and cons of a resource room.
9. Would you want to be a teacher of handicapped children in a setting other than a regular classroom? Why or why not?
10. Visit agencies and programs that provide services for the handicapped. Before you visit, list specific features, services, and facilities you will look for.
11. Visit a multicultural program. Compare and contrast this to other special programs. What changes would you make, if any? Why or why not?
12. Compare and contrast a gifted program to a regular classroom setting.
13. What programs does the federal government support for children with special needs in your area? Give specific information.
14. Identify the special needs of children in a mainstreamed classroom. What would you do to improve the program?
15. Visit with handicapped adults. From their school experiences, what do they suggest for improving classrooms, teaching, and attitudes toward the handicapped?
16. Discuss with people of another culture their culture's attitudes toward the handicapped. How are they similar or different from your attitudes?
17. John was convinced his 2-year-old son was gifted. His wife, Yvonne, disagreed; she said their son was not independent enough. John insisted that the boy's advanced language development was the mark of a bright child. What suggestions would you make to help these parents settle their disagreement about their son's giftedness? Why might some parents think their children are gifted while other parents might not?
18. Use Mary Wilson's match-up matrix with a handicapped child and the primary classroom he or she will attend. Report your findings to your classmates.
19. List the pros and cons of the transdisciplinary approach to meeting the needs of handicapped children.
20. Volunteer to teach a gifted child for six weeks. What special experiences did you provide? What did you learn? Would you want to teach the gifted? Why or why not?

12

Guiding Behavior at Home and School: Helping Children Become Responsible

As you read and study:

Determine the effectiveness of positive reinforcement in building desired behaviors

Discuss issues related to behavioral guidance of young children

Identify acceptable and inappropriate classroom and home behaviors

Consider different reinforcement systems for managing behavior

Compare reinforcers that children find motivating to those that adults believe are motivating to children

Analyze contingency management systems in parent-child relationships and teacher-child relationships

Compare teachers' reactions to appropriate and inappropriate classroom behavior

Evaluate the classroom as a behavior reinforcer

Develop a philosophy of guiding children's behavior

Compare and contrast different theories of guiding children's behavior

Identify the essential characteristics of effective behavior guidance

M anaging children's behavior at home and in the classroom has always been a concern of educators and parents. Now there is even greater emphasis on behavior management. Parents tend to interpret children's misbehavior as a sign that educators have gone "soft" on discipline and are demanding that schools and teachers return to a more fundamental system where control and authority prevail. Modern society is in a great deal of turmoil. There is national concern about the breakup of the American family, widespread drug use, rampant crime, and general disrespect for authority, all of which are seen as evidence that there has been a parental and societal erosion of authority and discipline beginning in the earliest years. In fact, many believe that current social ills are caused by parents' failure to discipline their children. These people believe a primary way to instill renewed respect for traditional values is to return to strict discipline, including physical punishment.

Another reason for the interest in behavior management techniques has to do with the emphasis on mastery learning in the skill areas of reading, writing, and arithmetic. Teachers realize that for children to learn the basic skills, they have to be motivated to learn and to spend time on learning activities rather than on misbehavior. Children and teachers need to use their teaching-learning time and energies on achievement-oriented goals. When children misbehave, they are not learning and teachers are not teaching.

BEHAVIOR

Behavior is an individual's actions. When we talk about behavior management and guidance, we are generally referring to behavior we can observe. We are concerned with what we see a child doing—not completing work, walking aimlessly around the room, or going for a drink of water—as opposed to what the child is thinking. The same is true for behavior at home. Parents should focus on the behaviors they can see, not what they think is going on in their children's minds. Focusing on overt behavior does not mean teachers and parents should ignore children's hopes, dreams, fears, and worries. They need to attend to the emotions, but it is external behaviors to which they usually respond and can therefore focus on.

DISCIPLINE

Discipline generally refers to correcting and directing children toward acceptable behavior. Other concepts of discipline have to do with getting children to obey, do what they are told to do, and "listen" to whomever is giving instructions. Results from a Gallup Poll indicate that when the public uses the word *discipline,* it means: "obeying rules/regulations, authority/control by teachers and respect for teacher."[1] This is a somewhat negative view of discipline that focuses on *control* rather than on helping children build positive behaviors.

Another view is that discipline should help children become self-guided and regulating, so they can control their behavior and become independent. In this view, discipline is a process of *guiding* behavior. Teachers' and parents' roles are to guide children toward developing self-control, encouraging them to be independent, meeting their intellectual and emotional needs, establishing expectations for them, organizing appropriate behaviors, arranging environments so self-discipline can occur, and, when necessary, changing their own behavior. Thus, effective guidance at home and school comes down to these points:

1. Helping children build new behaviors and skills of independence and responsibility
2. Meeting children's needs
3. Establishing appropriate expectations
4. Arranging and modifying the environment so that appropriate, expected behavior and self-control is possible
5. Modifying our own behavior and expectations where and when appropriate
6. Not creating or encouraging behavior problems

The goal of most parents and teachers is to have children behave in socially acceptable and appropriate ways. Since this goal is never really fully achieved, we should view guidance as a process of learning by doing. A child cannot learn to discipline himself by being told to sit still and behave. Just as no one learns to ride a bicycle by reading a book on the subject, children do not learn to discipline themselves by being told. Maria Montessori often remarked that "Discipline is not telling." Children must be shown and taught through precept and example. Children need encouragement and opportunities to practice self-discipline.

HELPING BUILD NEW BEHAVIORS

Helping children build new behaviors creates a sense of responsibility. As children are given responsibility, they develop greater self-discipline, so that teachers and parents have to provide less guidance and children are less of a "discipline problem." Ironically, many teachers and parents hesitate to let children assume responsibilities, and without responsibilities, children are bored, frustrated, and become discipline problems—the very opposite of what is intended. Discipline is not a matter of getting children to please the teacher with remarks such as: "Show me how perfect you can be," "Don't embarrass me by your behavior in front of other teachers," "I want to see nice groups," or "I'm waiting for quiet." The child's job is to learn how to behave so as to be able to learn.

Meeting Children's Needs

Abraham Maslow (1890–1970) felt that human growth and development was oriented toward *self-actualization,* the striving to realize one's potential. He felt that humans are internally motivated by five basic needs that constitute a hierarchy of motivating behaviors progressing from physical needs to self-fulfillment. Maslow's hierarchy

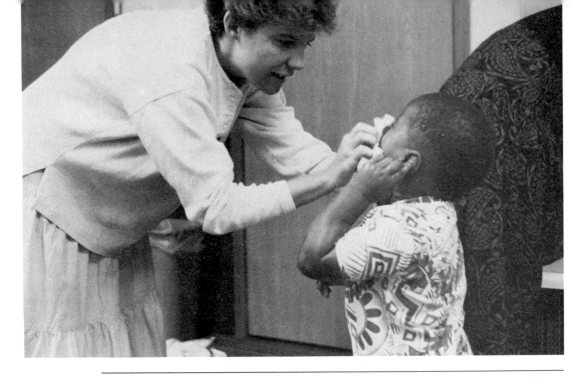

Children have a basic need for love and affection, and are more capable of responsible behavior when this need is met.

moves through physical needs, safety and security needs, belonging and affection needs, and self-esteem needs, culminating in self-actualization.

1. *Physical needs*—children do best in school when they eat a good breakfast. Parents should give them one, and teachers should stress the nutritional and health benefits of eating breakfast. The quality of the environment is also important. If classrooms are dark, smell of stale air, and are noisy, children cannot be expected to "behave." Children also need adequate rest to do their best. The amount of rest is an individual matter, but many young children need eight to ten hours of sleep. A tired child cannot meet many of the expectations of schooling.

2. *Safety and security*—children should not have to fear their teacher or principal and should feel comfortable and secure at home. Asking or forcing children to do school tasks for which they don't have the skills makes them feel insecure, and when children are afraid and insecure, they are under a great deal of tension.

3. *Belonging and affection*—children need love and affection and the sense of belonging that comes from being given jobs to do, from being given responsibilities, and from helping to make classroom and home decisions.

4. *Self-esteem*—when a child views himself as worthy, responsible, and competent, he will act that way. Children's views of themselves come from parents and teachers. Experiencing success gives them feelings of high self-esteem, and it is up to parents and teachers to give all children opportunities for success.

5. *Self-actualization*—children want to use their talents and abilities to do things for themselves and to be independent. Teachers and parents can help children become independent by helping them learn to dress themselves, go to the restroom by themselves, and take care of their environments. They can also help children set achievement and behavior goals ("tell me what you are going to build with your blocks") and encourage them to evaluate their behavior ("let's talk about how you cleaned up your room").

Establishing Appropriate Expectations

Teachers and parents need to know their expectations for children; and when children know what the expectations are, they can achieve them. Up to a point, the more we expect of children, the more and better they achieve. We really expect too little of most children.

Arranging the Environment

Environment plays a key role in children's behavior. For example, if parents want a child to be responsible for taking care of his room, they should arrange the environment so he can do so. Similarly, a teacher should arrange the classroom so children can get and return their own papers and materials, use learning centers, and have time to work on individual projects.

Modifying Adult Behavior and Expectations

Changing adult behavior is often one of the easiest ways to change children's behaviors. When expectations are beyond children's abilities to achieve, chances are that misbehavior will result. If teachers show children how to do a task, then have the children practice the skill under their supervision, there is a greater possibility that they will learn the skill. The teacher may have to change her behavior from telling to showing and demonstrating.

Avoiding Problems

Parents and teachers actually encourage a great deal of children's misbehavior. Teachers see too much and ignore too little. Parents expect perfection and adult behavior. If parents and teachers focus on building responsible behavior, there will be less need to solve discipline problems.

PRINCIPLES OF BEHAVIOR MODIFICATION

Another approach to guidance based on behavior rather than on feelings is *behavior modification.* An important concept of behavior modification is that all behavior is caused. Everyone acts the way they do for reasons, although the reasons may not always be apparent; in fact, the individual does not always know why he behaves a certain way. How often have you heard the expressions, "He didn't know what he was doing," "I don't know why he acts like he does," "I can't understand why I did that," and "I didn't know what I was doing"?

A second basic concept is that behavior results from reinforcement received from the environment. When we speak of reinforcements, we immediately think of psychologist Ivan P. Pavlov (1849–1936). Pavlov was concerned with the conditioned response. He worked with dogs in conditioning a reflex (salivation) with a new stimulus (a ringing bell). Pavlov conditioned the dog's salivary response by providing meat simultaneously with the ringing of a bell. After several occurrences in which the dog was presented with both meat and a ringing bell, Pavlov could merely ring a bell to make the dog salivate. Pavlov's procedure is called *classical conditioning.* The food is an *unconditioned stimulus* or primary reinforcer because it would normally stimulate salivation; the salivation is the *unconditioned response* because the dog does not have to learn (be conditioned) to do it. After several pairings of food and bell, presenting the bell alone causes the dog to salivate. The bell is then known as the *conditioned stimulus,* and the salivation becomes a *conditioned* (learned) response.

American psychologist Edward L. Thorndike (1874–1949) observed that the consequences of one's behavior influence the course of future behavior. The stimulus-response associations depend on response outcomes. He formalized this observation in his learning principle, the *law of effect.* If a satisfying condition follows a behavior, the individual tends to repeat that behavior, and the strength of the stimulus-response connection increases. If an unsatisfying condition follows a behavior, the individual tends not to repeat that behavior, and the stimulus-response connection weakens or disappears. The law of effect points out how important the quality of feedback is for behavior. This law has gradually come to be known as the Imperial Law of Effect, which says that the consequences of particular responses determine whether the response will be continued and therefore learned. In other words, what happens to an individual after he acts in a particular way determines whether he continues to act that way. If a child cries and is immediately given a cookie, he will probably learn to cry to receive cookies. Receiving cookies reinforces crying behavior. We should understand that this behavior is not always planned. A child does not necessarily say to himself, "I'm going to cry because I know my mother will give me a cookie." The child may have cried, and his mother, to stop the crying, gave the child a cookie. The child then came to associate the two events.

Figure 12–1 shows how a young child might be conditioned to have a fear of dogs (or anything else, for that matter). The child and mother are walking through the park. The mother, who has a fear of large dogs, screams when she sees a large dog. The scream frightens the child. Although the child may or may not have seen the dog the first time, on subsequent walks through the park, he associates his mothers screams with the dog, until after a number of occurrences, he, too, is afraid of dogs.

B. F. Skinner (1904–) is given credit for many of the technological and pedagogical applications of behavior modification, including programmed instruction. Skinner also emphasizes the role of the environment in providing people with clues that reinforce their behavior.

In behavior management, we are concerned with behavior modification, or changing behavior. As used in this chapter, behavior modification means the *con-*

Mother
(unconditioned stimulus)

Child
(unconditioned response)

1st occurrence — scream — cry

2nd occurrence — scream — cry

3rd occurrence — scream — cry

Conditioned stimulus

Conditioned response

4th occurrence — cry

FIGURE 12–1   Fear Conditioning

scious application of the methods of behavioral science, with the intent of altering child behavior. Teachers and parents have always been concerned with changing children's behavior, but it is implicit in the term *behavior modification* that we mean the conscious use of techniques to change behavior. Behaviorists maintain that all behavior is learned and, in this sense, that all behavior is caused by reinforcers from which individuals gain pleasure of some kind. The problem however, is that teachers and parents have usually changed children's behavior without realizing it. Teachers and parents should be more aware of the effect they have on children's behavior. To use power ignorantly and unconsciously to achieve ends that are basically dehumanizing to children is not good teaching practice. When you become aware of the power you have over the lives of children, try to use that power so children will benefit from it. For example, when a child first comes to school, he may not understand that sitting quietly is a desirable behavior that many schools and teachers have established as a goal. Therefore, the teacher scolds the child until he not only sits quietly, but sits quietly and bites his nails. The teacher did not intentionally set out to reinforce nail biting, but this is the child's terminal behavior, and the teacher is unaware of how it happened.

Reinforced Misbehavior

We must recognize that teacher and parent behavior, attitude, predisposition, and inclination actually cause a great deal of child misbehavior. Many children misbehave because their misbehavior is reinforced. For example, children enjoy receiving attention. Therefore, when a child receives any kind of attention, it reinforces the behavior the child exhibited to get that attention. A child who is noisy receives teacher attention by being scolded. The chances of his exhibiting the same behavior (talking to the child beside him) to elicit attention from the teacher is greatly increased because he has been reinforced.

We sometimes encourage children to do sloppy work or hurry through an activity when we emphasize finishing it. We may give the child a worksheet with six squares to color and cut out, and say, "After you color all the squares, I will give you a pair of scissors so you can cut the squares out." The child may hurry through the coloring to get to the cutting. We would do better to concentrate on coloring first, then cutting.

Positive Reinforcement

When we talk about positive reinforcement, we are talking about providing *rewards* or *reinforcers* that will promote behaviors teachers and parents decide are desirable. *Positive reinforcement* is maintaining or increasing the frequency of a behavior following a particular stimulus. What the child receives, whether candy, money, or a hug, is the *reinforcer,* the *reinforcement,* or the *reward.* Generally, a positive reinforcer is any stimulus that maintains or increases a particular behavior. These are verbal reinforcers: "Good," "Right," "Correct," "Wonderful," "Very good," "I like that," "Good boy/girl," "Hey! That's great!" and "I knew you could do it." Teachers can also use nonverbal behavior to reinforce children's behavior and learning; for example, a nod, smile, hug, pat on the head or shoulder, standing close to someone, eye contact, paying attention, or even a wink show a child that you approve of his behavior or are proud of what he is doing. The classroom can be set up to provide a positively reinforcing environment. If it is organized to help make desired behaviors possible, provides opportunities for novelty, gives children opportunities for control over their environment, and reflects children's desires, interests, and ideas, they will tend to try to live up to the expectations the setting suggests.

Understanding Behavior

Another extremely important concept of behavior modification focuses on external behavior rather than on the causes of behavior; that is, teachers and parents should generally not be concerned with *why* a child acts as he does. This idea usually takes some getting used to, because it is almost the opposite of what we have been taught. Teachers particularly feel it is beneficial to know why a child acts the way he does, and spend a great deal of time and effort trying to determine motivations. If Johnny is fidgety and inclined to daydream, the teacher may spend six weeks investigating the causes. He learns that Johnny's mother has been divorced three times and ignores Johnny at home. On the basis of this information, he concludes that Johnny needs help, but is no closer to solving Johnny's problem than he was six weeks previously. A teacher's time and energy should be spent developing strategies to help children with their behavior. Sometimes underlying causes help us deal with the behavior we wish to modify, but we need to recognize that the behavior a child exhibits is the problem, and it is behavior that we need to attend to.

Very young children can begin to learn responsibility by picking up and putting away their toys, but parents and caregivers must arrange the environment to promote that kind of responsibility.

Punishment

Is it possible to guide behavior without punishment? Most parents and teachers have punished children at one time or another; sometimes it seems necessary for the children's safety. In general, however, punishment does not guide children toward building new behavior. If punishment is necessary, make sure you explain why, and offer guidance for good behavior. Punishment also tends to build negative feelings in both individuals. If one must punish, the incident should be immediately put behind one—forgive and forget.

Teachers and parents sometimes seem to think a child behaves a certain way because he is innately bad. They also sometimes feel children do the things they do to disturb adults. Both attitudes show a lack of understanding of child development. Children are not born with a tendency to do bad things, nor do they spend their time plotting against teachers and parents. The responsibility for changing and directing behavior rests with adults.

Ignoring Behavior

Ignoring inappropriate behavior is probably one of the most overlooked strategies for managing an effective learning setting. Ironically, many teachers feel guilty when they use this strategy. They believe that ignoring undesirable behaviors is not good teaching. Although ignoring off-task behavior may be an effective strategy, ignoring behavior must be combined with positive reinforcement of desirable behavior. Thus, one ignores inappropriate behavior and at the same time reinforces appropriate behavior. A combination of positive reinforcement and ignoring can lead to *extinction* of the undesired behavior.

Providing Guidance

A child is generally not capable of acting or thinking his way out of undesirable behavior. Parents and teachers may say, "You know how to act," when indeed the child

Helping children and warmly supporting their efforts is the most effective and humane kind of guidance.

does not know. Teachers also often say, "He could do better if he wanted to." The problem, however, is that the child may not know what he wants to do, or may not know what's appropriate. In other words, he needs an organized procedure for how to act. Thinking does not build new behavior; acting does. Building new behavior, then, is a process of getting children to act in new ways.

A common approach to behavior control is "talking to" and reasoning. Reasoning doesn't generally have the desired effect. The child is likely to behave the same way, or worse. This often leads to a punishment trap, in which the teacher or parent resorts to yelling, screaming, or paddling, to get the desired results. The behavior we want children to demonstrate must be within their ability. A child cannot pay attention to and be interested in materials he cannot read.

REINFORCING BEHAVIOR

Appropriate Reinforcers

A reinforcer is only as effective as the child's desire for it. In other words, if the reinforcer has the power to reinforce the behavior that precedes it, then it will work. A method used to determine the nature of a reinforcer is the *Premack Principle.* David Premack determined that behaviors with a high probability of occurrence can be used to reinforce behaviors with a low probability of occurrence. Activities that children participate in when they have free time are what they like to do best, and teachers can use these activities to reinforce terminal behaviors.

In many early childhood classrooms, using the chalkboard or easels is a highly desirable activity. Therefore, time to use the chalkboard or the art easels can be used in reinforcing desired behavior. Rewards that children help select are most likely to have the desired effect. Privileges children often choose are getting the teacher's mail, watering plants, washing chalkboards, running errands, going outside, bringing books from home to read, playing games with friends, leading games, extra recess, passing out papers and supplies, using audiovisual equipment, watching TV, doing flash cards, and cutting and pasting. Table 12–1 shows typical reinforcers in an early childhood setting.

Praise as a Reinforcer

Praise is probably the most frequent method of rewarding or reinforcing children's behavior. Praise is either general or specific. Specific praise is more effective because it describes the behavior we want to build. The child has no doubt that he is being praised and what he is being praised for. For example, if a child picks up her blocks and you say "good, Laura," she may or may not know what you are referring to, but if you say "Laura, you did a nice job of putting your blocks away," Laura knows exactly what you are talking about.

Parents and teachers should approach children positively. A positive approach builds self-esteem. We help build positive self-images and expectations for good be-

TABLE 12–1 Reinforcers Used in Early Childhood Settings

Primary Reinforcers	Conditioned Reinforcers		
Reinforce behavior without the respondent's having much previous experience with the item	Reinforce as a result of experiences the respondent has had with the reinforcer		

Food

M & M's	Sugar-coated cereal
Cookies	Raisins
Juice	Popcorn
Peanuts	Gum
Celery	Cheese
Carrots	Fruit

Verbal—praise

I like the way you . . .

Great	Fine	A-Okay	Tremendous
Right on	Wow	Excellent	
Beautiful	Way to go	Fantastic	
Terrific	Super	Fine job	

Nonverbal

Facial	*Gestures*	*Proximity*
Smile	Clapping of hands	Standing near someone
Wink	Wave	
Raised eyebrow	Forming an A-Okay sign (thumb + index finger)	Shaking hands
Eye contact		Getting down on a child's level
	Victory sign	Hug, touching
	Nod head	Holding child's arm up
	Shrug shoulders	

Social (occur in or as a result of social consequences)

Parties

Group approval

Class privileges

havior by complimenting children and praising them for the things they do well. Every child has praiseworthy qualities.

Contingency Management

Teachers frequently find it helpful to engage in *contingency contracting* or *contingency management* to reinforce behavior. With this strategy, the child might be told, "If you put the materials away when you're done with them, you can use the chalkboard for five minutes." Sometimes contingency management is accompanied by a written contract between teacher and student, depending, of course, on the child's age and maturity.

When parents or teachers manage a contingency, they must be sure they have thought through its consequences. For example, if a parent says, "If you don't clean up your room, you have to stay there until you do," the child may choose not to clean up his room but to stay there and play with his toys. In this case, he doesn't have to do as he was told and is rewarded for not doing it.

Token System

Reinforcement works best when it occurs at the time of the behavior we want to reinforce. Also, the sooner reinforcement follows the desired behavior, the better it works. Particularly when building new skills or shaping new behaviors, it is important to reinforce the child immediately. To provide immediate reinforcement, some teachers use tokens, such as plastic discs, buttons, trading stamps, or beans, which the child later trades for an activity. If the children like to use the art easel, the teacher might allow a child to exchange ten tokens for time at the easel. When a child performs appropriate tasks and exhibits teacher-specified behavior, he receives a token.

While it is important in any setting to reinforce a child often, it is especially important in a token economy, because the child must be able to earn enough tokens to trade for an activity. Another strategy for a token economy is "time out." If a child exhibits disruptive behavior to the extent that it is impossible to ignore, the child is isolated in a booth or corner of the room. During this isolation period, the child is not able to earn tokens. The length of time out depends upon the behavior. The effect of this period is to associate the undesirable behavior with time during which the child cannot earn tokens. The consequence, of course, is that the child will not have the necessary tokens for desirable activities if he spends much time in "time out."

THE WAUKEGAN BEHAVIOR ANALYSIS FOLLOW THROUGH MODEL PROGRAM, WAUKEGAN, ILLINOIS

The Waukegan Resource Center is a nationally validated Follow Through Program in Behavior Analysis.[2] The Waukegan Follow Through Program has four basic goals:

1. Increased academic achievement and improvement in school and home environments for many children
2. Advances in development of comprehensive instructional approaches
3. Creation of alternatives for training and support of school faculty and staffs
4. Progress in involving parents in the educational and political process of schooling

These four goals are implemented through these major components:

Motivation—behavior analysis is designed to motivate students to learn through two systems, a token exchange system in grades K–1 and a contracting system in grades 2–3.

Curriculum—emphasis is on teaching the basic skills of reading, math, spelling, and handwriting.

Team teaching—all behavior classrooms are staffed by a lead teacher and a paraprofessional.

Continuous program measures—every month, students' progress is analyzed and progress prescriptions written. This analysis is conducted in cooperation with the University of Kansas. Standardized tests are also used to assess student achievement.

The Waukegan program not only demonstrates the behavior analysis model, but also provides technical assistance to school districts and programs that want to implement the model. So far, program adaptations have been introduced in St. Francis, Wisconsin; Midland, Texas; Milwaukee, Wisconsin; Sanford, Maine; Berwyn, Illinois; Marlin, Texas; Calumet Park, Illinois; Dallas, Texas (Wilmer-Hutchins I.S.D.); Zion, Illinois (Y.W.C.A. Key Kids); Cassopolis, Michigan; and Waukegan, Illinois (Lake County Head Start).

A behavior analysis classroom has elements of a number of educational strategies, including team teaching, individualized teaching, and a reinforcement system utilizing a token system in grades K–1 and contracting in grades 2–3. Instructional objectives are written for all children based on what they know and what they should learn.

The behavior analysis model rests on the assumption that many children are not naturally motivated to learn, but need to be taught. There are many things in a classroom and school day that children find rewarding, but these activities, such as recess, are not always immediately available to them. A reward is much more reinforcing when it immediately follows the desired or target behavior. The behavior analysis classroom uses a token exchange system to create and maintain a high level of motivation. Tokens are given immediately to every child for good behavior. The teacher and staff determine what they are going to reward the children for, and rewarded behaviors change constantly, depending on the child and the objectives of the learning program. For example, a child may be rewarded for making straight lines on his writing paper. Once he has learned to do this consistently, however, his learning objectives (target behavior) will change. In the same way, the things for which children exchange tokens change according to preferences and instructional needs.

Children who are engaged in on-task behavior are not interrupted, and continue to work until their tokens can be exchanged for enjoyable activities (called *backups*) of their choice. A token system motivates children, keeps them interested in their work, and teaches independence, since each child is free to earn the opportunity to engage in backup activities. A token can be any object, but it is best if it is something children can hold and put in their pockets. In the behavior analysis program, children wear aprons similar to a carpenter's apron with several large pockets in which they can put their tokens quickly and easily. The aprons have the children's names on them, so whoever is instructing them can always use first names when reinforcing.

Children are given or earn tokens only during an "earn" period. The behavior for which children receive tokens depends on the individual child and what each is being taught. Since children are working at many different levels, they are rewarded for many different behaviors; however, the procedure and rationale is the same for all: every child is reinforced, that is, given tokens. A token system won't work unless children have tokens to spend! All children should also have similar amounts of tokens to exchange. The implications for teachers are to have children involved in tasks they can accomplish, and to work individually with them so they can succeed. The period when children can earn tokens, the earn period, is generally when they are engaged in academic work; they are thus motivated to stay on task and work diligently to earn tokens.

Merely earning tokens does no good unless children have opportunities to exchange their tokens for items or activities that are attractive to them. How many tokens an activity is worth depends upon its value to children. If children prefer to have a story read to them rather than go out for recess, then the story time activity would cost more tokens. Children must exchange their tokens during each "spend" period; they cannot carry over tokens from one day to the next, otherwise, children could conceivably spend a day doing nothing but spending tokens on pleasurable activities.

Motivation is also kept high by varying the activities for which tokens can be exchanged, the length of the earn period, and the time when exchanges occur. In this way, children won't tire of the activities, and won't be tempted to earn a certain number of tokens and then stop working.

The purpose of a token system is to give children positive reinforcement for good behavior. Children enjoy the behavior analysis classroom because they can earn the opportunity to do things they find pleasurable. Also, since the emphasis is on achievement and positive reinforcement, the classroom is free from punishment, negative attitudes, and threats.

The second and third grade contract classrooms use a procedure called *contingency contracting.* Children select a particular activity they would like to participate in contingent on completing a certain amount of work. The amount of work a child contracts for and the length of time it takes to complete depends on the individual. Contracting provides incentives by giving children the opportunity to engage in pleasurable activities in exchange for a certain amount of work. It also involves children in planning and goal setting and helps them become more responsible for their work and behavior.

The Language of a Behavior Analysis Classroom

Earn—period of time children are working with academic materials (instruction in books)

Spend—time to use tokens to buy games and activities in the classroom

Token—a chip the teacher gives the child for good work or good behavior

Exchange—period when activities are announced, child counts tokens, and chooses an activity

Backup—activity or game offered during a spend time and at the end of a contracting period

Contract—a written agreement between teacher and student for pages to be done (used in second and third grade)

Red line—a mark to show completion of an assignment; time when teacher questions the child as to what he/she has done

Time out—three to five minutes when, because of poor behavior, a child cannot earn or spend tokens (kindergarten and first grade), or participate in contracting or backups (second and third grade)

The Classroom as a Reinforcer of Behavior

As mentioned earlier, behavior modification strategies can also be applied to the physical setting of the classroom. The classroom should be arranged so that it is conducive to the behaviors the teacher wants to reinforce. If a teacher wants to encourage independent work, there must be places and time for children to work alone. Disruptive behavior is often encouraged by classroom arrangements that force children to walk over other children to get to equipment and materials. A teacher may find that the classroom actually contributes to off-task behaviors. The atmosphere of the classroom or the learning environment must be such that new behaviors are possible.

Although teachers want to encourage independence, they often make the children ask for materials, which the teacher must then locate. This practice discourages independence. To promote independence, materials should be readily available. The same situation applies in the home. If a parent wants a child to keep his room neat and clean, it must be possible for the child to do so. The child should also be shown how to take care of his room. The parent may have to lower shelves or install clothes hooks. When the physical arrangement is to the child's size, the child can be taught how to use a clothes hanger and where to hang certain clothes. A child's room should have a place for everything; these places should be accessible and easy to use.

TEACHING BY PRECEPT AND EXAMPLE

We have all heard the maxim that "telling is not teaching." Nevertheless, we tend to teach by instructions and directions. The teacher of young children soon realizes, however, that actions speak louder than words. We encourage children to be discourteous by being discourteous to them. When we want them to move, we say, "Move!" instead of "Would you please move?" How will students learn what it means to be courteous if they are not shown courtesy?

The leading proponent of the modeling approach to learning is Albert Bandura, who believes that most behavior people exhibit is learned from the behavior of a model or models. A model may be someone whom we respect or find interesting and whom we believe is being rewarded for the behavior he exhibits. Bandura sees behavior modeling as similar to Skinner's concept of reinforcement. For example, chil-

Taking care of their environment teaches children responsibility and independence.

dren tend to model behavior that brings rewards from parent and teacher, and affection is a powerful reward.

Children see how other people act and store it in their memory system. The child then tries the act, and if this new action brings a reward of some kind, the child repeats it. Groups as well as individuals serve as models. A kindergartner sees a group of his peers rewarded for paying attention, so he does the same. Models children emulate don't necessarily have to be from real life; they can come from television and reading. In addition, the modeled behavior does not have to be socially acceptable. The teacher should use the following techniques to help children learn through modeling:

☐ *Showing.* The teacher shows children where the block corner is and how and where the blocks are stored.

☐ *Demonstration.* The teacher performs a task while students watch. For example, the teacher demonstrates the proper way to put the blocks away and how to store them. Extensions of the demonstration method are to have the children practice the demonstration while the teacher supervises and to have a child demonstrate to other children.

☐ *Modeling.* Modeling occurs when the teacher practices the behavior she expects of the children. Also, the teacher can call children's attention to the desired behavior when another child models it.

☐ *Supervision.* Supervision is a process of reviewing, insisting, maintaining standards, and follow up. If children are not performing the desired behavior, it will be necessary for you to *review* the behavior. You must be consistent in your expectations of desired behavior. Children will soon learn they don't have to put away their blocks if you allow them not to do it. Remember, you are responsible for the child's learning.

A CULTURAL BASIS FOR CLASSROOM MANAGEMENT

It is easy for teachers to believe that behavior and discipline are separate aspects of classroom management. This feeling goes along with the notion that children are children and will tend to misbehave. We must recognize, however, that it is almost impossible to separate the child and how he behaves from the cultural environment in which he is reared. Environment determines to a great extent the kind of behavior management the child expects and will respond to. Unless the teacher or caregiver is aware of these cultural conditions, she may not discipline the child appropriately, and the child will respond negatively to the discipline.

Some examples will help us understand this cultural reality. In a third grade classroom, a teacher asks Jorgé to sit in his seat and finish a writing project he began earlier in the day. His friend Roberto sneers at him and whispers, "Don't let the teacher walk on you." For fear of appearing subservient to the female teacher, Jorgé refuses to write, and taps his pencil on the desk as a further sign of his determination not to do what the teacher wants. Rather than force Jorgé to do his work, the teacher could assure him that he is not being "walked on"; discuss with the whole class the necessity for doing classwork and following directions; invite Jorgé's parents to talk with him and her about the situation; and manage her own behavior so that she is more sensitive to her students' culturally determined attitudes. It is always advisable for teachers to become aware of the cultural backgrounds of the children they are teaching. While it is true that awareness will come through teaching, some can also come through training programs conducted by colleges, universities, and other agencies.

In a second grade classroom, Ms. Anderson, a new teacher, has difficulty controlling the class. The class as a whole does not listen to her, although she uses many of the techniques taught in her college classes. She believes her colleagues are firmer with their students than she feels she should be. Finally, in frustration, she asks the teacher in the next classroom, "What am I going to do?" Her friend tells her that one reason for her difficulty is that the children come from families in which a "heavy hand" is the natural way of punishment, and the children are accustomed to feeling that an adult is not serious unless some form of physical punishment accompanies a command. The friend goes on to explain to Ms. Anderson that, while it is not necessary for her to paddle the children, it will be necessary, at least in the beginning, for her to be firmer in following up her directions. She cannot ask that something be done and expect it to be done until she is able to build a basis for this kind of behavior.

In a day care classroom, Ms. Smith is concerned about the three-year-old children's lack of independence. Many are still on bottles and cannot dress themselves, and some cannot use eating utensils. During a conference with the day care director, Ms. Smith learns that it is customary in the culture of the children's homes for parents to overprotect and extend the period of dependency. A mother is viewed as a good parent when she does many of the things for her child that other cultures expect the child to do for himself after he reaches three or four years of age. These parents value extended dependency.

In conferences with parents and staff, Ms. Smith will have to determine which areas are most important for the successful functioning of the children in the day care center and will have to teach those skills and behaviors. Although it is important that she understand the parents' attitudes, she must explain the necessity of certain independent behaviors in the center. She should also solicit the parents' help. She will concentrate her efforts in the beginning on helping the children dress themselves and learn how to feed themselves.

Guidance Tips for the Early Childhood Educator

Many of these ideas for guiding behavior apply to the home as well as the classroom, so parents should also find them helpful. The first rule in guiding children's behavior is to *know yourself*. Unless you know your attitudes toward discipline and behavior, it will be hard to practice a rational and consistent program of management and discipline. So, develop a philosophy of discipline. What do you believe about child rearing, discipline, and punishment?

Second, *know your children*. A good way to learn about the children you teach is through a home visit. If you do not have an opportunity to visit the home, a parent conference is also valuable. Either way, some of the information you should gather is a health history; interests of the child; the parents' educational expectations for the child; what school support is available in the home (for example, books and places to study); parents' attitudes toward education, schooling, and discipline; parents' support of the child (for example, encouragement to do well); parents' interests and abilities; home conditions that would support or hinder school achievement (such as where the child sleeps); parents' desire to become involved in the school; and the child's attitude toward schooling.

The visit or conference offers an opportunity for the teacher to share some of her ideas and philosophy with the parent. You should, for example, express your desire for the child to do well in school; encourage the parents to take part in school and classroom programs; suggest (if asked) ways to help the child learn; describe some of the school programs; give information about school events, projects, and meetings; and explain your beliefs about discipline.

You should plan to establish classroom guidelines from the first day of class. As the year goes on, you can involve children in establishing classroom rules, but in the beginning, children want and need to know what they can and cannot do. Rules might relate to changing groups and bathroom routines. Whatever rules you establish, they should be fair, reasonable, and appropriate to the children's age and maturity. Keep rules to a minimum; the fewer the better. Review the rules, and have children evaluate their behavior against the rules. You can have expectations without having rules. If you have a task ready for children when they enter the classroom, you establish the expectation that upon entering the classroom, they should be busy.

Establish a classroom routine. Children need the confidence and security of a routine that will help them do their best. A routine also helps prevent discipline problems, because children know what to do and can learn to do it without a lot of disturbance. Parents need to establish routines in the home; if the child knows the family always eats at 5:30 P.M., he can be expected to be there. A teacher must also be consistent. Consistency plays an important role in managing behavior in both the home and classroom. If children know what to expect in terms of routine and behavior, they will behave better.

You should also usually ignore off-task behavior. By ignoring off-task behavior, you are not reinforcing or rewarding it. Some authorities feel that by ignoring off-task behavior, teachers run the risk of also ignoring good behavior; however, a behaviorally aware teacher or parent *knows* what behavior to ignore and plans for the behavior he will reinforce. Make the classroom reinforcing. The classroom should be a place where children can do their best work and be on their best behavior. Components of an environmentally rewarding classroom are:

☐ Opportunities for children to display their work
☐ Opportunities for freedom of movement (within guidelines)
☐ Opportunities for independent work
☐ A variety of work stations and materials based on children's interests

At the same time, use positive reinforcement. When a child does something good, when he is on-task, reward him. Use verbal and nonverbal reinforcement and privileges to help assure that the appropriate behavior will continue. Look for good behavior. This helps improve not only individual behavior but group behavior as well. It can also be helpful to write contracts for certain work experiences. Contracting is a great way to involve the child in planning his own work and behavior. Rules to follow in contracting are to keep contracts short and uncomplicated; make an offer the child can't refuse; make sure the child is able to do what you contract for; and pay off when the contract is completed.

As we've mentioned, an excellent way to guide behavior is to be a good role model. Don't ask children to behave in a way you don't want to or are not willing to behave. Treat the children the way you want them to behave. But don't be afraid to be firm. In some instances, being firm may require physically punishing a child, and if you judge this to be necessary, do it.

Other techniques for positive guidance of children's behavior include keeping students busy and involved in a variety of interesting activities; developing and maintaining a good relationship with children; talking over classroom problems with the children; talking with the child who has a problem; and making and managing contingencies.

Above all, if you have a problem you don't know how to handle, seek help. Ask other teachers, parents, the administration, and experts in child behavior. You will be surprised how much good help is available when you begin to seek it out. Learning, teaching, and discipline go hand-in-hand. A teacher's success depends upon her attitude toward and methods of discipline. Teachers who master skills of effective discipline and promote opportunities for children to acquire self-discipline will be able to engage in individualized instruction and creativity.

THE MORALITY OF AUTONOMY

Implicit in guiding children's behavior is the assumption that they can be, should be, and will be responsible for their own behavior. The ultimate goal of all education, according to Constance Kamii, is to develop *autonomy* in children, which means "being governed by oneself."

Early childhood educators need to conduct programs that promote development of autonomy. One aspect of facilitating autonomy is exchanging points of view with children.

> When a child tells a lie, for example, the adult can deprive him of dessert or make him write 50 times "I will not lie." The adult can also refrain from punishing the child and, instead, look him straight in the eye with great skepticism and affection and say, "I really can't believe what you are saying because . . . ." This is an example of an exchange of points of view that contributes to the development of autonomy in children. The child who can see that the adult cannot believe him can be motivated to think about what he must do to be believed. The child who is raised with many similar opportunities can, over time, construct for himself the conviction that it is best eventually for people to deal honestly with each other.[3]

The ultimate goal of developing autonomy in children is to have them regulate their own behavior and have them make decisions about good and bad, right and wrong, and how they will behave in relation to themselves and others. Autonomous behavior can be achieved only when a child considers other people's points of view, which can occur only if they are presented with viewpoints that differ from their own and are encouraged to consider them in deciding how they will behave.

Rewards and punishment tend to encourage children to obey others without helping them understand how their behavior was appropriate or inappropriate. Even

To become self-directive and autonomous, children should be encouraged to do things for themselves from an early age.

more importantly, they have not had an opportunity to develop rules of conduct to govern their behavior. Children can be encouraged to regulate and be responsible for their own behavior through what Piaget referred to as "sanctions by reciprocity." These sanctions "are directly related to the act we want to sanction and to the adult's point of view, and have the effect of motivating the child to construct rules of conduct for himself, through the coordination of viewpoints."[4] Examples of sanctions by reciprocity include exclusion from the group, whereby the child has a choice of staying and behaving or leaving; taking away from children the materials or privileges they have abused, such as not allowing them to use certain materials while leaving open the opportunity to use them again if they express a desire to use them appropriately; and helping children fix things they have broken and clean up after themselves. A fine line separates sanctions by reciprocity and punishment. The critical ingredient that balances the scales on the side of reciprocity is teachers' respect for children and their desire to help them develop autonomy rather than blind obedience.

FURTHER READING

Bijou, Sidney, and Donald Baer. *Behavior Analysis of Child Development* (Englewood Cliffs, N.J.: Prentice-Hall, 1978) Somewhat technical but important reading for those who want to know more about behavior changes resulting from interaction between individuals and their environment; many insights into reinforcement theory.

Bisschop, Marijke, and Theo Compernolle. *Your Child Can Do It Alone* (Englewood Cliffs, N.J.: Prentice-Hall, 1981) Provides twelve steps for helping caregivers build new behavior in their children. The premise is that the more independent children are and the more they can do for themselves, the fewer problems they will cause caregivers and themselves.

Bluestein, Jane, and Lynn Collins. *Parents in a Pressure Cooker: A Guide to Responsible and Loving Parent/Child Relationships* (Albuquerque, N.M.: I.S.S. Publications, 1983) Helps caregivers rear responsible children who are self-regulated rather than dependent on others for external control. One premise is that to rear responsible children, one has to begin with responsible adults, so there is a chapter devoted to modeling; another useful chapter deals with expectations.

Canter, Lee, and Marlene Canter. *Assertive Discipline: A Take-Charge Approach for Today's Educator* (Santa Monica, Calif.: Canter and Associates, 1986) Lee Canter is the leading proponent of "assertive discipline"; based on principles of assertiveness training, this approach encourages teachers and parents to take charge of the discipline process; derives its popularity from the self-help movement of the '70s and '80s.

Charles, C.M. *Building Classroom Discipline* (New York: Longman, 1985) Seven models of classroom discipline. Helps the reader develop a personal system of discipline.

Essa, Eva. *A Practical Guide to Solving Preschool Behavior Problems* (Albany, N.Y.: Delmar, 1983) Based on the behaviorist approach to guiding behavior, provides practical ideas for caregivers, addresses specific behavior problems such as hitting, biting, tantrums, and whining. One section is devoted to social behaviors such as nonparticipation in play and group activities.

Fontenelle, Don. H. *Understanding and Managing Overactive Children* (Englewood Cliffs, N.J.: Prentice-Hall, 1983) Caregivers always have questions about how to guide the behavior of children they assess as overactive. Often, children are incorrectly labeled overactive; the first two chapters provide insight into the nature and causes of overactivity. Good section on general management techniques.

Schaefer, C. E., and H. L. Millman. *How to Help Children with Common Problems* (New York: Van Nostrand Reinhold, 1981) Information and strategies for helping parents deal with children's everyday problems. Addresses lying, stealing, shyness, overactivity, bedwetting.

Silberman, Melvin L., and Susan Wheelan. *How to Discipline Without Feeling Guilty: Assertive Relationships With Children* (New York: Hawthorn Books, 1980) Helps parents and teachers learn and apply techniques of assertiveness at home and school. Many situational and conversational examples to help you behave and talk assertively with children.

FURTHER STUDY

1. What are the advantages and disadvantages of using rewards to stimulate and reinforce desired behaviors?
2. Some critics argue that teachers need to devote so much time to managing student behavior because pupils are forced to engage in contrived learning. Discuss this claim.

3. What is the difference between normal behavior and acceptable behavior? Give an example of a case where normal behavior may not be acceptable and another where acceptable behavior may not be normal.

4. Visit a classroom that uses behavior modification. Interview parents, teachers, and students to find out how they feel about the program.

5. Observe an early childhood classroom. What reinforcement system (implicit or explicit) does the teacher use to operate the classroom? Do you think the teacher is aware of the systems of reinforcement in use?

6. Interview children to determine what they find reinforcing. How do their selections compare to the reinforcers mentioned in this chapter?

7. Behavior modification is practiced by parents and teachers without their being aware of what they are doing or the processes they are using. Observe a mother-child relationship for examples of parental behavioral management. What rewards does she offer? What was the child's resultant behavior? After further observation, answer these questions for the teacher-child relationship. In both situations, what are some ethical implications of the adult's actions?

8. Observe an early childhood classroom to see which behaviors earn the teacher's attention. Does the teacher pay more attention to positive or negative behavior? Why do you think the teacher acts the way he does?

9. A mother says her four-year-old daughter will not keep her room neat; it is always a mess, and she can't get the child to put anything away. Develop specific strategies you could give a parent to use in helping her keep the child's room in order. Design a floor plan and show furnishings that would help a child keep her room neat.

10. While observing in a primary classroom, identify and examine aspects of the physical setting and atmosphere that could influence classroom behavior. Can you suggest improvements?

11. List ten behaviors you think are desirable in kindergarten children. For each behavior, give two examples of how you would encourage and promote development of that behavior.

12. Interview five parents of young children to determine what they mean when they use the word *discipline*. What implications might these definitions have for you if you were their children's teacher?

13. How does a parent's behavior influence and affect a child's behavior? Give specific examples.

14. List five methods for guiding children's behavior. Tell why you think each is effective, and give examples.

15. Does a child's age make any difference in the method of discipline used and the kind and nature of guidance techniques? Give specific examples pro and con.

16. Do you believe in the adage, "spare the rod and spoil the child"? Where does this saying come from? What does it mean? Do you think the implications of this saying are appropriate for today's children?

17. Why is it important for caregivers and parents to agree on a philosophy of behavioral guidance?

18. Why is some children's behavior easier to guide than other children's?

19. Write a children's Bill of Rights relating to their care, guidance, and discipline in a child care center.

13

Parent Involvement: Key to Successful Programs

As you read and study:

Discuss current changes in the family and their influences on early childhood education

Examine the implications of changing family and parenting patterns for early childhood educators

Develop a personal philosophy of parent involvement

Define parent involvement

Examine procedures and practices for effective parent involvement

Examine a rationale for the importance of parent involvement programs

WHO IS A PARENT?

A parent is anyone who provides children with basic care, direction, support, protection, and guidance. Accordingly, a parent can be single, married, heterosexual, homosexual, a cousin, aunt, uncle, grandparent, a court-appointed guardian, a brother, a sister, an institution employee, a surrogate, a foster parent, or a group such as a commune. These changing patterns of who a parent is have important implications for early childhood teachers.

WHAT IS A FAMILY?

Families have undergone radical changes since the 1970s. Children are born into many different kinds of families, and parents create for children a wide variety of living arrangements. These family structures affect, in obvious and subtle ways, children's development and how early educators relate to them.

For statistical and reporting purposes, the U.S. Census Bureau classifies family households into three types: married couple families, families with male householders (no wife present), and families with female householders (no husband present). A *household* is defined as the person or persons who comprise a family unit. A *family* is defined as two or more persons living together who are related by birth, marriage, or adoption. The term *householder* has replaced "head of family." The number of family households increased by 8.9 million between 1970 and 1981; however, over 50 percent of this increase was in the number of householders with no spouse present. Also, in 1981, there were considerably more female family households (5.5 million) than male family households (666,000). Table 13–1 shows the dramatic ways families have changed.

Types of Families

Nuclear Family

Our concept of the family is undergoing radical redefinition. While the *nuclear family*, consisting of two parents and one child or more, is still the prevalent and probably preferred family unit, it is no longer the unit in which many children live. Although the nuclear family unit is undergoing tensions and strains, especially from divorce, it will probably remain the family unit of choice for most people. The first family unit most people form is the nuclear family; also, many divorced persons tend to remarry, forming a new nuclear family unit.

Extended Families

An extended family consists of parents, grandparents, aunts, uncles, brothers, sisters, and sometimes cousins, living together as a unit or sharing feelings of kinship

414

TABLE 13–1 Eight Ways Families Have Changed

		1970	1981	1984	Percent of Change, 1981–1984
1.	Married couples	44,728,000	49,294,000	50,090,000	+ 1.6%
2.	Married couples with children	25,532,000	24,927,000	24,339,000	− 2.4%
3.	Male householder (no spouse) with children	341,000	666,000	799,000	+ 20%
4.	Female householder (no spouse) with children	2,858,000	5,634,000	5,907,000	+ 4.8%
5.	Marriages	2,159,000	2,438,000	2,487,000	+ 2%
6.	Divorces	708,000	1,219,000	1,155,000	− 5.3%
7.	Average size per household	3.14	2.73	2.71	− 1%
8.	Average size per family	3.58	3.27	3.24	− 1%

Source: Bureau of the Census

through close geographical proximity and shared concern and responsibility for family matters. In an extended family, children may be reared by any other family members, particularly grandparents. In an extended family situation, it is not uncommon for a grandparent to respond to a note from a teacher for a conference about a child's school progress. Sometimes an unperceptive teacher interprets this as a sign that parents don't care, when it is actually a normal state of affairs in a family where everyone is willing to be responsible for children's growth and development. The extended family may well be the type to which more and more divorced spouses will turn as a means of support and assistance in child rearing.

Single-parent Families

With the increase in the divorce rate and new attitudes toward child rearing, single parent families are increasing, and single fathers rearing dependent children are no longer rare. The increase in single parent families has caused an accompanying increase in child care services, especially those supported by companies as part of their employment benefits.

Stepfamilies and Blended Families

A stepfamily is one parent with children of his or her own and a spouse. Instead of *stepparent*, some people suggest using the term *acquired* parent, or *recoupled* family. When two people, each with children of their own, marry, they form *blended, merged*, or *reconstructed* families. These families have "his" children and "her" children; if they have children together, a third level of sibling relationships is added with "their" children.

The number of single-parent families continues to grow, and early childhood educators must take into account the concerns of these families.

Foster Parent Families

Foster parents are those who care for, in a family setting, children who are not their own. Foster parents are usually screened by the agencies that place children with them, and sometimes the children are relatives. Foster parents occasionally adopt the children they care for, but even if not, the children sometimes remain in the foster home for extended periods. A major crisis facing many social service agencies today is a lack of qualified foster care families. Many agencies are vigorously attempting to recruit, identify, and train foster parent families, especially from minority groups.

Implications of Family Patterns for Early Childhood Educators

There are many ways for teachers to help children and parents in these days of changing family patterns. They may, for example, help develop support services for families and parents. Support can extend from being a "listening ear" to organizing support groups and seminars on single parenting. Teachers can help parents link up with other agencies and groups, such as Big Brothers and Big Sisters and Parents Without Partners. Through newsletters and fliers, teachers can provide parents with specific advice on how to help children become independent and how to help them meet the demands of broken homes, stepfamilies, and other family configurations.

Another way for teachers to be involved is in helping to make arrangements for child care services. More families need child care, and early childhood personnel are logical advocates for establishing child care where none exists, extending existing services, and helping to arrange cooperative babysitting services.

Teachers should be careful not to criticize parents or place extra demands on them. They may not have extra time to spend with their children, or know how to discipline them. Regardless of their circumstances, parents need help, not criticism. Similarly, teachers should not be judgmental; they should examine and clarify their attitudes and values toward family patterns and remember that there is no "right" family pattern from which all children should come. Teachers also need to address the issue of changing family patterns in the educational experiences they arrange. They need to offer experiences children might not otherwise have because of their family organization. For example, outdoor activities such as fishing trips and sports events can be interesting and enriching learning experiences.

Teachers need to adjust classroom or center activities and plans to account for how particular children are coping with their home situations. Children's needs for different kinds of activities depend on their experiences at home. There are many opportunities for role-playing situations, and dramatic settings help bring into the open situations that children need to talk about. Use classroom opportunities to discuss family patterns, parents, and the roles parents play. Make it a point in the classroom to model, encourage, and teach effective interpersonal skills.

There are also specific ways to approach today's changing family patterns. For example, avoid making presents for both parents and awarding prizes for bringing both parents to meetings. Avoid father-son and mother-daughter affairs. Replace terms like "broken home" with "single parent family." Be sensitive to the demands of school in relation to children's home lives. For example, when a teacher sent a field trip permission form home with the children and told them to have their mothers or fathers sign it, one child said, "I don't have a father. If my mother can't sign it, can the man who sleeps with her sign it?" Seek help, guidance, and clarification from parents about how they would like specific situations handled; for example, ask whether they want you to send notices of school events to both parents.

Request inservice training to help you work with parents. Inservice programs can provide information about referral agencies; guidance techniques; how to help parents deal with their problems; and child abuse identification and prevention. Teachers need to be alert to the signs of all kinds of child abuse, including sexual.

Finally, teachers should encourage greater and different kinds of parent involvement through home visits, talking to parents about children's needs, providing information and opportunities to parents, grandparents, and other family members, gathering information from parents (such as interest inventories), and keeping in touch with parents. Make parent contacts positive, not negative.

REASONS FOR PARENT INVOLVEMENT

The most compelling reason for involving parents is the effect it has on improving children's achievement: "According to recent studies, parent involvement in almost any form improves student achievement."[1] When children have a quality school program and supportive and involved parents, they do better on academic and social skills.[2] Children see parent involvement as a sign that their parents value education. When their parents are involved in their program, they recognize that their parents are not just "leaving them off" and forgetting them.

Educators have realized that their teaching and classroom efforts can be more effectively achieved by encouraging parent assistance. In turn, parents who believe discipline is one of the major problems schools face are more inclined to join the effort to improve the teaching-learning process. Every parent has a duty to be involved in some way in his or her children's educational program or in any program that provides a major service to them and their children. In fact, specific legislation, especially as it relates to programs that receive federal and state funds, mandates parent involvement. P.L. 94–142, the Education for All Handicapped Children Act (which we discussed in Chapter 11) mandates parent involvement when services are provided by federal funds.

Evidence shows that parents are more supportive of programs with which they have direct and meaningful involvement. If early childhood educators want support for quality programs, parent involvement is a certain way to achieve it. The rediscovery of the relationship between parents and schools is partly the result of political and societal forces. The consumer movement of the last several decades convinced parents that they should no longer be kept out of their children's schools. Parents believe that if they have a right to demand greater accountability from industries and government agencies, they can also demand effective instruction and care from schools and child care centers. Parents have become more militant in their demand for quality education, and schools and other agencies have responded by seeking ways to involve parents in the quest for quality.

What Is Parent Involvement?

Parent involvement is a threefold process; it is "a partnership between parents and teachers and their helpers in the community, . . . a developmental process that is built over a period of time through intentional planning and effort of every team member, and a process by which parents and teachers work, learn and participate in decision-making experiences in a shared manner"—a developmental process based on partnership and shared decision making.[3]

I have previously defined parent involvement as "the process of actualizing the potential of parents; of helping parents discover their strengths, potentialities and talents; and of using them for the benefit of themselves and the family."[4] This definition, however, did not totally recognize the three groups in the parent involvement relationship: children, parents, and early childhood programs. A more timely definition of parent involvement is: *a process of helping parents use their abilities to benefit themselves, their children, and the early childhood program.* Parents, children, and the program are all part of the process; consequently, all three parties should benefit from a well-planned program of parent involvement. Nonetheless, the focus in parent/child/family interactions is the parent, and early childhood educators must work with and through parents if they want to be successful.

Three Views of Parent Involvement

Task Orientation

The most common and traditional way to approach parent involvement is through a task orientation, aimed at completing specific tasks to support the school or classroom program. In this orientation, faculty, staff, and administration work to involve parents as tutors, aides, attendance monitors, fund raisers, field trip monitors, and clerical helpers. This is the type of parent involvement most teachers are comfortable with, and the type that usually comes to mind when planning for parent involvement. It can also include getting parents to help with areas the school traditionally has trouble with, perhaps asking parents to see that homework is done and that inappropriate school behavior is corrected.

Process Orientation

In a process orientation, parents are encouraged to participate in certain activities that are important to the educational process, such as curriculum planning, textbook review and selection, membership on task forces and committees, teacher review and selection, and helping to set behavior standards. Process orientation is not widespread because professional educators are sometimes unenthusiastic about sharing these responsibilities with parents. It is also a kind of involvement for which parents need a great deal of preparation and support. Teachers often think parents don't have the skills to help in certain areas, but with some preparation and opportunity to participate, many parents can be extremely effective.

Developmental Orientation

A developmental orientation helps parents develop skills that will benefit themselves, children, schools, teachers, families and, at the same time, enhance the process of parent involvement. This humanistic orientation is exemplified in cooperative preschools, community schools, and Head Start programs. Ideally, an effective and comprehensive program of parent involvement includes all three orientations. Diagrammatically, it would look like Figure 13–1.

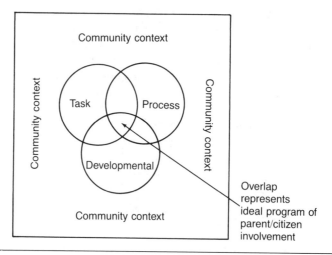

FIGURE 13–1   Parent/Citizen Involvement

Methods for Involving Parents

After teachers have become convinced of the wisdom of parent involvement, they wonder how to go about the process. A primary requisite for involving parents is the right attitude. Teachers have to *want* parent involvement in early childhood and school programs; otherwise, parent involvement won't be as effective as it could be. A teacher must not feel threatened by parents. The more self-confident the teacher, the less she will feel threatened. Self-confidence comes from being good at what you are doing.

The school and center administration must be ready for parents. When a program of parent involvement receives continuous support and recognition, it tends to be successful; without support, success is limited. Success also depends on how well teachers involve parents. Parents must have meaningful involvement, not just the custodial jobs.

Planning is critical. Determine what parents will do before they become involved, but be willing to change plans after determining parent strengths, weaknesses, and needs. Seek creative ways to involve *all* parents. Some parents, regardless of their level of education, are threatened by schools and schoollike settings. Help them overcome these fears. It may be unrealistic to expect all parents to participate, but it is not unrealistic to give all parents a chance. Be willing to go to the parents through home visitations; don't always make them come to you.

Provide for all levels of abilities, desires, and needs. Don't expect the same participation from every parent, nor all parents to want to do the same thing. Regardless of how much or little a parent can or wants to be involved, give them the opportunity to participate. Invite a group of parents to help organize and operate the program. The teacher's functions will be to develop a program rationale and structure, including philosophy and goals; train parents; supervise the program, including planning with the parent helpers and showing them specific teaching methods and tasks; and to evaluate the program, including each parent's performance and the overall effectiveness in the classroom. Parents can help operate the program by calling parents, setting up schedules, and matching children's needs with parent's abilities.

A well-planned orientation session should include the philosophy of the school; the teacher's philosophy of teaching/learning; learning goals and objectives for the classroom and the children; rules and regulations of the school and classroom; specific tasks of the volunteers, how to perform them, and any necessary special preparations; limits of responsibilities and duties; classroom management techniques; and a survey of parent interests and abilities.

Activities for Involving Parents

There are unlimited possibilities for parent involvement, but a coordinated effort is required to build an effective and meaningful program that can bring about a change in education and benefit all concerned: parents, children, teachers, and community. Parents can make a significant difference in their children's education, and with our assistance, will be able to join teachers and schools in a productive partnership. These are a sampling of activities for involving parents:

Schoolwide activities:

1. Workshops—to introduce parents to the school's policies, procedures, and programs. Most parents want to know what is going on in the school, and would do a better job of parenting and educating if they knew how.
2. Family nights, cultural dinners, carnivals, and potluck dinners—to bring parents and the community to the school in nonthreatening, social ways.
3. Adult education classes—to provide the community with opportunities to learn about a wide range of subjects.
4. Training programs—to give parents skills as classroom aides and as club and activity sponsors.
5. Support services such as car pools and baby-sitting—to make attendance and involvement possible.
6. Fairs and bazaars—to involve parents in fund raising.
7. Performances and plays—programs in which children have a part tend to bring parents to school; however, the purpose of children's performances should not be to get parents involved.

Communication activities

1. Telephone "hot lines"—hot lines staffed by parents can help allay fears and provide information relating to child abuse, communicable diseases, and special events.
2. Newsletters—newsletters planned with parents' help are an excellent way to keep parents informed about program events. Newsletters can also in-

422 | PARENT INVOLVEMENT: KEY TO SUCCESSFUL PROGRAMS

clude curriculum information and activities. Newsletters in parents' native languages also help keep minority-language parents informed.

3. Home learning materials and activities—a monthly calendar of activities is one good way to keep parents involved in their children's learning.

Educational activities

1. Participation in classroom and center activities—while not all parents can be directly involved in classroom activities, those who can should be encouraged. Parents must have guidance, direction, and training for these involvements. Involving parents as paid aides is an excellent way to also provide employment and training. Many programs, such as Head Start, actively support such a policy.

2. Involvement of parents in writing individual educational programs (IEPs)—for parents of special needs children, involvement in writing an individualized education plan is not only a legal requirement, but also a learning experience (see Chapter 11).

Service activities

1. Resource libraries and materials centers—parents benefit from books and other materials relating to parenting. Some programs furnish resource areas with comfortable chairs to encourage parents to use them.

2. Child care—parents may not be able to attend programs and become involved if they do not have child care for their children. Child care makes their participation possible and more enjoyable.

3. Respite care—some early childhood programs provide respite care for parents, enabling them to have periodic relief from the responsibilities of parenting a handicapped or chronically ill child.

4. Service exchanges—service exchanges operated by child care programs and schools help parents in their needs for services.

5. Parent support groups—parents need support in their roles as parents, and support groups can provide parenting information, community agency information, and speakers.

6. Welcoming committee—a good way to involve parents in any program is to have other parents contact them when their children first join a program.

Decision activities

1. Hiring and policy making—parents should serve on committees that set policy and hire staff.

2. Curriculum development and review—Parent involvement in curriculum planning helps them learn about and understand what constitutes a quality program. When parents know about the curriculum, they are more supportive of it.

PARENT-TEACHER CONFERENCES

Most parent involvement occurs through parent-teacher conferences, which are often the first contact many parents have with school. The conferences are critical from a public relations point of view and as a vehicle for helping parents and teachers accomplish their goals. These guidelines will help teachers prepare for conferences.

1. Plan ahead. Be sure of the reason for the conference. What are the objectives? What do you want to accomplish? List the points you want to cover. Think about what you are going to say.

2. When you meet the parent, spend some time getting to know him. This is not wasted time; the more effectively you establish rapport with the parent, the more you will accomplish in the long run.

3. Avoid an authoritative atmosphere. Don't sit behind your desk while the parent sits in a child's chair. Treat parents like the adults they are.

4. Communicate at the parent's level. Do not condescend or patronize, but use words, phrases, and explanations the parent understands and is familiar with. Do not use jargon or complicated explanations, and speak according to your natural style.

5. Accentuate the positive. Make every effort to show and tell the parent what the child is doing well. When you deal with problems, put them in the proper perspective: what the child is able to do, what the goals and purposes of the learning program are, what specific skill or concept you are trying to get the child to learn, what problems the child is having in achieving. Most important, explain what you plan to do to help the child achieve and what specific role the parent can have in the achievement goals.

6. Never leave the parent with a sense of frustration, not knowing what you are doing or what they are to do. Every communication with parents should end on a positive note so that everyone knows what can be done and how to do it.

7. Give parents a chance to talk. You won't learn much about them if you do all the talking, nor are you likely to achieve your goals. Teachers are often accustomed to dominating the conversation, and many parents will not be as verbal as you, so you will have to encourage parents to talk. You will have to learn how to listen. An active listener holds eye contact, uses body language such as head nodding and hand gestures, doesn't interrupt, avoids arguing, paraphrases as a way of clarifying ideas, and keeps the conversation on track.

8. A conference must be followed up. It is a good idea to ask the parent for a definite time for the next conference as you are concluding the current one. Another conference is the best method of solidifying gains and extending support, but other acceptable means of follow-up are telephone calls, written reports, notes sent with children, or brief visits to the home. While these types of contacts may appear casual, they should be planned for and conducted as seriously as any regular parent-teacher conference.

Among the advantages to parent-teacher conference follow-up are that parents see that you genuinely care about their children; everyone can clarify problems, issues, advice, and directions; it encourages parents and children to continue to do their best; it offers further opportunities to extend classroom learnings to the home; and you can extend programs initiated for helping parents and child and formulate new plans.

When it is impossible to arrange a face-to-face conference as a follow-up, a telephone call is an efficient way to contact parents. (Some families, however, do not have a telephone.) The same guidelines apply as to face-to-face conferences; in addition, remember these points:

1. Since you can't see someone on a telephone, it takes a little longer to build rapport and trust. The time you spend overcoming parents' initial fears and apprehensions will pay dividends later.

2. Constantly clarify what you are talking about and what you and the parents have agreed to do, using such phrases as: "What I heard you say then . . ." or "So far, we have agreed that. . . ."

3. Don't act hurried. There is a limit to the amount of time you can spend on the phone, but you may be one of the few people who cares about the parent and the child, and the telephone conference may be the major part of the parents' support system.

INVOLVING SINGLE PARENTS

Parent involvement activities are often conducted without much regard for the single parent. Teachers sometimes think of single parents as problems to deal with rather than people to work with. One-parent families need not be a problem in involvement if teachers remember some simple points.

First, most adults in one-parent families are employed during school hours, and may not be available for conferences or other activities during that time. Teachers must be willing to accommodate parents' schedules by arranging conferences at other times, perhaps early morning (breakfast), midmorning, noon (lunch), early afternoon, late afternoon, or early evening. Some employers, sensitive to parents' needs, give released time to participate in school functions, but others do not. Teachers and principals need to think seriously about going to parents, rather than having parents always come to them. Some schools have set up parent conferences to accommodate parents' work schedules, some teachers find that home visitations work best.

Second, teachers need to remember that working parents have a limited amount of time to spend on involvement with their children's school and with their children at home. When teachers confer with single parents, they should make sure (1) the meeting starts on time, (2) they have a list of items (skills, behaviors, achievements) to discuss, (3) they have sample materials available to illustrate all points, (4) they make specific suggestions relative to one-parent environments, and (5) the meeting ends on time. One-parent families are more likely to need child care assistance to attend meetings, so services should be planned for every parent meeting or activity.

Telephone conferences are a convenient way for teachers to keep parents informed and involved.

Third, illustrate for single parents how they can make their time with their children more meaningful. If a child has trouble following directions, show parents how to use home situations to help in this area—children can learn to follow directions while helping parents run errands, get a meal, do the wash, or help with housework.

Fourth, get to know parents' life styles and living conditions. It is easy for a teacher to say that every child should have a quiet place to study, but this may be an impossible demand on some households. Teachers need to visit some of the homes in their community before they set meeting times or decide what parent involvement activities to implement, or what they will ask of parents during the year. All educators, particularly teachers, need to keep in mind the condition of the home environment when they request that children bring certain items to school or carry out certain tasks at home. When asking for a parent's help, the teacher needs to be sensitive to the parent's talents and time constraints.

Fifth, help develop support groups for one-parent families within the school, such as discussion groups and classes on parenting for singles. Teachers must include the needs and abilities of one-parent families in their parent involvement activities and programs, otherwise they are ignoring part of society.

LANGUAGE MINORITY PARENTS

The developmental concept of parent involvement is particularly important when working with language minority parents. Programs for promoting parental involvement must consider this group. Language minority parents are individuals whose English language proficiency is minimal, and who lack a comprehensive knowledge of the norms and social system, including basic school philosophy, practice and structure. Language minority parents often face language and cultural barriers that greatly hamper their ability to become actively involved, although many have a great desire and willingness to participate in their children's education.

Because the culture of language minority parents often differs from the majority in a community, those who seek a truly collaborative community, home, and school involvement must take into account the cultural features that can inhibit collaboration. Traditional styles of child rearing, family organization, attitudes toward schooling, organizations around which families center their lives, life goals and values, political influences, and methods of communication within the cultural group, all have implications for parent participation.

Language minority parents often lack information about the American educational system, resulting in misconceptions, fear, and a general reluctance to respond to invitations for involvement. Furthermore, the American educational system may be quite different from what language minority parents are used to in a former school system. Language minority parents may have been taught to avoid active involvement in the educational process, with the result that they prefer to leave all decisions concerning their children's education to teachers and administrators.

The American ideal of a community controlled and supported educational system must be explained to parents from cultures where this concept is not as highly valued. Traditional roles of children, teachers, and administrators also have to be explained. Many parents, and especially language minority parents, are quite willing to relinquish to teachers any rights and responsibilities they have for their children's education, and need to be educated to assume their roles and obligations toward schooling.

INVOLVING FATHERS

More caregivers now recognize that fathering and mothering are complementary processes. Defintions of nurturing are changing to include the legitimate and positive involvement of fathers in children's lives. Many fathers are competent caregivers. More fathers, as they discover or rediscover their roles in parenting, turn to caregivers for support and advice. Fathers' roles are extremely important in parenting. Fathers provide direct supervision to children, help set the tone for family life, provide stability to a relationship, support the mother in her parenting role, and provide a masculine role model for the children.

There are many styles of fathering; some fathers are at home while their wives work; some have custody of the children; some are single; some dominate home life and control everything; some are passive and exert little influence in the home; some are frequently absent from the home because their work requires travel; some take little interest in their homes and families; some are surrogates. Regardless of the roles fathers play in their children's lives, early childhood educators must make special efforts to involve them.

FAMILY SUPPORT PROGRAMS

There is a movement in early childhood education to develop family support programs that look at the total family and design programs to help all members. These programs are not necessarily new; Head Start, through many of its programs such as Home Base, Parent Child Centers and the Child and Family Resource Program, considers the family the focus of its services. Now, more early childhood programs recognize that working only with children leaves the family—a critical factor in the child's development—out of the process.

National Organizations

National programs dedicated to parent involvement can be a good resource for information and support. Two of these are:

- ☐ Parents United, 401 North Broad Street, Suite 895, Philadelphia, PA 19108. This is an organization of parents working to help other parents work for better schools.
- ☐ National Committee for Citizens in Education, 410 Wilde Village Green, Columbia, MD 21944 (800–638–9675). This organization seeks to inform parents of their rights and to get them involved in the public schools.

FURTHER READING

Berman, Claire. *Making It As a Stepparent: New Roles/New Rules* (New York: Harper and Row, 1984) A guide for those considering the many challenges of creating a stepfamily; includes resources and many practical ideas for every family member.

Brazelton, T. Berry. *On Becoming a Family: The Growth of Attachment* (New York: Delacorte Press, 1981) Helps parents identify with the happenings when a family decides to leave a child in a child care center.

Brown, S., and P. Kornhouser. *Working Parents: How To Be Happy With Your Children* (Atlanta, Ga.: Humanics, 1982) Manual for working parents gives effective techniques for enhancing the time they spend with their children.

Brutt, Kent Garland. *Smart Times* (New York: Harper and Row, 1983) Over 200 appropriate activities for at-home fun and learning; defines "quality time" for today's active parents.

Bundy, Darcie. *The Affordable Baby* (New York: Harper and Row, 1984) Complete financial examination of having a baby, including charts and tables to demonstrate cost comparisons.

Coletta, Anthony J. *Working Together: A Guide to Parent Involvement* (Atlanta, Ga.: Humanics Limited, 1982) Based on the premise that parent/teacher partnerships should evince clear communication and reciprocity to help children meet their needs for survival, growth, and happiness; includes plans for parent participation in the classroom.

Duff, Eleanor R., et al. *Building Successful Parent/Teacher Partnerships* (Atlanta, Ga.: Humanics Limited, 1979) Authoritative solutions to problems that have led many parents and teachers to become disenchanted with parent involvement programs. Examines the changing nature of parenting and teaching and provides a comprehensive, workable plan for implementing a successful parent/teacher involvement program.

Ehly, Stewart W., et al. *Working with Parents of Exceptional Children* (St. Louis: Times Mirror/ Mosby, 1985) Helps caregivers know more about what to do and how to do it when working with parents of special needs children. Although main focus is parents of exceptional children, concepts and processes apply to all parents. The last chapter on the gifted is particularly useful.

Fitzgerald, Hiram E., and C. E. McCrean. *Fathers and Infants* (New York: Human Sciences Press, 1981) Up-to-date look at the father as caregiver of the very young child; special attention to the father-infant relationship and the social development aspect of this interaction.

Harris, Rosa Alexander. *How to Select, Train, and Use Volunteers in the Schools* (Lanham, Md.: University Press of America, 1985) Concise blueprint for recruiting, selecting, training, and evaluating a school volunteer program.

Kane, Patricia. *Food Makes the Difference: A Parent's Guide to Raising a Healthy Child* (New York: Simon and Schuster, 1985) Advocates a "nutritional/ecological regime," the process of finding the causes of disturbances in the body and finding answers to these biochemical puzzles; provides useful recipes and diets for parents to help their children overcome illness and behavioral problems.

Metzger, Peg, et al. *Parents Make the Difference* (West Falls, N.Y.: Just Sew Education Publications, 1984) Stresses parents' role in determining the direction of their children's growth and development. Chapters deal with how parents set the stage for learning and communicating with children.

Miller, Shelby H. *Children as Parents: Final Report on a Study of Childbearing and Child Rearing Among 12- to 15-Year-Olds* (New York: Child Welfare League of America, 1983) Deals with the need for caregivers to know more about the problems of teenage parents (children as mothers) and how to work with them; final chapter suggests how to help teenagers be good parents.

Morrison, George S. *Parent Involvement in the Home, School and Community* (Columbus, Ohio: Merrill, 1978) Practical approach to involving parents.

Moyer, Joan, ed. *Selecting Educational Equipment and Materials for Home and School* (Wheaton, Md.: Association for Childhood Education International, 1986) Part I is devoted to "Criteria for Selection Of Materials" and provides philosophy and rationale to guide decision making. Part II lists materials needed in infant groups, nursery school groups, kindergartens, and primary and intermediate grades.

Pantel, R., et al. *Taking Care of Your Child* (St. Paul, Minn.: Toys 'n Things Press, 1982) Guidebook to help parents through everyday childhood medical problems; what to look for and what to do.

Park, R. D. *Fathers* (Cambridge, Mass.: Harvard University Press, 1981) Shows how the father's role is changing in both traditional and transitional families; traces father's influence on a child's development from the prenatal to postadolescent periods.

Radeloff, Deanna, and Roberta Zachman. *Children in Your Life: A Guide to Child Care and Parenting* (Albany, N.Y.: Delmar, 1981) Covers areas of child development and parenting; combines theory with practical activities, projects, and case studies.

Rodgers, Joann Ellison, and Michael F. Cataldo. *Raising Sons: Practical Strategies for Single Mothers* (New York: New American Library, 1984) Looks at new roles of single parents, especially single mothers. Authors believe there are new "contracts" between men and women, and the same follows with mothers and sons. Helps others identify new rules and better meet the needs of their growing sons.

Schaefer, Charles E. *How to Talk to Children About Really Important Things* (New York: Harper and Row, 1984) Offers communication skills for parents of children between the ages of 5 to 10; also recommended for parents of preschoolers so they can plan ahead.

Swick, Kevin. *Inviting Parents Into the Young Child's World* (Champaign, Ill.: Stipes, 1984) Practical guidelines for facilitating parent involvement.

White, Margaret B. *Sharing Caring: The Art of Raising Kids in Two Career Families* (Englewood Cliffs, N.J.: Prentice-Hall, 1982) Accounts of parents who have chosen to share equally the responsibilities of work and child care.

Wilson, Gary B. *Parents and Teachers: Humanistic Educational Techniques to Facilitate Communication Between Parents and Staff of Educational Programs* (Atlanta, Ga.: Humanics Limited, 1974) Strategies to enable parents and teachers to work together effectively; series of structured experiences to promote increased parent/staff interaction.

Yablonsky, Lewis. *Fathers and Sons* (New York: Simon and Schuster, 1982) Examination of the roles fathers play and how fathers can develop significant relationships with their sons and families.

FURTHER STUDY

1. Arrange with a local school district to be present during a parent-teacher conference. Discuss with the teacher, prior to the visit, her objectives and procedures. After the conference, assess its success with the teacher.

2. Simulate a parent-teacher conference with your classmates. Establish objectives and procedures for the visit. Analyze this conference. (A good method for analyzing the simulation is to videotape it.)

3. Recall from your school experiences instances of parent-teacher conferences or other involvement. What particular incidents have had a positive or negative effect on you?

4. List the various ways teachers communicate pupils' progress to parents. What do you think are the most effective ways? Least effective? What specific methods do you plan to use?

5. You are responsible for publicizing a parent meeting about how the school plans to involve parents. Describe the methods and techniques you would use to publicize the meeting.

6. List six reasons why early childhood teachers might resist involving parents.

7. You have just been appointed the program director for a parent involvement program in grade one. Write objectives for such a program. Develop specific activities for involving parents in the classroom. What methods would you use to train parents? What classroom activities would you have parents become involved with?

8. How would a parent-home involvement program conducted by a public school be similar to or different from one conducted by a social service agency?

9. Write your philosophy of education. Explain it to a parent. What problems did you encounter in explaining it? In what specific ways did the parent agree or disagree with your philosophy?

10. What are your opinions and feelings about parent involvement in early childhood programs? Discuss them with your classmates.

11. Conduct a poll of parents to find out how they think early childhood programs and schools can help them in educating their children; how they think they can be involved in

early childhood programs; what specific help they feel they need in child rearing/educating; and what activities they would like in a home visitation program.

12. What functions do you feel the family should exercise but does not? What family functions could be better accomplished by other agencies? Do you think education about sex role and function is better accomplished in the home or by an external educational agency? What functions do you feel the family you came from should have performed but did not? What functions did they perform that you do not agree with?

13. Historically, families have assigned traditional roles to family members: the father earns money, the mother stays home and cooks. How are the emphasis on equality of the sexes and the feminist movement changing traditional roles? What problems/opportunities does this change create? What effect will these changing roles have on our concept of the traditional family?

14. How will the role of children in the family change? What new roles may be assigned to children?

15. Do you think the traditional family as you have known it is disappearing? Why or why not?

16. Do you think it is necessary to rear children in a nuclear family? Why or why not?

17. Do you think programs such as the Head Start Home Base program are effective forms of parent involvement? Why?

18. Develop a set of guidelines that a child care center could use to facilitate the involvement of fathers; language-minority parents; and parents with handicapped children.

19. Based on discussion with early childhood educators and your observations of programs, what do you think are the most effective means of parent involvement?

20. What are the most serious parenting problems facing parents today? How can early childhood educators help parents with these problems?

14

Contemporary Concerns: Educating Children in a Changing Society

As you read and study:

Assess the effects of poverty on children

Discuss what society can do to better meet the total needs of poor children and their families

Examine definitions of child abuse and neglect

Know and understand the role of the early childhood educator in identifying and reporting child abuse

Examine reasons that parents and caregivers abuse children

Identify behaviors and attitudes that tend to promote sexual stereotyping

Consider practices, procedures, and materials that are essential for nonsexist education

Assess the impact of television on children's lives

Identify procedures parents and teachers can use for dealing with children's television viewing

Examine humanistic education in the preschool curriculum

Identify conditions that promote a humanistic early childhood program

CHILDREN OF POVERTY

Although everyone imagines America as a land of opportunity, a large number of the nation's children may not realize the dream of becoming all that one can be. More and more children are subject to the disadvantages and long-term destructive consequences poverty engenders. To be poor means that one gets a poor start in life. Twenty-five percent of the children in the U.S. live below the poverty level. Nine million children have no access to basic health care; eighteen million have never been to a dentist; and two million children under the age of 15 are not enrolled in school.[1] Over 40 percent of New York City's young children live below the poverty line and the number is growing. In 1986, New York City alone had 11,000 homeless children, known as *boarder babies*, living in municipal shelters.[2]

Early childhood educators are seeking ways to provide educational and preventive social services to poor children and their families to enable them to develop their potential so as to lead healthy and successful lives. Certainly, agencies such as Head Start have done many good things for the poor and disadvantaged, but it is not enough. Only about 20 percent of the children who need Head Start services receive them, and Head Start services do not start soon enough. Many children actually need a head start on Head Start.

THE BEETHOVEN PROJECT

The Center for Successful Child Development (CSCD) in Chicago is undertaking an innovative program to provide intensive and comprehensive support services to all children born after January 1, 1987 in the Beethoven Elementary School attendance area. The CSCD, on Chicago's south side, serves the Robert Taylor Homes—the largest public housing complex in the U.S. with 20,000 residents. The Beethoven Project will concentrate on six of the complex's high-rise apartment buildings. Forty-eight percent of the residents of the six buildings are under age 14, and 68 percent are under age 25. Seventy-five percent of the households are headed by women; all residents are black, and median family income for 1983 was $4640.00. Besides poverty, residents face problems of a high crime rate, high unemployment, high drop-out rates from school, health and nutrition problems, and the highest neonatal mortality rate in Chicago.

The ultimate goal of the Beethoven Project according to its director, Gina Barclay-McLaughlin, is to equip poor children for success in school. The project will endeavor to prevent social, psychological, and physical dysfunction among these children so they will be fully prepared to enter kindergarten. The first group of approximately 120–150 children will enter Beethoven's kindergarten class in 1993. The CSCD will attempt to meet its goals by offering:

434

Infant and child health services
Infant screening, evaluation, and referral
Child care programs
Parent support groups
Classes in infant and child development, nutrition, health, and parenting
Family counseling
Employment counseling and training
A drop-in center (location for center activities)

These are unique features of the Beethoven Project:

1. It is the first program to ensure that an *entire* kindergarten class is ready for school so the children can take advantage of the educational system.
2. It is prevention-oriented. Many of the problems children encounter could be avoided if they were to receive adequate health care, nurturing, and stimulation in the early months and years of life.
3. It is a community-based project, which works to coordinate existing services of local, state, and federal agencies so that all children in the community have early and continuous access to services.
4. It works with and involves parents *before* the future kindergarten children are born so parents will have the nutrition, health care, and parenting information and skills necessary for bearing and rearing healthy children who will be ready for schooling experiences.

While programs such as Project Beethoven offer some children hope and opportunities, what about the rest—the majority? A former U.S. commissioner of education says:

> The overwhelming fact that must be faced regarding children in the U.S. today is that they are losing ground. Efforts to provide children with healthy and rewarding lives are declining even as the needs for such efforts are growing. The self-interest of adults is taking center stage, and the interests of children are being shoved into the wings.[3]

What, then, are the prospects? Will we keep any of our promises to our children? What can we do? Here is one suggestion:

> The problems of income, education, employment, and family functioning cannot be adequately handled piecemeal and through crisis intervention; many believe that there must be a national mandate, a service agenda to enlist the aid of both the public and the private sectors. According to this view, before government and the nonprofit sector can develop such complementary service priorities, there must be much greater awareness on the part of not only policy makers but also the general public of the needs of America's children and of the current constraints to fulfilling those needs.[4]

More and more of the nation's children are living in poverty. Poverty has many short-term and long-term consequences for children. Society needs to make many efforts to help children enjoy a reasonable standard of living.

CHILD ABUSE AND NEGLECT

Many of our views of childhood are highly romanticized. We tend to believe that parents always love their children and enjoy caring for them. We also tend to believe that family settings are full of joy, happiness, and parent-child harmony. Unfortunately for children, their parents, and for society, these assumptions are not always true.

Child abuse is not new to the 1980s and '90s, although it receives greater attention and publicity than previously. Abuse, in the form of abandonment, infanticide, and neglect, has been documented throughout history. The attitude that children are property is part of the reason for the history of abuse. Parents believed, and some still do, that they own their children and can do with them as they please. The extent to which children are abused is difficult to ascertain, but is probably much greater than most people realize. Valid statistics are difficult to come by because the interest in reporting child abuse is relatively new and because the definitions of child abuse and neglect differ from state to state and reports are categorized differently. It is estimated that there are probably as many as one million incidents of abuse a year, but that only one in four cases is reported.

Because of the increasing concern over child abuse, social agencies, hospitals, child care centers, and schools are becoming more involved in identification, treatment, and prevention of this national social problem. To do something about child abuse, those who are involved with children and parents have to know what abuse is. Public Law 93–247, the Child Abuse Prevention and Treatment Act, defines child abuse and neglect:

> The physical or mental injury, sexual abuse, negligent treatment or maltreatment of a child under the age of eighteen by a person who is responsible for the child's welfare under circumstances which indicate that the child's health or welfare is harmed or threatened thereby as determined in accordance with regulations prescribed by the Secretary.[5]

In addition, all states have some kind of legal or statutory definition for child abuse and treatment and many states are defining penalties for child abuse.

Just as debilitating as physical abuse and neglect is *emotional abuse*. Emotional abuse occurs when parents, teachers, and caregivers strip children of their self-esteem and self-image. Adults take away children's self-esteem through continual criticism, belittling, screaming and nagging, creating fear, and intentionally and severely limiting opportunities. Both abuse and neglect adversely affect children's growth and development.

The guidelines in Table 14–1 may help you identify abuse and neglect; however, one characteristic doesn't necessarily indicate abuse. You should observe the child's behavior and appearance over a period of time. Teachers should also be willing to give parents the benefit of the doubt about a child's condition. These are other ways to deal with suspected abuse:

> You should be aware of the official policy and specific reporting procedures of your school system, and should know your legal obligations and the protections from civil and criminal liability specified in your state's reporting law. (All states provide immunity for mandated, good-faith reports.)
>
> Although you should be familiar with your state's legal definition of abuse and neglect, you are not required to make legal distinctions in order to report. Definitions should serve as guides. If you suspect that a child is abused or neglected, you should report. The teacher's value lies in noticing conditions that indicate that a child's welfare may be in jeopardy.
>
> Be concerned about the rights of the child—the rights to life, food, shelter, clothing, and security. But also be aware of the parents' rights—particularly their rights to be treated with respect and to be given needed help and support.
>
> Bear in mind that reporting does not stigmatize a parent as "evil." The report is the start of a rehabilitative process that seeks to protect the child and help the family as a whole.
>
> A report signifies only the *suspicion* of abuse or neglect. Teachers' reports are seldom unfounded. At the very least, they tend to indicate a need for help and support to the family.

TABLE 14–1 Guidelines for Detecting Abuse and Neglect

Kind of Abuse	Child's Appearance	Child's Behavior	Parent or Caretaker's Behavior
Physical	Unusual bruises, welts, burns, or fractures Bite marks Frequent injuries, explained as "accidental"	Reports injury by parents Unpleasant, hard to get along with, demanding, often disobeys, frequently causes trouble or interferes with others; breaks or damages things; or shy, avoids others, too anxious to please, too ready to let other people say and do things to him/her without protest Frequently late or absent, or comes to school too early or hangs around after school Avoids physical contact with adults Wears long sleeves or other concealing clothing Version of how a physical injury occurred is not believable (doesn't fit type or seriousness of the injury) Seems frightened of parents Shows little or no distress at separation from parents May seek affection from any adult	History of abuse as a child Uses unnecessarily harsh discipline Offers explanation of child's injury that doesn't make sense, doesn't fit injury, or offers no explanation Seems unconcerned about child Sees child as bad, evil, a monster, etc. Misuses alcohol or other drugs Attempts to conceal child's injury or protect identity of responsible party
Emotional	Less obvious signs than other types of mistreatment; behavior is best indication	Unpleasant, hard to get along with, demanding; frequently causes trouble, won't leave others alone Unusually shy, avoids others, too anxious to please, too submissive, puts up with unpleasantness from others without protest Either unusually adult or overly young for age	Blames or belittles child Cold and rejecting Withholds love Treats children unequally Seems not to care about child's problems

TABLE 14–1 Continued

Kind of Abuse	Child's Appearance	Child's Behavior	Parent or Caretaker's Behavior
		(e.g., sucks thumb, rocks constantly)	
		Behind for age physically, emotionally, or intellectually	
Neglect	Often dirty, tired, no energy	Frequently absent	Misuses alcohol or other drugs
	Comes to school without breakfast, often does not have lunch or lunch money	Begs or steals food	Disorganized, upset home life
		Causes trouble in school	Seems not to care what happens
		Often hasn't done homework	Isolated from friends, relatives, neighbors
	Clothes dirty or inappropriate for weather	Uses alcohol or drugs	Doesn't know how to get along with others
	Alone often, for long periods	Engages in vandalism, sexual misconduct	Long-term chronic illnesses
	Needs glasses, dental care, or other medical attention		History of neglect as a child
Sexual	Torn, stained, or bloody underclothing	Withdrawn or engages in fantasy or babyish behavior	Protective or jealous of child
	Pain or itching in genital area	Poor relationships with other children	Encourages child to engage in prostitution or sexual acts in presence of caretaker
	Has veneral disease	Unwilling to participate in physical activities	Misuses alcohol or other drugs
		Engages in delinquent acts or runs away	Frequently absent from home
		Says has been sexually assaulted by parent/caretaker	

Source: United States Department of Health, Education and Welfare, Office of Human Development Services, Administration for Children, Youth and Families, Head Start Bureau, Indian and Migrant Programs Div., New Light on an Old Problem, DHEW Publication No. (OHDS) 78-31108 (Washington, D.C., 1978), pp. 8–11.

If you report a borderline case in good faith, do not feel guilty or upset if it is dismissed as unfounded upon investigation. Some marginal cases are found to be valid.

Don't put off making a report until the end of the school year. Teachers sometimes live with their suspicions until they suddenly fear for the child's safety during the summer months. A delayed report may mean a delay in needed help for the child and the family. Moreover, by reporting late in the school year, you remove yourself as a continued support to both the child protective agency and the reported family.

If you remove yourself from a case of suspected abuse or neglect by passing it on to superiors, you deprive child protective services of one of their most competent sources of information. For example, a teacher who tells a [children's protective services] worker that the child is especially upset on Mondays directs the worker to investigate conditions in the home on weekends. Few persons other than teachers are able to provide this kind of information. Your guideline should be to resolve any question in favor of the child. When in doubt, report. Even if you, as a teacher, have no immunity from liability and prosecution under state law, the fact that your report is made in good faith will free you from liability and prosecution.

In the absence of guidance from the protective agency, the teacher can rely on several general rules for dealing with the abused or neglected child:

Try to give the child additional attention whenever possible.

Create a more individualized program for the child. Lower your academic expectations and make fewer demands on the child's performance—he or she probably has enough pressures and crises to deal with presently at home.

Be warm and loving. If possible, let the child perceive you as a special friend to whom he or she can talk. By abusing or neglecting the child, someone has said in a physical way, "I don't love you." You can reassure the child that someone cares.

Most important, remember that in identifying and reporting child maltreatment, you are not putting yourself in the position of autocrat over a family. The one purpose of your actions is to get help for a troubled child and family; the one goal is to reverse a situation that jeopardizes a child's healthy growth and development.[6]

Causes of Abuse

Why do parents and guardians abuse children? Those who have been responsible for a group of young children will better understand the reasons for child abuse than those who do not know young children. Child rearing is hard work; it requires patience, self-control, understanding, and restraint. It is entirely likely that most parents, at one time or another, have come close to behavior that could be judged abusive.

Stress is one of the most frequent causes of child abuse. Stressful situations arise from employment, divorce or separation, income, quality of family life, moving, death of a family member, violations of law, sickness or injury, and other sources. We are learning more about stress and its effect on health and the general quality of life. Training is offered for dealing with and managing stress. Parenting and teaching are stressful occupations, and parents and teachers often need support from professionals to deal with the stress of their roles.

Lack of parenting information is another reason parents abuse or neglect their children. Some parents don't know what to do or how to do it; these cases more frequently result in acts of omission or neglect than in physical violence. Frequently, the child does not receive proper emotional care and support because the parent is ignorant of this need. Lack of parenting information is attributable to several factors. First, in this mobile population, young parents often live apart from their own parents, and there is little opportunity for grandparents to share child rearing information. Second, the greater number of teenage parents means that many parents are neither emotionally or cognitively ready to have children; they are really children themselves. We need a national effort to put parenting information into the curricula of every elementary and high school program. Fortunately, a trend is beginning in this area.

A third reason for child abuse is the parent's cognitive and emotional state. How people are reared and parenting attitudes that are modeled for them have a tremendous influence on how they will rear their children. Methods of child rearing are handed down from generation to generation, and people who were abused as children are often abusive parents.

A fourth cause of abuse relates to unwanted and unloved children. We like to assume that every child is wanted and loved, but this is not the case. Some parents take out their frustration on their children, whom they view as barriers to their dreams and self-fulfillment. Or, a parent may dislike a child because the child is a constant reminder of an absent spouse.

Some people believe a fifth reason for child abuse is the amount of violence in our society. Opponents of violence on television cite it as an example of people's callousness toward each other and poor role modeling for children.

What can be done? There must be a conscious effort to educate, treat, and help abusers or potential abusers. The school is a good place to begin. There are also organizations such as Parents Anonymous, a national, self-help organization that offers nurturing and therapeutic service to prevent child abuse. Parents Anonymous has chapters in every state. A national, toll free number (800–421–0353) is maintained for all who want and need help. Another source of help is the federal government's National Center on Child Abuse and Neglect, which helps coordinate and develop programs and policies concerning child abuse and neglect. For information, write to: National Center on Child Abuse and Neglect, Children's Bureau, Office of Child Development, Office of Human Development, Department of Health, Education and Welfare, P.O. Box 1182, Washington, D.C. 20012.

Child Abuse Prevention Curricula

Many curricula have been developed to help teachers, caregivers, and parents work with children to prevent abuse. The primary purposes of these programs are to educate children about abuse and to teach them strategies to avoid abuse. Before using an abuse prevention curriculum with children, staff and parents should help select the curriculum and learn how to use it. Parent involvement is essential. As with anything early childhood educators undertake, parents' understanding, approval, and support of a program make its goals easier to achieve. Parents and caregivers should not assume, however, that merely teaching children with an abuse prevention curriculum ends their responsibilities. A parent's responsibility for a child's care and protection never ends. Likewise, teachers and caregivers have the same responsibility for the children entrusted to them.

The National Child Abuse Hotline (800–422–4453) handles crisis calls and provides information and referrals to every county in the United States. The National Committee for Prevention of Child Abuse (NCPCA) is a volunteer organization of concerned citizens that works with community, state, and national groups to expand and disseminate knowledge about child abuse prevention. NCPCA has chapters in almost all states; its address is: National Committee for Prevention of Child Abuse, 332 South Michigan Avenue, Suite 950, Chicago, Ill. 60604 (312–663–3520).

Therapeutic Nurseries

How can one help abusing parents and abused children? One long-standing method is to remove the children from the home and place him in foster care; however, this method may not give the child the help he needs to learn new ways of behaving and of relating to others. An approach that is gaining popularity is the *therapeutic nursery*, of which a major goal is to help children learn ways to express themselves without resorting to anger and violence. These nurseries give children guidance needed to learn new methods of responding other than through the anger and violence they have learned from their parents.

Parents receive training in parenting skills, learning how to interact with, discipline, and guide their children without violence. Parents frequently spend time in the nursery observing and interacting with their children under the direction of counselors and teachers, who help parents break old habits of responding and develop new skills of interaction.

MISSING CHILDREN

Their faces stare out from grocery bags, milk cartons, and utility bills, representatives of the country's lost, missing, strayed, and stolen children. No one really knows how many there are. Many disappear from home; some are stolen by one parent or the other in custody disputes. Some run away from home because of what they think are intolerable conditions. Others are abducted, abused, and murdered. The tragic death of Adam Walsh in 1981 heightened public awareness of the plight of missing children and precipitated passage of child protection laws, including the Missing Children's Assistance Act of 1984. As a result of this act, the National Center for Missing and Exploited Children was established. The Center, created through a cooperative arrangement with the U.S. Department of Justice, Office of Juvenile Justice and Delinquency Prevention, serves as a clearinghouse for information on missing and exploited children; provides training assistance to law enforcement and child protection agencies; assists individuals, agencies, and state and local governments in locating missing children; and administers a national toll-free hot line (800–843–5678) to report information regarding missing children. The address is: National Center for Missing and Exploited Children, 1835 K Street, N.W., Suite 700, Washington, D.C. 20006.

The Center offers these suggestions to parents to help prevent child abduction and exploitation:

☐ Know where your children are at all times. Be familiar with their friends and daily activities.

☐ Be sensitive to changes in your children's behavior; they are a signal that you should sit down and talk to your children about what caused the changes.

☐ Be alert to a teenager or adult who is paying an unusual amount of attention to your children or giving them inappropriate or expensive gifts.

☐ Teach your children to trust their own feelings, and assure them that they have the right to say NO to what they sense is wrong.

☐ Listen carefully to your children's fears, and be supportive in all your discussions with them.

☐ Teach your children that no one should approach them or touch them in a way that makes them feel uncomfortable. If someone does, they should tell the parents immediately.

☐ Be careful about babysitters and any other individuals who have custody of your children.[7]

The Center also offers advice to parents to help them be prepared if their child is missing:

1. **Keep a complete description of the child.** This description must include color of hair, color of eyes, height, weight, and date of birth. In addition, the description should contain their identifiers—eyeglasses or contact lenses, braces on teeth, pierced ears, and other unique physical attributes. The complete description must be written down.

2. **Take color photographs of your child every six months.** Photographs should be of high quality and in sharp focus so that the child is easily recognizable. Head and shoulder portraits from different angles, such as those taken by school photographers, are preferable.

3. **Have your dentist prepare dental charts for your child, and be sure that they are updated each time an examination or dental work is performed.** Make sure that your dentist maintains accurate, up-to-date dental charts and x-rays on your child as a routine part of his or her normal office procedure. If you move, you should get a copy from your former dentist to keep yourself until a new dentist is found.

4. **Know where your child's medical records are located.** Medical records, particularly x-rays, can be invaluable in helping to identify a recovered child. It is important to have all permanent scars, birthmarks, blemishes, and broken bones recorded. You should find out from your child's doctor where such records are located and how you can obtain them if the need arises.

5. **Arrange with your local police department to have your child fingerprinted.** In order for fingerprints to be useful in identifying a person, they must be properly taken. Your police department has trained personnel to be sure that they are useful. The police department will give you the fingerprint card and will *not* keep a record of the child's prints.[8]

SEXISM AND SEX ROLE STEREOTYPING

The reasons for the concern about sex role stereotyping and sexism are essentially the same as those that have promoted our interest in early childhood education. The civil rights movement and its emphasis on equality provided an impetus for seeking more equal treatment for women as well as minority groups. Encouraged by the Civil Rights Act of 1964, which prohibits discrimination on the basis of race or national

Good early childhood settings are nonsexist and avoid sex stereotyping practices.

origin, civil rights and women's groups successfully sought legislation to prohibit discrimination on the basis of sex. Title IX of the Education Amendments Acts of 1972, as amended by Public Law 93–568, prohibits such discrimination in the schools:

> No person in the United States shall on the basis of sex, be excluded from participation in, be denied the benefits of, or be subjected to discrimination under any education program or activity receiving Federal financial assistance.[9]

Since Title IX prohibits sex discrimination in any educational program that receives federal money, early childhood programs as well as elementary schools, high schools, and universities cannot discriminate against males or females in enrollment policies, curriculum offerings, or activities.

The women's movement has encouraged the nation, educational institutions, and families to examine how they educate, treat, and rear children in relationship to sex roles and sex role stereotyping. There have been attempts to examine educational practices and materials for the purpose of eliminating sex-stereotyping content. At the same time, more and more teachers and agencies are developing curricula and activities that will promote a nonexistent environment.

This is how the Federal Register defines *sexism:*

> The collection of attitudes, beliefs, and behaviors which result from the assumption that one sex is superior. *In the context of schools,* the term refers to the collection of structures, policies, practices and activities that overtly or covertly prescribe the development of girls and boys and prepare them for traditional sex roles.[10]

On the basis of sex, parents and society begin at a child's birth to teach a particular sex role. Probably no other factor plays such a determining role in life as does identification with a sex role. It was once thought that certain characteristics of maleness or femaleness were innate; but it is now generally recognized that sex role is a product of socialization, role modeling, and conscious and unconscious behavior modification. Culturally, certain role models are considered appropriate for males and certain roles for females. Traditional male roles center around masculinity; traditional female roles around femininity.

Society imposes and enforces certain sex roles. Schools, as agents of socialization, encourage certain behaviors for boys and different ones for girls. Parents, by the way they dress their children, the toys they give them, and by what they let them do, encourage certain sex role behaviors. Parents also model behaviors for their children and tell them to act "like your mother" or act "like your father." Parents and teachers also modify, shape, and reinforce sex role behavior. "Don't act like a girl," or "Play with this, this is for boys," or "Don't play with that, only girls do that," are a few of the ways they modify behavior toward one sex role or the other.

Educators disagree as to whether children can or should be reared in a non-sex-stereotyped environment. Some say children have a right to determine their own sex roles, and should therefore be reared in an environment that does not impose arbitrary sex roles. Rather, the environment should be free from sex-role stereotyping to encourage the child to develop his or her own sex role. Other educators say it is impossible not to assign sex roles. In addition, they argue that development of a sex role is a difficult task of childhood and children need help in this process.

It is too simplistic to say one will not assign or teach a particular sex role. As society is now constituted, differentiated sex roles are still very much in evidence and likely to remain so. Parents and teachers should provide children with less restrictive options and promote a more open framework in which sex roles can develop. These are some ways to provide a less sex stereotyped environment:

☐ *Provide opportunities for all children to experience the activities, materials, toys, and emotions traditionally associated with both sexes.* Don't deny a male the opportunity to experience tenderness, affection, and the warmth of close parent and child, teacher and pupil relationships. Conversely, don't deny females the opportunity to experience aggressive behavior, get dirty, and participate in typically male activities.

☐ *Examine the classroom materials you are using and plan to use to determine whether they contain obvious instances of sex stereotyping.* When you find examples, modify the materials or don't use them. Let the publishers know your feelings and tell other faculty members about them.

☐ *Examine your behavior to see whether you are encouraging sex stereotypes.* Do you tell girls they can't empty wastebaskets, but they can water the plants? Do you tell girls they can't lift certain things in the classroom because they are too heavy for them? Do you give the female students most of your attention? Do you reward only females who are always passive, well-behaved, and well-mannered?

☐ *Have a colleague or parent observe you in your classroom to determine what sex role behaviors you are encouraging.* We are often unaware of our behaviors, and self-correction begins only after the behaviors are pointed out to us. Obviously, unless you begin with yourself, eliminating sex role stereotyping practices will be next to impossible.

☐ *Determine what physical arrangements in the classroom promote or encourage sex role stereotyping.* Are boys encouraged to use the block area more than girls? Are girls encouraged to use the quiet areas more than boys? Do children hang their wraps separately, a place for the boys and a place for the girls? All children should have equal access to all learning areas of the classroom; no area should be reserved exclusively for one sex.

☐ *Counsel with parents to show them ways to promote nonsexist child rearing.* If society is to achieve a truly nonsexist environment, parents will be the key factor, for it is in the home that many sex stereotyping behaviors are initiated and practiced.

☐ *Become conscious of words that promote sexism.* For example, in a topic on community helpers, taught in most preschool and kindergarten programs at one time or another, many words carry a sexist connotation. *Fireman, policeman,* and *mailman* are all masculine terms; nonsexist terms would be *firefighter, police officer,* and *mail carrier.* You should examine all your curricular materials and teaching practices to determine how you can make them free from sexism.

☐ *Examine your teaching and behavior to be sure you are not limiting certain roles to either sex.* Females should not be encouraged to pursue only roles that are subservient, submissive, lacking in intellectual demands, or low paying.

☐ *Do not encourage children to dress in ways that lead to sex stereotyping.* Females should not be encouraged to wear frilly dresses, then forbidden to participate in an activity because they might get dirty or spoil their clothes. Children should be encouraged to dress so they will be able to participate in a wide range of activities both indoors and outdoors. This is an area in which you may be able to help parents if they seek your advice. Or, you may want to discuss how dressing their child differently can contribute to more effective participation.

TELEVISION: TO VIEW OR NOT TO VIEW

Television is a fact of life; despite its critics, it is not going to go away. Television does serve many useful functions; it informs us of news events and political processes. It is also a companion and babysitter. Many people, especially the elderly, rely on television as a companion. On the other hand, many family conflicts revolve around who is going to watch what and how long they are going to watch it.

Action for Children's Television (ACT) is a nonprofit child advocacy organization that works to encourage diversity in children's television (20 University Road, Cambridge, Mass. 02138). It also discourages overcommercialization of children's programming and tries to eliminate deceptive advertising aimed at young children. ACT provides some interesting data about children's television viewing:

- ☐ The *average* American family watches more than seven hours of television *a day*
- ☐ Children watch an average of 27 hours of television each week, or almost four hours each day
- ☐ By the time they are 18, most children will have spent more time watching television than in school
- ☐ Advertisers spend over $600 million a year selling to children on television
- ☐ Children see about 20,000 thirty-second commercials each year, or about three hours of television advertising each week
- ☐ Most of the programs children watch are intended for adults
- ☐ Over a million young children are still watching television at midnight[11]

Parents and teachers tend to make one of two responses to the impact of television on children. One response is that we shouldn't try to fight it; we might as well let children watch what they wish whenever they wish. The second response is just as short-sighted: all television is bad and children shouldn't be allowed to watch it at all. But we cannot ignore television's educational value; rather, we need to use its best elements effectively and minimize the undesirable.

Two processes occur when a child watches television. One is the reaction to the content of the program. Whether the child is watching an educational or a violent program, he reacts to it on the basis of his experiences. The second process is the act of television viewing, including the environment in which viewing occurs. Environmental variables are where the viewing occurs, the people one watches with, the interaction that occurs with others while viewing, other activities that occur while viewing, and what the individual does while viewing. All these variables contribute to the child's viewing habits, which in turn determine how much, how long, and what programs he will watch.

Some critics try to make parents feel guilty about letting their children watch much television, and criticize parents for watching it themselves. We often say a child is better off doing something other than watching television, but this is not necessarily true. As parents or as teachers, we cannot say that all television is bad, or that not watching any television is good. The ideal is to guide children's viewing and to keep the viewing time within reasonable limits.

Advertising

One of the main criticisms of television is directed at its advertising. One frequently hears the complaint that the advertisements have become the program.

> What is happening—and what is fast becoming evident throughout children's TV—is that the medium has found an insidious new way to exploit its most impressionable audience. The practice of spinning off toy products from characters in kiddie entertainment is, of course, as old as Mickey Mouse ears and Dick Tracy rings. These days, however, the creative order has reversed; instead of deriving the product from the program, toymakers and animation houses now build the entire kidvid shows around planned or existing lines of playthings. The programs can become, in effect, little more than half-hour commercials for their toy casts.[12]

Specific criticisms center around these points: Television advertising places a great deal of pressure on children to buy, or to ask their parents to buy, the products advertised. Children have not learned to defer gratification, nor can they judge whether a product is good for them. They want immediate gratification, and they want the product. It is questionable to what extent children have the ability to distinguish between the commercial and the product it advertises. Young children, especially, may consider the commercial the program. Thus they are ingrained at an early age with the concept of immediate gratification, which is one reason critics seriously propose banning commercials aimed at children under the age of eight.

Television commercials also present an unrealistic view of the world. Most children's homes are not like those shown on TV. With millions of children living at or below the poverty level, many of the homes shown and products advertised are a fantasy world for children. Some psychologists claim that television commercials put pressure on parents because their children demand the things they see advertised. This pressure can lead to conflict between parent and child and can arouse guilt on the part of parents.

Many consumer advocates feel that television commercials aimed at children advertise products that are not good for them. A current objection is to products containing high proportions of sugar, many of which are low in nutritional value and can create health problems, such as tooth decay. Some advertising may contradict accepted or parental nutritional practices or customs; for example, many parents encourage children not to eat between meals or to eat only certain kinds of food at particular times, while television advertising can create the impression that it is all right to eat candy anytime.

Children's Responses to Commercials

Do the commercials children watch really influence them to be consumers of the advertised products? Apparently so, if not as direct consumers, then at least through their parents. In a controlled experiment, children aged three to five watched a twenty-minute children's cartoon program, complete with selected food commercials. Children and their mothers were assigned to one of three television viewing conditions: a mother-child situation, in which they watched the programs and commercials together; a situation in which the child viewed the television program and its commercials while the parent, in another room, viewed only the television program; and a control group, in which mother and child viewed the television program together, but did not see the commercials.

> First, children who were exposed to television food commercials emitted more bids for the advertised food products than children in the control condition. However, only children who viewed the commercial messages with their mothers bid on more different advertised products than did children in the control condition. What does this mean? It means that the television commercials were effective in getting the young viewers to nag their parents for advertised foods. It also means that when children and their mothers viewed the commercial messages together the children tried to persuade their mothers to buy more of the 6 advertised products than did children in the control condition. It could be that children in the *mother-child viewing* condition thought they would have a better chance at persuading their mothers to purchase more of the advertised products because their mothers had also been exposed to the appeal of the commercial messages.[13]

The investigators concluded that commercials for food are probably even more effective in the child's natural environment than in the experimental situations, and the commercials do influence parents' consumer behavior.

Television and Violence

A classic study of modeled aggressive behavior determined the extent to which children imitate aggression. In undertaking the study, the authors hypothesized that observed aggression would lead to a greater number of aggressive responses.

> To the extent that observation of adults displaying aggression conveys a certain degree of permissiveness for aggressive behavior, it may be assumed that such exposure not only facilitates the learning of new aggressive responses but also weakens competing inhibitory responses in subjects and thereby increases the probability of occurrence of previously learned patterns of aggression. It was predicted, therefore, that subjects who observed aggressive models would display significantly more aggression when subsequently frustrated than subjects who were equally frustrated but who had no prior exposure to models exhibiting aggression.[14]

As expected, the results of the study supported the theory that "exposure to filmed aggression heightens aggressive reactions in children." In a similar study to determine the effect on children of viewing aggression in cartoons, Ellis and Sekyra found that

> Overall, it can be concluded that viewing film-mediated aggression did have an influence on the *Ss*' behavior. It appeared that the effect of viewing an aggressive cartoon sequence was an increased rate of emitted hostile behaviors by the *Ss* when observed in his natural environment. These data suggest that serious consideration should be given to the content of children's cartoons.[15]

Television and its influences will continue to be a part of everyone's life. Parents and educators must attempt to capitalize on television as a vehicle to educate and inform. On the other hand, they must not let television become a child's constant com-

Because children frequently imitate the aggressive behavior they see on television, teachers should show them alternative ways to solve problems.

panion and baby-sitter. One solution to excessive viewing is to offer meaningful alternative activities. If children are busy with sports, household chores, and community and service groups, they really don't have time to watch much television. As we mentioned in our discussion of behavior management, children can't do two things simultaneously—they can't be involved in a community project at a local nursing home and watch television at the same time.

For preschool parents, the solution is even simpler: don't allow children to develop television habits that lead to excessive viewing and dependency. A general guideline is that if children are watching so much television that they don't have time for or are not involved in other activities, such as reading, household chores, or community involvement, they are probably watching too much. Parents need to understand, and early childhood educators need to help them realize, that parents are the ultimate key to their children's television viewing habits and, to some extent, the effects viewing has on them. Parents' viewing habits serve as a model for children's viewing habits:

It is clear that where mothers establish more rules about television, limiting viewing or allowing particular shows while forbidding others, the children are less likely to show the *negative* effects of television viewing.[16]

MAKING EARLY CHILDHOOD PROGRAMS HUMANE

Some classrooms seem to destroy children's personal dignity. In a dehumanized classroom, a child thinks less of herself than she ought to because of the conditions and atmosphere of the setting. On the other hand, a humane setting encourages children's full development and treats them as good and worthy human beings. A continual challenge to early childhood educators is how to make centers, homes, classrooms, and buildings in which they teach humane settings.

Interrelationship of Intelligence, Emotions, and Behavior

We tend to talk of the cognitive (intellectual), affective (feeling, emotional), and psychomotor (behavioral) domains as though they were separate and distinct. Table 14–2 shows the relationship among the three domains; all three areas must be accounted for in the instructional process and cannot be easily compartmentalized. Neither is it possible to assign topics or activities to one area with absolute assurance that they belong only to that area. Failure to integrate the three domains encourages fragmentation of teaching and usually emphasizes the cognitive domain to the exclusion of

TABLE 14–2 Interrelationship of the Cognitive, Affective, and Psychomotor Domains in a Humanized Early Childhood Setting

Domain	Intrapersonal	Interpersonal
Cognitive	Learning about body parts and how the body functions	Identifying likenesses and differences among people
	Learning right from left	
	Identifying the letters of one's name	
	Identifying colors of foods	
Affective	Identifying what foods one likes	Deciding what they want for snack time
	Deciding what one wants for a snack	Group discussions about favorite foods
Behavioral (Psychomotor)	Being able to walk well	Planning a grocery trip
	Playing games requiring knowledge of right and left	Shopping for food
	Writing one's name	Making cookies with everyone helping
	Eating favorite foods	
	Cutting carrots for snack	

Teachers are the key to making early childhood programs humane, and a sense of humanity should underlie all of our programs for and interactions with young children.

the other two, particularly the affective. There has also been a tendency to think education cannot have both achievement and humanistic goals. Now more educators are realizing that we need not choose between teaching the basics (achievement) or having a humanistic setting (values); it is possible and desirable to have both.

Requirements of Humane Settings

A humanized classroom is not so much a place as a condition or atmosphere in which a series of forces interact to enable meaningful learning and living. Specific items vary according to the social setting, different groups of children, and teacher attitude. We can, however, generalize about humanistic schools, learning settings, teachers, and curriculum. The school is open to the community; encourages community involvement; promotes student freedom; and encourages student growth toward independence. The learning setting is individualized and self-paced; is flexible in time (no rigid time schedule) and space (learning can occur anywhere); and provides an emotionally secure atmosphere. The teacher respects and trusts children; is honest and accepting; believes in, promotes, and provides for individual differences;

promotes a feeling of human warmth; and encourages children to express their own ideas. The curriculum is based on children's interests; learning is considered a life-long process; integrates subject matter with children's interests; is based on the whole student (not just as he exists in school); utilizes real-life problems in place of hypothetical ones; integrates the cognitive, affective and psychomotor; is based on planning by both teachers and children; and provides for development of the affective domain. At the heart of how to making early childhood settings more humane is the issue of child-centered education. When anything gets in the way of children's best interests, then children are pushed from the center and replaced by whatever is given priority, whether subject matter, testing, accountability, or something else. One of our roles as educators and caregivers is to continue our efforts to promote child-centered learning through humane environments, practices, and interpersonal relationships.

FURTHER READING

Arnet, Ruth P. *Stress and Your Child: A Parent's Guide to Symptoms, Strategies, and Benefits* (Englewood Cliffs, N.J.: Prentice-Hall, 1984) Comprehensive review and discussion of major factors causing stress in young children; also provides practical and useful suggestions for understanding stress and how caregivers can help alleviate situations that cause stress.

Blom, Gaston E., et al. *Stress in Childhood: An Intervention Model for Teachers and Other Professionals* (New York: Teachers College Press, 1986) A stress-intervention model for teachers and other caregivers to apply without becoming therapists; also suggests time-efficient interventions adaptable to a teacher's role. Describes children experiencing stress and their behavioral responses to it.

Brenner, Avis. *Helping Children Cope With Stress* (Lexington, Mass.: Lexington Books, 1984) Describes the many kinds of stress operating on and affecting children and ways that caregivers and parents can help children cope with stress.

Broadhurst, Diane D., Margaret Edmunds, and Robert A. MacDicken. *Early Childhood Programs and the Prevention and Treatment of Child Abuse and Neglect* (Washington, D.C.: National Center on Child Abuse and Neglect, Children's Bureau, Administration for Children, Youth and Families, Office of Human Development Services. DHEW Publications No. (OHDS) 79–30198, August, 1979) Discusses the large percentage of preschool children involved in cases of abuse and neglect.

Edwards, Carolyn Pope. *Promoting Social and Moral Development in Young Children: Creative Approaches for the Classroom* (New York: Teachers College Press, 1986) Describes a creative approach to social-cognitive development of children aged two to six based on Piagetian theory; seven areas of social and moral development.

Fernandez, John P. *Child Care and Corporate Productivity: Resolving Family/Work Conflicts* (Lexington, Mass.: D.C. Heath, 1986) Summarizes results of a survey of 5000 employees at five corporations regarding views and perceptions of child care; useful data to support decisions about meeting employee needs for child care.

Hill, S., and B. J. Barnes, eds. *Young Children and their Families: Needs of the Nineties* (Lexington, Mass.: Lexington Books, 1982) Expected trends for young children.

Landau, Hortense R. (Chairperson). *The Abused and Neglected Child 1982* (Practising Law Institute, 1982) Explores legal ramifications of child abuse with examples and case studies from judicial proceedings; helps reader understand rights of children and their guardians.

Liebert, Robert M., Joyce N. Sprafkin, and Emily S. Davidson. *The Early Window: Effects of Television on Children and Youth* (New York: Pergamon Press, 1982) Account of television, its effects, and how it operates. Many research summaries and statistical data.

Marotz, Lynn, Jeanettia Rush, and Marie Cross. *Health, Safety, and Nutrition for the Young Child.* (Albany, N.Y.: Delmar, 1985) Interrelates the areas of health, safety, and nutrition; focuses on prevention.

Miller, M. S. *Childstress: Understanding and Answering Stress Signals of Infants, Children, and Teenagers* (New York: Doubleday, 1982) Defines child's internal and external resources to cope with stress; lists signals to help adults identify stress in children.

Sarafino, Edward P. *The Fears of Childhood* (New York: Human Sciences Press, 1985) Describes what children fear, why fears develop, and how parents and caregivers can help children overcome anxieties; presents specific ways to prevent fears from developing and straightforward advice on helping children when fears do arise.

Singer, Dorothy G., Jerome L. Singer, and Diana M. Zackerman. *Teaching Television: How to Use TV To Your Child's Advantage* (New York: Dial Press, 1981) Encourages parents to use television programs to stimulate learning and creative activities.

Veitch, Beverly, and Thelma Harms. *Cook and Learn: A Child's Cookbook* (Menlo Park, Calif.: Addison-Wesley, 1981) Teaching aid to explore learning through cooking with children. Single-portion recipes develop sound nutritional principles and awareness of foods from many cultures, encourage oral communication, motivate language development, and introduce mathematical relationships.

FURTHER STUDY

1. Examine children's readers and supplemental materials to determine instances of sexism. What recommendations would you make to change such practices?

2. Watch children's television from 8 a.m. to noon on a Saturday morning. Cite instances of sexism. Write to the producers of the programs and advertisers stating your objections to such material and practices.

3. Observe children in both school and nonschool settings for examples of how dress reflects sex stereotyping, and how parents' behaviors promote sex stereotyping.

4. Survey children to find out what their favorite television programs are. Find out why they like the programs. What does this data tell you?

5. Contact organizations that are trying to reduce the amount and kind of violence and commercials on television programs aimed at children. Two such organizations are the National Parents and Teachers Association, and Action for Children's Television (46 Austin Street, Newtonville, Massachusetts 02160). Find out the purposes of these groups. Decide whether you agree or disagree with what they are trying to do.

6. We tend to ignore the role of the environment and materials in promoting sexism, but they do play a powerful role. Examine the environment of classrooms and homes to determine the extent of sexist practices. Make recommendations based on your findings.

7. Become familiar with the child abuse laws in your state. What are the responsibilities of teachers and other school personnel?

8. Interview social workers and other public service personnel who work with abused children and their families. Determine the problems, issues, and frustrations in working with these groups.

9. Interview people in your community to determine typical attitudes toward and means of punishment of children in different cultures. Be specific, so you can be aware of similarities and differences. What implications do these have for the teacher's role in reporting child abuse?

10. Visit child care centers, preschools, and primary grade classrooms. What features in the environments would you consider inhumane? Humane? Explain your opinions. What caregiver/teacher behaviors did you observe that contributed positively and negatively to a humane atmosphere? Provide specific examples.

11. What *effects* of stress have you noticed in children? Give specific examples.

12. Do you agree or disagree that today's children are being "hurried"? What can teachers and caregivers do to relieve or reduce stress in children?

13. What are five reasons for the increase in reported child abuse? Do you think the public's heightened awareness of child abuse will help reduce the causes of abuse?

14. As the director of a child care center, what would you do when hiring staff to assure that a person did not have a history of child abuse? How could you and your staff help parents protect their children from abuse?

15. Review a curriculum for young children designed to protect them from child abuse. Do you think the curriculum content is appropriate for the ages for which it is intended? Would you want the program used with your child? Why or why not?

16. What are six issues and concerns for children, parents, and the early childhood profession that emerge from the national attention to child abuse?

17. In addition to those mentioned in this chapter, identify five emerging contemporary concerns/issues associated with the education and care of young children. Defend your selections.

18. Why does it sometimes seem that this country does not treat children as its greatest asset?

19. List five of the most serious problems young children face today. Identify the causes of and reasons for each problem, and propose realistic solutions for each.

15

Responsible Caregiving and Teaching: Becoming a Professional

As you read and study:

Examine the relationship between an early childhood teacher's attitude and character and the healthy growth of children

Analyze qualities of early childhood teachers that are worthy of emulation

Analyze and understand the roles of early childhood educators

Discuss and evaluate trends in early childhood education as they relate to teacher training and classroom practices

Develop a philosophy of early childhood education

Begin to develop a personal plan for becoming a professional

A s we approach the twenty-first century, many people try to forecast what life will be like. The consensus of the forecasters is that learning will be considered a lifelong process and that more money will be spent on education. As an early childhood educator, you should be prepared to take your place in a world where learning is valued and respected.

CURRENT CHANGES IN EDUCATION

Minimum Standards for Teaching

There is a trend toward requiring teacher college graduates to pass minimum basic skills tests before they receive a teaching certificate. Testing for teacher certification is a direct result of the accountability movement, the back-to-basics movement, and the reaction against grade inflation and "soft" or "easy" education courses. Some state tests include items for assessing basic teaching and literacy skills. Critics of education contend that it only makes sense to require teachers to demonstrate that they know the skills we expect them to teach young children.

Closely associated with the testing movement in teacher education is the fifth-year training concept. Teacher training programs find it difficult to provide all the experiences a teacher needs in a four-year program; consequently, five- and six-year training programs are being developed. The fifth year may take place at the college or university, or in a school district as a probationary period. In some programs, the fifth year may result in a master's degree, so people who choose teaching as a career can expect to spend more time learning how to become a good teacher.

Changing Clientele

Early childhood programs will begin to serve different types of children in different ways. For example, as a result of P.L. 94–142 and P.L. 99–457, there will be more young (birth to age five) handicapped children in programs receiving federal money. This means new programs will have to be developed and teachers trained or retrained to provide appropriate services. Likewise, the gifted child will receive more attention, which also means retraining teachers and developing new programs.

Teacher Role

The role of the teacher will continue to be reconceptualized. Teachers will be trained to work with parents, design curriculum materials, and plan programs for paraprofessionals, such as teacher aides, to implement. Many schools currently operate a system of differentiated staffing that employs teachers and aides with differing role functions, levels of responsibility, training, and salary.

Differentiated staffing will be accompanied by differentiated teaching. There will be closer attention to different learning styles. Greater attention to learning styles will also involve greater use of concrete learning materials, self-selected activities, and use of students as tutors.

Field-Based Education

Until recently, most people agreed that teacher training should occur in colleges of education, but now the trend is toward training teachers in field settings. Critics of traditional approaches fail to see a relationship between theoretical college teaching and the real world of public schools, day care centers, and Head Start programs. The question is essentially one of relevance and effectiveness. For their part, students say that college classrooms are not relevant to the real world of teaching in good early childhood programs, particularly after they have experienced the exhilaration of helping or teaching in a classroom. Undoubtedly, more colleges will provide field-based settings for educating teachers. Many colleges of education have arrangements with public school districts for preservice teachers to spend blocks of time in the schools under the supervision of experienced classroom teachers. There is also a trend toward student teaching earlier in the teacher education program. The practice of reserving student teaching for the final semester of the senior year is no longer considered sensible because potential teachers may not discover until it is too late that they don't like children or teaching, and because it really requires more than one semester of working with children to gain the necessary basic skills for beginning teaching.

QUALITIES OF THE EARLY CHILDHOOD EDUCATOR

Anyone who has contemplated teaching has probably asked, "Am I the kind of person who is suited for teaching?" This is a difficult question to answer honestly. These are qualities early childhood teachers need: caring, compassion, courtesy, dedication, empathy, enthusiasm, friendliness, helpfulness, honesty, intelligence, kindness, loving, motivation, patience, sensitivity, trustingness, understanding, and warmth. Home and early school experiences are more responsible for developing these qualities than are teacher education programs, so we can conclude that if we want these qualities in our future teachers, we need to promote them *now,* in our teaching of young children. Toward that end, teachers might well concentrate on nurturing in themselves what are probably the most important of these characteristics: enthusiasm and caring.

As a teacher, you will live and work in a classroom where things don't always go well; where children don't always learn ably and well; where children are not always clean and free from illness and hunger; where children's and parents' backgrounds and ways of life are different from yours. If you truly care, teaching is not easy. Caring means you will lose sleep trying to find a way to help a child learn to read, that you will spend your own money to buy materials, that you will spend long hours planning and gathering materials. Caring also means you will not leave your intelligence, enthusiasm, or talents outside the classroom, but will bring them into the classroom, principal's office, and school board meeting.

Teaching is and should be a joyful experience.

Teaching: A Helping Profession

Teaching is an integral part of the broader range of human services and helping professions. The sharp lines that have traditionally separated social work, the health professions, and education are gradually blurring; however, members of all three professions are still reluctant to admit that the other professionals can provide meaningful services that complement their own. Before you make your career choice, you should know what careers are available in the helping professions. Many areas of expertise in these professions overlap and complement each other. There is also a trend toward resolving social problems through interdisciplinary programs, to which each profession contributes its particular expertise.

Saying a kind word to a child is helping. It helps him build a better self-image by showing that you care about him as a person. Teaching is also a helping process when the teacher takes time to be with and talk to children. We must not overlook the many opportunities in the school day to make teaching a helping profession in every sense.

The Preliminaries

Teaching can be a great and rewarding career for those who want it to be so. There are some things you can do to make your career happy and productive for both you and the children you will teach.

Go where the jobs are. The two factors most responsible for the declining demand for teachers are an oversupply of teachers and the trend toward zero population growth. But there will always be a job for the individual who is willing to go where the jobs are. Most problems of teacher oversupply are geographical; don't limit yourself to your hometown.

Seek every opportunity for experiences with all kinds of children in all kinds of settings. Individuals often limit themselves to experiences in public school settings, but there are also opportunities through church schools, child care, baby-sitting, and children's clothing stores to broaden and expand your knowledge of children. These experiences can often be work-related and can be doubly rewarding. Sometimes these positions pay little or nothing, but be willing to volunteer your services, because volunteer positions have a way of leading to paid positions. Many career possi-

The kinds of skills this young volunteer is learning can benefit a prospective teacher.

bilities and opportunities can become available through the volunteer route. Before committing yourself to training for one teaching specialty, volunteer in at least three different areas of education to find out exactly what age and field of education you are most interested in. Do other volunteer work with children in activities such as recreation, social events, or scouting.

Honestly analyze your attitudes and feelings toward children. Do you really want to teach, or would you be happier in another field? During your experiences with children, you should constantly test your attitude toward teaching. If you decide that teaching isn't for you because of how you feel about children, then by all means don't teach.

Explore the possibilities for educational service in areas and fields other than the public school. Don't limit your career choices and alternatives because of your limited conception of the teacher's role. Students often think teacher education prepares an individual only to teach. Other opportunities for service include religious organizations, federal, state, and local agencies, private educational enterprises, hospitals, libraries, and social work. Don't feel pressured to choose a major during your first year or two in college. Take a variety of electives that will help you in career choices, and talk to vocational counselors. Don't make up your mind too quickly about teaching a certain grade level or age range. Many teachers find out, much to their surprise, that the grade level they *thought* was best for them was not. You should remain flexible about a grade or subject level.

Employ every educational opportunity to enhance your training program and career. Through wise course selection, weaknesses can be strengthened and new alternatives explored. For example, if your program of studies requires a certain number of social science credits, use them to explore areas such as sociology and anthropology, which have fascinating relationships to education. Electives practicing teachers sometimes wish they had taken in college are typing, first aid, audiovisual aids and media, behavior modification/management, special education, creative writing, and arts and crafts. Of course, a teacher can never have too strong a background in child development.

AS I SEE IT

Linda Anthony, Toddler I Teacher

I became a child caregiver after working at Catholic Charities Day Care Center in Washington, D.C., as a summer youth employee in 1974. I enjoyed the job then and I still enjoy it now. What I like about my job is being able to watch children grow mentally, verbally, and physically and knowing that I have some part in their growth.

I think a good teacher is one who is willing to do anything to enhance learning. She should be creative, alert, and able to make learning fun and exciting. She should be able to give hugs and kisses as well as define limits. She should also have a good sense of humor. In day care the caregiver must be able to make a child feel comfortable enough to allow his mother to leave him. Once the child begins to trust you, he will also be willing to learn.

The most important thing about my job is keeping the children safe. There will always be little accidents in day care, like bumps on heads, bruised knees, and cut fingers. The staff must be alert enough to prevent any serious accidents.

A few things make me really mad about the policy makers for child care services. They look at caregivers as people whose role does not matter. There is so much disregard for how caregivers feel. Policy makers do very little to make one feel good about one's job. The pay is so low that many good caregivers must leave day care to survive and take care of their families. Sometimes I think all their talk about children being our greatest asset and making child care workers' pay more decent is so they can be comfortable with doing nothing.

My advice to others wanting to be caregivers is that when you work with young children, you must remember that children are people too, and you are their role model. Therefore, try not to do anything you are ashamed of in the presence of children, and always be conscious of your actions.

Deborah Robinson-Yarborough, Child Care Project Director

After receiving a Bachelor of Arts degree from Howard University in 1969, I accepted a position as a second-grade teacher with the Washington, D.C., public schools. The stringent curriculum guidelines made it difficult to create an environment that would foster creative and spontaneous learning. After two years in the school system I vowed to find a position that would afford me freedom of expression and self-satisfaction, a position that would allow for creativity and innovativeness. Before I accepted a position as director of a school-age day care center in 1971, I had not been aware of the existence of day care programs for elementary school children.

The center housed forty children, ages five to fourteen, whose parents worked or were in job training programs. It opened for children at 3 P.M. and closed at 7 P.M. during the regular school year; during Easter, Christmas, and summer vacations, it was open from 7 A.M. to 7 P.M. Activities included homework assistance, indoor and outdoor recreation, skills reinforcement by means of educational games, and other fun activities such as field trips. Other services for the children and their parents were in the health, social services, nutrition, and mental health areas.

The program was known as the National Child Day Care Association's Day Care After School (DACAS) program. It afforded me the freedom to create an environment that would make children want to learn and create. The center proved to be a vehicle for me, the children, and the staff to explore various methods and techniques of open education that allowed the children to be part of the decision-making process. Parent involvement was considered crucial to the program's success. Monthly parent meetings covered topics ranging from education and parenting to the more immediately relevant issues of landlord-tenant relations.

The program also provided career development opportunities for me. It helped give me the incentive to pursue a Master of Education degree at the Catholic University of America. After less than two years as a center director, I accepted the position as project director (the administrator for the entire five-center, 310-child, DACAS program). Still striving for new and innovative ways to operate school-age day care centers, I altered the existing program to accommodate children both before and after school. The "before school" concept, which began in 1977, grew out of a need for parents to have their children supervised in the early morning hours because of early work schedules.

The program I currently administer is now called the Day Care After School (DACAS)-Extended Day Care program of the National Child Day Care Association—hence DACAS-Extended Day. It operates from 7 A.M. to 9 A.M. and from 3 P.M. to 7 P.M. on regular school days. The "morning"/"before" program provides gymnastics and organized games and coordinates with the public schools breakfast program. The afternoon program continues to provide indoor and outdoor recreation, homework assistance, learning centers for fun and skills reinforcement, educational games, social services, health services, nutrition, psychological services, arts and crafts, drama, and field trips.

During the extended periods (summer, Christmas, and Easter) the centers operate from 7 A.M. until 7 P.M. Afternoon program activities are expanded to include three balanced meals, excursions to areas of interest such as amusement parks, Boy Scouts, circuses, and city park activities. Parent-involvement activities also increase during the extended periods. Parents are more likely to volunteer for classroom and center activities such as crafts and chaperoning out-of-town trips. Area merchants often donate items for program picnics and athletic awards programs.

In recent years, special projects—grants received, curriculum changes—have served to rejuvenate me as well as the program I administer. Several years ago I wrote a mini-proposal and received a small grant to put on a Black Jazz Concert for children featuring local singers and musicians. During the summer of 1982, I set up a program with the Capitol Children's Museum of Washington, D.C., to have all 318 children in the program receive six one-hour sessions for five- to seven-year-olds and eight one-and-a-half-hour sessions for eight to fourteen-year-olds on Atari 800 microcomputers. The younger children got their first introduction to computer literacy, while the older groups also learned computer language.

In January of 1985, I sponsored the first "Just Say No" to Drugs Club in the Washington metropolitan area and the second club in the entire nation. The charter members of the club, which included my 10-year-old daughter, Shelley, and my 9-year-old son, Shawn, accompanied me to all the school-age day care centers to talk to and recruit members to the "Just Say No" Club. In April of 1985 and May of 1986 the charter members led groups of day care center students and more than 2,000 elementary school students to the White House at the invitation of First Lady Nancy Reagan. These events, known as annual "Just Say No" walks have become national events. The First Lady is now the honorary national sponsor of "Just Say No" clubs. The Day Care Centers conduct "Just Say No" activities year-round, including swimming meets, bowling, and bake sales.

The "Just Say No" clubs have rejuvenated this project director for several more years of service. Having just completed fifteen years in the field, I have no regrets about leaving the "teaching" profession, for even though I am following a government-approved curriculum of activities, I designed the curriculum, and my students are learning extremely important lessons in life with their many opportunities for educational and cultural enrichment.

Being a project director of a school-age day care program has afforded me (within budgetary limitations) opportunities for innovation as well as personal growth and development that would not have been possible in a public school system. It has also opened up other avenues yet to be explored. Most important, it has taught me not to measure success by the size of a paycheck or the number of pluses on a performance evaluation. While these variables have a certain degree of importance, the greatest indicators of my success in this vocation have been the smiles, kind words of thanks, and other expressions of gratitude from students, past and present, and their families. These have given me the strength and enthusiasm to try for yet another fifteen years!

Start now to develop a philosophy of education and teaching. Your philosophy should be based upon what you believe about children and the learning process, how you think children should be taught, and your present values. A philosophy of teaching serves as a guide for classroom practice. Many teachers fill the school day and children's lives with unrelated activities, without considering whether they match their objectives. So much of teaching is based on no philosophy at all. In fact, your philosophy may be the only guide to help you teach, for as surprising as it may seem, many schools operate without a written philosophy. Basing your teaching on a philosophy will make the difference between filling children's school days with unrelated activities or with activities directed toward helping them learn and develop to their fullest potential. As you develop your philosophy during preservice training, discuss it with friends, professors, and inservice teachers, and be willing to revise your philosophy as you gain new knowledge and insights. Developing a philosophy will not automatically make you a good teacher, but it will provide a foundation on which to build a good teaching career. (An added benefit of developing a philosophy is that it will help you respond well during a job interview.)

Examine your willingness to dedicate yourself to teaching. Acquaint yourself thoroughly with what teaching involves. Visit many different kinds of schools. Is the school atmosphere one in which you want to spend the rest of your life? Talk with many teachers to learn what is involved in teaching. Ask yourself "Am I willing to work hard? Am I willing to give more time to teaching than a teaching contract may specify? Are teachers the kind of people with whom I want to work? Do I have the physical energy for teaching? Do I have the enthusiasm necessary for good teaching?"

In Practice

When you enter the teaching profession, several other suggestions will help you find your career more productive and rewarding.

Adjust to the ever-emerging new careers of teaching and society. All careers are molded by the needs of society and the resources available. Many teachers and schools waste potential and miss opportunities because of their unwillingness to adjust to changing circumstances and conditions.

Be willing to improve your skills and increase your knowledge. Many teachers choose to do this by returning to school, which is usually encouraged by state certification requirements for permanent or continuing certification. Many teachers fulfill the requirements through a master's degree. A trend in teacher certification is to allow accumulation of a specified number of "points," gained through college credits, inservice programs, attendance at professional meetings and conferences, and other professional involvements. Unfortunately, minimum requirements are often taken as maximum requirements.

Becoming a good teacher is a never-ending process and a lifelong quest.

Reading is one method of self-improvement; a less obvious method is to force change by periodically teaching at different grade levels. By changing grade levels, teachers gain new insights into and perspectives on children and teaching. Whatever method you choose for self-improvement, you should recognize the need for constant retraining. While some school districts do provide opportunities for retraining, most of the responsibility will be yours.

Be willing to try new things. Some new teachers get in a rut immediately upon entering the profession. They feel their college education has provided them with the one right way to teach children. This attitude results in a preconceived, fixed notion of what teaching is. These teachers become so preoccupied with fulfilling this image of good teaching that they seldom relax enough to try new ideas. Despite the number of new ideas and methods available, it is surprising how few the average teacher tries—although sometimes, trying something new may arouse opposition from your colleagues.

Be enthusiastic for teaching and in your teaching. Time and again the one attribute that seems to separate the good teacher from the mediocre is enthusiasm. Even if you weren't born with enthusiasm, *trying* to be enthusiastic will help a great deal.

Maintain an open-door policy in teaching. Welcome into your classroom parents, colleagues, college students, and all who want to know what schools and centers are doing. Teaching can be a lonely profession, but it need not be.

DEVELOPING A PHILOSOPHY OF EDUCATION

A philosophy of education is a set of beliefs about how children develop and learn and what and how they should be taught. Your philosophy of education will be quite personal. There may be similarities between your philosophy and that of another teacher, but what you believe is unique with you. You should not try to mold your philosophy to match another's; your philosophy should reflect your beliefs.

As we discussed earlier, your philosophy will guide and direct your daily teaching. Your beliefs about how children learn best will determine whether you individualize instruction or try to teach the same thing to everyone in the same way. Your philosophy will determine whether you help children do things for themselves or whether you do things for them. These are some ways to go about developing your philosophy:

- ☐ Read widely in textbooks, journals, and other professional literature to get ideas and points of view. A word of caution: when people refer to philosophies of education, they often think only of the historical influences; this is only part of the information available for writing a philosophy. Make sure you explore contemporary ideas as well, for these will also have a strong influence on you as a teacher and caregiver.
- ☐ If you have not written your philosophy, these headings will help you get started:

  I believe the purposes of education are . . .

  I believe that children learn best when they are taught under certain conditions and in certain ways. Some of these are . . .

The curriculum of any classroom should include certain "basics" that contribute to children's social, emotional, intellectual, and physical development. These basics are . . .

Children learn best in an environment that promotes learning. Some of the features of a good learning environment are . . .

All children have certain needs that must be met if they are to grow and learn at their best. Some of these basic needs are. . . . I would meet these needs these ways . . .

A teacher should have certain qualities and behave in certain ways. Qualities I think important for teaching are . . .

- ☐ Have other people read your philosophy. This helps you clarify your ideas and redefine your thoughts, because your philosophy should be understandable to others. (They don't necessarily have to agree with you.)
- ☐ Talk with successful teachers and other educators. (The accounts that follow are evidence that a philosophy can help one become an above-average teacher.) Talking with others exposes you to others points of view and stimulates thinking.
- ☐ Evaluate your philosophy against this checklist:

  Does it accurately relate my beliefs about teaching? Have I been honest with myself?

  Is it understandable to me and others?

  Does it provide practical guidance for teaching?

  Are my ideas consistent with each other?

  Does what I believe make good sense?

  Have I been comprehensive and stated my beliefs about:

  How children learn

  What children should be taught

  How children should be taught

  The conditions under which children learn best

  The qualities of a good teacher

TEACHERS OF THE YEAR

Russ Lofthouse, Kindergarten Teacher, Colorado Teacher of the Year, 1986; National Teacher of the Year Runner-up, 1986

> Lost, yesterday, somewhere between Sunrise and Sunset, two golden hours—each set with sixty diamond minutes.
>
> No reward offered, for they are gone forever.
>
> Horace Mann

Born second in a family of seven, I learned early to foster the needs and desires of young children. With both of my parents working, my older sister and I helped with the housework and with caring for our younger brothers and sisters throughout most of my adolescent years.

When I was in third grade, I was stricken with polio. Lying in an iron lung, there was not a lot I could do with myself. But during the nine months I was recovering, I made what was to me an astonishing discovery—I loved to read! Even now I still read two or three hours a night.

My high school experience was more positive because I was involved in athletics. One of my coaches, Don Strasser, befriended me. His geometry classes were interesting, and I was working hard and learning. He taught me geometry, but he also showed me that learning could be exciting. It was during my high school years that I also discovered the joy of teaching younger children. I was coach, umpire, advisor, and best friend to children ages seven to fourteen in my Chicago neighborhood. I was thinking seriously about becoming a physical education teacher as my high school experience drew to a close.

The Vietnam War put those aspirations on hold. I was drafted and spent the next four years in the United States Air Force. During those years I read, took college courses, and published some poetry and short stories, which influenced me to go to college full time to pursue a degree in English and to continue writing.

After an honorable discharge from the Air Force in 1967, I moved to Denver and attended Denver University. To finance my education, I worked for a corporation, writing, filming, and directing point-of-sale films. A few years later, while filming on location in Phoenix, I had the opportunity to visit some kindergarten classrooms. What I saw there reinforced my belief that school could be exciting as well as educational. From then on, whenever I had free time I visited classrooms, and shortly afterward, I quit my job and changed my major to Early Childhood Education.

In 1971 I began my career teaching kindergarten and first grade in the Cherry Creek School District in Colorado. I chose Cherry Creek because it was the only district in Colorado that had the courage and trust to allow me to teach kindergarten.

In 1977 I transferred to a different school in the district. There I team-taught in grades K–1, 2–3, and 3–4. I also made the change from single to married life that year when I married Ms. Pam Axelson. Pam has been a continual source of encouragement and understanding since the day we met, and I continue to learn from her. In addition, she brought to me a son, James, who continues to be the pride of my life. While at Ponderosa I received my Master's degree in Early Childhood Education at the University of Colorado at Denver.

Nineteen-eighty was a year of transition for my family. Pam and I received Fulbright teaching positions in London, England for the year. It was a wonderful year of new experiences and learning for the three of us. Best of all, it made me a better teacher. Upon our return from London, I began to teach kindergarten full time again. Meadow Point is a great school with a wonderful staff and a super principal, but most important, it has a supportive community with children who care about others and want to learn.

I am quite happy with my busy life. I keep active taking college classes in areas of need and interest as well as doing community service. I have a lovely wife, who's warmth and caring is a comfort to me. I have a great son, who tries hard at all he does. As for myself, I still try to fill each golden hour.

You see, my education is not complete, so it would be wrong to expect that children could gain all they need to know from me. I don't feel good teachers teach at all; rather, they guide and help children. Children do the learning; all we can do is guide them in their attempts and support them. The only real way to learn is to do. If I could teach a child one thing, it would be that learning is, by definition, never-ending—to stop learning is to stop living. I feel I teach children by helping them see their inherent worth.

When teaching, I try to give each child new experiences. I try to teach with excitement and enthusiasm so that children will find learning enjoyable. Someone once said, "One can learn from anyone . . . if they listen and accept." I believe this, but I don't want the children just to listen, to become passive learners. I want them to do and to become active learners, to help themselves, to use all the resources they have available. Just as there is no single way to teach, there is no right way to learn. It is a hard process, but the joy that shows in the face of someone who has learned something new is the same at five years of age as it is at fifty.

I have always felt there is more to teaching than helping a child learn the ABC's. We need to teach the whole child—the physical, social, and emotional as well as the intellectual. Modern children need love and understanding as well as help in achieving academic goals. It is more important to help a child toward creation and understanding of his or her own "self" than to impose my "self" on them. They need to be independent, and I encourage independence in all children, for only a child who is independent and free can develop his own unique personality.

I want children to learn how to learn. In these times of informational overload, it is all too easy to learn just facts. This is less important than having the ability to solve problems and make decisions. Criticism of education should not be directed towards the lowering of test scores, but toward the lack of teaching children critical thinking and decision making. Regardless of their ages, I give children the chance to make choices. Sometimes there is a hard lesson to be learned, but they are learning!

Finally, I strive to make each child trust me. At the same time I expect children to be worthy of my trust. They have never disappointed me, and I hope they can always say the same about me.

Janice Fitzsimmons, First Grade Teacher, New Jersey Teacher of the Year, 1986

Having taught for fifteen years, I have seen many changes occur in our schools. Techniques have changed, methods have changed, even curricula have changed; but throughout there has remained one constant . . . the children.

It seems to me that the key to working with children is creativity. By creativity, I mean touching or awakening that which is within each child waiting to be developed. We, then, as teachers must use our own creativity. We begin with an intuition, but it is our skill and training that carries us through to the end—to the enlightenment of the child, instilling a sense of trust, a desire to learn, and facilitating that growth through respect, understanding, sharing, and love.

There is a great need for excellence in all aspects of education. To train a nation of children who have begun at an early age to deal with ideas, who have come to recognize a system of values that includes the concepts of insight, compassion, understanding, and acceptance of human behavior—to do this carries an important responsibility. Children must be encouraged to think and to dream. As teachers we must allow students the opportunity, the time, and the avenues to express their thoughts, feelings, and ideas. For whether a child becomes a scientist or a secretary, a computer specialist, a mechanic, a teacher, a statesman, a factory worker, or a farmer, those values are basic to that child's fulfillment as a human being.

All children need to feel they have value and, as such, can make a lasting contribution by offering who they are to others. Leo Buscaglia states that maybe the essence of education is not just in giving you facts, but rather in helping you to discover your uniqueness, to teach you to develop it, and then to show you how to give it away. As teachers, we, along with their parents, prepare children for life, giving them the tools they need to develop their own futures. Preparing them for that future is a challenge to which teachers respond with enthusiasm and dedication. Each day, teachers enter their classrooms prepared to work with the greatest natural resource this nation has to offer—its children. From that labor comes the future of our world. We prepare them for the realities and the practicalities of that world, while trying to keep alive their dreams and childlike wonder. Teaching is sharing in those dreams. Teaching is a belief in the future.

Nanci L. Maes, Second Grade Teacher, Wisconsin Teacher of the Year, 1986

I made up my mind as a first grader that I was going to be a teacher and never changed my mind! My sister had the same plans, so I always had a partner to play school with. We had a teacher's desk and four student desks in our recreation room, and we spent many hours in role play. Today we are both second grade teachers, exchanging ideas and having our classes write one another as pen pals. My dad was also a high school speech teacher before he went into law.

As a teacher, I feel I must provide an atmosphere for growth and learning so effective that each child achieves his greatest academic, social, and emotional potential. I must go beyond imparting basic facts and devote time to helping children develop intellectually, socially, and personally. I must create a positive attitude toward learning and help each child develop a good self-image. I must stress the positive by using much positive reinforcement. I must provide the motivation necessary to make school a welcome place to be. The children must feel they are liked and like what they are doing. They must be happy about themselves and their work. Teachers, likewise, must have a good self-image, enjoy their work, and love children.

I must strive to actively engage all students. I must provide an atmosphere of enthusiasm with a high level of stimulating thought and interaction between teacher and students. I must allow for freedom of imagination and not stifle creativity. I must strive to individualize my instruction to meet the needs of all students, recognizing that each one is different. All groups of children should be kept heterogeneous to prevent a child from getting labeled or becoming "stuck" in one particular group. The longer a child remains in a group, the wider the communication gap between the groups becomes. Each child needs to be made to feel special and important.

I must strive to use good public relations ideas and techniques. I must continue to get many community members involved in my classroom as speakers and demonstrators so as to bring about good public relations between home, school, and community. I must continue to open important lines of communication between parent and child and between school and home through the weekly classroom reports.

I must never "reach my goals" but must continually strive for new ways of teaching, better methods of achieving success, and unlimited new challenges.

Donna Viveiros, Second Grade Teacher, Massachusetts Teacher of the Year, 1986

Why did I choose a career in education? My love of learning and the gift of sharing it have to be the prime reasons. From an early age, I enjoyed reading. When I was a young child my mother read to me every night at bedtime. The books she bought me were treasures. As I grew older, the library was my special haven. My father has always been an avid reader, and he has by example had a strong influence on me. His love of the printed word was contagious. He subscribed to fine periodicals that helped open my mind to current issues. He has a deep appreciation of history, and when I was a child, every summer we traveled the country and Canada visiting the historical, cultural, and natural wonders.

I was an outstanding history student in high school. I entered college as a pre-law major and worked my way through college. In my third and fourth years, I arranged all my courses into three days so that I could be available to substitute teach in the local school system. The minute I entered the classroom, I knew teaching was for me. I started taking the education courses required for teacher certification. In my senior year, I substituted in the federal Follow Through program. There were many disadvantaged children in the program, and the teaching style and materials were different from those I had observed. I was drawn to the program's child-oriented philosophy. I graduated with a degree in Political Science and began a teaching career as a Follow Through first grade teacher. I also began a Master's degree program in Early Childhood Education.

My philosophy of education is reflected in my teaching methods and the programs I have developed. I have an active parent volunteer program. I've created learning activities to correspond to my reading, math, language, and writing programs. I've developed a "Star Card" system of behavior modification that is positive, constructive, individualized, and effective. I also started a community program called the "Love Exchange," which involves the children in my class and residents of a nearby nursing home. The children adopt grannies and grandpas at the home and write, send art work, and visit regularly. The program has received national recognition, and Massachusetts has adopted it as an intergenerational model. This year I developed a program with a seventh grade science teacher called "The Big Student, Little Student Program," a collaborative effort between two school systems, one country and the other city, to share resources. The seventh graders act as mentors for my kindergarten students. (For the 1986–87 school year I exchanged classes with a kindergarten teacher.) It is a hands-on learning approach for the little ones and a motivational medium for the older ones.

I feel teachers, working within the bounds of their curriculum, should strive to have a positive impact on their students. The important job of educating today's youth to meet tomorrow's problems is what makes teaching special. Within the confines of the curriculum, an elementary teacher can teach respect for the environment, pride in community, good nutrition, the dangers of chemical abuse, and respect for the rights and differences of others. Teachers help shape history. They educate our future political leaders, researchers, professionals, scientists, and workers. Being a teacher is a joy, and knowledge is a gift to be shared.

Laurie Jones, Second Grade Teacher, Idaho Teacher of the Year, 1982

We have all been asked why we chose to be a teacher. I have received wondering looks when I've said I find it challenging, rewarding, and that I *love* it. The next question asked me is "How do you handle teaching—being crippled?" I explain that I let children help me and that they are open to learning new dimensions of responsibility and independence.

I began my teaching career 15 years ago. I've taught in private and public schools. I've taught third grade for 10 years and relish being with eight- and nine-year olds. They are eager, enthusiastic, exciting, and willing to learn.

Music seems to be a language that speaks to many hearts. Although I don't play an instrument, God has given me a talent for singing. So I make up songs and teach songs that fit the season, the situation, or the subject. I believe children learn better in a positive environment, so I try to make learning a happy experience. Music creates an atmosphere of warmth, love, and acceptance. Somehow, a feeling of unity and loyalty develops among us as we sing and learn together. Children respond quickly to music. They respond to me, the subject I'm teaching, and to new situations. I've seen sad faces light up, hostility wane, and interest spark. We experience a sense of "family"—a sense of working and growing together.

On the first day of school, expectancy fills the air as the children come in and find seats. I move around the room greeting each child. I then explain to the children that I had polio when I was young and that I walk with leg braces and crutches. I named my crutches Peter and Paul. I continue explaining that Peter and Paul are always with me, but during the day I leave one in the corner of the room and walk with only one. I walk with one stiff leg and ask the children if they would like to try to imitate me. They jump up and respond with "That's hard to do!" I show them how I must hold my pencil and chalk awkwardly because the muscles in my hands are weak. I always demonstrate and ask the children to try to write as I do. They eagerly grab their pencils and show me how well they do. I exclaim, "Oh! I'm glad you tried to do it. Your muscles aren't weak, so from now on you must write like you were taught in first grade." Children listen intently to my story, and when I finish I break into a song I made up that invites them to "echo" me in whatever I sing. So, the first day of school begins, and we are all feeling comfortable.

I decided I wanted to become a teacher in the sixth or seventh grade. I saw and knew teachers whom I respected and wanted to model. Just the next year I got very ill, however, and was diagnosed as having polio. Then I began an intensive therapy program and learned to walk with braces and crutches. I buried my desire to be a teacher because I felt helpless and dependent. After four years, I had gained strength and some independence, and I began to dream once again about being a teacher and giving to the world and to people. I attended a small private college for two years and got my preliminary teaching credentials. My first year of teaching was in a private school with a class of 50 second graders. I found children eager to learn and willing to accept that I was crippled.

Throughout my career I've found children accepting of me. I am honest and open about being handicapped. Each year a discussion occurs, often spontaneously, about different kinds of handicaps. I am open to their questions about how I got polio and how it feels to walk on crutches all the time. It seems children "forget" that I am handicapped after a short time. I emphasize to them that all of us have strengths and weaknesses. My vision is to continue to inspire children—to help them realize they *do* count. Their talents, great or small, are important to the world. Disabilities and weaknesses don't keep us back; abilities and good attitudes are what count!

My strength comes from my faith, but also from children who love and accept unconditionally. Children open their hearts and arms to me day after day. I return their love by being open, warm, honest, and by teaching them to the best of my ability. I feel so honored and happy to say, "I am an educator!" We make the world a better place by our good attitudes. I feel fulfilled doing the work I was chosen to do.

We meet so many children and are called upon to uncover so many talents. We could consider ourselves "talent scouts." Each day we encourage, compliment, assure, and stimulate, so our students will make the best of their potential. Our business is not just to teach, but to develop curriculum, advise, coach, counsel, nurse, and parent. We do so much more than convey knowledge—we enrich lives. As teachers, we affect eternity; we can never tell where our influence stops.

Becoming a professional means you will participate in training and education beyond the minimum needed for your present position. You will also want to consider your career objectives and the qualifications you might need for positions of increasing responsibility. The National Academy of Early Childhood Programs specifies staff qualifications and training appropriate for positions in early childhood programs that you should review to determine how they apply to your career and life goals (Table 15–1).

A Good Teacher: A Lesson from History

It is worthwhile looking at the history of early childhood education for ideas about good teachers; in fact, we need look no further than Froebel, father of the kindergarten:

> I understand it thus. She [the mother] says, "I bring my child—take care of it, as *I* would do;" or "Do with my child what is right to do;" or "Do it better than I am able to do it." A silent agreement is made between the parents and you, the teacher; the child is passed from hand to hand, from heart to heart. What else *can* you do but be a mother to the little one, for the hour, morning or day when you have the sa-

TABLE 15–1 Staff Qualifications and Development

Title	Level of Professional Responsibility	Training Requirements
Early childhood teacher assistant	Preprofessionals who implement program activities under direct supervision of professional staff	High school graduate or equivalent, participation in professional development programs
Early childhood associate teacher	Professionals who independently implement program activities and may be responsible for care and education of a group of children	CDA credential or associate degree in Early Childhood Education/Child Development
Early childhood teacher	Professionals who are responsible for care and education of a group of children	Baccalaureate degree in Early Childhood Education/Child Development
Early childhood specialist	Professionals who supervise and train staff, design curriculum, and/or administer programs	Baccalaureate degree in Early Childhood Education/Child Development; at least three years of full-time teaching experience with young children and/or graduate degree in ECE/CD

Source: From *Accreditation Criteria and Procedures* of the National Academy of Early Childhood Programs, Washington, D.C. (1984), pp. 18–20.

cred charge of a young soul? In hope and trust the child is brought to you, and you have to show yourself worthy of the confidence which is placed in your skill, your experience and your knowledge.[1]

A Good Teacher from the Parents' Viewpoint

In our discussion of becoming a good teacher, we should consider what the public thinks teachers should be. These are reasonable expectations:

1. Parents should expect teachers to teach their children.
2. Parents want well-planned lessons and a well-organized curriculum.
3. Parents want evidence of learning.
4. Parents want children to have an interesting school day.
5. Parents want teachers to be well-educated, literate, and well-spoken.
6. Parents want teachers who care about kids.
7. Parents want teachers to be adults of civility, maturity, and character.
8. Parents think powerful teachers' unions should use some of their muscle to weed out incompetents.[2]

A professional person is an ethical one, and fortunately, we have a set of ethical standards to guide our thinking and behavior. Developed by Evangeline Ward, these standards are both a guide and a challenge.

Preamble

As an educator of young children in their years of greatest vulnerability, I, to the best of intent and ability, shall devote myself to the following commitments and act to support them.

For the child

I shall accord the respect due each child as a human being from birth on.

I shall recognize the unique potentials to be fulfilled within each child.

I shall provide access to differing opinions and views inherent in every person, subject, or thing encountered as the child grows.

I shall recognize the child's right to ask questions about the unknowns that exist in the present so the answers (which may be within the child's capacity to discover) may be forthcoming eventually.

I shall protect and extend the child's physical well-being, emotional stability, mental capacities, and social acceptability.

For the parents and family members

I shall accord each child's parents and family members respect for the responsibilities they carry.

By no deliberate action on my part will the child be held accountable for the incidental meeting of his or her parents and the attendant lodging of the child's destiny with relatives and siblings.

Recognizing the continuing nature of familial strength as support for the growing child, I shall maintain objectivity with regard to what I perceive as family weaknesses.

Maintaining family value systems and pride in cultural-ethnic choices or variations will supersede any attempts I might inadvertently or otherwise make to impose my values.

Because advocacy on behalf of children always requires that someone cares about or is strongly motivated by a sense of fairness and intervenes on behalf of children in relation to those services and institutions that impinge on their lives, I shall support family strength.

For myself and the early childhood profession

Admitting my biases is the first evidence of my willingness to become a conscious professional.

Knowing my capacity to continue to learn throughout life, I shall vigorously pursue knowledge about contemporary developments in early education by informal and formal means.

My role with young children demands an awareness of new knowledge that emerges from varied disciplines and the responsibility to use such knowledge.

Recognizing the limitation I bring to knowing intimately the ethical-cultural value systems of the multicultural American way of life, I shall actively seek the understanding and acceptance of the chosen ways of others to assist them educationally in meeting each child's needs for his or her unknown future impact on society.

Working with other adults and parents to maximize my strengths and theirs, both personally and professionally, I shall provide a model to demonstrate to young children how adults can create an improved way of living and learning through planned cooperation.

The encouragement of language development with young children will never exceed the boundaries of propriety or violate the confidence and trust of a child or that child's family.

I shall share my professional skills, information, and talents to enhance early education for young children wherever they are.

I shall cooperate with other persons and organizations to promote programs for children and families that improve their opportunities to utilize and enhance their uniqueness and strength.

I shall ensure that individually different styles of learning are meshed compatibly with individually different styles of teaching to help all people grow and learn well—this applies to adults learning to be teachers as well as to children.[3]

THE FUTURE OF TEACHING

What does the future hold for early childhood teachers? As early childhood education changes, the changes will affect teachers as well as children. First, we will see a stronger move to professionalize teaching. Teachers continue to be challenged to become more professional. Professionalization of teaching is part of the national effort to improve education. The public recognizes, albeit belatedly, that real and lasting changes in education will occur when teachers are trained as professional and are treated as professionals. The emphasis on professionalism will require teachers to assume more responsibility for their own behavior and their professional development.

Second, we will see an intensification of teacher training, as professionalism brings a demand for higher levels of competence. Teachers who want a bachelor's degree may face a five-year program. Early childhood teachers and child care workers will probably have to take additional training through the CDA, inservice training, or college-related courses. Early childhood educators will be challenged and often required to demonstrate professionalism through courses, workshops, and certificate programs.

Third, a higher degree of professionalism will bring greater responsibility and decision making. There is a distinct trend to return to teachers much of the decision making about what to teach and how to teach it. Teachers have long said that they could get better results if they had the time and freedom to teach; now many will get this wish.

My wish for you as we end this book is that you will be the best teacher it is possible for you to be. Teaching young children is one of life's worthiest goals. Be proud and happy that you are an early childhood teacher.

FURTHER READING

Adler, Mortimer J. *The Paideia Proposal: An Educational Manifesto* (New York: Macmillan, 1982) A call to improve public and basic education; advocates the same course of study and quality education for everyone. (*Paideia* comes from the Greek, meaning "upbringing children.")

Bloom, Benjamin S. *All Our Children Learning: A Primer for Parents, Teachers, and Other Educators* (New York: McGraw-Hill, 1981) Selected papers by Bloom grouped under four sections relating to major aspects of education.

Brubaker, Dale L. *Who's Teaching—Who's Learning? Active Learning in Elementary Schools* (Santa Monica, Calif.: Goodyear, 1979) Shows that teachers themselves are still learners, and every teaching experience can also be a learning experience for the open-minded teacher. Guidelines and suggestions for spontaneous teaching.

Jorde, Paula. *Avoiding Burnout: Strategies for Managing Time, Space and People in Early Childhood Education* (Washington, D.C.: Acropolis Books, 1982) For early childhood educators who want to manage their total lives.

Kelly, James L., and Mary Jean Kelly, eds. *The Successful Elementary Teacher* (Lanham, Md.: University Press of America, 1985) For and about beginning teachers, these essays include intellectual development, motivation, humanizing the classroom, mainstreaming, multicultural education, classroom management, characteristics of good teachers, and classroom environment.

Kohl, Herbert. *Growing Minds: On Becoming a Teacher* (New York: Harper and Row, 1984) Practical, professional guide for growing into the profession of teaching; thesis is that, regardless of individual's motivations for entering the profession, one still has to learn how to become a good teacher. Author believes competence is acquired through careful and steady effort, self-growth, and experience.

Macrorie, Ken. *Twenty Teachers* (New York: Oxford University Press, 1984) Told by the teachers themselves, accounts of philosophies of teaching, how they teach, why and how their students do good work.

Ryan, Kevin, et al. *Biting the Apple: Accounts of First Year Teachers* (New York: Longman, 1980) Events during the first year of teaching/caregiving contribute to the gap between potential and accomplishment.

FURTHER STUDY

1. How important are the classroom teacher's character and attitude to a child's healthy growth during his primary years? Explain.
2. Recall the elementary teachers who taught you. List which characteristics you would imitate and which you would try to avoid as a teacher.
3. Some educators believe teachers are born, not made. Interview public school teachers and college professors to determine their opinions about this belief.
4. To teach young children, do you think teachers must be trained specifically in early childhood education?
5. For what specific roles do you think early childhood teachers should be educated?
6. Reflecting on your years in the primary grades, what experiences do you consider most meaningful? Why? Would these experiences be valid learning experiences for children today?
7. As a class, brainstorm and compile a list of competencies for early childhood teachers that are (1) generic, that is, applicable to all teaching; and (2) specific for early childhood education. Have professors of education and inservice teachers respond to your list.
8. Talk with other professionals about careers that relate to children and parents. How did they come to their jobs? Is there evidence that they planned for these careers? Do you think you would enjoy an alternative career in education? Why or why not?
9. List advantages and disadvantages of being an early childhood teacher. How will you overcome the disadvantages and capitalize on the advantages?
10. Share your philosophy of education with your classmates. Have them critique it for comprehensiveness, clarity, and meaning.
11. With your classmates, practice interviewing for a job. Develop a list of questions a job interviewer might ask. A good way to gather questions is to interview principals and find out what they ask. You might also want to practice your simulated interview with closed-circuit television so you can evaluate your performance.
12. Videotape yourself teaching a small group of children. You can take this videotape to job interviews as evidence of your teaching abilities.
13. List the reasons you have decided to go into teaching. Share and compare the list with your classmates. What conclusions can you draw from the lists?
14. After reading the accounts of Teachers of the Year, what impressed you most about their accounts? What outstanding qualities do these teachers demonstrate? Why were they able to become Teachers of the Year?
15. List four reasons you decided to become a teacher/caregiver, and rank them in order of importance.
16. List five ways early childhood professionals encourage others to become teachers and caregivers.
17. How can professionals assure that those who are not committed and dedicated do not enter the profession?
18. List ten characteristics and qualities of an early childhood professional.
19. How can early childhood teachers help "professionalize" the field?
20. How must the training of teachers and caregivers change to meet the changing needs of children, families, and society?

Endnotes

Chapter 1

1. National Academy of Early Childhood Programs, *Accreditation Criteria and Procedures* (Washington, D.C.: National Association for the Education of Young Children, 1984), p. x.
2. National Association for the Education of Young Children, *Early Childhood Teacher Education Guidelines* (Washington, D.C.: NAEYC, 1982), p. xii.
3. Urie Bronfenbrenner, *The Ecology of Human Development* (Cambridge, Mass.: Harvard University Press, 1979), p. 3.
4. David Elkind, "Formal Education and Early Education: An Essential Difference," *Phi Delta Kappan* 67 (1986), p. 634.
5. Susan Littwin, *The Postponed Generation: Why America's Grown-up Kids Are Growing Up Later* (New York: William Morrow, 1986), p. 21.
6. Neil Postman, *The Disappearance of Childhood* (New York: Delacorte Press, 1982), p. 80.
7. Vance Packard, *Our Endangered Children: Growing Up in a Changing World* (Boston: Little, Brown, 1983), p. xx.
8. John Locke, *An Essay Concerning Human Understanding* (New York: Dover Publications, 1959), pp. 92–93.
9. Committee for Economic Development, *Investing in Our Children: Business and the Public Schools* (New York: The Committee, 1985), pp. 1, 9.
10. AAP Child Health Goals, *News and Comment*, vol. 29, no. 3, March 1978. Copyright © American Academy of Pediatrics 1978.
11. Richard Farson, *Birthrights* (New York: Macmillan, 1978), p. 1.
12. Richard K. Kerckhoff and Jeffrey McPhee, "Receptivity to Child-Rights Legislation: A Survey," *Young Children* 39: 58–61.
13. "What You Should Know About Teen Parenthood," © 1982; "What You Should Know About Teenage Pregnancy," © 1983, Channing L. Bete Co., Inc., South Deerfield, MA 01373.
14. Brad Edmondson, "The Education of Children," *American Demographics* 8 (1986): 28.
15. John Naisbitt, *Megatrends: Ten New Directions Transforming Our Lives* (New York: Warner Books, 1984), p. 283.

Chapter 2

1. From *Luther on Education* by F. V. N. Painter, © 1928 by Concordia Publishing House. Used by permission, pp. 180–81.

2. John Amos Comenius, *The Great Didactic of John Amos Comenius,* trans. and ed. M. W. Keatinge, 1896, 1910 (New York: Russell and Russell, 1967), p. 58.

3. Comenius, *The Great Didactic,* p. 100.

4. Comenius, *The Great Didactic,* pp. 184–85.

5. Comenius, *The Great Didactic,* p. 127.

6. John Locke, *An Essay Concerning Human Understanding,* ed. Peter H. Nidditch (Oxford: Oxford University Press, 1975), p. 104.

7. *Émile; Or, Education,* by Jean Jacques Rousseau. Trans. Barbara Foxley, Everyman's Library Edition (New York: E. P. Dutton, 1933), p. 5.

8. Jean Jacques Rousseau, *Émile,* trans. and ed. William Boyd (New York: Teachers College Press, by arrangement with William Heinemann Ltd., London, 1962), pp. 11–15.

9. Alexander S. Neill, *Summerhill* (New York: Hart, 1960), p. 4.

10. Roger DeGuimps, *Pestalozzi: His Life and Work* (New York: D. Appleton, 1890), p. 205.

11. DeGuimps, *Pestalozzi,* p. 1691.

12. Friedrich Froebel, *The Education of Man* (Clifton, N.J.: Augustus M. Kelley, 1974), pp. 7–8.

13. Friedrich Froebel, *The Education of Man,* trans. M. W. Hailman (New York: D. Appleton, 1887), p. 55.

14. Friedrich Froebel, *Pedagogics of the Kindergarten,* trans. Josephine Jarvis (New York: D. Appleton, 1902), p. 32.

15. Froebel, *Pedagogics,* pp. 83–84.

16. Friedrich Froebel, *Mother's Songs, Games, and Stories* (New York: Arno Press, 1976), pp. 20–21.

17. Froebel, *Mother's Songs,* pp. 136–37.

18. Maria Montessori, *The Discovery of the Child,* trans. M. J. Costelloe (Notre Dame, Ind.: Fides Publishers, 1967), p. 22.

19. Maria Montessori, *The Montessori Method,* trans. Anne E. George (Cambridge, Mass.: Robert Bentley, 1967), p. 38.

20. Montessori, *The Discovery of the Child,* p. 28.

21. Montessori, *The Discovery of the Child,* p. 37.

22. Reginald D. Archambault, eds., *John Dewey on Education—Selected Writings* (New York: Random House, 1964), p. 430.

23. Henry Suzzallo, ed., *John Dewey's Interest and Effort in Education* (Boston: Houghton Mifflin, 1913), p. 65.

24. Archambault, *John Dewey on Education,* pp. 170–71.

25. John Dewey, *Democracy and Education* (New York: The Free Press, 1966, 1916), p. 158.

26. Edwin G. Boring et al., eds., *A History of Psychology in Autobiography,* vol. IV (Worchester, Mass.: Clark University Press, 1952; New York: Russell and Russell, 1968), p. 244.

27. Benjamin S. Bloom, *Stability and Change in Human Characteristics* (New York: John Wiley, 1964), p. 88.

28. J. McV. Hunt, *Intelligence and Experience* (New York: The Ronald Press Company, Copyright © 1961), pp. 362–63.

29. Christopher Jencks et al., *Inequality: A Reassessment of the Effect of Family and Schooling in America* (New York: Harper and Row, 1973), p. 254.

30. George W. Mayeske et al., *A Study of the Achievement of Our Nation's Students* (Washington, D.C.: U.S. Govt. Printing Office, 1973).

31. Burton L. White, *The First Three Years of Life* (Englewood Cliffs, N.J.: Prentice-Hall, 1975), p.4.

32. The account of a day in an informal classroom was written with assistance from Joan Wojdak, Mary MacArthur, Margaret Walsh, and Lynn Muto of Intermediate Unit 19, Dunmore, Pennsylvania.

Chapter 3

1. Maria Montessori, *Dr. Montessori's Own Handbook* (New York: Schocken Books, 1965), p. 133.
2. Maria Montessori, *The Montessori Method,* trans. Anne E. George (Cambridge, Mass.: 1967), p. 104.
3. Maria Montessori, *The Secret of Childhood,* trans. M. J. Costello (Notre Dame, Ind.: Fides Publishers, 1966), p. 20.
4. Maria Montessori, *The Absorbent Mind,* trans. Claude A. Claremont (New York: Holt, Rinehart and Winston, 1967), p. 25.
5. Montessori, *The Secret of Childhood,* p. 48.
6. Montessori, *The Secret of Childhood,* p. 46.
7. Montessori, *The Secret of Childhood,* p. 49.
8. Montessori, *The Absorbent Mind,* p. 6.
9. Montessori, *The Absorbent Mind,* p. 254.
10. Montessori, *The Absorbent Mind,* p. 84.
11. Montessori, *The Absorbent Mind,* p. 8.
12. Montessori, *Dr. Montessori's Own Handbook,* p. 131.
13. The account of a day in a Children's House is based on the program and activities of the Alexander Montessori School, Miami, Florida. There are nine directresses at the Alexander School, some of whom are AMI or AMS trained. Two of the staff come from Cuba, one from Italy, one from Hungary, and five are natives of the U.S.

Chapter 4

1. Mary Ann Spencer Pulaski, *Understanding Piaget* (New York: Harper and Row, 1980), p. 9.
2. P.G. Richmond, *An Introduction to Piaget* (New York: Basic Books, 1970), p. 68.
3. Richmond, *An Introduction to Piaget*, p. 68.
4. Deanna Kuhn, "The Role of Self-Directed Activity in Cognitive Development," in *New Directions in Piagetian Theory and Practice,* ed. Irving E. Sigel et al. (Hillsdale, N.J.: Lawrence Erlbaum, 1981), p. 353.
5. David M. Brodzinsky et al., "New Directions in Piagetian Theory and Research: An Integrative Perspective," in *New Directions in Piagetian Theory and Practice,* ed. Irving E. Sigel et al. (Hillsdale, N.J.: Lawrence Erlbaum, 1981), p. 5.
6. Constance Kamii, "Application of Piaget's Theory to Education: The Preoperational Level" in *New Directions in Piagetian Theory and Practice,* ed. Irving E. Sigel et al. (Hillside, N.J.: Lawrence Erlbaum, 1981), p. 234.
7. Hans G. Furth, *Piaget for Teachers* (Englewood Cliffs, N.J.: Prentice-Hall, 1970), p. 15.
8. Jean Piaget, *Genetic Epistemology,* trans. Eleanor Duckworth (New York: Columbia University Press, 1970), p. 21.
9. *The High Scope Early Elementary Program* (Ypsilanti, Mich.: High Scope Educational Research Foundation, 1973), p. 1.
10. Richard Lalli, *An Introduction to the Cognitively Oriented Curriculum for the Elementary Grades* (Ypsilanti, Mich.: High Scope Educational Research Foundation), pp. 2–3.
11. Lalli, *An Introduction,* p. 12.

12. Dr. Mary Frank Hancock, elementary supervisor, Ms. Patti Boyles, Follow Through curriculum specialist, Ms. Pat Todd, kindergarten teacher, and Dr. Gordon Eade, Associate Professor of Education at the University of West Florida, helped to prepare this section on a cognitively oriented curriculum in the Okaloosa County Public Schools.

13. Celia Stendler Lavatelli, *Piaget's Theory Applied to an Early Childhood Curriculum* (Boston: American Science and Engineering, 1970).

14. The sections Plan, Work, and Representation in this vignette were written by Donna McClelland, senior consultant, High Scope Educational Research Foundation.

15. Constance Kamii and Rheta DeVries, "Piaget for Early Education," in *The Preschool in Action,* 2nd ed., ed. M.C. Day and R.K. Parker (Boston: Allyn and Bacon, 1977).

16. Constance Kamii, "Why Use Group Games?" in *Group Games in Early Education: Implications of Piaget's Theory* by Constance Kamii and Rheta DeVries (Washington, D.C.: National Association for the Education of Young Children, 1980), p. 12.

17. Eleanor Duckworth, "Learning Symposium: A Commentary," in *New Directions in Piagetian Theory and Practice,* ed. Irving E. Sigel et al. (Hillsdale, N.J.: Lawrence Erlbaum, 1981), p. 363.

Chapter 5

1. "The Child Boom" (Washington, D.C.: The National Association for the Education of Young Children, 1985).

2. *Child Welfare League of America: Standards for Day Care Services* (New York: Child Welfare League of America, 1973), p. 9.

3. Bettye M. Caldwell, "What is Quality Child Care?" *Young Children* 39, 3 (March 1984), p. 4.

4. Pennsylvania Department of Public Welfare, Bureau of Child and Youth Development, *Regulations for Family Day Care Homes* (June 1981), p. 7.

5. P. Divine-Hawkins, Family Day Care in the United States: Executive Summary (Washington, D.C.: U.S. Department of Health and Human Services, DHHS Publication No. (OHDS) 80-30287, Sept. 1981), p. 1.

6. Family Day Care Standards (Florida Department of Health and Rehabilitative Services, 1985), p. 1.

7. Commonwealth of Pennsylvania Department of Public Welfare, Bureau of Child Development Programs, *Regulations for Child Care,* April, 1978, p. 8.

8. *Minimum Standards for Child Care Services* (State of Florida, Department of Health and Rehabilitative Services), p. 4.

9. John H. Winters, Human Services Center, *Minimum Standards for Day Care Centers* (Texas Department of Human Services, May, 1985), p. 2.

10. Dennis Meredith, "Day-Care: The Nine-to-Five Dilemma," *Psychology Today,* 20, 2 (February 1986), p. 38.

11. CDA National Credentialing Program, *Family Day Care Providers* (Washington, D.C.: CDA National Credentialing Program, 1985), p. iii.

12. *Children at the Center:* Final Report of the National Day Care Study, Executive Summary (Cambridge, Mass.: Abt Associates, March 1979).

13. The Southern Association on Children Under Six, *Position Statement on Quality Child Care* (pamphlet).

14. National Association for the Education of Young Children, *Accreditation by the National Academy of Early Childhood Programs,* p. 2.

15. T. Berry Brazelton, *Working and Caring* (Reading, Mass.: Addison-Wesley, 1986).

16. Deborah Fallows, *A Mother's Work* (Boston: Houghton Mifflin, 1986).

17. Burton White, *The First Three Years of Life* (Englewood Cliffs, N.J. Prentice-Hall, 1986).

18. Jay Belsky and Laurence D. Steinberg. "The Effects of Day Care," in *In The Beginning: Readings on Infancy*, ed. Jay Belsky (New York: Columbia University Press, 1982), p. 255.

Chapter 6

1. T. Berry Brazelton, *Toddlers and Parents: A Declaration of Independence* (New York: Delacorte Press, 1974); Benjamin Spock and Michael Rothenberg, *Dr. Spock's Baby and Child Care* (New York: E. P. Dutton, 1985).
2. S. I. Hayakawa, *Language in Thought and Action*, 3rd ed. (New York: Harcourt Brace Jovanovich, 1975), p. 30.
3. Eric H. Lenneberg, "The Biological Foundations of Language," in Mark Lester, *Readings in Applied Transformational Grammar* (New York: Holt, Rinehart and Winston, 1970), p. 8.
4. Eric H. Lenneberg, "A Biological Perspective of Language," in *New Directions in the Study of Language*, ed. Eric H. Lenneberg (Cambridge, Mass.: M.I.T. Press, 1964), pp. 66–68.
5. Alice S. Honig, "High Quality Infant/Toddler Care," *Young Children*, 4 (November 1985): 40.
6. National Association for the Education of Young Children, "Position Statement on Developmentally Appropriate Practice in Early Childhood Programs Serving Children From Birth Through Age 8," *Young Children* 41:1 (September 1986): pp. 4–29.
7. George S. Morrison, *The Education and Development of Infants, Toddlers, and Preschoolers* (Boston: Little, Brown, in press).

Chapter 7

1. George Foreman and Fleet Hill, *Constructive Play: Applying Piaget in the Preschool* (Monterey, Calif.: Brooks/Cole, 1980), p. 2.
2. Mildred Parten, "Social Play Among Preschool Children," *Journal of Abnormal and Social Psychology*, 27 (1932), pp. 243–69.
3. Texas Education Agency, *Priority '86: A Guide for Prekindergarten Education* (Austin, Tex.: Texas Education Agency, 1986), pp. 6–7.
4. Heritage Home is a program designed to intermingle preschool children with the aged or disabled. This section was written by Carolyn Morgan, former Nursery School Director at Heritage Home, Winthrop, Maine, and by Florel Steuerwalt, Codirector of Happy Day Nursery School.
5. "Position Statement on Quality Four-Year-Old Programs in Public Schools" (Little Rock, Ark.: The Southern Association on Children Under Six).
6. John R. Berrueta-Clement, et al., *Changed Lives: The Effects of the Perry Preschool Program on Youths Through Age 19* (Ypsilanti, Mich.: The High Scope Press, 1984), p. 1.
7. Lawrence J. Schweinhart and David P. Weikart, "Evidence That Good Early Childhood Programs Work," *Phi Delta Kappan*, 66 (8), p. 547.
8. Louise Bates Ames and Joan Ames Chase, *Don't Push Your Preschooler* (New York: Harper and Row, 1980), p. 2.
9. Alec M. Gallup, "The 18th Annual Gallup Poll of the Public's Attitude Toward the Public Schools," *Phi Delta Kappan*, 68, 1 (September 1986), pp. 55–56.

Chapter 8

1. Alec M. Gallup, "The 18th Annual Gallup Poll of the Public's Attitudes Toward the Public Schools," *Phi Delta Kappan*, 68, 1, pp. 55–56.
2. Sandra Longfellow Robinson, "Educational Opportunities for Young Children in America," *Childhood Education*, 59, 1, September–October, 1982, p. 42.

3. Robert Albrecht, *The Columbus Dispatch,* July 21, 1983. Reprinted with permission.
4. Arnold Gesell and Catherine Amatruda, *Developmental Diagnosis: Normal and Abnormal Child Development* (New York: Harper and Row, 1941).
5. Caroline Pratt and Lucile C. Deming, "The Play School," in *Experimental Schools Revisited,* ed. Charlotte Winsor (New York: Agathon Press, 1973), p. 23.
6. Friedrich Froebel, *Mother's Songs, Games and Stories* (New York: Arno Press, 1976), p. 136.
7. Reprinted by permission of the Nebraska Department of Education, Division of School Assistance and Support.
8. School Board of Dade County, Florida.
9. School Board of Dade County, Florida.
10. Highland Oaks Elementary School is in Dade County, Florida, the fourth largest school district in the United States.
11. Linda Garvey, Yukari Okamoto, and Teresa McDivitt, Stanford University.
12. Thanks to Louisa Birch, kindergarten teacher, Meadowbrook School, Weston, Mass. 02193
13. Texas Association for the Education of Young Children, *Developmentally Appropriate Kindergarten Reading Programs: A Position Statement,* p. 1.
14. Statute 2372, Section 703.
15. Statute 2372, Section 4A.

Chapter 9

1. Jean Piaget, *The Moral Judgment of the Child,* trans. Marjorie Gabin (New York: The Free Press, 1965), p. 395.
2. Lawrence Kohlberg, "The Claim to Moral Adequacy of a Highest Stage of Moral Judgment," *The Journal of Philosophy,* vol. 70, no. 18 (October 25, 1973): 630–646.
3. The School Board of Dade County, Florida, *Sample Assessment Items: Reading, Grade 3* (1983), p. 9.
4. Douglas H. Clements, *Computers in Early and Primary Education* (Englewood Cliffs, N.J.: Prentice-Hall, 1985), pp. 52–53.
5. Monica Overman, "Practical Applications of Research: Student Promotion and Retention," *Phi Delta Kappan* 67 (April 1986): 612.
6. R. A. Pendergrass, "Homework: Is It Really A Basic?" *The Clearing House* 58 (March 1985): 314.
7. William J. Bennett, *First Lessons: A Report on Elementary Education in America* (Washington, D.C.: Department of Education, 1986).

Chapter 10

1. Administration for Children, Youth and Families, "Project Head Start Statistical Fact Sheet" (Washington, D.C.: Dec. 1985), pp. 2–3.
2. U.S. Department of Health and Human Services, *Head Start Program Performance Standards* (45-CFR 1304) (Washington, D.C.: U.S. Government Printing Office, November, 1984).
3. *Head Start Program Performance Standards,* pp. 8–9.
4. Schedule from Franklin-Vance Warren Opportunity, Inc., Head Start Program, Henderson, North Carolina.
5. Sample daily schedule of the Metropolitan Dade County, Florida, Head Start.
6. *Head Start Program Performance Standards,* p. 58.

7. *Head Start Program Performance Standards,* p. 16.

8. *Head Start Program Performance Standards,* pp. 30–31.

9. *Head Start Program Performance Standards,* p. 53.

10. *Head Start Program Performance Standards,* p. 38.

11. E. Dollie Wolverton, "The Home-Based Option: Reinforcing Parents," *Head Start Bulletin* 12 (October/November 1986), p. 1.

12. From *Home Start Curriculum Guide,* Bear River Head Start Program, Logan, Utah.

13. *The Child and Family Resource Program: An Overview,* DHEW Publication No. (OHD) 76-31087 (Washington, D.C.: U.S. Government Printing Office, 1975), p. 1.

14. Child and Family Resource Evaluation, *The Effects of a Social Program: Executive Summary of CFRP's Infant-Toddler Component* (Cambridge, Mass.: Abt Associates, Fall 1982).

15. Linda B. Stebbins et al., *Education as Experimentation: A Planned Variation Model, Volume IV-A: An Evaluation of Follow Through* (Cambridge, Mass.: Abt Associates, April 15, 1977).

16. *Project Developmental Continuity: A Head Start Demonstration Program Linking Head Start, Parents, and the Public School,* Office of Child Development, Office of Human Development (Washington, D.C.: Department of Health, Education and Welfare, 1977), p. 1.

17. *Project Developmental Continuity,* p. 4.

18. John R. Bergan et al., *The Head Start Measures Project: A Summary Report on Full-Year Implementation, 1984–85* (Tucson, Ariz.: The Center for Educational Evaluation, The University of Arizona), p. 15.

19. *Head Start Newsletter,* 7, no. 2, DHEW Publication no. OHD 74-1068 (November–December 1973).

20. Stebbins, *Education as Experimentation,* p. 159.

21. Irving Lazar and Richard B. Darlinton et al., "Lasting Effects After Preschool," A report of the Consortium for Longitudinal Studies, Sept. 1979, Administration for Children, Youth and Families, Office of Human Development Services DHEW No. (OHDS) 79-30179.

22. L. J. Schweinhart and D. P. Weikart, *Young Children Grow Up: The Effects of the Perry Preschool Program on Youths Through Age 15* (Ypsilanti, Mich.: The High Scope Press, 1980), p. 63.

23. Lawrence J. Schweinhart and David P. Weikart, "What Do We Know So Far?: A Review of the Head Start Synthesis Project," *Young Children,* 41, no. 2 (January 1986), p. 50.

24. U.S. Department of Health and Human Services, Office of Human Development Services, Administration for Children, Youth and Families, Head Start Bureau. "Head Start in The 1980's: Review and Recommendations," September 1980, pp. 36–51.

25. Valora Washington and Ura Jean Oyemade, "Changing Family Trends: Head Start Must Respond," *Young Children,* 40, no. 6 (September 1985), pp. 12–15.

26. Francis Wardle, "Dangerous Suggestions for Head Start," *Young Children,* 40 no. 8 (November 1985), p. 18.

27. *Federal Register,* July 13, 1977, p. 36080.

Chapter 11

1. *Federal Register,* Tuesday, August 23, 1977, p. 42478.

2. U.S., *Statutes at Large,* vol. 89.

3. This section was written by Mary Wilson, Education Director, Orange County Cerebral Palsy Association, Inc., Anne Snead Deane Rehabilitation Center, Goshen, N.Y.

4. Ann E. Lupkowski, and Elizabeth A. Lupkowski, "Meeting the Needs of Gifted Preschoolers, *Children Today* (March/April 1985), pp. 10–14.

5. Michael Lewis with Leslie Kane, "Early Signals of Gifted," *Mothers Today* (January/February 1985), p. 14.
6. J. Gallagher, P. Weiss, K. Oglesby, and T. Thomas, *The status of gifted/talented education: United States survey needs, practices, and policies.* Los Angeles: National/State Leadership Training Institute on the Gifted and Talented, 1983.
7. Carol Johnson Parker, "Multicultural Awareness Activities," *Dimensions,* 10, no. 4 (July, 1982), p. 112.

Chapter 12

1. George H. Gallup, "The 14th Annual Gallup Poll of the Public's Attitudes Toward the Public Schools," *Phi Delta Kappan,* 64 (September 1983).
2. Special thanks to Bernice Hardman, principal, Oakdale Elementary School; Isabelle L. Buckner, principal, and Gwen Beckwith, Follow Through Coordinator, Carmen Elementary School, Waukegan Public Schools, for this vignette about the Waukegan Follow Through Program.
3. Constance Kamii, *Number in Preschool and Kindergarten* (Washington, D.C.: National Association for the Education of Young Children, 1982), p. 23.
4. Kamii, *Number in Preschool and Kindergarten,* p. 77.

Chapter 13

1. Ann Henderson, ed., *Parent Participation—Student Achievement: The Evidence Grows* (Columbia, Md.: National Committee for Citizens in Education, 1981), p. 1.
2. Irving Lazar, et al., *The Persistence of Preschool Effects: A Summary Report* (Washington, D.C.: U.S. Government Printing Office, 1976).
3. Kevin J. Swick, *Inviting Parents into the Young Child's World* (Champaign, Ill.: Stipes Publishing Co., 1984), p. 115.
4. George S. Morrison, *Parent Involvement in the Home, School and Community* (Columbus, Ohio: Merrill, 1978), p. 22.

Chapter 14

1. Save the Children Federation, *Hard Choices: Portraits of Poverty and Hunger in America* (Westport, Conn.: Save the Children Federation, 1985), p. 67.
2. Andrew Stein, "New York's Poor Children: A Tinderbox," *New York Times,* January 17, 1987.
3. Harold Howe II, "The Prospect for Children in the United States," *Phi Delta Kappan,* 68 (November 1986), p. 191.
4. Madeleine H. Kimmich, *America's Children: Who Cares?* (Washington, D.C.: The Urban Institute Press, 1985), p. 109.
5. United States Statutes at Large, vol. P. 88 part 1 (Washington, D.C.: United States Government Printing Office, 1976), p. 5.
6. United States Department of Health, Education and Welfare, Office of Human Development, Office of Child Development, Children's Bureau National Center on Child Abuse and Neglect, Child Abuse and Neglect, The Problem and Its Management, Vol. 2, The Roles and Responsibilities of Professionals. DHEW Publication No. (OHD) 75–30074, pp. 70–72.
7. National Center for Missing and Exploited Children, *Child Protection* (Washington, D.C.), pamphlet.

8. National Center for Missing and Exploited Children, *Just in Case: Parental Guidelines in Case Your Child Might Someday be Missing* (Washington, D.C.), pamphlet.

9. *Federal Register*, Wednesday, June 4, 1975, p. 24128.

10. *Federal Register*, August 11, 1975, p. 33803.

11. Action For Children's Television, *New Views on TV Viewing* (Newtonville, MA: ACT, n.d.).

12. "Toying With Kids' TV," *Newsweek*, (May 13, 1985), p. 85.

13. Gene H. Brady et al., "Television Food Commercials Aimed at Children, Family Grocery Shopping and Mother-Child Interactions," *Family Relations* 30 (July 1981), p. 439.

14. Albert Bandura, Dorthea Ross and Sheba Ross, "Imitation of Film-Mediated Aggressive Models," *Journal of Abnormal and Social Psychology*, 66, no. 1 (1963), p. 4.

15. Glenn Thomas Ellis and Francis Sekyra, III, "The Effects of Aggressive Cartoons on the Behavior of First Grade Children," *The Journal of Psychology*, 81, 1972, p. 42.

16. Dorothy G. Singer and Jerome L. Singer, "TV Violence: What's All the Fuss About? *Television and Children* (Spring 1984):36.

Chapter 15

1. Friedrich Froebel, *Mother's Songs, Games, and Stories* (New York: Arno Press, 1976), pp. xxxiii.

2. Francis Roberts, "The Ideal Teacher," *Parents* (December 1984), pp. 42–44.

3. Reprinted by permission from E. Ward, "A code of ethics: The hallmark of a profession," in L. G. Katz and E. H. Ward, *Ethical behavior in early childhood education,* pp. 20–21. Copyright © 1978, National Association for the Education of Young Children, 1834 Connecticut Ave. N.W., Washington, D.C., 20009.

APPENDIX A

Journals and Associations of Early Childhood Education

Action for Children's Television
46 Austin Street
Newtonville, Massachusetts 02160

Administration for Children, Youth and
    Families
Office of Human Development Services
Department of Health and Human
    Services
200 Independence Avenue, S.W.
Washington, D.C. 20201

American Academy of Pediatrics
141 N.W. Point Road
Box 927
Elk Grove Village, Illinois 60007

American Association of Elementary,
    Kinder-Nursery Educators
1201 16th Street, N.W.
Washington, D.C. 20036

American Association for Gifted
    Children
15 Gramercy Park
New York, New York 10003

American Association for Health,
    Physical Education and Recreation
1201 16th Street, N.W.
Washington, D.C. 20036

American Baby, Inc.
575 Lexington Avenue
New York, New York 10022

American Child Care Services
532 Settlers Landing Road
P.O. Box 548
Hampton, Virginia 23669

American Home Economics Association
2010 Massachusetts Avenue, N.W.
Washington, D.C. 20036

American Montessori Society
(AMS)
175 Fifth Avenue
New York, New York 10010

Association for Childhood Education
    International
11141 Georgia Avenue
Suite 200
Wheaton, Maryland 20902

Association for Children with Learning
    Disabilities
4156 Library Road
Pittsburgh, Pennsylvania 15234

Beechnut Infant Hotline
P.O. Box 127
Fort Washington, Pennsylvania 19034

Big Brothers/Big Sisters of America
117 South 17th Street
Suite 1200
Philadelphia, Pennsylvania 19103

Black Child Development Institute
1463 Rhode Island Avenue, N.W.
Washington, D.C. 20005

Bureau of Education for the Handicapped
U.S. Office of Education
Department of Health and Human
  Services
7th and D Streets, S.W.
Washington, D.C. 20036

Child Care Employee News
P.O. Box 5603
Berkley, California 94705

Child Care Information Exchange
P.O. Box 2890
Redmond, Washington 98052

Child Care Quarterly
Human Sciences Publishers
72 Fifth Avenue
New York, New York 10011

Child Care Law Project
625 Market Street
Suite 816
San Francisco, California 94105

Child Development
University of Chicago Press
5801 Ellis Avenue
Chicago, Illinois 60637

Child Development Associate
  Credentialing Commission
1341 G. Street, N.W.
Suite 802
Washington, D.C. 20002

Child Study Association of America
9 E. 89th Street
New York, New York 10028

Child Welfare League of America, Inc.
67 Irving Place
New York, New York 10003

Childhood Education (Journal of ACEI)
3615 Wisconsin Avenue, N.W.
Washington, D.C. 20016

Children Today
Children's Bureau, Administration for
  Children, Youth, and Families
Office of Human Development Services
U.S. Department of Health and Human
  Services
P.O. Box 1182
Washington, D.C. 20013

Children's Defense Fund
1520 New Hampshire Avenue, N.W.
Washington, D.C. 20005

Children's Foundation
1420 New York Avenue, N.W.
Suite 800
Washington, D.C. 20005

Children's Rights Group
693 Mission Street
San Francisco, California 94105

Children's Rights, Inc.
3443 17th Street, N.W.
Washington, D.C. 20010

Citizen's Committee for Children of New
  York, Inc.
105 E. 22nd Street
New York, New York 10010

Council for Exceptional Children
1920 Association Drive
Reston, Virginia 22091

Day Care and Early Education
Human Sciences Press
72 Fifth Avenue
New York, New York 10011

Day Care U.S.A. Newsletter
Day Care Information Service
United Communications Group
8701 Georgia Avenue
Suite 800
Silver Springs, Maryland 20910

Developmental Psychology
American Psychological Association
1200 17th Street, N.W.
Washington, D.C. 20036

Early Years
Allen Raymond, Inc.
P.O. Box 1223
11 Hale Lane
Darien, Connecticut 06820

Educational Resources Information
    Center/Early Childhood Education
(ERIC/ECE)
805 West Pennsylvania Avenue
Urbana, Illinois 61801

Exceptional Children
Council for Exceptional Children
1920 Association Drive
Reston, Virginia 22091

Family Journal
W.J. Wheeler Publishing Inc.
RD 2, P.O. Box 165
Putney, Vermont 05346

Family Service of America
44 East 23rd Street
New York, New York 10010

Food and Nutrition Service
U.S. Department of Agriculture
Alexandria, Virginia 22302

Foster Grandparents Program
ACTION
806 Connecticut Avenue, N.W.
Washington, D.C. 20525

Foundation for Child Development
345 East 46th Street
New York, New York 10017

Growing Child
Dunn and Hargitt
22 North Second Street
P.O. Box 620
Lafayette, Indiana 47902

Harris Foundation
120 South LaSalle Street
Chicago, Illinois 60603

Head Start Bureau
Department of Health and Human
    Services
P.O. Box 1182
Washington, D.C. 20013

High/Scope Educational Research
    Foundation
600 North River Street
Ypsilanti, Michigan 48197

Infant Stimulation Education
    Association
UCLA Medical Center
Factor 50942
Los Angeles, California 90024

Instructor
The Instructor Publications, Inc.
P.O. Box 6099
Duluth, Minnesota 55806

International Concerns Committee for
    Children
911 Cypress Drive
Boulder, Colorado 80303

Journal of Family Issues
Sage Publications, Inc.
275 South Beverly Drive
Beverly Hills, California 90212

Journal of Learning Disabilities
5615 West Cermak Road
Cicero, Illinois 60650

Learning
Education Today Company, Inc.
530 University Avenue
Palo Alto, California 94301

Legal Services for Children
149 Ninth Street
San Francisco, California 94103

National Association for Child Care
    Management
1834 Conn. Ave. N.W.
Washington, D.C. 20009

National Association of Homes for
    Children
104 East 35th Street
New York, New York 10016

National Association for Retarded
    Citizens (NARC)
2709 Avenue E East
Arlington, Texas 76011

National Black Child Development
Institute
1463 Rhode Island Avenue, N.W.
Washington, D.C. 20005

National Committee for Adoption
2025 M Street, 512
Washington, D.C. 20036

National Committee for Multi-
Handicapped Children
239 14th Street
Niagara Falls, New York 14303

National Committee for Prevention of
Child Abuse
332 South Michigan Avenue
Suite 1250
Chicago, Illinois 60604

National Council for the Gifted
700 Prospect Avenue
West Orange, New Jersey 07052

National Easter Seal Society
2023 West Ogden Avenue
Chicago, Illinois 60612

Office of Early Childhood Development
(OECD)
Office of Education
Department of Health, Education, and
Welfare (now U.S. Department of
Education)
1200 19th Street, N.W.
Washington, D.C. 20506

Parents
Parents Magazine Enterprises, Inc.
80 New Bridge Road
Bergenfield, New Jersey 07621

Parents Anonymous
7120 Franklin Avenue
Los Angeles, California 90046

Play Schools Association
120 W. 57th Street
New York, New York 10019

Rosenberg Foundation
210 Post Street
San Francisco, California 94108

Southern Association on Children Under
Six
P.O. Box 5403
Brady Station
Little Rock, Arkansas 72215

Teacher
Macmillan Professional Magazines, Inc.
262 Mason Street
Greenwich, Connecticut 06830

Today's Child Newsmagazine
Edwards Publications, Inc.
P.O. Box 98
Roosevelt, New Jersey 08555

Today's Education (Journal of NEA)
National Education Association
1201 16th Street, N.W.
Washington, D.C. 20036

Totline
1004 Harborview Lane
Everett, Washington 98203

USA Toy Library Association
1800 Pickwick Avenue
Glenview, Illinois 60025-1377

Young Children (Journal of NAEYC)
National Association for the Education of
Young Children
1834 Connecticut Avenue, N.W.
Washington, D.C. 20009

Zero to Three
Bulletin for the National Center for
Clinical Infant Programs
733 15th Street, N.W.
Suite 912
Washington, D.C. 20005

APPENDIX B

Follow Through Models

Adaptive Learning Environments
   Model
Temple University
Center for Research in Human
   Development and Education
9th Floor, Ritter Annex
Philadelphia, PA 19122

Bank Street Model
Bank Street College of Education
610 W. 112th St.
New York, NY 10025

Behavior Analysis Model
Support and Development Center for
   Follow Through
Department of Human Development
University of Kansas
Lawrence, KS 66044

Cognitively Linguistic Curriculum Model
High/Scope Educational Research
   Foundation
600 N. River
Ypsilanti, MI 48197

Cultural Linguistic Approach
Center for Inner-City Studies
Northeastern Illinois University
700 E. Oakwood Blvd.
Chicago, IL 60653

Direct Instruction Model
University of Oregon
Department of Special Education
College of Education
Eugene, OR 97403

Interdependent Learning Model
Fordham University
St. Robert's Hall, B13
Bronx, NY 10458

Language Development Approach
   (SEDL)
Southwest Educational Developmental
   Laboratory
Follow Through Division
211 E. 7th St.
Austin, TX 78701

Mathemagenic Activities Program
University of Georgia
427 Aderhold
College of Education
Athens, GA 30602

New School Approach
University of North Dakota
Center for Teaching and Learning
Box 8039, University Station
Grand Forks, ND 58201

Non-Graded Follow Through Model
The Hampton Institute
Follow Through Program
Department of Early Education
P.O. Box 6418
Hampton, VA 23368

Tucson Early Education Model
University of Arizona
College of Education
Room 409
Tucson, AR 86721

Index

The Author

George S. Morrison, Ed.D., is Professor of Early Childhood Education in the Division of Curriculum and Instruction at Florida International University—The State University of Florida at Miami. Professor Morrison teaches courses in early childhood education, curriculum development, and urban education and directs the Graduate Urban Education Program. He has a broad background in program development and implementation in child care, Head Start, parent/ community involvement, bilingual/multicultural programs, and adult education.

Dr. Morrison is extensively involved in teacher training programs. He chaired the State of Florida writing team for Prekindergarten and K–4 certification. He had overall responsibility for determining teacher competencies, content outlines, and specifications for Florida's Initial Teacher Certification and Master Teacher programs.

Some of Dr. Morrison's accomplishments include a Distinguished Academic Service Award from the Pennsylvania Department of Education and an Outstanding Alumni Award from the School of Education, University of Pittsburgh. Dr. Morrison is the author of *Parent Involvement in the Home, School and Community* and *Education and Development of Infants, Toddlers and Preschoolers.* He is a frequent contributor to journals in the areas of early childhood/elementary education and community and social affairs.